CW01460669

BUDDHA

ON THE DANCE FLOOR

BUDDHA
ON THE DANCE FLOOR

living **awareness**

Buddha on the Dance Floor
is published in 2015 by Living Awareness
PO Box 447 Frenchs Forest Sydney NSW 1640
ABN 30 596 615 132

Originally published in 2006 as *Isira – A Journey of Awakening*
by Delphian Books (a division of New Frontier Creative Services Pty Ltd)
Epping, NSW, Australia

© Isira Sananda 2006, 2015
www.isira.com

This book is copyright. Apart from any fair dealing for the purposes of private study, research, criticism or review, as permitted by the Copyright Act 1968, no part may be reproduced by any process without written permission. Enquiries should be addressed to the publisher.
All rights reserved.

National Library of Australia Cataloguing-in-Publication entry:
Author: Isira Sananda
Title: Buddha on the Dance Floor
ISBN: 9780994218001 (pbk)
ISBN: 9780994218032 (epub)
ISBN: 9780994218049 (Kindle)
Subjects: Sananda, Isira. Spiritual biography.
Spiritual life. Meditation. Spiritualism. Enlightenment.
Women and spiritualism. Self-actualization. Self-culture.

Dewey Number: 204.092

Cover art: Danijela Mijailovic
Internal design: Ronald Proft
Back cover photography: Nicholas Sutcliffe

For all,

as the ONE.

In endless love and gratitude.

Acknowledgments

There are so many I wish to thank ... everyone who has been a part of my journey has helped in the making of this gift. First of all, my parents: this journey wouldn't have happened without you! I so love, honour and thank you for my life.

Thanks to my brother and sister for putting up with me in our younger years!

And, to all the people along the way who helped in the shaping of my journey: my love and gratitude to you all.

Glowing praise to my 'team': Leelani, Frances and Joya Rose. Without you this gift could not have been birthed. From the bottom of my heart: thank you for your commitment, endurance, patience, sharing, love and humour!

Thank you to the 'extras' team: Jim, Jacqueline and Christo. Your support has enabled the very necessary fine-tuning of a very big book!

Beloved service support: Kooshani and Lili-Shaili, who have lovingly cared for and nurtured us through this commitment.

The names of some of the people and places in this book have been changed for the benefit of privacy.

Contents

Preface

Coming into this world and the journey of life have always been steeped in mystery. We have all heard that we come from the world of Spirit, the source of creation, the home of God. Yet we remain bewildered and sceptical, spending most of our lives searching for an answer.

Why? Because although we have been told we come from 'above', most of us don't remember. Somewhere in the passage between the spirit world and our life on earth, our memory is temporarily displaced. It is simply part of the process of assuming a body. It is as if each soul takes a nice big sleeping potion before coming, and forgets its true nature and its true source. But I must have been one of those cheeky souls who, having taken one little sip, threw away the potion in disgust, because for some reason I was still quite awake when I came into this world for this lifetime. And yet, that little sip of the potion of sleepiness meant I wasn't fully awake yet knew there was something more. For many years the consequences of that were both a curse and a blessing: it was the perfect cocktail for a relentless quest to remember – and why my experience is both ordinary and extraordinary.

So I have known the journey of doubt, fear, confusion and longing for transcendence in this life. I have known sorrows and have overcome them. I have faced violation and come to know peace. I have looked into the face of death and found eternal life. By remembering who I am, I have found freedom. It is this experience, of coming again to remember who it is that I have always been, that I hope will be of value and encouragement to you on your path.

It is now widely recognised that all experience is relative to perspective. *How* we see, colours *what* we see. The variety of human life is endlessly magical, like a giant shifting kaleidoscope. And given that we are all encountering varying perspectives, it is only fair to acknowledge that no one person's experience is ever the same as another's.

What I share with you here is the journey I have encountered through the vast spectrum of my perspective. To some this may seem outrageous, perhaps even fictional. To others, it may seem incredibly familiar. I respectfully acknowledge that my account may seem contrary to that of others, who have been a part of my journey. And by sharing what the experience was for me, I have no intent to offend anyone in any way. I have endeavoured in every way possible to respect each individual and have therefore chosen to change names of people and places (where appropriate) for the benefit of privacy. I simply seek to share the gift that has come to me through each and every encounter. Indeed, I count every one as a blessing.

In recounting my experiences, whether in infancy, childhood or other-life memories or visions, I am in the eternal now, utterly present to each moment. In my sensory and extra-sensory perception of 'mundane' events, my comprehension is not dampened or dulled. This sense of immediacy and the intensity of my perception will indicate the paradox of my ordinariness and extraordinariness. The contrast between the human aspect and the higher Self can make them appear even contradictory and incompatible. The process of integrating these different aspects is both awe-inspiring and humbly human.

You may be one of those who have asked me to write this book or perhaps we have not yet met. I deeply believe that it is no coincidence that you are holding this book in your hands; for you have come to create this experience, this looking glass, as a part of your own journey. You, the reader, may also in another sense have been a part of the creation of this book – this story, since many of you have called, prayed and pleaded to know the very thing that I am blessed to experience. This is what I am here to share. This story is an invitation to know your own true Self. And, like many signs along our path, may you see it as a marker, a confirmation, of your own homecoming.

Jonva

Introduction

From the moment of birth to the moment of death, life unfolds through a series of stages: infant, child, teenager, adult, elder, and deceased. Every culture has recognised these as significant passages and has provided teachings or myths using symbols, images and characters to help each person understand their own life's journey. Carl Jung and Joseph Campbell documented these cultural stories and evidence of the common human challenges using the term *archetypes*. We encounter these archetypes through our interaction with life. Archetypes are many and varied. They may represent our passages of life, like the teenager or elder archetype; our models of living, like the mother or friend archetype or our ideals, like the archetype of the lover or hero. It is these archetypes, and our universal desire to understand and reconcile them in our lives, which has inspired countless stories from Aboriginal Dreamtime myths to fairytales to epics like *Star Wars* or *Lord of the Rings*.

Each of us will experience some, if not all, of these archetypes in some degree within a given life. This is because the archetypes are often synonymous with life's course from birth to death. Each of us encounters these as mini-stages of growth (or initiation). We all face certain 'tests'. And, according to how we respond or interact with the circumstance, we either 'learn' and attain a higher state of understanding from the experience, or we continue to attract the same encounter, again and again, until we do reach a completion of understanding and are able to move forward.

Although we all face the same archetypes in our life, the level of our encounter with them varies significantly according to our stage of evolution. An example is the archetype of death. A child could begin to understand the part that death plays in the process of life through discovering a dead bird. An adult may be faced with the death of a loved one or a terminal illness. And again, according to the stage of the soul's evolution, one person may be caught in great pain and misery, feeling victimised by life, whilst another may awaken to a transcendent awareness that there is life beyond death and that death represents a process of transformation within eternal life.

Regardless of what level we are experiencing, our soul is also on a journey through a much larger passage. It is important to understand that these experiences are not occurring only in a linear sequence. We encounter our life journey as loops within loops, with the overlapping of archetypes occurring and re-occurring. Very often we are unaware of how much 'growth' is actually happening, because we are commonly caught in a narrow perspective: we lose sight of the bigger (and multi-directional) picture. Through many lifetimes we encounter the same archetypes to a greater and greater degree which eventuates in a state of completion. Through these encounters we come to complete experience, complete feeling and complete knowing. It is this alchemy that results in our ultimate completion: what the mystics refer to as Enlightenment. It is the moment of return: the remembering of who we are. That moment is the end of all within us that had taken on the belief in separation: it is that moment in which we are totally merged again with the ALL ... God.

THE USE OF ARCHETYPAL KEYS IN THIS BOOK

I have recognised these stages within my own life and have chosen in this book to highlight these passages through a particular set of keys. These keys appear in many archetypal stories throughout the world and are used as universal tools of insight. Composed of twenty-two major archetypes, this unique set of keys uses the symbols and imagery that have been meaningful to me in my connection with nature and the spirits of this land.

These keys provide significant indicators: markers that give a clear map of the journey. It is like walking up a series of steps and unlocking a door into another room and into another stage of life. Each key indicates the essence of what my soul is encountering and 'learning' through the living experience. During the unfolding course, the experience is digested through feeling and insight which results in a state of knowing or realisation. This marks a point of completion which is integrated into the soul as an attainment. Although the attainment indicates a point of significant completion the same experiences may be seen occurring again on another level at another time.

The keys begin at zero and reach completion at twenty-one, giving a total of twenty-two keys and twenty-two attainments. You will notice the numerical sequence differs between the keys and attainments. Although the keys start at zero, the attainments start at one and complete at twenty-two. The completion of the twenty-two keys and attainments reunites the journey with zero – the beginning and the end: the alpha and omega.

It is inevitable that we will all attain our own realisation and completion. I hope that the journey I now share with you will inspire you, and perhaps serve as a mirror for the wonder of your own homeward passage.

May you recognise the keys that are in your own life.

KEY 0.

The Fool

KEY 0. *The Fool*

This is the game of Creation: we start out on a journey innocently, full of faith, seeking an end, yet to discover that the beginning and the end are forever united – always in the instant of Now.

Zero is the circle, the alpha and omega that contains all.

In mystery we enter this world. Having forgotten what we are, we feel lost, as if we have left home. We are separated from our womb of safety, cast away from God, abandoned. Like fools, unknowing, we stumble along the path, aching to find our way home again.

Like a fool, I stepped off the edge of knowing into the mystery, seeking a way home.

From no-skin we come and to no-skin we return.

Isira

1. *Where Did I Begin?*

Our birth is but a sleep and a forgetting:
The Soul that rises with us, our life's Star,
Hath had elsewhere its setting,
And cometh from afar:

Not in entire forgetfulness,
And not in utter nakedness,
But trailing clouds of glory do we come
From God who is our home.

William Wordsworth

Every person's life is dominated by a central event which sculpts and colours everything that comes after it and, in retrospect, everything that came before it. Mine was at the age of twenty-nine when I discovered that my life story was just that: a story. Suddenly I had taken a rocket-ride beyond my mind and discovered that I was something limitlessly beyond the idea of a separate ego-self.

My story was that I had left 'home', but that was a lie, a clever mirage. I discovered that I was always have been, and always will be the untouchable, unshakable presence that the mystics have talked about as our true Self. And in that central moment every doubt, every question and every longing was consumed – returned to an infinite ocean of bliss, resting at one in the eternal life of the One Self that is God.

I returned to zero. I returned to the place of no time in which all of life's events are in the one same eternal instant, where the beginning and the end are a circle and *life* is forever home.

How I arrived in that liberated moment was an odyssey of wonder and a quest of consciousness which had its first beguiling power upon me even at the tender age of eight months.

•

My life had mostly been a blur of light, sound and strangely mixed-up images since I had left the womb on that cold, startling day in May 1967. Eight months later, when I lay on a baby blanket in a backyard of suburban South Australia, as the hot air played around my soft skin, I was gripped by a penetrating attention. My consciousness had fully entered. In that moment my mind reached out and in, spun by a wheel of insatiable enquiry. How had I come to be in a tender new body again, on earth? And what for? I was determined to find the answer in anything: from the ground upon which I lay, to the sky that stretched endlessly above, to the strange new eyes of the family I had come to be with.

I searched in my awareness. But there was no beginning and no ending. Even then, as a baby, my awareness flitted between past and present and between images and impressions of other worlds, places and times. On the ground my plump body was dressed in a pale pink chequered bikini and matching bonnet. Next to me lay a pale blue spade – a body of plastic the same length as mine. I lay staring up to the sky. Inside, my consciousness was alive and alert, buzzing with curiosity. I could just as easily have been a grey-haired Plato, contemplating the meaning of life.

Before my eyes, the endless space of clear light was now filled with form and colour, as if painted. I blinked. The light, now brightly golden yet somehow also dampened by a blue curtain, burst sporadically through a tapestry of green shiny patches. An apple tree arched above my tiny body like a giant umbrella collage. Its leaves shimmered and tinkled in a play with sun and breeze. I blinked again and rolled my eyes, in an attempt to focus.

Somewhere from the past, a valley surrounded by majestic snow-capped mountains stretched before my eyes. Colours danced, flashing by in sliding screens. Rich blue, gold and maroon. White and grey. Their silhouettes were outlined by vivid blue skies and interrupted by repeating images of beads, bells, robes, statues and temples – golden, shining visions. Chanting filled my being and echoed out across the valley.

Then leaves rustled above my body again. I reflected on the passage that led me to this body. Out of a vastness of light, traversing other dimensions, times and places, I had come to sense the presence of the world again: sounds, colours, scenes, voices.

From the very beginning I felt different from my family. I was aware that I had lived before and that I had lived with different people. This father and mother were not the parents I knew. Yet I found myself held in a growing connection to them. I was gradually drawn down a funnel into their world – into Mother's internal furnace, warm, light and liquid, an enclosing body of life. Inside her body I had floated, engulfed in luminous orange-carnelian light. Occasionally a sound rippled through me. Then my watery carriage would gently rock and wobble me as a muffled string of voices and music surrounded me and Mother danced to *The Baby Elephant Walk*. It was the only thing that seemed to give her any joy as I lay heavily inside her.

Then the watery womb broke open. The warm cradling ceased. Cold air, harsh light, rubber gloves, and clashing steel. They were the signs of the world's coldness about to come down on me, taking me from my sweet place of embracing warmth.

Mother lay unconscious. Father reached out, his arms stretching, yearning to bring out from his heart the tenderness he knew lay hidden deeper within. Yet somehow it eluded him, staying caught behind his mind's reservations. Nothing was comforting or reassuring. This new passage failed to reflect to me the Divine Love I had known so deeply before.

My attention shifted again away from my mind's reflections to my baby body. I became acutely aware of my physical enclosure. I adjusted my senses and kicked my feet in the air. I was pinned to my back without much control. My senses said this was all new. Yet my awareness was not. Somehow a strange familiarity emerged from the conscious life-current flowing deep within me. As I lay under that swaying apple tree I was gripped by the recognition that something new had begun; yet it had all unfolded from a place that had always been.

Everything that would follow that moment – watching the wind ripple the grass like the sea, my fifth birthday candles going out, seeing the all-connected light between each and every thing, looking into my schoolteacher's eyes, struggling for friendship and seeking a place of belonging – everything was shaped by that penetrating awareness. That awareness held me in a constant embrace, an influence that seemed to move me towards an already spoken destiny: to that momentous fulcrum in time, the event of my ultimate liberation, and beyond.

•

So there I was as a baby, suspended between an ancient eternal awareness and the beginning of a new life. I slept and woke and slept and woke. My mind was carried on the thread of a time-line: its moments shuffled, woven from memories and an awareness of the present. I seemed to lose track of where I had really come from.

As I grew older I felt an increasing loss of control, frustration with my body, and confusion about identity. Everything seemed at odds with my being. Even eating. The business of eating was a mixture of disgust, occasional delights and torture. Just the thought of food gave me a sick, dropping feeling in the pit of my belly from a jumble of nerves and the juices of repulsion. That food certainly wasn't what I was used to eating. And yet, to my frustration, I couldn't remember what food I was used to eating. So I felt helpless, and my mother's annoyance grew at my stubborn unwillingness to eat all my food. It all compounded a growing sense of myself as an alien.

I often sat staring solemnly at my mother. My expression was what the adults called a sour-puss. They often taunted me. Their words bore a certain weight – belittling and cruel. I couldn't work out who *she* was and how she had come to be my mother. I had many thoughts and images of life and lifetimes that I had lived before. I knew I had always existed. And in all those memories I didn't have any image of this mother. How then had she come to get me and where had she got me from? I started to wonder if it had been some devious scheme that she and the other adult of the house, my father, had arrived at. Was it a plan to fill some hollow need that ached in them like a gaping wound? This deep uncertainty about my surroundings grew and grew.

It became evident very quickly that I was somehow 'less' than my mother and father. My thoughts and expressions didn't seem to be acknowledged or worth anything. I was either laughed at, with comments that I had a vivid imagination and was a strange child, or there was an onslaught of angry yelling.

Inside the house, the air was often thick with tension along with smells from soaking nappies, smoking and cooking. My mother insisted on presenting strange food: soggy vegetables and seared flesh – lamb, bacon and beef, all dismembered parts of other creatures! It all pressed upon me like an unpleasant blanket that threatened to suffocate me.

I also shared the house with another child, who, I was told, could do things I wasn't allowed because he was a boy and he was older. My brother Jackson was six. I was only three. Sometime after I had found myself in this house, I remember mother mysteriously disappearing for a while and returning with a little bundle: her new baby girl. I was told I now had a sister, Merrilyn. She seemed to take up most of my mother's interest from then on.

I sensed a warmth extending from my mother to the baby that seemed to be mostly absent in her engagements with me, and soon I developed a longing, and a resentment that I felt so unnoticed. These strange feelings twisted my heart and stomach in knots, provoking me to do and say things: anything that might give me a taste of the sweet love that shone from my mother's eyes to her baby. And when it did come to me, in a rare moment, it seemed to melt away the sense of dislocation that seemed to pervade my being.

But soon I would be back in a world that seemed to grow ever more hostile. Strangest of all was the knowledge that, even so, deep inside me, was a vast and bottomless presence of peace and love and joy. It seemed to have an existence all of its own, untouched by this foreign dream of events.

2. *Believe It or Not?*

It matters not what you believe,
Only that you believe.

Unknown

A sudden and violent bang in the kitchen brought me back to my senses. My poor body jolted, adding another strand of tension to my already jangled nerves.

'Stop dreaming and eat your food!' Mother commanded.

I stared down at my plate. I sighed as I smelled the soggy, over-cooked food. The flat yellow dish seemed oddly large for the small collection upon it: a few green peas, those funny shiny balls that I couldn't balance on my fork; limp, orange rings which Mother called carrots; and a charred lump of stiff, hard, smelly lamb chop, the taste of which sent my stomach heaving.

The more I watched and searched for the way that I knew life was meant to be, the more bewildered I felt. I knew the joy, the light and the love inside me. That light gleamed from a fire deep within, which burned with unstoppable passion. I could see the joy, the light and love in the world of nature all around me. I could even see it in the people around me. For some reason, however, they kept putting on dark cloaks that hid the light.

Each day was like a mysterious dance in a strange place. The roller-coaster ride of emotions in the family had me spinning, trying to find a foothold of joy that could last more than a few fleeting moments. It eluded me.

From within this little body that housed me, I looked out at the world feeling increasingly perplexed. The more I looked for some sign of belonging – something familiar – the more sure I became that I was somehow lost. I must have taken a wrong turn somewhere.

These people couldn't be my real family because they didn't look with me through the same windows of light. Their eyes were distant and cut off. They were dull panes that reflected a world of fear and limitations. They weren't the windows that shone with a knowing of sacred communion. I implored with my own eyes, reaching out to them, aching to find even a fleeting reflection of what I knew existed somewhere. Where were the eyes of ancient wisdom? What happened to the mountain peaks? Where were the fields of light and the chants so divine? Where were my friends who knew me?

I took solace in the garden. As I sat quietly with aching questions, I became aware that I was not alone. A beautiful golden angel was by my side. I looked at him in wonder, hopeful that he could help me.

'Where are my friends?' I asked. 'What happened to the world I knew? Why did I have to come here?'

'You are always surrounded by friends,' he said. 'Look, see the other angels?'

I nodded. 'Yes, yes, I can!' I squealed with delight.

'Even though you cannot always see us, we are always by your side. And the flowers and creatures are your friends, too. You talk to them too, don't you?'

My eyes opened wide. I *did* talk to them. He knew. I thought: he must be real! I was so excited that I ran inside to tell Mum about my friends.

'Mum, Mum!' I called out. 'I'm not alone. The angels came to visit me!'

Mum looked down at me, bemused, and chuckled, shaking her head. 'Oh dear, angels aren't real. It's just your imagination,' she said, and went on cleaning the cupboard.

I felt even more puzzled. If it was my imagination (a big word for something that meant my thoughts weren't real), then how did my imagination know about something that *was* real? Something inside decided to ignore my mum's words. I didn't care if she thought my friends weren't real. They were. And I was going to keep talking with them. I ran back out into the garden.

And sure enough, there was my angel waiting for me.

'Mum told me you're not real,' I said.

'Yes, but it's up to you. You can choose to keep believing or not. If you keep believing, you will keep hearing my voice. If you don't, you will forget your own inner voice too.'

Oh no, I don't want that, I thought. 'I do believe.' I said.

And with that my angel disappeared.

It was in those moments that I felt appeased, that I was not completely lost. The flowers' faces smiled at me, the sunshine warmed me, the trees whispered to me, the creatures greeted me and my angel comforted me. It was in these moments that I felt Presence in the world. The depth of love and communion filled me with such joy that I felt as if I was bursting into oneness with all around me. It was so intense that somehow the light in this love would ignite again a flame of faith in me. The sense of the conflicting family behaviours that tore at my soul instantly dissolved in this field of joy. For hours I would rest and play in the reprieve of nature. Yet it became so starkly evident that it was temporary relief. Soon enough the demands of household existence would once again call me.

3. *A Divided World*

You are a child of the universe no less than
The trees and the stars; you have a right to be here.
And whether or not it is clear to you,
No doubt the universe is unfolding as it should.

Max Ehrmann

From a very early age I had a growing awareness that my world was constructed of apparently extreme opposites. One was my inner world, the other was the outer world. I also noticed that the outer world seemed far more contradictory and unstable. In many ways it was the opposite of the *oasis* within. Hearing this word one day and liking the sound of it, I enquired about it. I learned that it was almost like a fairytale, a place of great bounty, life and beauty in the middle of a harsh land. So I claimed it as my secret name for my inner world.

Indeed, the oasis was a place of great beauty and seemed to stretch on forever. And as long as I sat in the middle of my inner world, I had some salvation from the harshness of my outer reality. I discovered that my inner realm was always full. Full of love, beauty, peace, joy and boundless adventure and wonderment. There were no limitations. I could visit angels in far-off fields of light. I could melt into endless seas of radiant flowing colour. I could play with creatures and beings of every kind who had no fear, who were gentle and loving and kind. I could fly to distant places, leaving my body behind, to experience myself in endless ways. And best of all, I could meet with my spirit friends, my 'real' family – the ones who knew and understood me, and with whom I was at one.

One day I posed a question: I wonder if I could make myself leave my body? That question wasn't really *to* anyone, it was just a curious wondering, yet I immediately saw the scene of imagining myself floating above my body and watching it lying on the bed. So, when I went to bed, that's what I did.

Three nights later I consciously left my body and was *really* watching it. Once I felt comfortable with this conscious shift I was able to travel with a Tibetan yogi spirit to many different dimensions and places around the world. We most frequently visited caves of light surrounded by majestic mountains and valleys.

With the experiences of other dimensions I became aware that 'I' was something more than just the body. I discovered that *this me* was not attached to the four-year-old, little-girl body I now had. Instead, I was without fixed identity, often appearing in other ways: sometimes as a man with a shaved head in robes of gold; sometimes as a being of unshakable power and love; sometimes as an angel-being of sparkling light; and sometimes as the Self that knew the mind without the need for words, that laughed in the simple joy of loving divine service for my fellow companions.

Feeling bored and frustrated with this world of so many *no's* and *don'ts,* I went to my bedroom. My brother was outside with Mum and Merrilyn. I could still hear an occasional shriek so I pushed the door across and sat on the floor next to my bed. Folding my legs up in the way I always did with my little pink soles pointing up at my face, I closed my eyes. Instantly I felt soft and warm as I retreated into silence. The familiar feeling of openness transported me. I soon found myself with my inner circle of friends. Amongst them were angels, saints and yogis, who would come and go. But most constant was the presence of several Tibetan masters.

The sight of their shaven heads, maroon and gold robes, and smiling faces, always filled me with a sense of peaceful belonging. No words were uttered, yet much was spoken. We did not need to speak to hear and know our songs of loving wisdom, accompanied by a celestial orchestra of chanting and heavenly music. It was enough to simply sit in this circle of wonderful beings that I knew so well. These ones were my Self, the one Self looking at me – as I looked back, at myself.

And yet, there was a sense that some of the pieces were still missing. If these radiant beings were who I knew them to be, then why were they not with me now? Why was my body different now? The beloved lama[1] who sat next to me smiled knowingly yet silently as if to hold the door shut on this mystery.

I couldn't help but feel puzzled. Why was I so knowing yet not-knowing at the same time? As this dilemma tugged at me, my inner world started to dissolve. Bewilderment remained in the little girl's mind that I had somehow acquired. My body jolted as the back door slammed and my father's voice followed: loud and red and hot like the air and sun outside.

'Keep the door CLOSED!'

I got up with a sigh and roamed down the hall. Finding my drink of water now warm, and sweeter from the slobbery saliva I had left in it, I flopped down on the lounge-room floor. The carpet was hard and rough under my bare knees and I could smell all the tiny particles of dust that danced, alight in shafts of sunlight. My pencils were still scattered, next to the paper I had been drawing on. My father sat brooding, looking at me with flashing eyes.

'If you're not going to use them, put them away, young lady,' he grumbled.

'I aaammmmm,' I said with a whine. But instead, I began to draw again. It was one of the things I loved most to do. I already felt an ambition to be a great artist. It was one of the things I could do that seemed to take my mind away from the volatile emotions that surrounded me. But before long it was all turned upside-down again.

The door opened and in came Mum. Her face was flushed tomato-red and the light around her body was all jangly. In her aura I

[1] A Tibetan Buddhist who is recognised as having a certain degree of spiritual attainment and authority to teach.

could see, hear and feel her anger: the light streams were all jagged, sharp and tangled and the sound was a clanging noise of grating and squealing. It sounded like a host of screaming demons, grinding and scraping on the walls. Its ominous vibration pulsed out from her body like arrows reaching at me – poking, stabbing and paining.

I was experiencing two distinctly different dimensions. One was the state of awareness in which I was the observer, the other was the mind and feelings of the little girl. As the little girl I felt confused by the events around me. As the observer I witnessed the events that were occurring around me with curiosity – like a scientist in a lab.

The intensity to which I experienced these 'subtle' dimensions had even greater weight than the solid world. To me, the apparent normality of the world was alive in even greater depth than the way it was perceived by others. The world was also translucent. It was a scintillating field of streaming light and energy waves of vibrating sound that reflected the state of each thing. To others, these dimensions were inconceivable. To me, they were commonplace. Whilst the people around me seemed to take in the surface of reality, I was taking in its vastness.

I was quickly brought back to focus on the surface again. Mum growled at me.

'Tidy up your mess, young lady, or you won't get any dessert!'

'Huuawh,' I sighed. My last speck of simple joy slid away. I realised that I had to stop what I was doing if I was going to be able to eat at least one tasty thing that night!

With dessert in my belly and tired legs, I dragged myself willingly to bed: another opportunity for peace. That night I dreamed.

I looked out from my great mountaintop across the valley to the other peaks and gave thanks for the light of the heart in all life.

I felt deeply at peace. In the back of my mind, I cherished

the love of my people, all following this path of compassion.
My weathered hand moved instinctively over my mala[1] as
I called for this Buddha[2] within to be awakened in all.

•

I woke up in the little-girl body again. I felt a slump in the pit of my belly – disappointment, confusion. But it is so real ... and now it's not? I thought to myself.

I got up. In the bathroom was a stool with high legs. I slid it across next to the bench where I could climb up to look in the mirror. I stared at the face, with great disbelief. I directed thoughts to the body. Move, frown, squint, growl, gasp, surprise, eyebrows up, eyebrows down. Hmmm, I thought, unfailing response. Complete obedience at every thought! Well, it was evident, this body was somehow now *me*.

I looked down between my legs as I had done many times with shame, confusion, disappointment and concern. I didn't seem right in this department. My brother had the extra dangly bits. What had happened to mine? I was sure I remembered having them before. This really was a mistake. If I was missing this part, something must be wrong. I had contemplated this often. It was one of the things that caused me to frown and brood a lot.

I couldn't stand it any more. It was silly that I couldn't wee with as much gusto as I should, and it couldn't happen without that little extra bit. I climbed down from the bench determined to rectify this grave mistake. My mind scanned this new time and place for a suitable instrument that might make it easier for me. I thought of all the objects behind cupboard doors. Suddenly I thought of the rubber gloves under the kitchen sink. That would be perfect! I thought. I hurried to the kitchen, careful not to draw attention from the sleepers that still occupied nearby rooms. I stole a pink glove and then climbed onto a chair to reach the kitchen scissors.

---

[1] A string of prayer beads.

[2] This word literally means 'awake'... one who is realised.

I heard Mum and Dad's door open suddenly. I gasped, leapt down and, feeling as guilty as a mouse caught in the cupboard, ran through the back door. I felt my mother's voice chasing me up the corridor.

'What are you up to?' she called.

'I'm just going to play outside,' I yelled back, and scuttled off into the yard at the back where I couldn't be seen. Once there I got to work on the rubber glove. An oddly half-neat surgery of the little finger resulted in a nicely dismembered tube with a small hole in the tip. It was just the right size to reclaim my weeing status. And so, with determination and curiosity, I held my newly claimed part and did a pelvic thrust as I poised myself to pee.

A sudden warm wet mess splattered my assumed pride. My elation at the thought of being clever enough to solve my handicap slid down my legs into the ground, together with my golden warm wee!

There were so many unsolved questions in my mind. Where did I really come from?

4. *Growing Pains*

The most blessed thing in the world is to live
By faith without imputation of guilt;
Having the kingdom within.

Paul Goodman

At the age of six I began to feel a sudden increased awareness of my physical body. I stared down at my skinny legs and knobbly knees: 'chicken legs' had become the most commonly used description for them. I worried about it, but Dad just smiled.

'Don't worry love, you can't fatten a thoroughbred,' he quipped.

But I did worry. It seemed to me that something was quite wrong about my long, skinny legs. They began to stretch so fast they brought me deep and painful torment. My tears in the middle of the night only brought more. Mum was the one who had to attend to my cries. And, caged in her own suffering, she could only offer me her anger.

This additional pain piled upon me like an inescapable mountain. Day followed night. Innocent moments of play and discovery were interrupted by emotional thrashings from my parents. I could not understand the words and beltings: the irrational meting out of punishment. Day after day, the words of rage, belittling and tyrannical, rained upon me. And rhythmically, through the cycle of days, the waves of anger would swell into a crescendo that would see my mother or father reaching for a wooden spoon or a belt. I would run like a hunted rabbit. The chase would end with a loud crack or a resounding wallop.

I saw that I could not escape this body. Nor could I see how I could escape this house and family. It was becoming clear that I was under their command and could not survive without them. I was trapped in a system of exclusive dependency: a society structured so that I could not reach out to anyone else for support – a society that would only send me back to my family where I 'belonged', to a place filled with pain, to a place where I didn't want to belong.

•

I lay awake in bed at night, breathing, feeling alive, alert. I listened to the sounds of others sleeping, longing to be there myself, but held captive by my own intensely conscious presence. I tossed and turned, heaved and sighed, with no sign of the curtains of sleep. As I turned on my side, I curled my legs, knees to my chest and tucked my hands between my thighs. My fingers touched the soft fleshy mount of my pelvis. A sudden rush of energy arose between my legs and ascended to my tummy. It was such an incredible vibration of aliveness and excitement that in an instant I was transported again into the magic and wonderment of my body. A trickling warm light washed over me and a sweet familiarity enveloped my mind. And before I could even notice, the curtains of sleep had drawn themselves upon my weary soul.

That night I dreamed of my family, my other family, when our skins were dark and glossy like the rich dark chocolate my dad liked to eat.

I was happy playing with the other children in our village. The songs of mothers and aunties and grandmothers floated across the red sands. Their tones were weaving into the song of the land.

Every now and then a wisp of smoke swirled above the wurlies[1] in the backdrop and the old man's voice rose to command attention to the goanna in the hot coals.

[1] Aboriginal shelters.

In the warmth of the sun and the sweetness of the waterhole, we splashed and played; exploring everything about our bodies with delight, naturally and innocently. The differences between the boys' and girls' bodies were cause for great cackles of laughter. The adults, well aware of our exploration, echoed the music of our playful discoveries with their own occasional burst of laughter. All was sweet and natural. All was pure and beautiful.

•

After such a tender dream I awoke with a heavy sense of trepidation. It seemed there were already conflicts within my awakening sexual awareness. The messages all around me in this world and in this family were loud and clear. This 'private' part was out of bounds, not to be seen or touched by anyone, not even myself.

For some strange reason when I turned six, my freedom to play naked like the rest of nature was suddenly and inexplicably condemned. I wondered if it was all to do with the Church's devil that seemed to favour the number six. The Church seemed to think it was a sin to talk or even think of our natural naked truth, until the day we would marry. And all sins were governed by this one creature called 'the devil' who was against all of our God's creation and was the nastiest critter imaginable! Well, for someone who already had an 'overactive' imagination, that was a very scary thought.

And then, as if that wasn't enough, if we were tempted and took part in the devil's game, God would punish us and – just like Adam and Eve – we would be cast from the safety of the beautiful Garden of Eden and sent to burn forever in Hell, with the devil.

Could it be that because I had played with my other family and friends and laughed in joy at the delight of our private parts, I had now woken up in Hell? Could all this suffering be the orchestration of the great and terrible devil? Had we all turned white out of fear?

Or maybe I was simply the only one who knew that God loves us all, that we are all forever in his garden as children of nature, and everyone else was asleep in some deeply obscure nightmare of their own creation.

The question rolled around in my mind for days. On the third day, I concluded that I was existing in this life, with this family and this world's rules. And since I was here, I may as well try and play the game. As I loved to play and as I loved the dance of life, I wanted to explore all its riches.

Somehow, however, I couldn't quite digest all the rules. What was supposed to be 'right' just didn't fit me. I felt like a bewildered actor on a stage, determined to play my part, yet finding the script was in a foreign language. My script was of unconditional loving embrace, wisdom, divinity, unity and spirit. The world's script was one of duality, fear, lies, conditions, judgment and punishment. And so the question remained, haunting me, plaguing me. Where did I come from?

It wasn't long before this question met my resounding resignation – mind-racking, heart-wrenching resignation. I simply could not see how I belonged in this alien setting. I must have come from elsewhere. And now I simply had to accept my lot.

Having watched other children and their families, I concluded that I could not have come from this family. The love extended to others was something that seemed denied to me. When I dreamed or sat quietly with closed eyes, I would see all the beautiful beings that I knew. When I opened my eyes, I saw strangers. I longed for the ones who loved me. Not just in the light, I wanted them with me in the world. I began to feel indignant. My soul's loneliness and sense of displacement grew so heavy that one day it took a spill.

I walked across the road to the neighbour's house. I looked at Bradley and Jacqui laughing happily. They were children who seemed to know they belonged.

Blatantly I asked: 'Where did you come from?'

The boy and girl looked at each other quizzically, and then giggled.

'From our mum and dad,' came the definite answer.

I stared at them with vacant eyes – a reflection of the gaping hole I felt inside. 'I don't come from my mum and dad.'

The boy and girl looked surprised. 'Don't you?' they asked together.

'No. No, I don't. I don't know how they got me. But I do know it was from somewhere else. They don't love me.'

'Ohh,' sighed the children.

'Hey, maybe you're adopted,' said the boy. He looked at his sister. 'You know that boy around the other block? He's adopted. His mum and dad got him from an orphanage.'

I looked at both of them in amazement. I wasn't sure if I felt relief or anger. My mind felt a sense of victory in the certainty that I had come from somewhere else. Yet a burning question followed. Then where and how did they get me? I walked away feeling overwhelmed at the thought that I might never know.

Over the space of the next few hours, Bradley and Jacqui had told their mum my forlorn story. And, naturally, she went and told my parents. Of course, all of this was unknown to me. That was ... until I came in again from the backyard. In an instant, I could feel rage was about to target me. Mum stood in the kitchen, looking at me, fire in her eyes.

'Ry-an!' she called, with a pitch that scaled from low to high. 'Kathryn's here.'

Through the doorway, Dad's body appeared. Fire in his eyes. They both loomed over me with red raging auras.

'What do you mean by telling our neighbours you're not our child and that we don't love you?' Her words were so harsh; I felt the anger tearing my tummy into fear. There wasn't a moment to think; just an instant response.

'Well, you don't love me. You're not my parents! I didn't come from here. Where did you steal me from?'

The two adults, horrified, looked as though they might explode. Only a fine line of physical control contained them. But rather than hitting me physically, this time it remained as shooting words and red hot light. Blows that defied space and form.

Merrilyn and Jackson stayed in the lounge room behind the thick glass door. Through the spotted seventies' glass, I could still see their faces like mottled mirages. As much as they were captured by the intrigue of it all, it was as close as they dared to be.

'What are you talking about, you stupid child? Of course you belong to us. WE had you. I went through all this pain to have you. How dare you embarrass us like this! What do you think you're doing, telling our neighbours such a stupid thing?' she screamed. She was almost senseless. I just stood there feeling like a fool.

But I couldn't hold it together anymore. I burst into tears: burning, aching, pleading tears to take it all away. I wanted to run. But where? The only plaçe that seemed safe was under my bed covers. So there I huddled, wrenched by tears.

That night I dreamed that I was flying high above the earth. Then all of a sudden I began to fall, fast and hard ...

Terror shocked me awake. My heart beat furiously. Like a drum, it pounded in my chest, it beat in my ears. Outside the bedroom, a blackbird began to whistle its sweet morning melody, the call of dawn. I lay flat on my back, staring at the ceiling. The sunlight began to creep through the edge of the blinds. Then the bedroom door opened. Mum came into the room.

Her morning smell arrived well before her body, a pungent stench of cigarettes and coffee. She sat on the edge of the bed, her eyes swollen and puffy. She put her hand gently on my arm. Her energy was a mixture of soft, jumbly, nervous, weary, caring; her words, the same.

'Oh Kathryn, I don't know, dear. Why do you feel these things? We do love you. And we want the best for you. Why do you make it so hard?'

I stared back at her, wanting to drink up the possibility of love in this tenderness. But inside I still quaked like a lamb. I couldn't help but think of Little Red Riding Hood: I felt just like her. I wondered whether these words were just disguising the wolf. All I could muster up was a shrug. I turned on my side facing the wall. But Mum stayed present. She lay down next to me. Her warm, soft breast cradled against my back. Her arm enfolded me as she sighed.

I released my breath as I realised that something in me was so still, it was untouched, present and watchful. It was deeply unattached, oddly at home in the mystery of my life.

The 1st Attainment

The Fool, having once stepped over the edge of the cliff, cannot turn back. Either she will fall deeper into unconscious sleep or she will keep her head up, moved by her pure-hearted faith in the mystery, and take one step at a time, willing to enter the game of creation.

KEY 1.

The Magic Man

KEY 1.

The Magic Man

Holder of mysterious power, the tools and intelligence of creation, he contains all knowledge of how to create. He is the bridge between consciousness and form. He moulds the world in the image of his choosing.

The world is the work of one great Magician – the play of the real and unreal. One is the Master; the other is his own trick, the illusion that one is not the Master.

Alert and watchful, I looked closely for the signs and tools of creation.

5. *Seeing*

> Dew evaporates
> And all our world
> Is dew ... so dear,
> So refreshing, so fleeting.
>
> *Issa*

As a young child, I was very often in deep contemplation, my thoughts reflecting on the landscape of life. This deep focus and concentration earned me a reputation as a very 'serious' child. Jackson, my brother, seemed to delight in supporting this portrayal. My sister seemed to remain oblivious.

I found this label, and the many other references, odd, and it quickly became obvious that no one understood me at all. The more I tried to explain, the worse it got. The more others tried to explain to me how it all 'really' was, the more I felt deceived. In the purity of my soul, the explanations felt like a mass of lies offered behind shady masks, from those who pretended to be loving and wise. The integrity of my soul was put before the bench of illusion and convicted of deception and delusion. I could see that the world's idea of reality was contorted by fear. I felt heavy at the idea that I might never be understood, and my truth might forever be judged as a lie.

With a growing sense of entanglement, I retreated. My inner contemplations seemed to move me in a very direct way. The more knotted up I felt, the more I would direct my body into very specific poses, turning upside down, back to front and almost inside out.

With my legs behind my ears, I turned into a human pretzel. With my back arched and toes clasped to the top of my shoulders, I was a rocking boat. With legs fully crossed and with arms looped through and around my body, I made myself into a human knot. With my body folded neatly in half upon the floor, I became like freshly folded laundry.

I would dissolve deeply into a pose, sometimes for ten minutes or longer. At other times, I would take to waddling around the house on my knees with my legs crossed and feet folded up to my hips. To everyone else, it appeared that I was as knotted up in my body as I was in my mind. Yet, as troubled as it all appeared to the outside world, these body bends and knots led me to a deeper pool of peace within. Somehow the act of focusing and coming into a stillness in the body's twists and contortions soothed the pain of my soul. And in this stillness came a new contemplation, which led to wonderful surprise discoveries and to more questions ...

•

I was particularly contemplative when we went for drives in the car. We had a house in the suburbs and a beautiful family shack on the coast, so we were often on the road for hours. One day, as we were driving, I had grown tired of the usual game of 'I spy with my little eye'. My ability to read my brother's and sister's minds wiped out the fun of guessing and added to their agitation since I always exposed them so quickly.

I sat wide-eyed staring out of the window. I watched the swirling scape[1] with amazement ... parts within parts within space, all connected, all moving, all changing. I felt a deep stirring, an ancient knowing. It was the voice of this Self, which had always been. The thought was clear: It's all connected. Nothing at all is a part by itself. And still there are all these parts! And it's all changing, all moving ... Then an even deeper consciousness stirred, like a deeply soft and full explosion of light that sent a gasp to escape my lips: And it's still the

[1] A word I use to convey a vastness of expanse that is without defined form and yet can include form.

same … ! Hmmmm.

I sat reflecting again on my inner thoughts and watched the moving landscape.

Dad was a slow driver. I noticed how most cars would pass us on the road, sometimes quickly, sometimes slowly. I enjoyed this because I got to watch all the drivers and their passengers. The thing that had me most intrigued was how the spokes on the wheels appeared to spin in the opposite direction. I once asked Dad why they did that, but received a disappointing reply.

'They aren't, they are moving forwards.'

'But why?' I asked.

'Because.'

I knew that reply well enough. It meant *end of story.* So I figured I'd have to work it out myself. So there I was, just turned seven, contemplating physics.

As I watched, I paid great attention to the direction of the cars going forwards, the landscape passing, the spokes spinning in the opposite direction and the horizon getting closer while it was still distant. Suddenly the sound of a fly caught my attention. It was struggling with the invisible barrier of the back window. My awareness then opened. I was no longer watching from the usual perspective, relative to the objects. I realised that there were many more layers to the illusion of moving objects. The apparition of the spokes had caught my attention so deeply that I moved into a wider state of awareness. In an instant, I understood the optical illusion. But that witnessing went further. I began to see a wider play of illusion as the realisations rolled through my awareness: All these directions are just a name. Dad says we're travelling forwards, but to the fly, the car is travelling backwards. That's it! There is no fixed state of forwards or backwards or up or down. It just *looks* like that. Nothing is fixed! It's all moving up, down, in, out, left, right, all in the same moment. Direction is relevant to perception. Wow! Clever! A smile spread across my face and I drifted into no-time as I continued to watch, mesmerised by it all.

My trance was broken as a car moved up beside us and slowed down to the same pace. There, was the face of a little boy who was looking out of the window just like I was. It startled me as I realised I was looking at another 'me'.

Suddenly I was *seeing*. I gasped out loud and, without a pause, my thoughts came tumbling out of my mouth.

'Oh my! It's all me's, we're all me's. It's all myself! Everything! And everything has a different thought, but it's all me. Wow! How amazing!'

A feeling of such oneness and completeness filled my being. I sighed into silence, overwhelmed by the beauty, the magnitude, the normality and the strangeness of it all mixed together. In that moment I realised I was experiencing all of life, multi-dimensionally at the same time! It was as if a sliding door of the mind had opened into a space that had no walls. The mind was no longer fixed to any one direction, time-line or dimension. I was the awareness, not the 'room' that I had been in. In that space I could see that I had chosen everything that I was experiencing. My life was something I had created from a place of great consciousness, not something that was simply happening to me. I felt the immense joy of being a child of creation. Its power was in me and a part of me, and I was choosing it. I was like a child placed before an endless, beautiful white sheet of paper, and offered the paints of life, with endless possibilities of what I could paint. I could paint anything I chose!

But before long, my amazement was broken by laughter from Mum, Dad, my brother, and then my sister. I half began to laugh but stopped in my tracks when I realised that this laughter wasn't light and tickly. It was 'that' laughter, the one that was dark and sticky and poked at me. I suddenly saw that my family was viewing my outburst of wonder from a totally different perspective. I had been seeing the wonderment of the all-connected creation – the One Self that is all ... that I AM. They were seeing a silly little girl who thought the world was centred around her. Then Mum spoke to Dad as if I wasn't there.

'Well, that's not surprising. She is selfish, after all.'

I felt a twist in my tummy as the heavy slicing energy sent me plummeting once again into the world of my family.

'No, I'm not!' I cried, 'That's not true!'

'Yes it is,' my brother sniped.

I started to cry. Why don't they understand? How can I be selfish when it's all the same Self? I just love. That's not the way life is, I'm not meant to feel this. My sense of being different from everyone else became more solid. I cried. I felt so alone. I'd rather be all by myself! I thought. Mum's angry voice lunged at me.

'Stop crying or we'll take you home and you can be there all by yourself. See if you like that, then, little miss selfish!'

I stopped crying out of sheer shock. No. How could that be? Did she know what I was thinking or did I make her say that? It rattled my mind.

And so I sat with my tears, wailing inwardly. Best I stay silent, I thought.

My deep inner voice echoed back at me. 'The magician must keep silent.'

Then before I knew it, I was back in the little room of my body and mind. Why do I have to be here? I thought, I don't belong here. It's not meant to be this way. What happened? Why did the dream have to change?

My sobbing thoughts were interrupted by the sweetness of my beautiful friend, my angel, shining blue and golden light. He was my true friend, my angel love, the one who would come when I was lost, the one who could calm my fretting mind. His voice was like a gentle song and his face shone with golden light.

'Beloved, I am always with you. You are not alone. Do not forget what you see and feel. It is truth. Remember you are here because you are meant to be.'

He disappeared in a cloud of light, leaving me feeling soothed and restful.

Yet somewhere deep inside, my heart sank as the knowing dawned on me that this could only mean one thing. I was here to stay for a long time. I wasn't so sure that I liked the idea of that. And yet even deeper in my soul was an awareness that was so untouched – so still, it was like a rock. A rock that knew it would all be fine, that it was all for a grand purpose.

It was only two weeks later that I discovered how liberated that 'rock' inside of me was. We happened to be staying at my Nanna's house for the weekend. At that age I had a particular liking for things that were sweet. And in Nanna's cupboards I discovered a favourite: a dish filled with snow-white sugar cubes. Nanna (my mother's mother) was fairly liberal with sweet treats. She was quite happy to give us cake, jelly or sweet biscuits as snacks. But one thing she was firm on was: no more sweets once we were bathed in the evening.

Yet on this particular evening, I had a relentless desire to take two of those little snowy cubes to bed. My taste buds watered at the thought of the hard packed sugar dissolving on my tongue. I managed to sneak to the cupboard just before going to bed. As I snuggled in I felt the cubes in my hot little hand. Some crumbs were starting to fall onto the sheet. My little mind urged Nanna to hurry up; she always came to kiss us goodnight once we were tucked in.

Then the unexpected happened. In came Nanna. But instead of just a quick kiss, for some reason she pulled back the sheets a bit in order to smooth the bed out more for me. And as she did her hand brushed over the little sugar crumbs.

She stopped abruptly. Her dark eyes began to squint.

'What's this ...? Sand? How did sand get in your ...?'

Her words trailed off as she looked more closely.

'Sugar!'

She grabbed at my pink hand as it squeezed hard around the cubes, trying to hide them. Her dark Spanish eyes glared.

'You wicked little girl!' she yelled. And with that she wrenched the cubes from my grip and gave my backside a hit that stung.

I burst into tears. Nanna stormed out of the room leaving me to cry myself to sleep. And there under the covers as I cried and sobbed heavily, I suddenly realised that 'I' was watching. 'I' was a 'rock' of deep calm and peace just watching the act of crying. In fact, that one watching was even totally consciously amused.

Hmm ... look at all that noise! I thought. 'I' am not even sad. In fact 'I' am not any thoughts. 'I' am endless peace!

So there I lay in the wonder of knowing the immovable 'rock' within. And from that moment, no matter what act occurred, no matter what happened, I was aware of the permanence within – the 'I' that knew it was all okay, the 'I' that remained forever clear, forever unmoved by life's events.

A week later, I found myself temporarily outside the prison of the normal perception of time. We were experiencing a typical South Australian heatwave: the temperature had been hovering around 40–45°C for five days. In such weather, we would occasionally get the treat of walking to the local delicatessen to buy an 'icy pole' (an ice block).

As we stood under the shade of a tree, I lavishly sucked on the orange icy treat, enjoying its cool lusciousness. The air was so hot that the ice block began melting and running down my wrist. Then, as I tried to lick up the bottom and slow down the rapid melt, the top of the block broke away. With wide eyes, I watched it falling, in slow motion, into timelessness. It fell to the ground and dissolved before my eyes. Suddenly I became aware that the very thing I had enjoyed as so real, no longer was. In fact, *everything* that I thought was real in each moment was destined to completely disappear!

The truth of this struck me so deeply that I felt a simultaneous disappointment that all pleasures would never last or fulfil me, and yet a liberation that all the suffering would also pass.

6. The Fairytale

I have been here before,
But when or how I cannot tell:
I know the grass beyond the door,
The sweet keen smell,
The sighing sound,
The lights around the shore.

Dante Gabriel Rosetti

My summer months were filled with outdoor adventures. The sun danced as stars on the emerald sea and baked the earth, on which I loved to play. And it turned my skin dark and rich – 'as brown as a berry', my Nanna used to say. My straw-blonde hair bleached white to the tips.

I was slowly, tentatively, beginning to embrace this body. Yet it still caused such confusion. I felt neither boy nor girl yet was beginning to yearn for the feminine power to ripen. And equally I could not imagine giving up all the things that made me such a tomboy – like climbing to the very tops of trees and taking in the great horizon, traversing cliffs, and running so wild and free that my hair was like a screaming fright.

My golden tendrils gave me perhaps my deepest sense of a physical female quality. In my daydreams I considered myself to be like Cinderella, with my life resembling a chore directed by the horrid stepmother (about whom I still had suspicions). Or I would see myself waiting in the tower, like Rapunzel – ready to lower my great long golden tail of hair for my knight in shining armour. But I didn't imagine a white knight. My knight was a man of the land, with dark skin and eyes like midnight. I longed to be freed of the cage of the house, to be returned to the place my spirit knew ... the heart of nature. This little girl felt trapped in the modern world and dreamed of her ancient roots, her world that had been born from red earth.

I thought my fairytale was about to come true when two new Aboriginal boys arrived at the school. They were the only black children and were immediately the target of cruelty. But to me they were a godsend, especially Barry, the older one, who was in the same class as me. At that age all the girls were getting curious about boys, giggling and fantasising about kisses and weddings. The other girls were only interested in the white boys. I was totally uninterested in the white boys. It was the black boy who caught my attention. Before long we were meeting at the local playground.

There in the warm sunny haze we would climb up in the slippery-dip tree. Old and weathered, the conifer had grown long sloping branches that provided hours of delight. Inside the tree were wonderful nesting forks and broad arms to sit on. It was there that I had my first kiss. Barry and I were laughing and staring into each other's eyes when we suddenly grabbed each other and planted our lips together. It took my breath away, but the other children groaned in disgust. However, my first 'knight' was only in my life for a few months. Before long, Barry Williams disappeared out of my life forever and I became Rapunzel again.

The princess syndrome suited my desperate longing for freedom until one day, in one fell swoop, my living connection to this fantasy was taken. My mother decided my hair was too much to deal with. So, taking a bowl from the cupboard, she sat me on a stool. I looked down at the cool tiles. They were black like the sudden hole inside me. She sprayed my hair, placed the bowl on my head and began. The sound of the scissors severing my hair echoed my heart's sentiment. I watched my long golden tendrils flop onto the floor. And along with them my young and tender feminine identity fell away.

As I looked in the mirror, my self-confidence about becoming the woman I was destined to be took a great leap backwards. The tears rolled down my flushed, freckled cheeks. Once again, I looked like a boy.

I stood there puzzled that I felt some strange attachment to the thought of being a girl. How could I, when I could not see any lasting reality in these bodies? I thought I had been a boy, a girl, a boy ... a man, a woman. A sensation like some distant chord[1] in an ancient memory tugged at my mind. Yet the song lay too deep to understand.

My mind stood on the frontier of a question. Wasn't all of this just another fairytale? I could see that all of this life, as with people's hopes and dreams, was just some great myth of the mind.

The knowing was like a dropping, a plummeting through cosmic space. It was a knowing I had had for eternity. I felt like I was twisted inside out, in a rapid flip from dreaming to awake and back to dreaming. Somehow, I wasn't really asleep and was aware that what seemed as reality to everyone was, to this deeper awareness, only dreaming.

I teetered on the spinning edge of my mind and, in one instant of conscious glance, stopped dead still. I was nothing but a gap.

From the timeless, I suddenly snapped back out of it and saw my body's reflection again in the mirror. I stood in a daze. My skin was dark from long days in the sun ... This body bore a striking resemblance to those of Aboriginals, whom I had watched with fascination and a sense of familiarity. I looked at my broad nose and strong forehead, the squarish jaw, my skinny arms and legs. I thought of Uncle Rej and Granddad with their dark features. I thought of my brother with his dark eyes and hair, broad nose, and skin that turned even darker than mine in the sun. Then I thought of Merrilyn, fair with blue eyes like my mum. Something didn't add up. I sensed a secret, hiding behind the closed doors of our family heritage.

Questioning thoughts passed through my mind at lightning speed. Yet it was impossible to pin them down, at least for the time being.

---

1 All experiences include a sound vibration or a particular harmonic, like a chord played on an instrument. Occasionally I experience a sympathetic vibratory response, a resonance, with such sounds.

7. Red Roo

And a little child shall lead them.

Isaiah 11:6

From about the age of seven, it seemed that the other levels of awareness began to overlap with life even more. The fuzzy lights I was aware of, surrounding every living thing, suddenly seemed even more vivid. And not only light – the voice of the conscious Self was in each. I heard the animals, the birds, the flowers and the trees, with such deep openness that it was completely natural to have delightful conversations with them all. I also noticed that many spirits would start to gather around whenever these little garden chats lit up. It was there in nature that I felt most alive and most real.

I didn't feel I belonged in a house. A house to me was like a cage, a box that represented a kind of death, where the spirit of life was blocked. My spirit felt most at home on the naked earth, surrounded by the trees, rocks and nature spirits. Somehow I didn't feel like a white person. I'm sure that if I didn't have a mirror, I would have believed myself to be a little black girl. And, there on the land, I often found myself comfortably surrounded by the presence of Aboriginal spirits. The old skinny man who stood to my left made me feel safe and protected. The old womens' round faces made me feel embraced in perfect innocence, natural beauty and something more – a quiet power. I spent many hours dreaming of life in nature, imagining myself in a world surrounded by my native family, living off the land.

To me it was the greatest romance imaginable: being free to live on the land and roam as a wild nature spirit. I spent many hours making little shelters and gathering precious things from the bush and praying that somehow I could be transported again into that reality, away from the prison walls of modern life. Something ancient in me just couldn't comprehend the modern world.

Along with this came an increased sensitivity. I felt so completely aware and awake in nature that my sensitivity would be overpowering in moments. It reached a climax one day when Dad started the lawn-mower. As he rolled the great growling machine onto the lawn and set its blades upon the grass, my body reeled in pain. It was as if every cell was connected to every blade of grass. The spinning slicing blades brought the sound of screaming tears. The sound of this pain was too much. I ran to my room, leaped onto my bed and buried myself under the blankets in a frantic attempt to escape the sound of a million souls being slaughtered. But how could I escape? It was all in me. I realised that everything lived within this awareness.

My eyes made me want to believe in the illusion that I was separate – to be free of the cries of everything and everyone. But in my soul I knew I could not divide from me what seemed outside but was really within me. Everything was ONE. So where then was freedom from suffering if not somewhere deeper within? I knew that if I was to expose the Magician's trickery, the great mystery, I would have to watch closely. Deep within, my God-voice spoke.

Everything is a sign pointing you there. You are free. If you watch closely enough you will see the Magician's trick. He hasn't made anything disappear. He just distracted you for a moment. That's when it happens.

My mind conjured up an image of a giant Wanjina being,[1] white like a great wizard spirit. He wielded great power and danced between the world of spirit and form. It was then that I first felt the profound truth that God IS always watching, through the eyes of creation. The

---

[1] Guardian spirit and keeper of creation dreaming in the Kimberleys (a region in the north-west of Australia).

ancestor spirits hovered over me, protecting me, guiding me.

My spirit felt the power of some urgency arising from this insight. Even greater now was my determination for freedom. Over many months I had felt the need to be on my own, to be away from the entrapment of a family who so completely misunderstood me. I desperately wanted freedom from the screaming, the punishments, the confinements and the tears. I plotted my escape. I dreamed of a life in the bush: roaming beside rivers, sheltering in caves, lazing under the trees and gazing at the stars.

I began collecting supplies of food and pocket money, and earning extra coins for odd jobs. Behind the drawer under my bed, I hid all that could sustain me: cookies, lollies, coins, a few one- and two-dollar notes, and packets of dehydrated soups and noodles. I started researching escape routes to the parks and train station. I planned to make my way in the middle of the night when the rest of the family were sleeping. I could easily get out of the bedroom window, as stealthily and quietly as a cat.

I applied myself diligently for weeks. It all seemed to come together beautifully in my exciting vision of freedom, until I decided to let my brother in on my getaway plan. He seemed the perfect partner in crime; a willing accomplice. Deeply spellbound in a sense of a brotherly bond, I trusted our pact of secrecy. And in the hope that my brother was going to aid my escape, I exposed the time and 'D-day'. As an ally, he learned every last detail of my plan – only to betray me.

The next morning I was summoned to the kitchen, where Mum and Dad confronted me. I felt hauled backwards and forwards between their admonishing fury and my own growing anger at having been 'turned in'. I struggled to understand this betrayal. My vision of freedom was quickly tied down by the heavy hand of my parents' discipline. And whatever camaraderie had existed between my brother and me was turned upside-down.

What had been confusion and bewilderment at life was now taking a turn. Rather than a solemn brew of compassion and willingness to have hope again, my pot now seethed in wilful anger. Yet, to my amazement, the awareness remained that the anger was not even real. I knew that it was really a motivating force for me and that underneath it all was an ever-present love. And so I pivoted on a point of awareness in which I yearned to be free of the world yet saw the non-reality of the world. In fact, the world and its events were no less (or more) real than the dreams that continued to emerge, fresh and startling.

Amongst all the vivid, bizarre and prophetic dreams that I had consistently as a girl, there was one that kept recurring. I would be walking through a park, the city or shops, when all of a sudden the scene would start changing. I saw the fast-forward of consumerism and the self-sabotaging fate of society. Everything was speeding up with a sense of urgency. Then I would be running. I'd run, faster and faster, bearing a great torch. And the torch would become brighter and brighter: a beacon, a flaming light, as if I was carrying the sun. People would start following, with more and more coming, until there was a great crowd coming after me.

My skin was golden brown and my wild golden hair flew out behind me as a north wind blew strong. Then suddenly I was running so fast that I became a great red kangaroo, and the earth beneath me became a passing landscape changing from city to far-off places. The land beneath me became red sand; the sky, vivid blue. People of every race followed me away from the cities, away from the walls of concrete, into the heart of nature, into stillness, into silence, into the dreaming, where the world, as it was known, ceased to be. We were in the heart of Australia, surrounded by the perfect beauty of nature, of mother earth in all her glory. There, in that perfect beauty, there was a return ... to a life of purity and innocence.

Where life had been held in the grip of the monster of greed and corruption, I saw ghost towns and barren cities. And then I saw the renewal of life: an awakening, a new way of living, where people lived as one again in love and light and divine consciousness.

•

There were three occasions when this dream changed shape and I found myself as an ancient black grandmother, sitting on the red sand.

My old woman's body felt the power of my earth mother and the ancestors of creation. Many men and women were seated around me as I told the dreaming story of a girl with golden hair who would carry a great fire stick and run as the red roo. It was the prophecy, the promise, to be born again to bear a light and speak of the lore of creation.

I spoke of a time when white men would come with a book and take us from our land. People would fall asleep, walk blind, talk hate, take and not share. Great illness, destruction and death would follow. Our mother would be violated and her life would be at risk. Her rivers would die and forests and creatures would disappear and piles of grey stuff would suffocate her. The light-bearer would be born in the time of destruction to bring unity again amongst the people and respect again for the sacred way.

•

The red roo dream remained consistent, occurring once or twice a week for years. It was one of many dreams that were to occur repeatedly.

I began to recognise a pattern. Very often, the dreams that

repeated were a message to help me understand my life and memories from other lifetimes. And increasingly they became a reality, dreams of prophecy. Yet there was no consistency to the timing between the foresight and the actual encounter in physical reality. Sometimes my dreams would all unfold in exact detail the very next day. Sometimes they would unfold weeks, months and even, I was to discover, years later.

Aside from the dreams and visions, I also seemed to have a constant trail of 'visitors'. My family called it my imagination at first. But then the more I tried to explain the reality of these spirit beings that would come and talk with me, the more my family took to the opinion that I had a few 'problems'.

Amongst these visitors were beings of great light, wonder and wisdom. Their forms were evident, yet not distinctly outlined by a body. Instead they emanated in orbs of golden, white or flame-blue light. There were two yogis who frequently appeared. One was in the form of an Indian sage, the other was a Tibetan. In their presence I felt nothing but loving embrace and encouragement to be myself. Sometimes I would start talking out loud to them or speaking in other languages, which would seem like a great stream of babbling to anyone else who might be listening. I chanted for hours, whispered and sang – sometimes to the spirits, sometimes simply in the bliss of connectedness to God – all in a warbling language foreign to my family. (It wasn't until my adult years that I discovered one of these chants was the Gayatri[1] mantra.) And, naturally, the more I talked to these things that no one else could see, and in words that didn't make sense, the more I was considered to be mentally disturbed. Furthermore, I would even talk to the trees, flowers and creatures. I didn't even know how to begin explaining this because it was something totally other than human thoughts and words. So I was often referred to as being 'off with the fairies' – which oddly enough was true! Yet no one else wanted to believe they were real.

[1] Considered the supreme mantra of the Indian yogis.

And so I was often chastised, humiliated and ridiculed, which provoked a deeply emotional state within me. I was not able to hold a constant connection to the higher levels of awareness. Despite a very powerful aspect that was 'awake' there was also the part of me that experienced confusion as a girl. This contrast amplified my sense of frustration and confusion. And as a consequence, my volatile emotions only served to validate the theories that something was actually wrong with me.

In my increasingly 'open' state I seemed to attract a lot more than just light-beings. Lost souls would visit me at night, pressing upon me, wailing to me, hassling me – all for attention. For the first two years, I found this terrifying. So terrifying, in fact, that even when I tried to scream, nothing would come out of my mouth. By this time, I had learned mostly to keep quiet about these things, which were beginning to take a toll on me emotionally. As a consequence, I started to lose even more faith in my own sanity, and in life's reality/non-reality. This only compounded the emotional roller-coaster of my family life.

However, I eventually came to understand that these dear souls (the distressed spirits at night), no matter how ugly, smelly or agitated, were lost souls of God who were seeking love. They would first appear to me as dark, disturbed presences. But as I accepted and embraced them, they would leave in lightness and peace.

Aside from the emotional pain in many areas of my life, I still had a deep sense of wonder about this world.

•

My sense of confusion wasn't all so bad either. The emotions were there, yes, but they would pass again so quickly. They also compelled me to make a deeper investigation into myself. So I became very present to my body and feelings. Spontaneously I would have 'ideas' that I would experiment with in order to settle into deeper awareness.

I began breathing in rhythmical patterns. What seemed to work best was a count of four with the in-breath and six with the out-breath.

At first my attention focused on the rhythm. Then gradually that focus created a 'slowing down' of my mind. It was as if my mind was melting, like the ripples on a lake dissolving into stillness. My awareness then simply flowed with the breath. I became the alert 'witness'. Over the days, as I witnessed the breath I became aware of the converging space between the in and out breath. In that space I could hear an ever-so subtle sound ... *so hum, so hum, so hum: so* on the in-breath and *hum* on the out-breath. The more I practised this, the more I experienced stillness. The awareness of my body ceased and I expanded into pure consciousness.

On several occasions I was visited during these breathing states by the Indian yogi who appeared in a brilliant ball of light. He reminded me that So Hum (or SãHaṃ) *is* the sound of the breath and that I had used it as a mantra[1] in previous lifetimes to develop stillness and conscious awareness.

This practice increased my alert awareness within the worldly happenings. So self-awareness and decisiveness were intensely awake and developed in me. However, according to my parents and teachers, that usually deserved no acknowledgment because it was inappropriate or simply 'not allowed' in one so young. When I attempted to assert myself, it evoked fear and anger in others. I nearly always ended up in a crying mess, having been screamed at or hit.

It seemed I was causing problems. Innocently and diligently I confronted, questioned, asserted and determined, in order to walk my own path. For a seven-year-old that was unthinkable – let alone in Sunday school. I remember those moments so vividly ... the smell of the church, the cool air in the hall, the hard carpet under my knees.

Miss Dawe was prim, upright and like a little bird, except that her movements were stiff. To my mind, she had just been giving us a ridiculous sermon about overcoming sins: saying that God was always watching and we should fear his name, which was why we had

---

[1] Sacred Sanskrit words or phrases, often used repetitively to assist in stilling the mind's chatter.

to pray everyday.

'Now, children, let us pray,' she said. The other ten children, along with my ever-obedient sister, dutifully followed suit. They kneeled on the floor, closed their eyes and put their hands together. I just sat there staring, totally refusing to do something I didn't need to do.

Miss Dawe must have sensed me because she opened her eyes, stared and nodded at me as if to say now close your eyes and pray. I held my ground and shook my head.

'Kathryn. Why aren't you praying?'

'Because I'm not afraid.'

Her body stiffened and she pressed her lips together tightly. She looked at me indignantly. The stuffy church air pressed in around me.

'What do you mean?' she snapped.

'You said the Bible says we should fear God.'

'Yes, dear, and we should pray to be free of our sins.'

'But why would God make his children bad if God is good? I'm not afraid. I haven't done anything wrong. I am not bad. Why should I be afraid? And why do you want me to lie? Even the Bible says I should not lie.'

For a moment she looked taken aback. Then her look became firm. 'Now, dear, if you want to be a good girl, you should pray.'

I felt my toes curl inside my shoes.

'No!' I retorted. 'I don't need to pray. I am good already and I'll be good my own way!'

With that she took me firmly by the arm and led me out of the room to sit in the cold silence of the foyer. I sat in my own stern defiance. I haven't done anything wrong, I thought to myself. Why should I fear God? That would mean I would have to fear myself and that would be horrible. I had to live with me – if I was afraid, I wouldn't feel the joy in my heart and that would be terrible. I loved the joy in my heart. Why would I admit I had done something wrong when I hadn't? Then that would be a lie and then I *would* have done something wrong. The thoughts rolled around and around until I became aware of my aloneness. But it was not a sad thing. It was a beautiful thing, because there in my aloneness I could just be myself, untouched, unspoiled by others' thoughts and demands.

Of course, Mum was furious when she came to pick us up. The whole way home she rebuked me: 'You are such an embarrassment. How could you be so rude and obnoxious?'

Her words went on and on. But they just rolled off me, like rain off an umbrella.

•

My mind became stronger and my awareness of my body's wants and my soul's desires more powerful. I seemed to have an endless reserve of strength to pick myself up and carry on, no matter what happened. And despite the efforts of others to bring me under their control, I only seemed to develop an even greater sense of my own will. I simply refused to conform to any one else's demands of how I 'should' be and instead formed an even greater resistance to society's expectations.

Aside from differences about goals, priorities and life's meaning, I found even the most ordinary matters confronting. Food continued to be particularly challenging, except for the sweets. The smell of meat in the grill was so nauseating that I used to try to pretend I wasn't hungry or that I felt sick. I began to consciously develop my acting skills. But this didn't bring me much power of self-choice either.

One day I sat considering the charred lamb chop on my plate, feeling sure that if I ate it I'd be sick. But my usual attempt at debate with Mum was failing – once again. Her temper was escalating. It was something I hated to feel so much. It was so strong and painful. With her last demand that I eat it before I left the table, I finally carved off a piece and put it in my mouth.

But before I had begun to chew it, I felt the familiar sensation of heaving in my stomach that sent pre-vomit saliva rushing to my mouth. Trying to hold it back, I clamped my teeth onto the stinky bit of tough leather. But before I could move, my stomach did one great lurch and my dinner left my mouth in a great sloppy heap of chunky projectile soup. My mother who was standing by the fridge did a leap that almost put her in the category of some superhero's villain, with one great swoop, she smacked me on the back of the head.

'You filthy little animal!' she screamed.

I remember feeling so afraid and hurt and yet, at the same time, a comical rebel rose up in me with a comeback thought that no, she was wrong. She wanted me to *eat* the 'filthy little *dead* animal'! I left the table, went and wiped my face and went to bed sobbing.

8. Into the World

Our normal reality is like each of us living in a tiny,
Windowless cell in a house
That contains a hundred thousand rooms
And covers a thousand acres of land.

Michael J Roads

I woke up feeling fresh and ready for school. I had great enthusiasm for school because I found I was acknowledged for my capabilities. Even in grade three it was evident I had a high IQ: I was in the top three and made A's in each subject. It was also a totally different environment. There was no moody mother, no stern father and no teasing brother. At home, nearly every day was disturbed by some factor that griped my parents or siblings – and to which I had already developed strong reactions.

School also meant weekends and holidays, which had become a regular treat for me, mostly because we would journey to our family shack in Hidden Valley. Here, indoors, the aroma of Granny's home-baked pies wafted. And outdoors, the hills were huge and endless, the ocean was sparkling like turquoise and emeralds, the valleys were forested and the cliffs offered a dare-devil challenge for my wild spirit.

However, this particular year different plans arose.

My father had remained an enigma to me. Even though he wasn't around much he was a mysterious presence of power. He worked long hours, sometimes being called out at night and sometimes for longer periods, to faraway places. Despite his long periods of absence, I discovered that his return from distant places brought more wonderment into my life. My eyes opened wide as I listened, excited by the knowledge that the world was so big and filled with so many different things.

He would could home with stories about China, where the Chinese people all had black hair and almond-slanted eyes, food was exotic and delicious, streets were bumping with people and rickshaws, stalls overflowed with dried fish and chickens' feet (surely they didn't really eat them?) and houses were full of mysterious objects. Dad must have spent time looking in the shops and strange-smelling market places too, because he would bring little surprises home for us: battery-driven toy dogs that yapped, little skull caps with long tassles, satin pyjamas with dragons and flowers chasing each other all over the cloth, and little black 'happy' shoes. I was very happy to have happy shoes! I had a thought (it didn't last many days) that maybe they had magic power. Maybe if I wore them all the time then everything, including my grumpy mum, would be turned into 'happiness'.

But the thing that fascinated me most was the collection of Chinese astrological marble seals, one for each of us. I thought it incredible that these animal symbols actually seemed to suit our characters. Dad was born in the year of the rat and loved cheese and nuts. Mum was the ox, the burdened domesticated worker. I could see she felt chained to her duty. Merrilyn was the rooster, except her crow came from a trumpet. Jackson was a dragon who liked to hide away in his lair and would breathe fire if it was invaded. And me? – I was very happy to be a goat, with my head in the clouds and my feet on rambling rocky cliffs!

•

Then one day my father came home from work to tell us he had been asked to go to America for a period – to the United States of America, and that we would *all* be going. America! I thought. This caused great excitement for my curious spirit. I imagined giant buildings and 'just as giant' people.

Mum and Dad made sure we understood that this still meant work – that it wasn't just a holiday. We got the drilling that we would still have to do work from our own school as well as the school in the States. My brother whined about it but I actually felt excited and very confident about this challenge. When we got there I discovered it was also a breeze. In fact, at eight I was advanced for my age and had to be placed in a class with kids one and two years older than me. This proved rather interesting socially because, albeit I was more intellectually advanced, it seemed they were way ahead of me in terms of the social stakes and other things ...

When working in class one day, drawing a diagram, I discovered my pencil work needed a few alterations, so I raised my hand.

'Yes, dear?' the teacher queried.

'Could I please have a rubber?' To my shock the classroom burst into laughter. I didn't understand why, which must have been evident from the look of confusion on my face.

'There ain't no rubber,' yelled a boy. 'Eraser, dummy!' he laughed.

The teacher settled the class down and later on had the task of explaining to me, a naive eight-year-old, that a rubber was a condom, which she also had to explain. Judging by the look on her face, I think she was as embarrassed as I was.

When I told the family, my father burst into uproarious laughter. Somehow, that made me feel like it was all okay. I loved that about my father. Despite his discipline he had a tendency on occasion to burst out in fits of wacky wit. Unlike my mother, I had an immediate attunement with his quick, dry humour. I exercised my own humour often just to feel the delight of laughing banter with my father. And despite my father's lack of emotional communication, it was in those moments that there was no distance between us.

There were many things about America that delighted, inspired, amazed, shocked, humoured and horrified me. Incredible landscapes that took my breath away; the exhilaration and pain of snow on bare fingers; the funny accents that were as amusing as mine was in turn; high speed chases of cops after criminals; tulips massed in long gardens; exquisite patterns of ice crystals on windows; armed hold-ups and thieves grabbing granny-bags; the thunder of Niagara Falls; the funny smells in our upper New York State home, followed by strange ghosts that no one else could see; skipping rope with cute girls, white and coloured; and a terrifying moment that remained in the depths of my soul, dark and secret – my first encounter of sexual violation.

The house where I played with my friend turned out to be the place of cruel interruption to my completely virgin anatomy: a painful change thrust upon me by the groping fingers of my friend's father. It was also the first time I understood that it wasn't only adults who were the subject of gaping, drooling mouths. In horror I soon realised some tried to eat up children as well. It was a waking nightmare that I carried in deep fear, remembering my tormentor's words.

'You tell anyone and I'll come kill you ... No one else needs to know ... It's just our secret.'

I felt so violated, so confused. How could my friend's daddy do that? What about her? My mind ran over and over the experience every day. And to the rest of the family my emotional balance seemed to tip sideways – for no reason at all.

The other person who seemed to have an impact on me, and profoundly so, was an old Navaho Indian man. We met in Arizona near the Canyon.

Our family outings eventually led us to some of the stations where the native people produced collections of craft, jewellery and pottery for sale. I remember looking at my mum, thinking it was the happiest I had seen her. She seemed to be alight in this place. Her excitement over all the beautiful native artwork kept her buzzing and in a more loving mood. It was also when she was most generous, which made me glad because I liked all those things too.

While I was looking at everything, I felt a familiar vibration come over me, and my inner vision switched on. In the background I could hear the call of a soulful flute that had been haunting me from a great distance. It was deep in my soul. I saw many Indians, but not like here in the deserts. I saw grassy plains and tepees, regal faces, long-fringed clothes, bright beads and blue skies. I could see how connected that way of life was. It was even connected to this place, to these people, and I felt a deep warmth inside.

Just then I spotted a little bag on the shelf in front of me. Its soft golden deer suede and bright beads beckoned me. It was almost as if it called me to pick it up. Inside me, my soul felt very glad to be getting 'another one of these'. Gladly Mum bought the little bag for me. I held it to my heart and walked outside into the glaring sun. That's when I saw him, sitting on a crate against the wall.

His long grey hair hung over his faded black western shirt. His skin, wrinkled brown and leathery, was adorned with big silver and turquoise rings. His eyes, sharp and bright, looked into the distance, staring out from under a furrowed brow. And his nose pointed in regal pride at the horizon. Just then a gust of wind swept up the dust, tossed his hair and he turned his face to me as if the wind had encouraged him beyond any resistance.

In those eyes was a wisdom I had not seen in this life. They drew me in to a place of oneness. Yes, he was family, to me he was grandfather. I just stood there staring. Our eyes locked, our souls met. Then out of his mouth came soft and raspy words that flew to me on the wind: powerful, pointed words, sent like an arrow to my soul.

'Your medicine too big for that little bag ... but it will do to start.'

Intuitively I knew what he meant. This medicine was the spirit power in my soul and the gifts I would gather, reawaken and give through life. I definitely knew he didn't mean the antibiotics that Mum gave me regularly. I knew he meant the magic kind.

That's when I felt a giant tug: a struggle between my destiny in a modern world and my love affair with the ancient ways. It was also a tug between the little world I was in and the awareness that I was a part of something much bigger.

We returned to Australia. I brought home the collective impacts upon my spirit: my soul more awake; my intelligence activated; my innocence raped; worldly eyes opened; the rebel rumbling. Two very different realities were escalating, and stretching further apart, both as driven as the other.

It wasn't long before I started to take a progressive slide at school. The cruelty of kids in the classroom began to outweigh my tolerance. They teased and taunted not only the fortunate ones (who were well-off, good looking and 'cool') but also the poor, the different and the 'unfortunate' (who lacked looks, skills or intelligence). I wanted to protect them all, to take them under my wing and show them how beautiful they really were. I cried for their loneliness, reflected in my own struggle with identity. For that, the other children boycotted me.

And to add further to the other children's dislike of me, I myself was different and fortunate. I couldn't really understand how my friendly spirit was something of such disdain. It seemed that my enthusiasm was not appreciated. It led to constant prods and jibes from rulers in my back, hands that tugged my hair, eyes that encased me in ice, words that reduced me to tears and exclusions that left me lonely. I often went home with bruises, marks from the sharp pointy elbows that were deliberately dug into my body or from kicks to my shins. But it wasn't just the physical attacks that pained me. It was the underlying emotional dig that really hurt, like a hit straight to my heart. With each blow came a deeper sinking feeling, like my heart was trying to crawl into some dark hole where it couldn't be found, only to wait on the border for renewed hope. Yet with each little leap of hope, expressed by my efforts to fit in, I was only dashed on the rocks again.

I felt deeply isolated. I wanted a sense of belonging, not just to sit next to or play with someone who would talk to me, but to share in my deep connection and curiosity with life. And I wanted to share in loving innocent joy, simply who I was. I ached to be accepted only to find all my efforts thwarted. Most of the children thought I was simply weird, or too good at everything. And the children who would take the time to listen didn't have the capacity to understand. So, I was often left alone, pushed to the back of the line. Now I felt even more deeply ostracised, not just by my family. School became a place I wanted to avoid.

So, in my attempt to be away from school and receive some type of caring, I began practising lies. I was acting even more and with better success. Several times I managed to convince Mum I was sick. I even went to the extent of spending two painstaking hours making a measles-like rash all over my body with my pink texta marker. Unfortunately though, after the second day and a trip to the doctor, my cover was blown. The doctor wasn't as gullible as my mum, nor was he anywhere near as angry.

I surmised that I would have to improve on my magic powers.

9. *Hidden Valley*

And forget not that the earth
delights to feel your bare feet
And the wind longs to play with your hair.

Kahlil Gibran

In my early years, my greatest sense of freedom in the world was found in the life of Hidden Valley's rolling hills. With every return to the valley my spirit would lift. Even the thought of the sacred land would set my soul free.

As the car made its way along the winding roads, the hills and cliffs etched their faces in my mind. It was a route so well travelled, it became a permanent map in my memory. A giant gum tree, twisted and twined like an old rope, marked the last bend. Once around it, my heart would skip to the rush of joy dancing in my soul.

I could hear the white cockatoos screaming in the treetops. A magpie swooped over the car. An old crow, perched on a hay shed beam, cocked its head as it watched us drive past, its soot-black feathers contrasted strongly in the scene of golden hay and blue skies. I knew the character of these birds so well. They were as unique as people: the cockies with their antics and screeching cacophony, the magpies' warbling melodies in the first rays of the morning sun and the crows' glinting eyes – a penetrating presence.

I turned my head and looked out across the hills to the right, searching the scene for my favourite landmark, the 'faraway' tree.

With this in sight, I knew the open world of freedom and adventure was only seconds away, well worth the ninety minutes of travel in a stuffy car. Over the rise, the country road dropped down the hill, dappled in shadows thrown by the old pine trees.

Dad turned the car into our little dirt road, passing behind the colourful row of beach shacks, each one painted a different colour. I found their simple rustic character charming, inviting my thoughts to escape into a world of fantasy, where elves dug up old sea treasures and fairies darted between shadows. Most of the time the shacks stood silent, empty and mysterious in the play of spotted light, creaking branches, cactus flowers, abandoned beach pebbles, shiny shells and fallen pine needles, whispered to by salty winds.

The engine stopped and in an instant the whole family spilled languidly from the car. The smell of the sea, the pines and the rolling hills intoxicated me in a single breath.

'Aaaahhh!' I sighed in relief, then ran through the gate.

The yard never changed much. And yet with each season came a distinct play of flowers and colours. Tall pink hollyhocks and bright orange cactus flowers appeared in the heat of summer, surrounded by clumps of golden grass and little pussy-tails, with the persistent buzz of flies in the background. Autumn brought long shadows in the golden light, and black, brown and spotted cows ambled along the hillside paths. Gusting winter winds delivered great clouds, thick with mist and rain, and earthy smells burst forth with the bright green grass. And with spring came splashes of lavender, yellow daisies, and fluttering wings – most often the swoop of a magpie!

I loved each season with a passion of such gratitude – gratitude for the gifts of lush and vivid changes, buzzing at my senses. I took it all in with a sweeping gaze. Then my ears switched to the sound of the creaky hinges as the front door opened. Granny's round, smiling face poked out.

'Hello!' I called excitedly.

'Hello!' she mimicked back and stepped outside onto the sunny porch. The stones laid in concrete were baked warm by the sun. I leaped up the steps into her arms. Her short, tubby body was always wrapped in an apron. Her big bust was like a warm pillow to my face as I hugged against her. I looked up into her shiny eyes. She looked through her glasses at me and chuckled. Her round nose and cheeks were always rosy, but even more so when she chuckled.

Granddad was inside sitting at the table reading, the dogs at his feet. His dark smoky eyes peered at us over the book and he uttered a short greeting. We threw our bags in the bedrooms and caravan, grabbed a drink of cold lemon water and a couple of Granny's freshly baked cookies, and ran outside into the bright morning sun. With a good couple of hours before lunch there was plenty of time to amble down the beach, over the hills and around the cliffs.

This was the place where we children enjoyed each other's company most. We swam together; snorkelled; turned over rocks; watched and collected crabs; jumped off the jetty; climbed the hills, cliffs and rocks; dug in the sand; and lazed in the sun. We laughed in the simplicity of our innocence, dancing in nature, singing songs and playing like wild creatures. I delighted in our time together, yet more than anything, I loved to roam by myself.

After a good hearty lunch I wandered out the back. Our yard stretched down into a gully at the foot of a massive hill. The back half was a steady slope that grew steep, the front half a vertical ascent of sheer cliff face, a jagged layering of silty soil, shale, rocks and the occasional bristly coastal plant.

The gully was a welcome sanctuary from the midday sun, shaded by a grove of pine and native trees. The layers of pine needles made a spongy carpet to walk on and with each step their sweet, sharp scent escaped into the air. It was there in the gully that I spent many hours in a state of natural delight, feeling as if I had returned to my native roots as I wove baskets from long wide grasses, made little shelters and collected nature's treasures. It was in those surroundings that I felt most at home. In that place I felt my natural native self was my true being. It far surpassed my single bed in a brick box surrounded by walls and the imprisoning attitude of a family that had resigned itself to a 'civilised' life: 'we weren't meant to live like animals in the wild'. To me it was odd that nothing much seemed civil about our life at all. It seemed devoid of the things that made life truly civil: mutual respect, love, gratitude and acknowledgment would be a good starting place. And all I could do was daydream of the lifetimes and places that were so woven into communion with the greatest master of all that is civil: nature herself. Those times reflected to me the true peace and respect of a life lived in harmony and accord with the laws of nature ... a time when people were truly civil to each other and all creatures alike.

I climbed around the edge to find my retreat ledge. Nestled in the cliff face it overlooked the gully's base several metres below. There, in the afternoon heat, I found cool shady rest. I collected fresh clumps of soft golden grass to make a bed and laid myself down. I stared up through the splay of branches at the pale blue sky, letting my thoughts disappear into its never-ending space.

The lowing of cows sounded in the distance and the afternoon breeze gently rustled the grasses on the ledge above me. Time disappeared. There was only the flowing living moment. And there, in that moment, all of life swam in me. There was no death, no thoughts, no tomorrow – no starting, no stopping, just life *being*.

Then the cool of the shadows moved across my skin. The sun had disappeared behind the giant hill, making its way to dip into the ocean. I sat up and stretched my arms above my head. A few yoga *asanas*[1] were the natural link for me between sitting, playing and sleeping. I stood up tall and bent at the hips, leaning over until my body folded in half, head down on my knees and fingers sweeping at the ground beneath me.

As I arrived back I could smell dinner well on the way. The back door creaked as much as the front. I walked through the back porch across the cool floor, breathing in the sweet dampness of the ferns as I passed all the boxes of Granddad's rocks and gemstones and stepped

---

[1] Yogic postures.

into the light of the doorway.

Reliable as ever, Granny was in the kitchen tucked in between the skinny row of lemon and white painted cupboards, her slippers scuffing on the speckled lino.[1] Pots and jars lined the walls, the most favoured collection kept up high for consumption control, Granny's best: dried figs and an assortment of coffee, jam and almond kiss cookies.

Dad, Granddad and the rest of the family were playing cards in the dining room. The last of the afternoon light shone through the glass-slatted windows and cast a soft glow on the setting. Shadows stretched across the golden hilltops and the trees murmured in a deep calming whisper. And yet the strange stillness of it all was broken again with the returning flock of raucous cockatoos, squabbling in the trees as they caught the final rays of sunlight. By the time I lay in bed my body was ready for rest. And a deep rest I had. Unlike in the suburbs, I always slept well in the valley. Its sweet air and nature songs lulled me into peaceful sleep.

•

The days and nights would pass in timeless wanderings as I lost myself in the rolling continuum of wonder. From my perch on the hill, I could see the great expanse of bays and cliffs meeting emerald seas which rolled out far below me. There I had many moments of silent revelations seeing the true presence of life undisturbed: melting into the vastness of it all; drowning in the sounds of waves, lapping and crashing; floating on the song of sea birds and disappearing into the stillness of earth beneath me.

Sometimes I would sit in such stillness myself that the creatures would visit me as if I were just another piece of the landscape. Lizards would laze next to my feet and birds would dance and fly around me. I had come to know the habitat well, understanding the intricate web of life in this environment. To see the play of such inter-

[1] Linoleum – a vinyl floor covering.

being was to see perfection: perfect cooperation. Not a stone, a tuft of grass, an insect or bird on the breath of wind was ever out of place. Life supported life.

It was there on the cliff top that I had my first experience of 'shape-shifting.' A young kitehawk was hovering only a few feet from where I sat, hanging in the air with the slightest occasional flicker of its feathers. The great ocean glistened like a stretch of silk encrusted with diamonds and the sky swept out before me, an empty stage in God's set. I sat in stillness, consumed by the power and beauty of the scene.

Quite suddenly I felt a dropping, dissolving sensation followed by an expansion and a sudden pointed awareness. I was no longer the experience of the girl on the cliff watching the hovering hawk. *I* was the hovering hawk watching the girl on the cliff! And yet there was still the 'I' awareness, the 'I am' watching. And what was so incredible was that it was both amazing and yet not at all amazing – it felt completely ordinary and normal as if I had known this before.

I revelled in the lightness – the freedom of height – the feeling of oneness with the wind and air as I hovered there. And then, in another instant, I was back in the body as the girl on the cliff. The little kitehawk darted towards me, stopped two feet from my face and tilted its head to look me directly in the eyes. But it was myself looking at me!

Then, as suddenly as it had come close, it turned and flew away, swooping down along the cliff face and out across the sea. The sunlight sparkled on the ocean's tidal patterns and the distant roar of the swell rose beneath me.

It wasn't only transcendence that the cliffs brought me. There was also terror. Courage was not something I lacked. In fact, I seemed to have an unusually high level of it. But to me it wasn't driven by a need to go beyond fear. It was driven by an inherent confidence that was suffused with an extensive degree of presence, focus and perception.

I seemed to have a natural capacity to perceive life and situations with great accuracy, giving me an advanced edge – not just in sports, education and arts, but also in adventure. I was often told I was 'too big for my boots' meaning I was somewhat 'cocky' and overly confident. This seemed like a precursor of the teasing that followed in the wake of shock, disgust and cruelty that our surname, Cocks, provoked. And a day came when I started to understand those words that tugged at my spirit as it reached for the sky.

I had mastered many of the cliff faces already. I could run across the rocks like a mountain goat and scale the cliffs with speed. It delighted me that I was as nimble as my Chinese star sign. Of course, most of the cliffs I had taken to were in the lower range, and having mastered the terrain, I began to feel an itch for more adventure. Even my brother, whom I thought matched me in courage, decided to rescind the idea of joining me in the next big quest.

I stood at the base of the revered and feared cliff: the face of the backyard hill. It reared up before me, an awesome scale of three hundred feet. The large rocks beneath me had taken their plunge over the years, great crashing slabs and smatterings of shale. They lay there defeated by the forces of nature: gravity and erosion. Their stark, jagged shapes were in dark contrast to the water-polished, pale-grey rocks of the beach. The sound of pebbles, moving against each other under the push and pull of lapping waves, rattled and rumbled behind me.

I stared up at the cliff face. It reached up into the vast blue sky. I scanned it with my keen eyes, taking in the possibility of a track of hand and footholds for ascent. Noting a series of ledges, I began my climb. Straight up first, then diagonally to the right, straight up, a quick left, a drop down, then right again. I zigzagged my way easily over the first hundred feet. Then I noticed more loose shale. The cliff face around me had turned into a conglomeration of fine, dry clay silt, shale and scraggly plants. But, determined to make it to the top, I pushed on, negotiating my way between the stronger ledges and bands of shale – until I suddenly realised I was stuck.

I couldn't see the next move. I felt like a piece on a vertical chessboard, but now I wasn't the queen, the ruler on the cliff: I was the pawn, dominated by circumstance. I stood, pinned to my last footholds. The more I looked, the less I could see a way up. Or down. I was a good two hundred feet from the ground and the rocks and ocean looked distant and life-threatening. I began to tremble, first my arms, then my legs.

I burst into tears. I cried in terror. I thought I was going to perish for sure, that I would lose my grip and be dashed upon the rocks below. I clung there with my body shaking and tears streaming down my cheeks.

Then suddenly the voice of awareness within switched on like a bright light.

'Stop ... be still, silent ... just breathe ... deep, slow breaths ... feel the breeze ... now be at one with the cliff.'

So I responded. The tears stopped. I closed my eyes. I breathed deeply, and opened my eyes in a steady gaze at the cliff.

Without a thought I turned my head in slow motion and there, just to the right and up, was a clear track of handholds. I was surprised that I hadn't seen them before and even wondered if the cliff had suddenly changed its body out of compassion for this child who wept upon its face.

Slowly, surely, I made my way up. Then, with about fifteen feet to go, my foot slipped. My heart leapt and the instant thought of a bloody end flashed through my mind. I imagined the bronze plaque: **K. R. Cocks 1967-1977** laid into the rock upon which I had landed. But my fall was stopped by my foot as it connected with a jutting rock, and my hand managed to grab a sturdy bushy root. My heart pounded and I heaved in a great cloud of dust. I blinked my eyes trying to refocus through dusty grit, my eyes and mouth full of it. I spat, trying to rid my teeth of the unpleasant grittiness.

I regained my balance and finally took the last steps. Those last steps were so much easier, albeit risky. The cliff top ended in a slope between sturdy ledges that rested finally on the top of the hill. I turned around and sat down with a huge sigh of relief ... and victory.

As I sat looking down at what I had just scaled, I shook my head in disbelief. I was amazed to still be alive. A strange mix of satisfaction and hazard swirled around inside of me. My itch for a challenge was gratified and the thought of further escapades sank into my gut – my first real sense of caution that tugged my spirit back from invincibility.

Then I realised the sun had gone past the zenith, which meant I was very late for lunch. That was unusual for me and would be a sure giveaway that I was 'up to something'. Being late for meals was considered a reason to question what I had been up to, especially as I voluntarily made sure I was on time, if not early, to the table – mostly due to my ravenous appetite and love of Granny's home baking.

So I leapt up and started down the back slope of the hill. Even though it was mild compared with the cliff face, it still took artful negotiation – especially at increased speed. Within minutes I was in the yard and ran inside to the table. But before I could sit down I was met by stunned stares.

'Where have you been?' Mum asked firmly.

'Have you been crying?' came a duet of questioning.

'No,' I said with a quick high cut-off note. 'I just lost track of time.'

'Go wash yourself,' said Granddad.

I ran to the bathroom, went to the toilet and then stood at the basin to wash my hands. There, to my shock and horror, in the mirror was the image of my face, covered in brown dust with great trails of dried tear-tracks running down my cheeks and neck!

My face turned red as I realised how obviously fake, my denial had been. Oh God, I thought to myself, I'd better wash and keep quiet or I'll probably be banned from the cliffs and hills. I couldn't bear the thought of that. To deny me the hills and cliff tops was like denying a bird its wing tips.

Thankfully, nothing more was said. I ate my cold meal in silence – delicious, sweet silence.

That same year, my Granddad died, aged seventy. I watched his spirit shining brightly over us all. Although I knew he wasn't really 'gone', I knew that I would miss his solid power and presence. He was like a sentinel, keeping watch over my tender spirit, nourishing the valley with his reverence for nature. He had planted countless trees and spent hours watching the native birds, delighting simply in existence. And he was full of mystery. I knew he had a secret deeply locked away behind those eyes. I used to look into them longingly, as if he held a secret key to my own life's mystery. But he was a closed man, keeping his thoughts to himself. He was never particularly close to me. That was – until he left his body.

In the middle of the milky-way that stretched across the sky like a great serpent, he was suspended like a bright star. The first thing he told me was that he loved me. Then, as his light burned brightly above me, he wrapped me up in his power.

His face came close to mine.

'I am watching over you,' he said. 'I will guide you. You must return to your roots, bring the power of our ancestors from the dark.' As he spoke it was radiantly clear that he was finally revealing the thing I had always suspected: his Aboriginal ancestry. I could see them – men, women, children and elders, strung out in great lines of ancient culture behind him.

Of course it was still something steeped in mystery and uncertainty. The door to his past had been truly locked. Yet through spirit I had begun to see the tragic history. A dark secret of genocide, the stolen generation. His passing had become a doorway of access to his ancient culture. Perhaps that is why I am such a nature child, I thought. From the other side my granddad became a mentor for me. He guided me in the ways of lore[1] and ancient dreaming. He was a magic man. And he relentlessly reminded me that inside me was a magic woman.

---

[1] The indigenous system of knowledge and wisdom that sustains sacred respect, awareness and balance in the relationship of all things in creation.

The 2nd Attainment

Albeit I knew I was somehow intimately connected with the great Magician of life, imbued with His powers, I humbly, yet willingly acknowledged that I had a long way to go before I mastered the magic.

I was willing to see and do whatever it took.

Somehow, I knew everything I needed was already within me. All I had to do was trust, focus and take action.

KEY 2.

Silver Star Woman

KEY 2.

Silver Star Woman

Although many things are hidden, the Silver Star Woman is attuned to the higher purpose in all. She sees all experiences of light and dark as good. Each contains a message, a sign that points the way, assuring us that there is a hidden purpose in the mystery. She understands that the journey is multi-dimensional, not linear. Therefore she has the power to see beyond polarity. She is consciousness.

To understand and have faith through the passage of life, we must open and attune to the signs revealed within us.

10. *In the Fire*

> The clouds are in danger, not the sky.
> The river is in danger, not the ocean.
> The body is in danger, not the soul.
>
> *Isira*

Among the few friends our family associated with were the Hogan family: Uncle Bob, Aunty May and their two children, Alice and Jamie. It made for interesting play for us children, as we were suddenly a group of five. What made it even more interesting was their home. It was a large house situated in bushland at Flora Heights. The surrounding native forest that ran along the top of the gorge was a place for great adventures and a favourite game, hide-and-seek.

One afternoon we were playing in the trees and rocks. I was one of the 'hiders'. The late afternoon sun was casting a dusky pink glow over the treetops and the air was sweet with a warm gentle breeze. I found a crop of rocks surrounded by clumps of long golden-dry grasses and lay down on my side. I could hear the 'finder' in the distance, evidenced by an occasional crack of twigs on the dry ground. Feeling safe from being found, I propped myself up on one elbow and looked out across the swaying grasses, breathing in the fragrant air and the peaceful sounds of the bushland. Then I heard a sound nearby. It sounded like the 'finder' was getting closer, so I went to lie low again.

But as I flopped my arm on the ground, I was gripped by an

intense biting pain. It sliced through me like a fire-hot clamp. I screamed. I looked down in time to see a fat brown scorpion. I screamed louder. The sensation of burning, clenching pain increased as my arm began to swell. My heart started pounding. I leapt up and ran, wailing frantically. I ran all the way to the house. I could hear the others thrashing after me through the bush calling out,

'What happened?'

I ran in the door, a crying, screaming mess. Mum, Dad, Uncle Bob and Aunty May looked up, surprised and disgruntled that I had interrupted in such hysteria. Aunty May was the first to respond with genuine, sympathetic concern. She stood up and stepped towards me.

'Oh dear, now what's happened?' she asked.

'I, I, I've b-been b-b-bitten by a s-s-scorpion!' I stammered through heaving tears.

Their eyes all opened wide but Uncle Bob, always the cynic, said 'Ah ... Naah ... it was probably just a centipede. There's big bush ones here.' The others nodded and agreed.

'B-b-b-but ... the pain,' I cried.

'Yeah ... they can hurt,' he said. 'But you'll be okay. Just sit down.' He looked at his wife.

'May, get some ice and give her a drink of water. She'll be right.'

Aunty May looked at me with loving concern and ushered me to the lounge sofa against the wall.

I fell into the seat, my body heaving with pain. I looked at my arm. It was swelling up, from my fingers to my shoulder. I felt helpless. I knew it had been a scorpion that bit me. I saw it as clearly as the rocks and the grass and the trees. And, at twelve years of age, I had expanded my knowledge of the bush, animals and insects, to know it without a doubt. But no one else seemed to believe me.

So what could I do but surrender. I felt the fire moving inside me, as though my arm was going to combust. And slowly, deeply, it crept through my veins until I could feel it in my heart. I shook and breathed heavily and closed my eyes.

There was a sudden *whoosh,* and blackness engulfed me. In an instant I was out of my body. The scene suddenly changed. While my body slept feverishly, I entered vivid states of awareness, experiencing myself in other times and places.

I was standing in the middle of a fire, looking through the eye-holes of my mask at a scene of dancing flames leaping into a black sky. Dust was billowing up around the feet of shamans dancing, stamping, drumming, chanting, wailing. Their long black legs leapt up and down. Feathers, bones and masks jerked in a frenzied rhythm. I felt myself being consumed in the fire, becoming the fire, igniting in a maddening height of trance, until I was taken and nothing remained but fire.

Then suddenly everything went black again. I disappeared down the chute of deep, deep unconscious void.

When I came to, I was dripping with sweat and my breath was shallow. I felt nauseous. I looked at my arm. It was still swollen. I sat staring at the wall opposite. The shamans' fire dance flashed repeatedly through my mind. I tried to place it in some order in my mind. Where had I gone? Was that just a dream? It felt so real. It seemed to stir from within that deep corner of a long lost conscious past.

Over the following days I stared at the painting of a fire spirit in the dining room of our house. I looked at other pictures of the Aboriginal Dreamtime fire spirit. And I looked through books and some pictures of Africans in the same type of shamanic ceremonies.

Something seemed to be unlocking inside of me. All the dimensions of this life seemed to be unfolding from, and weaving back into, other places, other times. I began to see the connectedness in so many directions. Then the dreams came and over the following nights I re-encountered a series of other lifetimes.

11. *Between Worlds*

> Am I a girl, dreaming of the fire in all things and beyond,
> Or am I the fire, dreaming I am a girl dreaming?
>
> *Isira*

Over the succeeding days and nights my body fell into heavy sleep as it fought the scorpion poison. I had hours of lucid dreams, interrupted by fleeting moments of wakeful awareness. And in those moments, I had the penetrating realisation that those dreams were not from my imagination. They were startlingly vivid scenes – of other lifetimes. The streams of visions played out in frames like grabs from a film and I was the actor in the scenes upon the screen.

I found myself floating, swirling in light, looking back at Earth. And from this vantage point I could see the spinning story of life on earth. My own experiences flashed before me – past, recent and future – and continued to expand into a tapestry of unfolding history. It was a history of cultures and civilisations, races and religions: all an orchestration of galactic proportions.

I could see so many roles of apparent reality, so many parts in the play. It seemed so incomprehensible that I was simultaneously a star; spinning galaxies; an angel of far-reaching love; an earth child, simple and primitive; a mother, strong and tender; a shaman, powerful and limited; a student of life; a priestess of high temples; a starving thief imprisoned; a daughter of a murderer; a rebel with a cause; an ancient Aboriginal song master; a hermit; a yogi and ascetic; a Chinese sage; a goddess of Tantric[1] rites; an emissary of God; a wandering consort; an Ascended Lady of Light; a master of many seekers; a Red Indian's wife cum wizened white-haired crone; a laughing Tibetan lama; a dancing shimmering deity; a daughter of God – messenger of eternal love and freedom.

So after several lifetimes of adapting to earth culture and the dynamics of simply being human, I began to further unravel what appeared as vast complexities of my multi-dimensional consciousness and God-Self. The earth play seemed to be evolving at an increasing speed. What was such a simple way of life, imbued with magic and mysteries, became entwined in the advance of the mind and civilisation, amidst an uprising of barbarism. I saw the forthcoming beast of ignorance forever served by bodhisattvas[2] and awakened beings. And in it all I saw Self – one great creation and the Divine play of compensation.

•

Then I fell into a deep, dreamless sleep for what seemed to be forever, until I was stirred again by another scene ...

In a daze I sat on the giant gateway stone. The sun's heat was intense upon my face. Its searing, blinding light flashed on the Nile in the distance. I turned my head as I heard the bare footsteps of my head maid behind me. It

---

1 Referring to Tantra – subtle, secret and mystical teachings of consciousness and sexual transcendence.

2 Bodhisattva – One who is enlightened or committed to attaining enlightenment and has taken a vow to assist in the awakening of all beings. The emphasis is on compassion and service for others.

wasn't only her body that was large and noticeable. For the first time, I recognised the aura of energy that preceded her. Quite suddenly I felt as if my life had been but a dream and that now all of a sudden I was awake in it. There appeared a tangible sharpness, openness and clarity in my perception. Everything seemed to be converged so closely upon me; in the moment it was as if time had stopped and yet all things were occurring in the same instance.

'The Pharaoh has requested the presence of Your Highness. You must be appropriately adorned. There is talk that you must now enter the seventh chamber,' she said.

The seventh chamber, I thought. An image arose of my father passing me an ankh,[1] which until now he had kept at a distance from me, albeit he had shown me the use of its conduction powers in healings. And yet a sense of puzzlement passed through me as I wondered why I was summoned to the seventh chamber – entry was only the right of a Pharaoh. A bolt of light shot through my inner eye, followed by a singular flash of a multi-dimensional overview of the pyramids and a giant ankh that seemed connected to an infinite source of light. Within it was a brilliant point of light, the beacon of Isis.[2] It approached as if from a distant past and, as it swept before me, I saw the sands of time part like a veil.

Without a second thought I arose. Then I walked, the gentle feminine swish of my sixteen-year-old body now quickened by an ancient conviction of timeless knowing. I strode with a determined pace through the courtyard and along corridors lined with giant inscribed pillars. The stories of our starry ancestors and the God of Life spiralled up from deep within. How magical, I thought, this inner knowing

---

[1] An Egyptian ritual item, a cross with a loop at the top, representing the feminine power; often used in healing and initiation.

[2] The Mother Goddess of Egyptian religion and mythology; worshipped as great magic; mother of Horus (Hawk-head God); protector of children; associated with the sun gods; represented with the sun seated in cow's horns.

dialogue displayed all around me, yet knowing ... knowing there was still more to come.

I turned the corner, following the cool air currents that pervaded the long stone passages, into the vast open chamber. There he stood, the Pharaoh, tall, regal and powerful. His long gleaming chin-piece stood out from his angular jaw, defining a set expression of royal command. I stopped at the customary twelve feet from his royal presence and stooped to bow. He stood patiently, lovingly, knowingly, as he embraced my gesture of honour.

'Father, my Pharaoh,' I spoke.

'Come ... stand here beside me,' he invited.

As I stood, my father turned and began to speak, naturally and gently, casually commenting on the reports he had received from the priest of my progress through the initiation halls.

'The Priest tells me you hold well the conscious vibration of the laws of prophets ... that indeed you display the love awareness of the eternal Self. Because it is that you know the true nature of the varying energies of manifestation, you are now ready to be trained in your role of destiny.'

'And what is that, my Father?'

But, without answering, my father asked me a question.

'Tell me what you know about life and death.'

'I know that life is love and that in the conscious embodiment of love all that appears as death is nothing more than a transformation of energies. To the unconscious one, life without love is fear. In fear there is the lower identification with form and thus an apparent entrapment in its appearing fixed form. It is this which breeds all that is hate, duality, illness and death. To such a one, death is a lapsing of the manifest experience. The unconscious one does not know that the manifest form is yet again to re-form for the ongoing upraising of conscious evolution.

'To the one of conscious love, it is the duty and power

granted by the eternal life of God that healing is imparted to the unconscious field, and the service is to raise the vibrations of the creative field of life so that the highest potential of God-conscious man may be fulfilled. Such a one is supremely conscious and radiates the divine creative forces through the power of intent that transcends the physical realms. In this love-knowing, there is only One life ... eternally.'

My father looked into me with eyes that transcended time and place.

'It is in this truth that you are now to pass through the initiation of the seventh chamber that you may embody the full conscious intent to direct the divine creative forces. You are a healer and a prophet ... but you will also be a supreme one of God's will.' As he spoke I saw wisps of scenes other than our time and place ... somewhere in the future.

'But Father ... my Pharaoh ... when is this? How can it be when it is the law that only a Pharaoh has the power or divine right to take such a level of initiation?'

'My dear daughter ... of God, you are being prepared now for a time that is yet to come for you in your earthly incarnations. You are to be available now to manifest the full power of your healing radiance. This is required of you now in this time. But the fulfilment of this initiation shall not have its full rights until such time that you pass through other lifetimes and dimensions, serving our galactic forces. By then it will be such that you will incarnate in full conscious awareness as a daughter of God in the self-realised form, to serve the raising of consciousness for the world. Such a time will be known as the twenty-first century for mankind.

'It is not the first time you have manifested as such. Yet it is the first time, in such synthesis of all your previous incarnations, that you shall serve for earth as the feminine power of realised love. For in such time you are to be 'self-born'. You shall not be brought forward by any lineage in that life, but through the authority of all lineages that you have come to know and serve through each incarnation. These have only served as a bridge for human understanding, for you are that which has come from a spirit far beyond this world. You will enter bearing those gifts already awake in your soul, and your role will be to teach, not through lineage, but through the power of truth that remains always in the Now. It is that power, beyond name and religion that you will speak of.

'It is that power alone that will save humanity from the atrocities of war, poverty and dissension. Through revealing that power awake in your heart, you will be as a mirror for others to remember that power as their true Self also. That power must be seen as the presence within each person. It can no longer be seen as a separate exclusive power of which one is only a channel or a messenger. For each soul must come to stand as the Divine.

'Although you had realised the Divine Laws before and lived to inspire others to remember life's gift, as a woman you had not been placed in a role of leadership. Yet women's time to lead is coming. In this life you shall take the throne upon my passing and serve our people of earth and stars as the Queen that you are. For this you must be ready.'

As he spoke I could see the shining beauty of the Pleiades – the seven bright sisters. Their celestial song stroked my soul, arousing in me a tender homesickness.

The Pharaoh then turned to the centre of the chamber where an altar radiated a great field of luminous light. It seemed to come from within and above, radiating in shafts of golden rays. As he turned again, the rays of light engulfed my form.

In an instant I felt the field of my conscious awareness expanding at the speed of light, transcending the gravitational field of form. I became the light, consciously moving, freely, in and around the play of particles of form and space. There, in that oneness, I felt the power of infinite love consume me and unfold from the innermost recesses of being. There within, was nothing less than God. And in the radiant height of such ecstatic at-one-ment, I saw the unravelling of the codes of creation and healing powers – the maps of resonant manifestation – forming, dematerialising, and reforming in perfect harmonic illumined intelligence. I was as it, as it was as I.

In that instant of full conscious knowing was the almighty flash of the eye of Ra[1] ... sealed within my being, and along with it, every code of the laws of creation.

Then, through the chute of instantaneous consciousness, I dissolved from form into the far reaches of infinity. I was no longer a body that was breathing. I was breath, breathing the body in and out of a vast and limitless source creation. And unto a billion billion light-years in eternity's evolution I saw the always abiding ONE presence, for I AM that which is, has been and always will be – forever I AM being. I watched the play of Self – God as stars of gases and galactic passion in a dance of creation, a play of always being. From particles of infinite space I gathered the stardust to form stars and galaxies in evolving grace. From planets and worlds of rock and ice, to oceans and lands of creations fair ... I AM the journey in all creation ... born of stars and galaxies gone before.

In the all-pervading presence of awareness lay a love and gratitude for all existence in God. A love and gratitude beyond a scribe's count. A love that had always been. A love destined for conscious realisation in all humankind, the supreme One of pure awareness ... God-One.

I saw the passage of time, and the play of creation unfold through billions upon billions of light-years. And I saw the joy, the majesty, the miracle ... the magnitude of love that is life! It overfilled me to flowing, surrendering, willingness, sacred-

---

[1] The Sun God; chief god of the Egyptian religion and mythology.

ness and gratitude ... to serve ... to radiate Divine creation.

Every particle of light had dissolved into a field of oneness. I was gone ... gone into love ... light ... the source of creation itself.

When I came to I was lying on the altar in the middle of the chamber, alone. Shafts of light from above illumined minute particles of white gold swirling all around me, and upon my heart-centre my hands clasped the golden ankh; but my father was gone. My body vibrated as if made of pure light ... a frequency beyond limited form. Deep in my heart was peace and gratitude. Then I cried tears of joy, and blessedness flowed ... for life, for love ... for all of creation.

I suddenly found myself dressed in warm maroon and saffron robes. The mala of beads, polished from many prayers, felt warm and smooth in my old weathered hands. A month's growth of silvery hair kept my old skull warm as I gazed out of the open window at the glistening snow-capped peaks in the distance. The sun cast its last golden rays upon the great valleys as I felt a deep heart-stirring contentment with a life fulfilled. The last of my scriptures were bound and left in the cave where I had spent most of my lifetime. They were deep meditations of life's eternal play which moved me so deeply that its liberating bliss could only pour from my hand upon golden pages: pages left to be discovered by those keen of heart, keen for a conscious life of liberation.

I was ready. My time had come to leave this world yet again. And so I sat upon my pillow of woollen cloths, an old, fulfilled man, closed my eyes and breathed into eternal light ... a rainbow ... cast into eternity.

The dreams and visions had unravelled in a seemingly endless stream as if time's own linear play of assumed reality had disintegrated. Then from within a vast light of pure presence as I sensed a form again, I was almost at a loss to know which was my body or my time of being.

Strangely enough, Mum and Dad didn't seem to link my illness and fevers with the bite in the bush. The swelling had been thought of as a reaction to a 'centipede' and my illness was just a coincidental 'flu' that followed.

Eventually it all slid again into the apparent normality of a linear journey in South Australian suburbia. After all, I was just another 'white girl,' 'middle class,' and 'Australian', who was born to be another number in the system. At least that was what our family and society assumed. But I was determined to follow my own song.

I found myself tumbled around by my mind's enquiry. I was undoubtedly somehow a part of the world's normality and the dominant culture that was considered to be the reality. And yet I was even more deeply entwined in events and experiences that were considered to be unreal. Most of my life I had managed to hold a steady inner conviction that, no matter what anyone else thought, I knew I was not crazy; and that what I experienced was perhaps a larger reflection of reality than others were able to see. And then there were moments where I teetered dangerously on the edge, wondering if I really was insane.

I had noticed a strange sensitivity about my neck, experiencing discomfort when anything was too close to it. But when Mum followed the fashion trend and bought me a skivvy, I almost 'lost the plot'. I didn't want to put it on. I dreaded the thought of this thing clamping around my neck. But of course, Mum had to have her way. She had chased me from my bedroom to the lounge-room. Her mood heated and I became hysterical as she forced the skivvy over my head. I started screaming, pulling and tearing at this thing, fighting to get it off.

'It's choking me! Stop!' I screamed.

'Oh for God's sake, you wretched child, behave yourself, it's just a top!' she yelled back at me.

I began sobbing and heaving frantically. I felt like I was being strangled. I struggled to breathe until I couldn't fight anymore. I just flopped on the lounge room floor and curled up in a ball. When I finally caught my breath I realised I was surrounded by an horrendously foul smell. It was the worst smell I had ever encountered. It was rotten, like the excrement and decay of a body left to die.

'What's that smell?' I asked as I sat up, blinking my eyes. Dad who was sitting in the lounge room just shook his head.

'Nothing,' he said. 'I can't smell anything.'

I blinked again but everything was becoming fuzzy. Oh God, I thought to myself, what's happening to me? The smell got thicker and thicker and the strangling feeling drew in ever more tightly. I started to squirm, trying to escape the feeling and smell, but the more I moved the more I felt pinned to the spot. Then as I realised the sensation was also around my wrists and ankles, I began to see myself, feel myself and know myself, in another time and place.

I was a man, naked, with iron bands clamped around my neck, wrists and ankles, chained to the wall of a small dark cell. My body was almost dead, the life drained out of it, rotting in its own excrement as I was left to die. I had lost track of the days. The cold stone walls and the echoing wails of distant people in pain and misery had been my only companions for days upon days. No food came, no water. One tiny window that let in the daylight reminded me that the days were passing.

The scene that had led me to this place, rolled through my mind. The cobbled lane, potato carts, bread stands, beggars, death trolleys, gloomy sky. I had thought to myself: If the plague doesn't kill me, hunger will. I couldn't bear another day without food. And so as I ran past the bread stand I snatched a loaf. It wasn't long before the law had chased me down, beaten me, chained me and dragged me to the small cell where I was now chained to the wall. And here I would die. That was the end of my life in that world.

•

I shuddered, still half aware of the sensation as I adjusted again to my girl's body in the lounge room. As I struggled to feel present I heard my deep God-voice, echoing as if from a great, distant place.

Remember, you are all life, pauper and king, saint and sinner, light and dark ... one whole.

I recognised again the feeling of the transcendent – that all of this is passing, and that, even in moments of forgetting, *I* remain always as pure spirit, an endless eternal presence. That which I truly am remains a power untouched by any world, by any event.

That brought me fully to my senses. I pondered at the contrast between the higher Self awareness and the more limited understanding of my child mind in the experience I was having. Once again I found myself caught between a place of knowing and faith, and one of bewilderment and doubt. Then, right in the moments that I was about to seriously take up the doubts, something would happen to give me a jolt – unmistakably linking the transcended powers and states with apparent worldly realities.

One sunny Sunday, as I was walking home from the tennis courts, I stood at the side of the main road. The lights had just turned red and traffic was starting to slow down. I was about twenty feet down from the lights and decided to step out and cross between the stopped cars. The lane closest to me had several cars, whilst the one closest to the middle of the road had less. But just as I stepped forward into the gap I turned to see a car heading towards me at break-neck speed. Time seemed to disappear as I became aware that I was right in its path. I heard the car's tyres screeching as it was almost upon me. Then suddenly I felt a force lifting me. I was literally picked up in the air and pulled backwards out of the car's path!

I stood there in awe, not fully comprehending how I had been moved. I quickly stepped up onto the path and without any further glance, the drivers moved on as the lights turned green again. I stood on the pavement in bewilderment. I knew I had just been saved and it was not a physical thing, yet it had the power to affect my physical world.

From that day, even though doubts continued to plague me as the rest of the world tried to convince me that life was only real if it could be measured logically or scientifically, I returned to a deep inner knowing that life is immeasurably more real in ways that most choose not to see.

•

As my body finally grew out of the growing-pains phase, I found a sense of joy and power in my legs. I felt inspired to run, to jump, to swim and to hurl my body into challenges of speed and agility: gymnastics, sprinting, long jump, high jump and hurdles. I finally found something through which I could feel more 'normal.' With great determination I dedicated my body to physical excellence. It seemed to come easily. But there was still dissatisfaction in me. Out of all these physical endurances, it was running that I loved the most. I wanted to run the fastest. The faster I ran, the more I felt a sense of freedom in the spirit of my body. When I ran, all my confusions about physical life dissolved in a breeze of exhilaration. So I ran – every day.

I trained hard, sometimes before school, at lunch and after school. When it came to the race days it became obvious I was the fastest in my league. But it still wasn't enough for me. I wanted to break through my own boundaries. I was sure there was yet some deeper latent power that I could tap into. And if I could just do that I could go beyond this sense of limitation in body that seemed to weigh me down. Somewhere inside I knew it was my indomitable spirit that drove me on. It pointed the way to the supernatural. That thought was followed by an unexpected insight. But all insights are unexpected of course!

The sound of the television caught my attention. My spirit lit up when I sat down in front of it: the David Attenborough nature documentary had me captivated. Nature seemed to illumine the qualities I yearned to master. I watched it in the perfect orchestration of a bird in flight, soaring to great heights. I watched it in the power of beasts claiming their prey for survival. And then I watched it in the unparalleled artistry of a cheetah in high-speed chase. It was as if its every muscle and bone cooperated in perfect conscious precision. And the power of that consciousness was anchored in the centre of its being. The speed born in its fluid power enthralled me. I watched in absolute engaged wonder. I thought: That's how I want to run, as fast and fluid as a cheetah. I took in every detail of its motion, power, timing and speed. Every second was a display of potent precision. And I breathed deeply in my knowing of its spirit from the stirring remnants of an African life gone by.

The next day I went early to the school oval. I stood at the edge of the great grassy expanse. I breathed into my body. I felt the muscles, ligaments, joints and bones. I felt into the relationship of energy, movement and power as I began to stretch. Then I envisaged myself as the cheetah. I felt myself to be as sleek and stealthy. I imagined my body to be just as finely tuned, connected and empowered. Then I began to run, stretching and pacing my body, maximising movement through space and breath. I felt a new dimension of power. It was as if my body was changing.

At the next school race I blitzed it to the line leaving the others behind. A wave of surprise and wonder moved through the Year 9 fraternity. Before long, there were rumoured debates and bets as to whether I could beat the fastest runner in the school, James. He also happened to be an outcast and the butt of many jokes, due to his unkempt body and clothing. He was certainly the most shabbily dressed kid at school.

I assumed his family was too poor to provide him with any better presentation and so I silently regarded him with compassion.

However, my softness to him suddenly took a sidestep one day when he walked up to me and goaded me with a challenge.

'You can't beat me,' he scowled.

And, before I even realised what I was doing, I rose to his challenge.

'Yes I can!' I retorted.

'Huh!' he grunted. 'We'll see about that.'

Two other kids overheard the challenge and ran off to find the Physical Education teacher. And before long a race time was set. Wednesday, at going-home time.

I felt ready to meet the challenge.

So, after a few stretches and a warm up, we stood on the oval, surrounded by a group of kids eager to watch their bet in action. I stepped up to the line, closed my eyes and breathed deeply. I felt a rush of energy flooding my veins and, in the pulse of inner power; I felt my body become a cheetah. I poised myself ready, ready to run with stealth, with speed, with fluid precision.

'Ready ... set ... GO!' called the PE teacher.

My legs stretched, my feet seemed to barely touch the ground. It was as if I were the wind. And in a flash of wind, legs, feet and breath, I reached the finish line with James flailing, following in my tracks. The group yelled out a flurry of exclamations. I stood there, bent over, surprised and fulfilled. I felt as satisfied as a cheetah that had caught its prey. A shiver moved through my bones at the thought. A deep memory had swept through me.

•

That run awoke a deeper thirst in me. I wanted to know how much faster I could go. When the time came for State trials, I was selected for our school in the 100 and 200 metre sprints, and in hurdles and long jumps. I trained every day and before long I found myself at the SA State Stadium warming up for my events. A lot of talk was circulating about how tough some of the other schools were, with unbeatable records. I found this out first hand: I was up against girls who must have found a greater mentor than my inner cheetah.

I came in fourth and fifth for 100 and 200-metre sprints, only to be encouraged by my teacher to be even more prepared next year.

But then the hurdles took me by surprise. I came in third and as a result got nicknamed the 'gazelle'. Then when it came to long jump, my confidence took an even bigger leap. My first jump (which was usually my worst) set me well in the lead. The second jump kept my position strong. Then, as I strode out ready for my best and last effort on the third jump, I stood poised at the line, already feeling victory. I took the run up and with full force leapt from the line, projecting my body towards the other side of the pit. I landed just over my last mark, feet thudding in the sand.

But then, the unexpected happened, with breathtaking shock. As my body fell forward I landed on my knees and a pain struck me in the right kneecap as if I was being stabbed. I screamed in agony then fell on my side rolling breathlessly. I pulled my knee up to see what had happened. There, jutting out of my flesh was the top of a rusty stake that had come off a pit rake. It was driven into my knee like a nail into a post. I fell back in shock and disbelief.

That brought an abrupt and painful end to my athletic ambition. My knee took two years to fully recover and another two before I could really run again. By then, however, my passions led me elsewhere.

•

Next came the torment of further abuse at school because my surname was a common sexual term, particularly inappropriate for a girl. My achievements in arts and sports as much as reading, writing, and arithmetic seemed another reason for most kids to dislike me. How was it that jealousy and insecurity could be so rife in children? Even those I thought were my 'true and trusted' friends often seemed to turn sour for reasons that were beyond my grasp.

Yet no matter how cruel the torments were, or how much they pained me, I still offered my loving hand of friendship. And so it was puzzling to me: I couldn't understand why friendship and love could be rejected so harshly. At the age of twelve I had recognised consciously, with deep presence, that I loved every person and creature with the same immense love. And I saw that others had forgotten, denied or were afraid, of such love.

By the time I entered my second year of high school my tolerance threshold hit overwhelm. Even with this love and awareness, there was only so much I could endure. I was so obviously 'different'. What I hoped were immature behaviours that the other children would soon grow out of, proved only to ripen into greater maliciousness and mockery.

They laughed at me because I was different and dared to dream. I screamed and cried inside at their games of conformity – their flock mentality. And I ached to be accepted, simply as myself. That was something I could find only vaguely – even in the strangest of circles.

I hung out with 'smart asses' and the uncool, had the attention of most of the boys (to the further annoyance of girls), was weird yet unconventionally confident, was unafraid of pain, and did strange things. I spent a lot of time reading about mystical and paranormal phenomena and had even developed such a high meditative ability that I could consciously astral travel.

I also knew beyond any doubt that I was gifted with premonition, as very frequently I would have a dream or vision of an event before it happened. And it seemed that most of these premonitions were related to rather disturbing events.

It also fascinated me how often I was disturbed by things that seemed inconsequential to others, while those things which were disturbing to others were of no concern to me at all. One such moment had been the news of my Granddad's death. There had been tears and great sorrow about his parting, yet I had just taken it all in, remaining unmoved by the affair. At the funeral I had been struck by such a sense of the beauty and freedom of spirit, and the absurdity of all the sorrow, that I couldn't help but laugh. Everyone had turned and stared at me. Mum had muttered at me under her breath, 'Stop it. Be quiet.'

Dad had given me a ferocious stare. Death was not something to laugh about. I was an embarrassment. But I couldn't help it. I laughed even more. I knew Granddad wasn't actually 'dead'.

I could still see him. His spirit was shining bright and strong and free. And all around the coffin was an air of humour, a fragrance of delight.

When I had finally stopped laughing, I just sat there staring, in a trance. The family looked at me suspiciously as I sat there unmoved in any way. But I didn't dare tell anyone why. In their view I was about an inch away from a mental institution.

My life seemed to be mostly entwined in fields of the collective psyche of unconscious fear and judgment. It was only briefly and sporadically illumined by some fresh hope, creative camaraderie and genuine communion. It was dog-eat-dog, all around me. Yet I wouldn't join in such a game, as another hungry, competitive, fearful dog. And that only exposed me to even more attack.

Gradually, the consistency of love, tolerance and patience I had displayed towards even those who persistently abused me began to falter. I struggled. I felt trapped in a hostile world of futile agendas. And it seemed that the more I understood from a higher plane of awareness, the less the world made sense to me and the less I made sense to it. I began to lose my tolerance, feeling like I was a pawn on a board where I did not belong. I felt the toll of harassment growing into a harrowing state of pain as my family and society tried to squeeze me into a box. School was no longer a sanctuary or place of discovery. It was a place filled with nonsense (non-sense): stuff that had no relevance to me.

The students were immature and concerned with things that seemed non-essential to me. And the system was designed to program us all into a mechanistic mentality that could be easily controlled. Anything creative was considered of less importance. It wouldn't result in a job. But I didn't care about logic and society's idea of making a living. My idea of success was to be fully expressing me. I didn't want to be suffocated by society. I wanted to give myself to everything in each unique moment.

I cared about the spirit of life, the way creation danced in all its natural flowing beauty. I cared about freedom and the truth of the soul. I think even then I was seeking enlightenment, not education. I cared about fully living, not *making* a living. But in school there was no interest in the unique path of each person. We were a flock. I may as well have been locked up with the key thrown away. This wasn't living. It was a place of alienation and cruelty. And I wanted out!

I made it a point that, whatsoever the consequence, I would not deviate from myself. I could only be true to my self, even if I were to make many mistakes and even if that meant I had to walk to hell and back. How else could I know what was true other than through my own experience? My determination to know truth (the big Truth!) had me on course like a homing missile.

Before long my brooding behaviour began to affect my work and the teachers started noticing my contrary attitude. Not only did I feel trapped in a place that was not my truth, I suffered the emotionally immature harassments of the other children every day. To the teachers it seemed odd that a student who had generally been well behaved and a good scholar should become increasingly moody and unreliable.

My parents finally gave in to my pleas and moved me to another school. They thought my problems were probably due to the school's poor standards, which resulted in its bad reputation. But Dad refused to accept that our name had anything to do with it. He took the stance that it would only make us stronger.

'Sticks and stones will break your bones, but names will never hurt you.'

Yeah right! (NOT!) Especially when attached to strong fists, toe-capped boots that could land between your legs, and ready-made weapons like compasses! And all of that catalysed by a surname.

Well, you know that great truth that your problems follow you wherever you go? I learned this by the not-so-ripe age of fourteen.

Those problems were much more complex than what appeared

on the surface. The implications of so many confusing elements extended much further than just a troubled teenager's world. I was profoundly aware of my life as a series of threads in a much larger tapestry. Somehow I felt deeply responsible for the world yet terribly incapacitated at the same time. I struggled to find my place in it all. I yearned to have a path of significance – a path of the soul. On the one hand, I was frustrated that I was 'too young' to be or do what I knew was significant. On the other hand, I had a feeling that time was running out. It wasn't long before something in me had to be expressed.

In art class as I sat drawing, I was turning this feeling over and over inside of me. I liked the boy whom I most often sat next to. He was considered a 'nobody'. I liked that he didn't try to be a 'somebody'. I liked who he was – just himself. And maybe it was his anonymity that magnetised me, compelling me to speak. I turned and looked at him. He looked up in the same instant, his sad puppy eyes openly gazing at me.

'I don't have long to live,' I said.

A slight look of bewilderment passed over his face.

'What do you mean?'

'I might not live past the age of thirty,' I said nonchalantly.

A heavy look of concern spread over him.

'But why?'

In that moment, as I paused briefly, I had a strange realisation that I didn't really know why I was saying any of this and yet some deeper 'knowing' in me was speaking.

'Well, I've got some rare medical condition that could become fatal. No one really knows what it is. But it'll make me get sicker. And I'll probably die around thirty.'

'But that's terrible!' he said, looking appalled.

I sat and stared silently at my sketch. I felt totally neutral. Nothing inside was sad or worried. I just felt a calm, a knowing, that the life we really are was beyond the fleeting acts on this stage.

I looked up with an expression of 'end of topic' and, brushed it off, 'Nah ... it just is.'

He looked down at his paper as if he had just heard something he shouldn't have, and with a sigh, returned once again to anonymity.

I looked around the room. All the faces reflected so many variants – happy, bored, frustrated, confident, lonely, focused, depressed and suppressed. It was like looking at life's human emotional diversity right there in one room. Life's journey, like a roller-coaster ride, streamed out before my eyes.

The world around me continued to reflect an extreme dichotomy between Granny's humble, genuine love and the seething violence at home and school capped mostly by controlled rage. Then there were the niceties of socially good behaviour which, while not overtly violent, were not expressions of truth, either. So I began to retreat into my deeper most secret self. My own dichotomy followed. The deeper I retreated, the greater was my inspiration for heights of love, friendship, creativity and success in the outer reality. I began to discover that despite the appearance of a great gap between these realities, they were somehow intimately connected and affecting each other. This took my interest, intensely. I focused deeply on the power of mind and awareness.

One day, as I was experimenting, I discovered a new dimension in my inner visions. I decided to strengthen and heighten my powers of conscious concentration.

Not only could I experience these as a spontaneous adventure, I could direct the focus of my awareness to such a concentrated point that I would 'become' the point itself and that point was, simultaneously, infinitely vast. This was so immensely peaceful and powerful that it took my fancy to explore further. I focused my awareness, the inner vision, on the point between my eyes. As I watched, a disk suddenly emerged. I watched it spinning. It was so luminous and beautiful! Swirls of emerald light and violet turned into leaping starbursts of silvery white light.

It was a delightful dance yet something in me determined to gain even greater focus. So I decided to visualise a triangle. Its tip pointed up and its three sides looked like bright green neon light tubes. The more I stared the brighter it became. Every day I sat, closed my eyes and stared into this green triangle. As my concentration increased I found I could easily control its form, making it really small, then really large. Sometimes I even found myself sitting inside it.

Then one day something happened. The 'me' that was watching disappeared into the triangle 'being'. I found my self-awareness had simply become the triangle of light. Then, suddenly, the light burst. It was like a great explosion. And in an instant, within this field of light was a transformed scene. I then discovered that I was not alone. My Indian yogi friend was floating in the light in front of me. He reminded me that the form of the triangle is a powerful tool of concentration. It awakens the inner eye[1] and assists in centring the awareness. Through this centring one can move into the source of consciousness itself and experience events of many different dimensions and, ultimately, the state of omnipotence.

Following this event I experienced another quantum shift in my meditative states. I experienced an acceleration of visions that filled me with wonderment, joy, peace *and* questions. How did I know so many things that I had never encountered in this life if we only have one life? The church was emphatic that we only had one life. Reincarnation was considered to be a false and dangerous belief. Yet all I could do was recognise and know the profound awareness of life before and beyond this one.

Repeating visions and dreams flooded my awareness. Temples, pilgrimage, sacred rivers, endless streams of people praying, surrounding me, my brown-skinned body in a loin cloth, white cropped hair and beard. Then ... snow-capped mountains, chanting, prayer beads, maroon and gold robes, and shaved head. Then ... wide open fields, horses, haunting flute, sacred circles, wild deer and antelope, tepees, smoke and long plaited hair. Then ... glaring sun, river boats, pyramids, initiation chambers, anointing baths and royal jewels. Then ... swirling light, bright angels, vast galaxies and love eternal.

---

[1] This relates to psychic and clairvoyant powers.

Suddenly I found myself in a field of endless blue light, blue like a soft flame. And from within the light a shimmering brilliant white point emerged. Then I realised it was coming from the exquisite form of an Elephant-God. It was Ganesh.[1]

He sat upon a fully open lotus on a golden throne. His body glowed like the luminous blue light and was adorned with radiant gems. One white tusk shone with lustre, the other he held in his hand; and upon his lap a golden sacred book began to open. From its pages poured a great stream that flowed from his lap, over his toes and straight towards me. Then a little rat, who was clearly Ganesh's companion, leapt up upon the book, which the Elephant set upon the stream.

The rat floated along on the book until it reached my hands. There, on the book, were written ancient scriptures and symbols. They seemed to float into my mind as if they had come from there to start with and were now making their natural return. Then the little rat took an equilateral cross and placed it on my palm. Each branch had an arm on it that pointed to the right. I stared at its glowing red form. I knew it well. It was the stamp of wisdom, the key of truth that would bring liberation from the pain of forgetting.

As that vision dissolved I was left with mixed feelings. Power, wisdom, certainty, expansion, awe, guidance, protection, purpose *and* confusion, bewilderment and helplessness. It was evident that these things were all showing me a sacred story that had been sung around the world through all ages. It was the song of our same soul, uniting us all. I had seen how I had been touched and even touched others with its wondrous truth. Yet I started to feel quite annoyed. Why was

---

[1] A Hindu aspect of divine incarnation, with the head of an elephant, known as the remover of obstacles and holder of wisdom.

I supposed to know all of these things? Of what use were they to me? And, why couldn't anyone else around me understand them?

Although I watched and experienced these things from a place in me that was ageless, it was very obvious that a fourteen-year-old girl was not supposed to know anything about life. In any moment that I would offer some 'wise' insight I was either given a blank stare in return or was asked,

'How do *you* know?'

All I could muster was simply: 'I just do.'

Somehow I knew that my soul was trying to reveal symbols that it understood, pictures from other lifetimes that were to help me understand the greater plan of life. Yet all the pictures didn't seem to connect up yet. It was like trying to complete a dot-to-dot painting with several numbers missing.

It wasn't until many years later that I was to make full sense of all the pieces of my visionary puzzles. And so until then they remained – like the rest of my life – another mystery adventure.

12. *Divided Worlds*

> Pain is inevitable.
> Suffering is optional.
>
> *Isira*

Two years later, after daily abuse at school and home, my patience ended. I was trapped in a world of judgments. Those limited perceptions, the views that everyone had dressed me in had already grown into a heavy cloak of history that seemed to enclose me. I felt a desperate urge to escape. I simply could not live in such heaving conflict. It seemed almost impossible to find a moment's rest from my mind, which ached for understanding. My spirit longed for freedom and my heart for a place of belonging where I was no longer an alien in a strange land. I wanted to be free of my life's history, free just to be me.

It was as if I had made a cut-and-dried decision. I would no longer accept abuse. I was determined to face anything that denied what I knew to be truth. I felt baffled that I was treated like a child as if I knew nothing. I was so wilful because I knew that what everyone said I was supposed to believe was a lie. I was not young or unaware despite my youth. The 'me' inside was as old as life itself and determined to assert independence. I knew I had my own unique purpose, one that I must fulfil. And so I vowed that I would not let anything or anyone stop me.

Well, that was a choice that sent my family relationships reeling. From that moment I decided to do as I chose. I would be who I wanted to be. The next morning as I put on my school uniform I stared at my legs. Unshaved legs were the schoolgirls' taboo. And, as I looked at mine, with strong blonde hairs that shone on dark brown skin, I cringed at the thought of another rude comment. Some things in life were guaranteed – teenagers' harassment of each other was one of them.

I looked at the cupboard. Dad's shiny metal shaver sat up there. I'd investigated it many times. I sat on the edge of the bath, soaped up my legs and shaved off every hair from my ankles to my knees. It was an act that was to dramatically rock the mother-daughter relationship when it seemed it couldn't be rocked any further.

Mum was outside hanging up the clothes. Merrilyn and Jackson were already through the back gate. I grabbed my school bag, closed the door behind me and collected my bike. As I wheeled it to the back gate Mum stepped forward and looked down at my shiny legs, freshly shaved with a bright red-pink pit from a nick. I hesitated to stop to say goodbye. But in an instant she noticed and looked up with eyes like lightning.

'You shaved your legs, didn't you? I told you, you weren't allowed to do that!' she hissed.

'You little SLUT!'

And with that she raised her arm back with an open hand and swung it full force across the side of my face with a heavy, stinging blow to my ear and cheek.

Before I could even think, I struck back at her and screamed,

'Don't hit me! You'll never hit me again!'

She reeled back from my blow, as shocked as I felt. I ran out of the gate feeling that despite how much I hated the treatment I encountered at school it seemed like a good escape from home.

From that day, my life at home seemed to spiral into deeper insanity. My sister remained the 'good girl', a stark juxtaposition that only emphasised the growing problem that I posed to my family. And my brother seemed entitled to a respect and freedom that I could only long for. I rebelled against all the boundaries. I stayed out late, went out when I was told I couldn't, hung out with people I wasn't supposed to be with and refused to do as I was told. My life felt like a constant field of tension between my quest to go beyond confinements and the rage that rained upon me in return for such rebelliousness. I couldn't seem to make sense of anything much any more and existed moment to moment with fleeting dips into my inner sanctuary.

I tried to make sense of it all, of myself, and yet the pieces just didn't fit. Despite the confusion and pain, I was acutely aware of something beyond these moments, a much bigger plan. And so I became a rebel – seeking a cause.

The 3rd Attainment

Once again the God-voice spoke within, 'Remember each step in the light and the dark is of purpose, leading you to the place you seek. Be sure to retain what you see and learn, for these are the tools by which you will fulfil your purpose.'

I had watched closely. I was aware of all the signals in my environment. They were pointing to a place far beyond the little world I lived in, yet every step within it was carrying me forward.

From the inner place, the eye of consciousness watched. I had to follow the signs.

KEY 3.

Venus

KEY 3.

Venus

The world is a Goddess of form, all abundant ... gestating whatever is imagined. She is the thunderous power of sexuality, the darkness of temptation, the nurturing embrace of a lover's arms and the sweetness of love's perfect beauty – all, waves in her vast ocean.

My time had come to understand the power of being woman – all-attractive and desirable, the power of love's infinite ocean ...

13. *Beyond Normality*

> When the most important things in our life happen
> we quite often do not know, at the moment,
> what is going on.
>
> *CS Lewis*

The sounds of morning penetrated my sleep. I sat up, startled, temporarily unsure of where I was. Which world, what time was it? Just a moment before, I was in a wonderful and vast valley, surrounded by mountains, listening to the song of the flute that had echoed throughout my life. My dreams were vivid and lucid and so real that the boundary between being asleep and awake became non-existent.

Premonitions warped my sense of the time and place of life's happenings and my psychic senses seemed to grow more intense. That intensity could rip me from my silent and secret world. For many years I had mostly kept it all quiet because I had learned that it only made people consider me to be less normal, less stable and possibly requiring a bed in a psychiatric ward.

Then, one night I dreamed the school was on fire. I woke up completely convinced it was real. But despite my attempts to convince people, I was once again brushed aside with cynicism. However, that afternoon, the school *did* catch on fire. I thought it strange that everything about the fire, except my last night's dream, was discussed. It was 'too difficult to explain'.

Only a few months after that, I woke up at about four o'clock in the morning to a terrifying sense of being strangled. It was so physical I felt like I was suffocating. In the same instant I saw the stark white face of a young man before my eyes. He then turned grey and purple and I felt the shocking strangulation around my throat suddenly release. About two hours later the phone rang. Mum ran to the kitchen mumbling surprise and annoyance about the phone ringing at six in the morning. Her best friend at that time was on the other end with tragic news. Mum's friend said her son had hanged himself in the front tree early that morning.

The tragic news hit me like a semitrailer. I knew I was directly linked to this. My sense of reality took another spin. I was beginning to wonder if I was somehow responsible. My God, I thought, how is all of this possible? Maybe I *am* insane. I searched with my heart for an answer. I prayed for my angel to be by my side, but nothing happened. I was all alone, on the edge of madness. I tried to tell it all to my mum but she just looked at me, half-blank and half-confused.

My life had three theatres: school and home, where the drama of violence, excitement, confinement and discoveries played; and my inner scenes, the release of expanded meditations and the crossover of the inner seeing in the outer world.

I tried desperately to establish friendships. I longed for communion, togetherness, playfulness and joy. My attempts to find acceptance amongst the girls seemed to leave me in a void looking not at no-man's land, but rather at the boys' corner. This only led to greater turmoil. My agenda was a bit of fun, friendship and philosophy. Theirs was below the belt.

They were thinking: How can I get her to bed?

I was thinking: How can I show them the meaning of life?

They were thinking: P for puberty, peer groups and pubs.

I was thinking: P for philosophy, purpose and penetrating presence.

Albeit I didn't fully understand why, the boys incessantly viewed me as an attractive, desirable sex object. But one thing I did understand went way beyond that. They thought my surname was enough evidence that I deserved and even asked for their sexual advances. I soon became the subject of sexual harassment. I was met frequently, sometimes daily, with offensive words and grabbing hands.

'COCK sucker!'

'COCK *head!*'

'Kathy sucks ... *cocks.*'

Girls pretended not to see me, deliberately colliding with me in corridors. Boys made sure their actions weren't seen. Hands grabbed my backside and reached up my crotch.

I retreated to the library or the art room, seeking relief in the creative escape of drawing or reading. I also discovered a deeper sense of intelligence, openness and friendship in the teachers. They had no girls' bitchiness, no boys' silliness, no jealousy, and no overactive testosterone. Yet still the plague of harassments seemed unavoidable.

One day I found myself lured by some of the older boys with what looked like innocent fun. I was caught behind the shed by a three-point trap: the 'Italian trio'. Before I could even guess the next move they had me pinned down between Tony's legs on the grass. One hand was thrust between my legs, the other pushed my face to his. His groping mouth stung my lips. I let out a muted scream and struggled to kick myself free. He pulled back a bit and laughed.

'Ha ha, you're a fiery one, aren't ya? I bet your pussy's hot!'

I felt his finger's force and let out another scream,

'Let me go! STOP!'

All three boys laughed.

'Hey, she wants more. Look, she's thrusting!' said the short fat one.

'Yeah ...' cajoled Tony. 'I like 'em feisty, you're a real little fighter – I like it like that.'

After a great thrashing and clashing of arms and legs, I finally broke free.

Meanwhile the news had spread like wildfire that I had 'got it on' with the 'Italian trio'. The word 'slut' echoed between the girls. I was so shaken, shaken by a force I felt no control over. The memory of my past seemed to ricochet in the shock of the present. For days I retreated into the back corners of the rooms and yard. I really wanted help. I wanted to be free of this pain. I thought about Mum. But that was of no use, she would only abuse or reject me.

I then thought of the school counsellor. I'd talked to him before. He always seemed kind and caring. I finally got to the point and told him what happened.

'Oh now, Kathy, I don't think that's what really happened,' he said solemnly, without a second thought. 'I know Tony. He's a respectable, good boy. Now how 'bout you just settle yourself. Be sensible, life is okay. Why don't you stop trying to mix with the boys? They can be a bit rowdy. You should have some nice girlfriends, shouldn't you?'

I looked at him in disbelief. His response was point-blank denial. Tears welled in my eyes. I got up and left the room.

I felt like I wanted to leave the world, yet desperately ached to be united with it. I wanted to embrace the beauty of love, of my womanhood, of sexuality. But so many moments had shown me its brutality: the mysterious power was a thing both light and dark that seemed to tug at every soul. And I knew the same conflict within me, for I too felt rocked between feelings of repulsion and longing. The brutal and lustful force that sought woman as a prize disgusted me. Yet the divine power within yearned for the gift of sacred union. And still yet another place in me felt a profound stillness, a beauty of quiet aloneness, like a sage who had found the ultimate lover that lived within.

In that moment I couldn't make sense of it anymore. So I walked out of the building, went to the toilet block and took out a half squashed, bent cigarette. I'd started pinching them from Mum. I couldn't really explain why I started doing that because I thought they were disgusting and stank. But I stuck it in my mouth and lit it. I sucked hard. I knew the harder I sucked the dizzier it would make me. And in that dizziness was some kind of sweetness, a momentary sense of escape. Then I passed out briefly and my head hit the wall.

When I opened my eyes I was staring at the speckled conglomerate concrete. A little trickle of blood left my nose. Now I was late for the next class.

Lateness became a regular thing for me. Over the next few months I stayed quietly in the background avoiding what I could. The torments of gossip still spat at me. Eyes chased me. Energy brewed. I felt the hatred of the leading girl gang escalating to a threat. Then the volcano blew.

I walked into English class and took my seat in the back row. I was feeling exhausted, at the end of my tether. The daily taunts at school had piled up in a great, buried heap within me. I felt ostracised by the world around me. Fears of my family's domination over my spirit also wreaked havoc on my mind. I had felt such confidence in my states of other-worldly awareness. To me those insights had shown a greater reality beyond ordinary perception, yet I was actually beginning to wonder if the world's opinion of me was really true. The daunting thought that maybe I really was a candidate for insanity challenged my heart's wisdom, threatening to drown it in a sea of confusion. It felt like I was teetering on the edge: the fine line between madness and transcended awareness.

Mrs Hilberdink was busy writing on the board and the pile of study books had been given to Kaz, the leader of the girl gang, for passing back. I watched her going through the pile, reading each name, then smiling and handing it to each person at their desk. In that instant I knew the next one would be mine. Sure enough, the look on her face confirmed it. Her smile turned to an insidious smirk. She looked at me with malice, and, in one motion picked up my book and flung it full force across the room. It hit me right in the eye. My body responded before I could even think. I leapt towards her like lightning. And as she raised her brow in surprise I drew my fist and ploughed it into her stomach. It was a one-inch punch. It sent her body flying – airborne – into the wall.

A shock of silence hit the room. Time stopped. Then, gradually, murmurs rippled around the room. I looked up at Mrs Hilberdink.

There was a smile behind those eyes that looked in quietly contained surprise. It seemed to reflect a thought of congratulations: that my silence was finally broken.

All those years of taking the abuse: swallowing my pain, turning my back, forgiving, forgetting, offering friendship, accepting rejection, quiet resignation. That was it. Finished. The leader of the girl gang was humiliated. The mind set of the girls shifted from group power to a disquieted, unwilling respect. The students parted as I left the room. Nothing in school meant much any more.

I didn't care about grades. I didn't care what future they were meant to bring. Art was my only remaining passion: passion for the freedom to express my life the way I wanted it to be; passion for the love inside me; passion for a life somewhere else. And still, life's confines only allowed for a freedom to be found within. So I dived ever deeper, probing the depths of consciousness.

I would sit in the middle of the asphalt at break-time, cross my legs, close my eyes and dissolve in the light. I began to dissolve so deeply that my body would pass out. On numerous occasions I found myself being shaken by hands trying to wake me up. Temporary confusion was rapidly brought to order with the slumping realisation that I was still in this world. I struggled, desperately aching to find my own place of true belonging. My body seemed to be the only thing in this world that I could call home, where I could express my own authority.

I stood staring into the mirror in the school toilet block. I looked at my face. My eyes were blue-green and lined heavily with black makeup. My broad nose sat solidly in the middle of my face which was square, no, slightly round, actually maybe a little bit heart-shaped, I decided. I stared at the dimple in my chin, my high cheeks. What a weird face, I thought. What's the big deal about me? I frowned heavily, incensed and bewildered that I seemed to be such an object of fascination and desire. But then I caught a little feeling of paradox. Yes, I did want to be desirable. I wanted to be loved. I wanted to be accepted. But then, back to the frowning me. That wasn't what I had come to the toilet for.

I took out the needle that I had squirrelled away from the home economics class and had carefully tucked into the pocket of my school bag. Next I took out the cigarette lighter. Striking the flame I held the needle in the heat of its blue fire. And, without a moment of hesitation, I proceeded to pierce my nose.

One of the girls from my English class walked in.

'Ooooo!' she exclaimed, squirming and screwing up her face. 'What are you doing?'

I flashed her a silent stare and continued my operation. The needle was through and blood was seeping out of the hole. I reached into the pocket of my jeans (black, in rebellion against conformity) and pulled out the stud with a fake red ruby setting. Pushing forcefully, I finally managed to get it through the smaller hole the needle had made.

The girl had stood there, wide eyed and transfixed, until that moment. Then, as if the spell had been broken, she screwed her face up again.

'You're sick' she scowled, and walked out.

I sighed out heavily, inspecting my new apparel. I had already added three piercings to my ears, much to my parents' disgust. Yet I had gained some satisfaction, knowing that what I was now doing to my body was something that no one else could control. My reputation changed from being too clever to 'a slut', to 'weird', to 'sick'. It seemed no one could really make any sense of me, just as I could make no sense of the world.

Then, my psychic awareness took another quantum leap. No longer did I merely experience spontaneous moments of insight into people's thoughts and future events. Now, it seemed that the boundaries of 'me' dissolved completely into some surreal meltdown. There was no longer inside/outside, and I had no apparent control over it. I had the awareness that everything was all in me. Everyone's thoughts and feelings – and all actions and events – unfolded in my awareness even before the physical reality followed. It was as if I was in some kind of time/space warp.

In class I would leave my body and watch from the back of the room – watch my own body sitting at the desk. At home I would dodge the rest of the family in favour of the sunrise and sunset. I felt my sense of reality dissolve into the apparent reality of the world and then beyond – far, far, far beyond. I felt like I was flung into infinity and back in a single instant. I was rocked by the mind-shattering pains of humanity and into the ecstatic bliss of eternity. I dissolved in tears – rivers of pain, rivers of joy, rivers of life.

•

I took more and more to sitting quietly in every moment possible. I was quietly present, quietly watching and contemplating. Somehow I could see that it was all so different – not what it appeared to be – not the play that seemed to be a never-ending wheel of up and down. I opened my consciousness to the world.

This time when I sat I didn't close my eyes. Instead I looked in the same way, but instead of into the eternal within, I looked into the life around me. Just then an ant began to make its way across the path. I focused my gaze while at the same time I expanded my vision. It seemed as if the cracks in the path, the ant and the grains of sand were suddenly so absolutely small within the vast scape, yet so infinitely large in themselves.

I found my self pulled into the scene and in a sudden flash as I watched the ant walk into the crack, I *became* the ant. The crack that I had just walked into, head first, was a cliff face half lit, half engulfed in shadow. I heard the whirrs of the other worker ants: the navigation vibrations, a pulse of collective intelligence. My feet moved precisely and easily within the terrain. Then as I stared into the dark crevice I found myself engulfed in an endless void.

The ring of the school bell suddenly blasted three times. With a jolt I found myself sitting in my body again. I got up, brushed myself off and raised my eyebrows with a sigh as I contemplated how totally 'normal' yet completely extraordinary and unusual that experience had just been.

I started to walk home, feeling a bit dazed. The sun warmed my face as I drifted along the footpath. However my sense of a natural everyday stroll home from school was suddenly interrupted. I stopped dead as I saw an image of my brother's terror-struck face flash before me. All in the same instant I saw *and felt* the scene unrolling with a full-on sensory impact.

The scene played in slow motion, with my role switching from observer to being my brother driving his VW 'bug' through a round-about ... a car slamming into the front ... a sudden sharp pain in the knees and chest ... breathless shock. I screamed. Realising what had happened I blinked in the bright light. I looked around me but couldn't see the accident anywhere. So I just started running, crying.

I ran all the way home, through the gate, into the house, screaming, crying.

'Accident ... Jackson's in an accident!' I cried.

I was hysterical.

Mum was in a foul mood. In her attempt to find relief from the heat, she had the fan spinning wildly. She took one look at me and yelled:

'Oh, for goodness sake, stop that noise, you silly little bitch! Sit down and shut up!'

She grabbed my shoulders and shoved me down in the chair. Somehow my foot was under one leg of the chair and as my body weight landed, it pushed down on my foot. I screamed louder. Mum slammed a cup of water in front of me and yelled again.

'Oh, stop it. I've had enough today without your nonsense!'

By this stage I was simply a heaving, sobbing mess. Mum walked out of the room, slamming the door behind her. I was still shaking and sobbing fifteen minutes later when the phone rang. Mum came back into the kitchen and picked up the phone.

Her racing angry energy just stopped flat. She pulled a chair to the phone and sat down, in slow motion.

I watched her face drop.

'Yes …' she said.

'… Oh …'

I watched her mind's sense of reality break. It fell into a thousand pieces. Just dropped like pieces of a puzzle onto the floor.

She looked up from the phone to me, a stare of blank shock on her face. Her mind entered a gap. She looked back at the phone.

'Oh … yes … okay,' she said, 'I'll be there soon.'

She hung up the phone and looked at me, then stared at the floor.

'Yes,' she said. 'Jackson's been in a car accident.'

Mum left the house.

In that moment I felt overcome with compassion and understanding for her. I could see her own innocent struggle as a woman, as a wife, as a mother. Inside I felt a deep appreciation as I recognised the soul's journey in the sacrifice and offering of motherhood. And I began to understand my own quest as a woman.

I sat quietly. Inside was a flutter: a feeling of some relief, some gratitude, some triumph and some hope. Well, that was the beginning of a change – even if only slight. Mum began to realise there was truly something else about me. And it wasn't all fantasy; it was real. She also started to realise that something was terribly wrong with her: with her life, her attitude, her anger and her pain. Following that realisation, she became depressed, and that state was somehow broken by a staccato beat of her recurring anger, confusion and yearning to escape.

Yet our relationship, albeit changed, only slid further as I strode towards independence with even more determination. I refused to conform to the expectations of someone else's story: how I should live, who I should be and with whom I would spend my time.

I rebelled in the face of morally righteous conformity, demanding the right to love all beings equally – hippies, Aborigines and bikies alike. I spread my flight for freedom further afield. The local tram gave me a wider territory to explore. On hot afternoons I would take to the beach. There were plenty of locals: mostly drunk; happy; happy for friendship; and happy to share. On cooler days, I took to the city. There also, were plenty of locals: mostly drunk; happy; happy for friendship; and happy to share.

But it wasn't only incidental. In moments I became profoundly aware that something else was orchestrating my moves, leading me to places, revealing little clues in my life. It was like a trail of breadcrumbs.

One day, when I stepped off the bus at Victoria Square, my eyes immediately gravitated to the local group of Aboriginals gathered in a circle in the park. I began to walk towards them, as if pulled by a magnetic force. The older woman of the group noticed me.

'Ay!' she yelled across to me.

'Ay! Cum 'ere! Ay, you! Yer one of us! Cum 'ere!'

I watched her long, dark, skinny arm wave and her head tilt back in an inviting gesture.

'Cum 'ere,' she said again as I approached.

She patted the ground next to her in a command for me to take my place in the circle. She looked at me again. Her eyes penetrated right to my soul. Her voice deepened and her face was overcome with a sense of sincerity.

'You're one of us, ya know.' Spittle sprinkled on my arm as her mouth came closer to my face.

I stared at her. My heart raced. My spirit began to soar.

Seeing I had paid full attention she then sat back and looked at me with a big, round-faced smile.

'What's ya name, love?' she asked.

'K..K..Ka ...'

'Katja!' she finished. 'That's ya name,' she laughed, 'Katja!' Her big round belly jiggled and her long skinny drunken legs sat still on the ground as she laughed heartily.

'You just call me Auntie, ya hear?'

She looked at me intensely again.

I nodded.

'Now pass that blagon 'round 'ere a'gin!' she called out across the circle of people. 'Pass it 'ere fa ya sista, ya cuz!'

The flagon of sherry was passed around with quick swills into mouths along the way. Once Auntie received it she took a big gulp then, with great gusto, passed it to me.

Before I could even think about it I took a swig. I tried to repress the impulse to cough, making a bit of a splutter instead. The hot, sweet liquid moved down the back of my throat. The image of my Granddad's face swept across my mind and I felt his spirit surround me as I took a deep breath in.

To the passersby this was just another drunken scene of the disgraced local Aboriginals and I was an unfortunately misguided teenager. To me, it was the first breadcrumb on the trail to understanding my Aboriginality.

It was there that I began to understand why I had felt so different and why I had instinctively connected to Aboriginal culture.

14. *Seeking Freedom*

> If you shut your door to all errors,
> Truth will be shut out.
>
> *Rabindranath Tagore*

The sound of the tram, rattling along the tracks, clacked out a monotonous rhythm. All I could see were the images of my life. But something else was there, a deep feeling that had been touched in me. The new world I had entered with all its scenes and people had given me a taste of freedom. It wasn't long before I wanted to have that sense of freedom all the time. And along came an opportunity.

The tram pulled to a squealing stop at the end of its tracks. I stepped out into the bright sky, breathed in the ocean air and wandered across the grass to the wall that ran along the beach. People regularly gathered there and sat on the wall, watching tourists passing by, children playing in the sun, sexy girls swimming in the sea. It was a place filled with so many faces, so many expressions. It woke up my senses and reflected life's joy, friendship and openness.

I turned back around and looked at the grass. A group of local Aboriginals had gathered there. Without a thought I was drawn to them. In their drunken delight they welcomed me cheerfully, inviting me to sit with them. Not long after I sat down, two men and a young woman approached. Her long hair was bottle-blond, shining in the sun. She stood with her arm around the waist of the tall man.

The other guy stood a little apart, closer to me and smiled. His eyes were starkly blue under brown eyebrows. His smile widened in response to my little 'hello'. We just seemed to click. I heard the others asking if there was any 'stuff'.

'What stuff?' I asked naively.

'You know ...' said blue eyes ' ... stuff, the good stuff.'

'Oh', I said.

I didn't want to look dumb so I just made out I knew.

Within a few minutes we were all laughing and chatting. There were no judgments, no history. We were just four people united in the moment and enjoying the freedom of it. I sighed with relief and a feeling of arrival.

Next thing I knew, I was invited to the farm. It turned out that Mick, Donna and Paul were all living together in a farmhouse on the route towards the hills that I had loved so dearly as a child. I felt excited at the idea of the hills, bush, birds, dogs, cats, horses and 'good stuff' for fun. It seemed like a welcome escape route – perhaps a new life.

Those were the days when FJ Holdens, Chargers and Monaros ruled the roads and rock music was live. Life for the young was fast, loud and furious. We were all in a Holden. The tape deck was thumping, the engine revving and the tyres were burning. I was enthralled by the wild and exciting ride. No sooner did we get to the farmhouse than the alcohol was being poured, pipes were being lit, Roxy Music was blaring and more friends were arriving.

This was a leap in a new direction, one my body and my mind weren't prepared for. I might have had a couple of sips of the 'black fellas' brandy before but I had no idea what it was like to slip down milky vodkas. They tasted like an exotic milkshake – easy to swallow. But it was much harder when it came back up and out of my mouth.

Drunkenness was something I had only watched till then. I wished it had stayed that way. Before I had laughed, but now I was being laughed at. I was still staggering when I got home, and my staggering was not met with any further humour. A full force of fury sent me reeling to bed.

I woke up trembling: trembling in sickness and pain, trembling in excitement at the possibility of a new life, a new home; trembling with a deep intuitive fear and trembling with the thought of the reactions to follow. Yet a magnetic pull drew me again and again.

I threw myself into the dance of life, hungry for its vast array of experiences. Over the following months I entered deeper into a new domain. A world away from home. It was there that 'blue eyes' innocently took me into my first experience of a loving embrace. Tenderly, he wrapped me in the sensual beauty and sexual passion of our bodies, and in the freedom of two surrendered hearts, we simply danced together for whatever moments were given. Those moments were fleeting. It was not long before my first love was taken from this world. He was killed in a head-on collision.

The world around me changed, dramatically, rapidly as if it was being spun by the kaleidoscope of a mad god.

My life seemed to be hung out on a thin line. It was now a balance between the seething rage at home for which my endurance was fading and keeping the brakes on as I started careering into my own life.

I took my final stand about school. I refused to go past year eleven. Already I was rarely at school any more. I preferred to wander around aimlessly, on green pastures, sandy beaches, city streets and parks. I'd taken a part-time job at the local garage to further my independence. But I began to discover my independence came with a new set of consequences.

I was finally finding a sense of friendship – in circles that embraced work colleagues, locals and strangers alike. It seemed that life was drawing me ever more deeply into its diversity. I felt fascinated by all the varying faces, cultures and expressions of life's paths. I watched the bankers banking, the fashionable women prancing, the drunkards drinking, the mechanics driving, the bogans[1] fighting, the

---

1 A tag name for the average roughneck male who is renowned for fighting, driving dangerously and 'living life on the edge.'

dancers dancing and the street people shuffling. I could see the same pulse of life in every being. I felt the same longing, saw the same seeking and knew the sameness of journeying.

My heart was full with love and wonderment; my mind, thirsty, aware with a strange maturity beyond my years, yet naive and determined. I was ready to accept all, free of the hatred or judgment which others had so readily thrust upon me.

Mum and Dad were of course greatly reticent to give me consent to leave home.

Mum spoke first. 'You're not old enough yet. You need to think more about it. It's a big mistake.' The rest of the words drowned into blah blah blah in my mind.

'Why do you want to keep holding my hand?' I demanded.

'Because you keep tripping over your own foolishness,' came my father's quick reply.

'So what? So what if I fall. Let me fall. It's not going to kill me. I need to fall over so I really know how to walk my life. It will give me knowing. It will make me more alert. You can't think for me. You aren't always going to be here. I am here for myself. I am here to know myself. You can't do it for me.'

'Why are you so determined to waste your life?' my father asked angrily. 'You're intelligent. If you keep studying you could go to university and get a degree. Your life will just amount to nothing. Why don't you become ...'

'Become what?' I interrupted. 'Become what you want me to be? What society says I should be? I am ME. Why do you keep trying to make me something else? I'd rather be nothing than be something I'm not. That's what has happened to everyone. That's why this world is sick and crazy and angry. Everyone is made to be everything except themselves. I won't be. I am here to be me. And I am going to make sure I encourage everyone else I meet to escape the prison and be free to be their true self too!'

My father took a quick breath in readiness to launch at me again but I was too fast.

'And why do you keep pressuring me about 'becoming', about tomorrow? I'm not there yet. I'm here. I can only live here. Now. Tomorrow will take care of itself ... and I will meet that 'then' in another now. If you don't let me fully live now I won't *understand* what I really am and then I won't know how to take the next step. You can't take that step for me!'

My mother shook her head in exasperation. 'Why can't you be like ...'

'Like who? Like Merrilyn, like Jackson, like ... like you, all miserable? Like who? I'm no one but me. Don't compare me. You can't. No one can be compared to me and no one can be compared to anyone else. Each person can only be themself. Even if I end up as a 'bum', at least I'll be a real bum instead of a phoney 'star'. At least I'll be happy. So leave me be. Let me be me.'

I stood up ready to leave. There was nothing left to say. My parents simply huffed and frowned.

For me it was no longer a matter of choice. For a long time I had seen myself as nothing more than a caged, tormented animal. And I may as well have been, there seemed to be such a great divide in our understanding of each other. I could not understand the degree of suppression, control and depression my parents seemed to ascribe to life. And they could not understand the expansion and freedom of spirit I demanded. I knew there was so much more and yet, in this world I had been brought to, it appeared lost. But I was determined to find it and, as it seemed, no matter what.

With every new situation I found myself in I could feel a heavy dissatisfaction. I was not looking for the temporary gratifications of sex, drugs, and cars, or of boy-meets-girl, making babies, drinking in pubs and working in factories. I was looking for the power and communion of spirit. It was something in this world that I had only felt deeply when I was in nature and yet in the vastness of conscious Self-presence I knew it existed within humanity.

Once again I wondered if I had taken a wrong turn, or perhaps come in at the wrong time. It all seemed so dramatically wrong.

Simultaneously I had no resistance, for a deep part of me knew that it was all in perfection. And in this sense, I was like a river flowing, simply flowing, as was my destiny: to dance over rocks, to lap on the banks, to flow so deeply. Therein was a stillness, and in letting go so freely, I experienced the journey with a lightness that tickled and giggled.

My wonder at this and my sense of adventure was such that I was free from the inhibitions that most people had. I would dive into every moment, experiencing it to the fullest, to know this discovery of self knowing Self in such diversity, in such freedom – just to be the play. And what satisfaction could there be for Hamlet if he did not fully play the part of Hamlet?

And so, I took the leap. I flew the nest. I set off with little idea of the 'real' world and it was only a matter of months before I felt disillusioned with this apparent freedom. The drugs, alcohol and sex were games of destruction that degraded my soul. I felt a tug between the part of me that loved to be included and the part in me that felt so different. The modern renegade and the ancient Buddha collided. The play of experience enticed me and its futility flung me away, deep into renunciation. I seemed to be tugged to and fro, running head-on into the game then withdrawing, seeing the illusion in it all.

I woke up one morning and after sharing the morning ritual of a pipe, looked myself in the mirror and with an undeniable conscious stare, asked myself,

'What are you doing?'

I already had the answer. This scene was opposed to my soul. I knew I was beyond the game. I couldn't play here anymore. I looked at the people I loved with a twist of pain. It was a pain of hopelessness, knowing there was nothing I could do but watch them drowning in destruction and leave them to their own path. But I had to move on. I felt the claws of their desperation wanting to cling to me, wanting to hold me back. They were afraid to see me taking flight for it revealed the pain of their own immobility. But I had no choice. I had to go.

I tried calling home but I received the outcast lecture. Dad had disowned me and Mum refused to count me in.

I'd made my bed so I must lie in it. That was their story, but mine was another. Suddenly I realised I had *unmade* the bed and now I didn't have one to sleep in. That was my first day as a homeless adolescent. I was just sixteen and on the streets.

I took the bus to the city thinking of finding a friend to hook up with. But every person I knew seemed to play the same game I had just left: a struggle for freedom in the haze of dope, alcohol and sex. I was tired of the power struggle, the constant command of energy it took to say no to the incessant harassment of those who wanted to convince or control to gratify their own desires. I just wanted peace, freedom, independence and acceptance. Struggling to find those things in my world, I turned to my meditative practices again. Despite the chaos of the city I was always able to find a quiet place. With closed eyes I could quickly find a state of inner focus.

Within the open space of awareness I began to see a singular point of brilliant white light. That point was so saturated that it was almost blinding. But, with regular practice, every day, I learned to focus in this one direction, holding all of my attention on the point of light. Once the state of my attention was steady I began to merge with the light until the awareness dissolved into IT. That resulted in blinding flashes and explosive states of expansion into ALL light. Huge rushes of energy would course through me, rushing up out of the top of my head, sending my whole being into an all expansive presence. Years later I came to understand that this point of light was a central originating source of pure consciousness. But despite these incredible inner experiences, when I opened my eyes, I was still in a world of challenges. In moments, all I could think of was survival. I felt my power caving in for briberies of food and rest.

I found myself moving from house to house, constantly attempting to escape the lusts of men. I was juggling with their jealousy and plays for power and attention in scenes of drugged debauchery. I even found myself acquiring greater comfort bus-hopping, bench-sitting and café-roaming. But winter was coming. Over a period of three months, I grappled with one discomfort after the next. I was succumbing to some dulling of the senses and occasional obliteration. I caught snatches of sleep and catnaps on benches or in cafés. Occasionally I was offered a place to stay. But my sense of rest was becoming more disturbed.

My sleep had turned into a disturbing broken record: a repeating dream which became a bloodbath of a nightmare. During that three months my dreams were brutally unsettling.

It was the same each night.

Fists were coming at my face.
Blood splattered across walls and carpets.
There was no way to escape ...

And the words, 'I'm gonna kill you,' were echoing.

Then suddenly, I would be awake.

And still I smiled. I smiled at strangers, at the bus drivers, at the drunkards, the café owners and the people I met every day.

15. *Awakening the Dream*

> All the world's a stage,
> And all the men and women merely players:
> They have their exits and their entrances;
> And one man in his time plays many parts ...
>
> *Shakespeare*

The season changed its mood, turning harsh. It became so cold that I felt my face harden to a frown. The winter wind of Adelaide came in slicing sheets, cutting through my remaining selection of clothes, pushing me to seek shelter. So, rather than street roaming, I took to the all-night cafés. I found one that had a rare selection of herbal teas – chamomile taking my fancy.

After one such night I found myself sitting on a wall opposite the train station. It was a nice spot to soak up some warmth in the morning sun. I turned and saw a man in a leather jacket. He was walking towards me with hands in pockets. I had seen him in the same vicinity nearly every day. He'd nodded with a short hello a few times. Now he walked straight up to me.

'Hey,' he said in a greeting, 'How you doin'?'

'Oh, okay,' I said ... 'You?'

'Yeah, good,' he drawled in an accent that sounded strongly Italian. 'What you doin'?' he asked.

'Ah, nuthin' much,' I said, 'just warming up.'

'What, you need work? ... a place to stay?' he asked.

'Yeah, I 'spose,' I said, 'it might help.'

'Yeah? ... I can help, come'n have a look,' he said. 'Come with me.'

I followed him back down the street a few yards to a door that led downstairs. Its neon lights flashed on the walls: 'Cocktails' and 'Girls'. I felt uneasy and suspicious but curious at the same time. Once inside, it became obvious it was a bar and entertainment space. A well-dressed lady came up to me straight away.

Before me stood a woman, rotund and buxom, of not much more than five foot in height and a good six inches of that was taken up with a great pile of silver curls rinsed with a lavender dye. She looked like an eighties remake of a town aristocrat from the eighteenth century. A soft musky, pink velvet cloak covered her body from its pert upturned collar, tightly buttoned around her neck, to its ruffled fringe that fell around her feet. As she walked her plush velvet cloak swished behind her, revealing slip-on court shoes with beads that sparkled.

'Hello, sweetheart, how are you?' she asked.

'Hi,' I spoke softly, giving away my unsure state.

'Do you want a drink, honey?' she asked.

'Sure,' I said. 'Umm, a juice please.'

She took my hand and led me to the bar, stepped behind it, got out a bottle of juice and poured it into a tall glass for me.

'You want some work, honey?' she asked, and just as I was about to ask doing what, a tall, leggy lady stepped out from a door next to the bar, wearing not much at all.

I must have looked both scared and shocked. Until that moment I'd thought of cleaning tables or dishes.

'Oh, don't worry love, she's here to entertain. You can wear clothes, just some waitress work. Don't worry,' she said. 'Miss Velvet'll look after you.'

'But ... what?' I asked. 'What clothes?'

'Come on. I'll show you,' she said. She then led me into another room. It was full of costumes and outfits, mostly frilly lingerie, with a few aprons and tops. She selected a few items and handed them to me.

'See, you don't have to expose anything, just a little apron skirt and top to show your sexy legs,' she winked at me.

I had a mixed response: some fear, some 'fun', some survival instinct, some 'plot to earn money' and some desire to run.

I thought to myself, maybe I could just do a few days, just enough to get some money together.

'Okay,' I said.

She winked at me with a cheeky grin. It was warm and friendly. 'Okay, love, you go with Vince and he'll get you some nice new high heels.'

Suddenly, I saw the whole situation as a game. I thought I could see the moves and I was the director, but there was something much more sinister waiting behind the screen. It was as if the nightmarish dream were pressing ever closer.

I returned with Vince with a pair of beautiful, sleek high heels. They did make my legs look even longer and yes, perhaps even sexy.

Miss Velvet gave me an 'oooh' and smiled sweetly.

'So, sweetheart,' she said, 'do you need somewhere to stay?'

'Maybe,' I replied cautiously.

'Well, honey,' she said, 'you can come and stay with me and have a nice plush bedroom to yourself and a beautiful big bubble bath to soothe yer bones.'

She described a place that sounded like heaven to me, and after weeks of roaming around the streets it sounded irresistibly welcoming.

That afternoon I served maybe half a dozen beers to two men who were polite and friendly, was fed a hot meal and given $200 in cash. I was amazed. It was the most money I had ever held in my own two hands. Miss Velvet said it was more than the usual for waitressing but she wanted to give me a good head start. It all seemed rather easy. Then came the drive in a big old ivory Bentley, complete with a driver. He took us all the way to Miss Velvet's, which, she said, was in Paradise.

I thought to myself, Wow, I really am going to a heavenly place!

We arrived at a mansion, all lit up with fairy lights. Once inside, I was given a plush room and made a hot bubble bath, just as promised. In the middle of my steamy soak Miss Velvet came in with a spare gown and a fancy drink in a tall cocktail glass.

'Enjoy,' she said as she sat it on the edge of the giant tub. She turned and looked over her shoulder at me, then left, her plush velvet gown flowing out behind her. I drank it down in sweet gratitude. By the time I got out and dried I felt somewhat dizzy. I didn't even manage to put the gown on but instead fell, face first, onto the bed.

A few minutes later I heard the door open. I tried to turn over to get up and grab the gown but my body felt heavy and tingly and my head, all fuzzy. When I finally managed to roll over I saw one of the 'security' men sitting on the bed. He started to touch me, moving his hands up my legs. I tried to say 'stop', but only a mumble came out. It was very clear to me now that I had been drugged. I heard the man calling someone else. The door opened and in came another man. They both started pressing themselves on me. I kept muttering until finally a loud 'No!' came out. But they didn't stop.

'No!' I called again.

But they kept pressing. I finally managed to thrash my body over and screamed at the top of my lungs. The door opened and Miss Velvet came in.

'Okay,' she said 'leave her be.'

The men got up and left.

'Don't worry, sweetheart. It's okay. Just have a sleep now.'

I passed out almost instantly.

By the morning I had a hazy memory of the night before but my instinct for danger was on high alert. But I had to play my cards right. I decided to play along until the end of the day, collect my tips and pay, and do a runner. So I did.

With an extra $300 in my pocket, I said I was just going to the shop for a few things. I walked out of the door, around the corner and ran. I didn't want to look back. I desperately hoped that I had managed to escape the full fury of my prophetic nightmare. I shivered at the thought of how closely such a violation had breathed upon me.

I felt disgusted with myself. I felt shame and abhorrence at the game I had played, and still a sense of victory filled my mind. I had played to the edge and escaped. I had made it by a hair's breadth.

It was a toss of the dice whether or not survival meant soul destruction, a vicious loop for so many women. Words echoed through my relieved mind. 'There but for the grace of God go I.' The stories I had heard of prostitution and dirty dancing were no longer just a moral debate in my mind. Some women know nothing but the moves of a victim. The only power they think they have is the magnetism of their bodies: that feminine mystery that can use its force for gain. Over those few months I had come to see another side of Adelaide. The city of churches was not altogether a holy place.

So I took to quiet and secluded places, still driven by survival. The dream came again, like the night that follows day. Steadily pressing, the omen bore upon my mind. Fists, blood, blackness.

•

I was in an all-night café at 3 am, sipping a cup of camomile tea when the door opened. An icy wind rushed in, followed by a couple in their mid-thirties. They took a seat in a booth on the opposite wall, gave their order and then sat staring at me. I knew by their whispers that it wouldn't be long before they would approach me. Sure enough the lady got up and came over. Her plain face was framed by mouse-brown hair and her eyes looked weary.

'What's a young girl your age doin' in a place like this at this hour?' she asked.

So I told her my homeless story, straight up and honest.

'Ohhh,' she said with genuine sympathy.

'Look – oh, my name's Vicky, by the way – why don't you come back to our place? We've got a log fire in our living room and the lounge is cosy,' she said.

Well, I felt a sense of relief. My body ached from the cold and the hard benches. I was tired and longed for a decent sleep, and the couple looked friendly and caring so I happily accepted the invitation. Their home was only fifteen minutes from the city, a small red-brick house sitting in the middle of a shabby yard. The porch light was on and once inside I could see the glow of the fireplace.

As I was shown the lounge a wave of deja vu swept through my body, sending a ripple of prickly goose-bumps up my spine. Yet I had still not learned to honour all of the signs that my intuition sent me. So, feeling tired, I quickly pushed it aside in preference for some rest. Then Vicky gave me a blanket and wished me a peaceful sleep. And sleep I did. A deep, undisturbed, dreamless sleep.

I fleetingly wondered if I had been freed from the dark omen that seemed determined to send me into a room of murder. I woke to the sound of the front door banging: opening, shutting, opening, shutting. It sounded like a lot of coming and going. I got up and walked down the corridor. I could hear voices in the kitchen. When I walked in the door I saw three tattooed men sitting at the table and Vicky rescuing half-burnt toast from the toaster.

Bags of powders and marijuana were strewn on the table. As I looked, part of my response was disappointed, part surprised, and part not surprised. Altogether it was a view free of judgment. I just saw it for what it was.

Obviously this was a drug-trafficking ring. It wasn't where I wanted to be. I had seen enough of the aggressions, depressions, violence and ignorance that were the disturbing jangled reality of this sort of scene. Yet it was where I was, and all I had for now. And as for the people, well, I just accepted everyone as they were.

I sniffed at the selection of distasteful breakfast foods – cold, half- burnt toast, butter and jam. Instead I opened the fridge, hoping to find an apple, a carrot or a stick of celery, and smiled at the memory that I had often been referred to as a rabbit. But I soon discovered that I was out of luck. So I went hungry.

•

The men suddenly noticed me. I just stood there smiling gently amongst the rough, haggard and grumpy faces.

'Hey ... look at you,' said the guy with a missing tooth, 'ain't you a breath of fresh air.'

I found this a line that amused me, the speaker, and anyone listening. I'd heard it several times before. Even though they couldn't work out what it was, they sensed something different about me ... the air of peace around me, the lake of all-embracing love that filled every cell in me, the innocent childlike joy that had remained so present for all I met.

I smiled and asked for the bathroom, took my bag of things and went to wash up. One day rolled into the next, all pretty much the same except that I began to feel relief as my recurring nightmare had disappeared from my sleep. Yet, as I looked at the scene and the people who surrounded me, I thought perhaps it was premature to consider myself safe. And still, trapped by my needs for survival, I didn't know where else to go.

I saw probably thirty different people regularly come and go for their drugs. They gave up offering any to me, accepting my disinterest. And I accepted their indulgence. I met bikers, thieves, waitresses and factory workers and despite all their hardened masks, tough stances and rough manner, I saw the sweetness in their hearts. Soft, loyal and kind, they were ready to give all in friendship wherever there was acceptance. I saw their pain in the lines on their faces. The lines of drugs they took to dull it all reflected a desire for escape. Society saw these people as filth, but I saw the hearts of gold hidden behind the suffering masks of pretence, fear, victimisation and persecution.

Friendships grew in this field of acceptance. The couple who owned the house came and went a lot, mostly on night-shift, together with pub-crawls and partying. Chris lived in the backyard shed that had been turned into a living space. He was a small but strong man with ginger hair, freckles and a short, cropped beard, whose wardrobe seemed to consist only of blue levis, western shirts, steel-capped boots and big silver biker rings.

Chris was around most of the day. We 'clicked' and a friendship grew. He took me to different places: places filled with bikers, drunk or drugged; places filled with toothless grins, tattoos, bloated bodies, smiling eyes and loud, raucous laughter. The stench of cigarettes and beer was infused in the walls and carpets.

The music was loud. Midnight Oil was at the top of the charts and Angry Anderson was at the local gig. The energy was high and full of camaraderie. The women took me under their wing, instinctively mothering me, desiring to protect me from any untoward harm.

The more time passed in Chris's company the more I sensed an urgency. I was seeing signs of obsession, a desire to possess and consume. So, I started to withdraw. But the more I pulled back, the more he pursued me. Again I felt like a hunted creature, now smelling the ever-present scent of my predator. I tried telling him I wasn't interested in a relationship or intimacy. But it fell on deaf ears.

Then one afternoon, I returned home from the city. The house was empty. It was so still and quiet, I welcomed the silence. It was the first moment I had encountered of peaceful solitude in months. I walked into the lounge room and sat down. The quiet was so unusual that I responded with the compulsion to turn on the television but no sooner did my finger touch the button than I heard the back door swing open. I knew it was Chris. I sensed him loud and clear. Within seconds he entered the lounge-room.

A shiver ran through my body. Like a wild animal I sensed great danger. He began to push himself at me, wanting sex. I asked him several times to leave me alone, but he persisted. He persisted with so much force that I began to raise my voice.

'No. Stop!'

He reached out to grab me so I yelled:

'Stop! Just leave me alone!'

He snapped. He drew his hand into a fist and in that instant I realised I was in the dream. It had returned. But this time I was awake. The dream was now the reality.

Time slowed down.

His fingers were loaded with large silver biker rings. I watched them in timeless motion coming straight at my face. His fist shattered my nose instantly. The echo of the splintering, shattering crunch resounded through my head. I reeled back and blood burst from my nostrils.

'FUCK YOU!' he yelled.

'I'm gonna fuck you!

You're DEAD, bitch!

I'm gonna kill you!'

His fists hammered his words into my body.
He tore at my clothes.
The force of his lusting body entered me.

Not a sound came from my mouth. I entered a timeless zone of no thought. I was gripped by presence, yet fear eluded me. It was so surreal. Just like the dream in exact detail and yet I was so aware of the physical reality. It was happening to me and yet it was as if I was just watching a movie. His fists flew at me viciously, incessantly, blow after blow, shunting my body around the room.

Then with a crashing thud, he smashed my head against the wall. I watched the blood splatter, bright red against the pale cream paint. My body dropped and he laid his steel-capped boots into me. I tried to pick myself up but was beaten down with the iron fire-stoking bar.

He beat me continuously for two hours. He toyed with me like a cat with a mouse as he seethed, his mouth foaming, his red eyes bulging, possessed by ravaging rage.

His voice reached a maddening, demonic crescendo.

'DIE, BITCH ... I'm gonna kill you ...

You'll never get outa here alive!'

I watched my bright blood pool and splatter in between the flowers on the carpet pattern. I was amazed that it was exactly as it had been in the dream. I took a gasp for breath. My lungs were seizing up. My mouth and nose were full of blood. When he realised I was looking at the carpet, he looked down and saw my blood everywhere – sprinkled and splattered in pools and droplets – bright red and turning dark.

He screamed in rage.

'AAAGH, YOU FILTHY LITTLE BITCH! Look at the mess you're making. Clean it up!'

And he grabbed me by the hair, shoved my head down and started scrubbing the carpet with it. I tried to escape his grip but to no avail.

He hurtled fists and boots at me again and threw me across the room. My body lay crumpled on the lounge, broken. Blood filled my eyes, my cavities. I felt my consciousness slipping.

In that moment I realised that if I didn't stay conscious I was going to die. So I drew upon my powers of focus and concentration.

It came swiftly and naturally, after years of practice. As I breathed into a state of one-pointed awareness, I felt a familiar shift of vibration, then, suddenly I sensed complete open merging with the entire scene.

I opened my eyes.

There was no longer any sense of separation. Everything was connected as one field of energy. And, right before me I saw Chris, but no longer a separate reality. I was looking at myself.

It was the one all-connected Self. I saw the one same presence. I saw the Divinity within. And, I saw pure presence, shrouded by the body and mind of Chris, shrouded by the pains and wounds of disconnection. I saw his hopelessness: such aching for love, love he had never felt or been given, and in that instant I realised it was out of such pain that he acted so desperately. It was the only way he knew to find love. He would rather take it or kill, than be denied and left without it. And I knew it was not me he violated, but himself. What he was blind to was the knowing that there was only the *one* Self. All he knew was the pain and the belief of separation.

The compassion welled up inside me like a lake with no shores, an infinite ocean of love. It was so immense. I prayed. I prayed for him to know love – to know love as I knew it, to feel love as I felt it, to know that he is love, that he is lovable and loved. I felt the love of a thousand million mothers aching for the child, to know he is held in love. I prayed with all my soul.

Then, in a flash, the room lit up, bright as a golden sun, and I saw within the room a thousand thousand angels. The entire room was illumined! Instantly he dropped to his knees, this dear soul who had never been loved or ever known a second of spirituality in his upbringing. He put his hands together in prayer and turned his face heavenward. With his eyes wide, he raised up his hands and cried out,

'Oh, my God! My God! Oh, what have I done? I'm killing an angel. I've killed ... Oh God! Help me!' He implored with tears.

His soul cried forth.

He then turned to me, my body broken, bloody and swollen.

'Oh God! Please forgive me! Oh, please help me. Quick! You have to move. Someone help!' he cried.

Chris picked up my body and carried it to the hall and sat me next to the phone. He picked up the receiver and dialled 000.

'Tell them,' he said. 'You have to tell them or you'll die.'

The operator answered. And without a thought, the words blurted out of me, a bloody, gurgling stutter,

'He's killing me ... 10 Barr Avenue, Ashfield ...'

But then Chris suddenly realised his fate and snapped again to rage. He slammed my head again into the wall. The crunch echoed in my head, drowning into darkness.

Void. I went down the chute into an eternal space.

There, in that vastness was limitless *being,* beyond thought, beyond form, beyond light and dark ... beyond anything ever thought of in this world.

Nothing remained but pure peace ... love ... stillness ... light ... eternity. I was home with God. Then that state of vastness took on a vibration again. I felt all-embracing warmth. And there, all around me, were angels of every kind. Then, within that light I heard the voice of God.

Do you want to stay or return?

That question marked a split second in which my life stretched on forever like an ocean of time. All the possibilities ran through my mind. What then followed unfolded all in the same instant. I felt my sense of self re-forming and found myself floating through a tunnel yet watching from the ceiling above the hospital bed, looking over my sleeping body.

Mum was sitting in a chair at the foot of the bed. Dad was standing next to my unconscious body. There was no separation between objects or thoughts. I could feel and hear everything telepathically. Dad was lamenting in remorse. His steely blue eyes stared at the cold floor, only to blink and half close as he looked heaven-ward. His soul ached for everything that had gone wrong, ached with the thought of lost opportunity, ached with anger, ached with humiliation ... and love. What if he never got to tell his own daughter that he loved her? What if she didn't live? His soul cried.

•

I was watching it all from a vast space, like a glowing corridor. It was as if I was suspended in time, floating between worlds, between life and death. In that instant I saw an unravelling of images like a stream of movies. I saw the past lives I had experienced, the present life I had come to experience and what was yet to unfold. It was all strung out before me, punctuated in beautifully concise yet complete freeze-frames, filling me with a profound knowing and understanding of all the symbols that had been popping into my world. I understood then that the images of other times, places, bodies and beings had all been part of the rich tapestry of my eternal life.

The dreams, the visions, the scorpion bite, the meditations, the astral travels. They had all been precise messages from my soul, placed like signposts in my life, pointing me to the place of remembering my eternal being.

What was most startling amongst all those things my soul could now see and understand was the awareness that the souls of both Chris and myself had chosen our encounter. He had chosen to encounter love that was truly whole and free of judgment. And I had chosen to give such love for another. It was a power of love that dissolved the fear in the separation, the pain and wounds of the victim and perpetrator. It served for both our souls to fulfil the expression of knowing and experiencing the divinity of love.

I welcomed a feeling of profound wholeness, depth, lightness, relief, understanding. Finally the dot-to-dot painting was joining up.

I suddenly realised I had not yet finished what I had come for.

'Oh, that's right,' I thought, 'I'm not done yet.'

And with that I slipped back into the body, jolted with a twitch and took a breath.

Dad turned when he realised there was movement. I squinted up at him through very swollen eggplant eyes.

He burst into tears and said 'I love you' for the first time in my life.

I lay there in deep peace. The body broken, bloody and bruised yet I – *I* was in a state of clear light. I lay there in blissful awareness with the knowing that I am not the body ...

I AM THAT WHICH IS UNBROKEN, UNTAINTED.
I AM ETERNAL LIFE.

There is no victim, no perpetrator. All this, which appeared, was simply the scene in an act in a play that was a passing dream.

The freedom of self-awareness was a state of such stillness it was unfathomable. I felt nothing but peace. I saw the perfection in it all. I felt no anger, no resentment and nothing to forgive. And, as I thought of Chris, all I could feel was compassion.

Years later, when I looked back upon that incident, I realised that I had entered the state that many sages had referred to as the transcendent realm, a place beyond all fear and judgment. I knew then what it meant to 'walk in the shoes of our enemy'. Only then can we truly understand who they are, so that we may truly forgive them. Then our heart bears the fruit of compassion. It is the lack of compassion that feeds the pain of mankind, originally incubated in the Petri dish of fear.

•

Then came a freight train of agendas: the demands to press charges; the anguish, anger and pain of my family; the reality of bodily violation that provoked the universal claim of justice. My brother was ready to buy a shotgun and hunt down the man who had so violently abused his sister. He wanted to 'blow his head off'. Suddenly his coldness and indifference to me was shaken into the rage of a vengeful protector.

My mother kept shaking her head, only to drop it into her hands as she cried tears.

'I'm so sorry ... I'm so sorry.'

She sobbed those words over and over again. She charged herself with her own guilt. I looked at her forlorn face. Her years of anger and torment were catching up with her.

My sister just looked at me through tearful eyes, not really knowing what to say, yet knowing how dearly she loved me and how much it pained her that someone had tried to murder me. And my father sat, withdrawn, behind the closed doors of the lounge room. I sat in a daze, knowing all those reactions were valid for such an event, yet also knowing how unbroken I truly was.

And still, I knew it could not be left. Such an action was beyond condoning and required justice: the responsibility of reaping a crop that had been sown. I knew my assailant must face the consequences. And yet I could feel no judgment in my soul. The love and compassion I realised was beyond it all.

The line was thin as I stretched my mind and heart around it. I was strung out on a tightrope between compassion and jurisdiction. Society had taught us it was one or the other. How then to find the union of both? Over the following weeks my body healed rapidly. It was considered miraculous. Despite my nose requiring reconstruction, not a single scar remained. At the age of sixteen I knew the power of love could heal all.

However, the incident did leave its mark on the family. The collision of emotions toppled any remaining complacency or refusal to face and deal with our life. Change began. It was a turning point, a fork in the road. Each of us in our own way made the choice to travel the road, together. We were now on a track to greater understanding, building bridges, albeit still with minimal tools to meet each other. Yet, nonetheless, there was determination. And so, growth began.

The 4th Attainment

I came to understand the infinite power of the great Feminine as being like the ocean. Indeed all waves of Love's longing, from lovers' struggles to lovers' embraces, were mere ripples moving in Her vast, untouched ocean. No matter how stormy, no matter how sparkling, the waves all fulfil Love's expression, only to pass again, leaving Her love untainted.

I had emerged from the chrysalis of the girl into the power of a woman. I knew that being female is a calling in itself and that the deeper inherent love and wisdom within the great Feminine can transform the world. I also understood that Her power is so great that most people find it threatening. And so my quest to establish myself comfortably in that power continued to unfold.

KEY 4.

The Elder

KEY 4.

The Elder

He is the keeper of social knowledge, higher order, stability, balance and security. He imparts the knowledge of responsibility.

To draw from his strength we must understand the difference between force and power. Force controls, power harnesses.

In understanding the relationship between the large and the small, he guides as the Father to set the world in order. He administers order and lore for the keeping of sacred balance.

16. *From the Ashes*

> If you want to become whole,
> let yourself be partial.
> If you want to become straight,
> let yourself be crooked.
> If you want to become full,
> let yourself be empty.
> If you want to be reborn,
> let yourself die.
> If you want to be given everything,
> give everything up.
>
> *Lao-tzu*

I walked from the silence of my bedroom, along the dim corridor and into the kitchen. The house was filled with a strange sense of void, an air of coldness and bewilderment. What had been before had been radically altered. Each person in the family was at a fulcrum point in time, faced with a death (of old ways) and with the possibility of new life. But first, the old structures had to be abolished and remade. What followed for me was the demolition of my naiveté, ignorance and disregard for mindful discernment.

I realised that freedom, friendship and joy were elusive qualities often paraded by impostors. Whatever world I wanted to experience could not be explored without discrimination. I had to build my life from a place of knowledge and strength. It seemed totally daunting. I was only sixteen years old and had yet to understand the building blocks of this world.

Just then, when I least expected it, my angel arrived by my side. He spoke immediately and commandingly.

'Seek stillness to see clearly. Build your world in the image of your choosing.'

His words resonated deep in my soul and filled me with curiosity. Me? Create? It seemed to be truth yet appeared to be beyond me. I wondered at the possibility. I looked into his light, searching again for the strength I had felt before. But something inside me knew it was up to me to create it, that somehow I had to draw it out of my own being. So I retreated again into my sanctuary, into the oasis within.

I raided every corner of my mind with penetrating enquiry. As I reflected back upon the last few years I observed the chain of consequences that had arisen. From an immature search for freedom, confined ideas of options and a foolish slathering of excessive curiosity, I saw the light of awareness, like a phoenix, hovering over the ashes. For six months my pendulum swung wildly in the opposite direction. I was happy to have silence and solitude. Still my mind remained thirsty, and my soul hungry. I ravaged my mind until it lay, like ploughed soil, ready for new life.

From the seclusion of my room and the depths of meditation, slowly I began to surface again. Mum also was reaching for the surface, having plummeted to the depths of a depression. Her search began, though for what, she didn't know. I followed her. We walked into a bookshop with a sign above the door that read 'The Theosophical Society'. Its mystical symbol intrigued me.

I turned to the shelves. My eyes landed on the spine of a book. It was as if it leapt off the shelf at me. I reached up and took it down from the shelf. The cover read: *Yoga, Youth, and Reincarnation: a modern step by step approach to the ancient art of yoga* by Jess Stearn. The photos of a lady in balanced poses struck me. The images were more than familiar. Excitement welled up inside me as I flipped through the book. There was more excitement in those pages than I could have ever imagined. Page after page displayed photos of yogic postures and spoke of the practices of breath, energy, meditation and the soul's journey through lifetimes.

I felt an enormous relief and gratitude well up. Finally, here was something tangible to explain all the 'strange' things I had done since I could sit and stand. It was what I had been doing all my life. Then spontaneously, moved by a vivid inner knowing, I felt a rush through every cell in my body as a deep thread of memory connected with past lives unrolled itself like a filmstrip in my lucid awareness. There were images of myself, as a yogi, absorbed in profound states of yoga and concentration.

'Mum!' I called excitedly. 'Mum, look! Look in this book. This is what I've been doing. See, it's here, all explained. I know all of this! It's how I see life.'

I opened the pages to her. She looked with her eyebrows raised up.

'Oh, yes,' she said 'how fascinating,' and she turned back to the desk.

She was too busy to notice the profundity of that moment, the power of what that meant in my life. She was engrossed in a conversation with the lady behind the counter.

It turned out that Mum had found out about astrology and tarot. She decided to have a 'reading'. That was enough to stoke her fire. She signed up for courses and soon made new friends.

Dad was hardly ever home because he worked long hours. But when he was in the house he would sit in the corner of the lounge room in the brown leather armchair. With suit coat, shoes and tie discarded, and with his hot sweaty socks filling the air with a smelly leather shoe scent, he would read *National Geographic* and drift off to sleep. It was as if he fitted into a few limited frames: the man who worked long hours and was even called out in the middle of the night to fix magical machines called computers; the man who demanded silence at dinner as he listened religiously to the news; the man who donned green Dunlop rubber thongs, shorts and a sun hat as he dug weeds from the lawn, leaving it in a constant forlorn and bedraggled mess; and the man who gave more pride and attention to his shadehouse full of orchids than he did to his wife and children.

And yet, despite his walls of silence, I saw the searching, the softening in his eyes. He so dearly wanted to understand, to embrace me. He was no longer just the staunch man, the king of the house, the ruling authority. He was now painfully aware that life was ruled by something beyond his own power of control. Yet he desperately wanted to understand it, to find a way to regain a stable world, to make the house right again. So I watched him teetering on the edge of the firm boundaries of his own conditions, knowing yet resisting the truth that his little empire had crumbled and was beckoning him to build anew. All that he had been taught was so rigid and now he had to face a world, a daughter and a wife that demanded a wider view.

My brother finally left home. His room had become silent. The blaring sound of AC/DC's *Hells Bells* no longer shook the house. He was emotionally drained, unable to support our mother any longer in her great depression. He had his own. He was left scarred and shocked by a dark journey into the underworld of a black magic coven. I had stayed on the edges of his bizarre passage, watching from a distance, yet had unavoidably stumbled into the thick and horrid space in which he dealt.

Mum had asked me to fetch him one evening, but the moment I opened his door I knew I had entered a forbidden and secret zone. The air was so thick it felt like I could slice it with my arm. I closed the door quickly behind me. On his bedroom floor was a cloth, marked with a six-pointed star. Candles were alight at each point and in the middle sat a silver goblet containing a dark and syrupy liquid. His eyes glared at me.

'Now that you have entered my space you must be sworn to secrecy,' he growled.

I nodded vigorously, insisting I would uphold his secret. I left the room as quickly as I could, desperately pushing what I had seen to the back of my mind.

Six months later, after a dark and debauched journey, he finally cracked. Jackson exposed his secret to Mum, desperately seeking solace for his disturbed and tormented soul. Whatever spirit had previously been open and curious in him seemed to disappear behind a closed door. From that moment he did everything he could to don a persona of 'normality', yet he was tired of trying to become what Mum and Dad wanted him to be. He wanted freedom, but his idea of freedom was no longer in the world of 'spirituality' – 'all that weird stuff'. He now sought freedom in the world of the 'ordinary', in his own quest in the streets of Melbourne.

My sister seemed to slide from her seemingly oblivious naiveté into a struggle for her blossoming womanhood. I watched her, trapped between the 'good girl' persona and the longing to be beyond the 'square' box. From the time she had been fitted with 'geeky' glasses as a little girl she had been trapped in the slot of the 'geeks', the ordinary, the 'square' ones. And now she was squirming, like an emerging butterfly with wings still wet, reaching for the sun, yearning to take flight.

Mum was no longer happy with life just as a suburban mother and housewife. I watched her mind's map of references expanding rapidly. Her perceptions were no longer confined by conditioned ignorance and confusion. Life began making more sense to her. Along with her new ideas and friendships came new challenges. She suddenly found herself caught between two realities. Dad still held on tightly to the logically formed view of life. His view of this world was one of harsh cynicism.

Dad was resistant to change. He found Mum's awakening, with her rapidly changing thoughts and beliefs, all too much to understand or accept. It was a confronting situation creating upheaval between my parents. Mum was breaking out of her repressed mould. Dad found it unsettling. All he could do was react with antagonism, constantly provoking her compulsive subconscious behaviours. It was like a game of 'hot potato'. Neither of them wanted to hold the heated energy. And so it became a vicious loop of accusations, judgments and defences.

Mum's frustrations burned in the awareness of wider fields that were now available. I watched her struggle to find a meeting point with Dad in the process of transformation. Somehow, despite the enormous conflict, she kept going.

The 5th Attainment

I committed to watching and learning from all around me in order to create a world in the image I chose. Structure, order and discipline were no longer things of bondage. They were a framework upon which I could establish outcomes. That masculine power was a complementary part in the building of experience.

Most of all, I prayed that such a world could be in peace and highest order for all.

KEY 5.

The Message Man

KEY 5.

The Message Man

He is the voice within: the inner messenger. He is the keeper of higher learning, the student and teacher, the guru within: the voice of the soul. His communication is on the level of spirit.

In the light of visions, in the feeling of the heart, in the touch of a spirit guide – our path is made Divine.

I stood on the bridge between the inner and outer, listening to the inner messages, watching the outer symbols, eager to learn.

17. A Willing Heart

I have learned silence from the talkative; tolerance from the intolerant and kindness from the unkind. I should not be ungrateful to those teachers.

Kahlil Gibran

Mum's new friends meant a lot to me. They provided the beginning of greater understanding and confirmation of my life. I felt mostly disillusioned with friendships in my own age group. Young women were too jealous, fickle, insecure and competitive to discover a deeper sharing, and young men seemed to have tunnel vision. In their eyes I could see through to the file of their mind. Their view of who or what I was, read – Mmm ... young, blonde, dumb, sexy chick. It was a clear-cut case for the dismissive mind that judged by appearances. There was no open consideration (let alone interest) that perhaps there was something deeper, something ancient and wise hiding inside an unlikely package.

To my mother's friends I was a wise old crone trapped in a seventeen-year-old body: 'Seventeen going on fifty-seven.' I was finally understood. The aching plea of my soul that cried to be seen and share the seeing was finally being met. So in every moment I could, I would join in or tag along.

In moments this annoyed Mum. It raised a new set of emotions for her to deal with: jealousy and competition. She was desperate for her own sense of belonging and identity. And it was becoming very obvious that I actually had what she wanted. It was a strange sense of push and pull. Part of her wanted me near, out of her deepest desire for our own reconciliation, and another part of her didn't, because it took the attention away from her. And that was what she craved. But with her, I went.

On one such afternoon we visited Maria. I loved seeing this cheery little lady. She was married to a Turkish–Greek man and hence had been initiated into 'coffee cup reading'. And, she had a gift for it. Mum was keen to learn and develop the skill. I sat watching, quietly contemplating the endless streams of these 'clairvoyant' visions I had experienced already. Maria looked at me astutely.

'I reckon you got something, love. Why don't you look?'

She pushed a little cup towards me. Its dry powdery remains lay like an etching inside. Instantly the images danced before my eyes. Clearly I could see symbols, faces, scenes and events. I started talking, just speaking what I could see. Mum and Maria sat wide-eyed. As soon as I took a breath, Maria leapt in.

'Hmmm!' She exclaimed. 'You got the eye! You're gifted, a true clairvoyant.'

Mum looked on in amazement. Our relationship took another turn. She started turning to me for insight.

Next came the tarot cards. They came like a strum of synchronicity, reflecting a language that my soul already knew. No sooner did I learn the basics of symbols by watching Mum and her friends, than I was able to give vivid and accurate interpretations. I found the cards to be another trigger for the high voltage of psychic awareness that already flowed in me. And they provided a profound set of universal symbols that could connect the language of the soul to the trials and adventures of our life. Most startling of all was this unshakable feeling that I already knew them.

It seemed that the twenty-two symbols of the major Arcana, the master archetypes of the tarot deck, perfectly reflected the stages of my life. Like a series of initiations, life presented me with experiences from which I could attain insight and remember my higher Self. And it seemed a little 'coincidental' that I was born on the twenty-second day in the month. According to numerology that was a 'master number', indicating a soul taking a journey of, and for, mastery or a higher purpose.

When I started telling Mum's tarot friend, Marjorie, about all the dreams, visions and experiences I had been having she responded with great enthusiasm and affirmations which finally gave me peace of mind. She was the first person who understood me and had words in the English language to explain it all. I began reading voraciously. Mum brought home a constant array of books on metaphysics, yogic consciousness, theosophy,[1] sutras[2] ... I read the complete set of Alice Bailey and HP Blavatsky, comprising weighty volumes of high level metaphysics and esoteric verses, hardly putting them down. It opened up an even deeper channel within me. I found I already knew everything I read! I was amazed yet not surprised. In fact it was as if they were my own words. So then my own writing began.

I poured out poems and verses. I was finally free to express. My fascination for life and its processes grew deeper as I began to understand my own physicality more. And along with it came another power switch. I could feel energy pouring through me into my hands. I could see streams of light pouring out from my palms and fingertips. Mostly it was greenish but sometimes it would be white with gold, pink or blue, like a flame. I felt drawn to people when they were in pain. Sometimes I would just put my hands on their head or neck and within minutes they would be feeling better, and surprised.

Then one day my cat came towards me from the garden. I could see he looked a bit under the weather. His aura looked dull and his body a bit limp. He leapt up onto my lap. His eyes were full of pus, his nose dribbly and his chest rumbling. He really sounded sick. So I sat there with my hands on his chest feeling an endless stream of love and healing energy pouring through me and into him. After about half an hour he got up, stretched and went and curled up. He slept until the next morning. When I saw him sitting at his food dish I could

---

[1] The study of truth, God, religion and spirituality based on the idea of the unity of all things.

[2] Short teachings on consciousness and creation, usually Buddhist or Hindu.

hardly believe it. He looked even better than normal. His eyes were sparkly, his aura bright and he sat up fully with his ears all perky.

Later on I sat in the garden where I had loved to sit as a child. As I sat quietly I realised I was not by myself. I saw the light field of a familiar presence. It was the divine light of my beloved angel. My journey with him had been so intimate, and so deeply synonymous with my growth. As a child he had reflected to me the sweet, innocent simplicity of life. And now as I moved into my adulthood he reflected the ancient and ageless power of wisdom. Then I heard clearly the words,

'You are this love. The power that I am, you are. This is the One. Remember who you are. Let your powers flow, for you are here now, reborn for the world. Many wait your healing presence. They will come to the light that you are. We are the One. You serve the One.'

I sat in a daze. There were still moments of doubt – doubt in the power and the truth of what I experienced. And yet it was a power beyond me that in the depths I knew I could not question.

The next day I went to sit again in the garden. Just as I passed beneath the tree a snow-white dove landed right next to me on the fence. It cooed and blinked at me. I experienced a strong sense of deja vu, then peace engulfed me.

From that day on I noticed an even greater sense of communion with all living things. The sense of unity flowed as a river of love and sacred respect. Each creature I saw was family to me, like an old friend. There was no sense of the unknown. No living thing was a stranger. I felt deep gratitude. Friendship was to be encountered everywhere.

This seemed really quite ordinary to me. It wasn't at all something strange. To me it was simply the true nature of existence, the web of life. Yet to others, it was mysterious and unexpected.

In the following weeks the visions in meditation and my dream states were even more frequent and vivid.

I vigilantly practiced yoga and pranayama,[1] sometimes spending

---

[1] A practice of directing the breath with specific depth and rhythm to move energy through the channels of the subtle body.

my entire day breathing, meditating, sitting and posing. I would be visited frequently whilst in these states, always by the same beings, yogis and masters. Their light fields were powerful. It seemed to accelerate my own energies. Sometimes the frequency was so high I thought I was going to take off. The kundalini[1] would swirl and pulse through my chakras[2] and channels.[3] It was like watching a new dimension of a neon laser light show of luminescent streams of white, silver and golden light. My third eye flashed with blue discs which sometimes turned to green or amethyst. My heart centre blossomed with petals of radiant rose pink. There were periods when I was just completely flooded in gold and white light. Sometimes it would quiver for an hour then reach a sudden explosion. Other times there would be one great sudden *whoosh* and everything would dissolve into endless light.

My bedroom was engulfed in the darkness of night. Silence had descended with the rest of my family who were sleeping. But I lay on my bed, deeply alert. My body vibrated in a state of expanded energy when suddenly I became aware of an intense light in my room. I opened my eyes.

There, on the end of my bed was a glowing orb of light emanating from a being of such radiance the light was almost too dazzling to look at. But as my eyes adjusted I could see more clearly. It was a yogi, floating above the bed, seated in full lotus posture. I sat straight up and folded my legs likewise.

From within the vastness of energy a mantra suddenly began to emerge. It was coming from both of us! We sat together chanting for what seemed like hours until I dissolved into deep bliss and everything disappeared into deep stillness. It wasn't until years later that I would discover this yogi was the famous Baba Muktananda.[4] It then became a frequent happening that I would emerge within the light

---

1 Energy that lies dormant in a chakra or energy centre at the base of the spine until spiritual awakening, when it begins to move upwards eventually stabilising in the crown chakra.

2 Energy centres in the subtle body aligned in a path corresponding to the spine.

3 Pathways within the body for the movement of spiritual energy.

4 A great yogi, saint and spiritual master, who introduced Siddha Yoga to the west in the late twentieth century.

in another place and find myself in company with another particular yogi. He was cloaked in maroon and gold, sometimes appearing in regalia and other times with his shaved head bare. But always he had something to show me or to communicate to me. I would find myself chanting with him. In consciousness it was not at all foreign, yet in my life it was a mysterious language.

Sometimes I would find myself travelling through space with him, traversing many planes of different realms. Often we would fly over great snow-capped mountains and descend into a cave overlooking great valleys lit by a golden light. Once there we would sit quietly, share a drink of thin warm water flavoured with herbs, eat a seed[1] each, and then dive deeper into timeless meditation. He took me through initiations of higher awareness and informed me that I was being prepared for my physical quest. The initiations were of such a high level that they cannot be conveyed in human language. Despite this I felt deeply saturated with the conscious 'knowing' I had been held in. Finally he conveyed that it would not be long before we would meet on the physical plane.

So my days unfolded in great expanding ways.

As much as I felt the increase of inner growth, I hungered for the same in my physical life. And despite the gift of such healing and closeness that my mother and I were sharing I still felt so alone in the world. It was becoming almost unbearable that I was left without any integration in the world that could support me or give me the degree of clarity that I needed on a physical level. I ached desperately for true communion in the world.

•

My interest in the physical world seemed to also enter another level. I took to studying natural health. First nutrition and herbs, then acupuncture, reflexology and massage. I felt compelled by society's

---

[1] The drink and the seed was an ancient formula that sustained energy for long periods of time which meant the body did not need to take food. I was re-encountering this experience as something I had known in a past life.

demands to acquire some type of accreditation in further education. However this study choice wasn't considered a worthy option by most, especially my father. Once again I found myself unsupported and unaccepted. Nonetheless I was determined.

I took to working as a waitress to finance myself. I worked hard. I studied hard.

I found myself being drawn more and more to the unorthodox. For most people I was still an oddball, on occasions classified 'a witch'. Yet there were those who were attracted beyond any debate.

I started giving consultations and healings using crystals, energy and clairvoyance. At the same time that I healed others I focused on healing myself. My body had suffered from years of an abusive environment. First a mother who had smoked heavily, next a diet that was less than sufficient and which filled my body with toxins, candida[1] and allergens, and then my short but hard-core trial of self-obliteration with drugs and alcohol.

So I took to fad health diets. Vegan, raw food, macrobiotic, vegetable juicing, brown rice fasts, coffee enemas ... I tried the lot. It made an enormous difference. I regained vitality, vigour and a seemingly endless sense of physical power. The juvenile arthritis that had seized my fingers up disappeared and I could finally breathe free of mucous. I had so much energy I had to find an outlet for it. So I took to sports again. I joined Surf Life Saving (inspired by the notion that it also served the community) and launched myself into serious training. Surf skis and triathlons were proving to be a suitable challenge.

The passage of solitude became obsolete as I burst forth on a new stage of social adventures. But just as I came to feel confident that I had left the traumas behind me, I found myself in a scene of sudden contrast.

I was walking down Jetty Road when there, across the road, I saw Chris heading towards me.

His aura was dark and intense. I felt immediate shock and fear.

---

[1] A gut bacteria which can become overgrown with a poor diet, especially excess sugar and yeast.

I knew that if he saw me he was bound to chase me. I had come to realise that, despite his 'awakening' after nearly killing me, he nonetheless was driven by fear – fear for his survival. And that could mean killing me in order to protect himself from the fate of prison. I also had grave concerns that with such an unstable mind he might affect the lives of others.

The court case had dragged out due to his absence until it was finally passed by a representative of the courts. He was charged with attempted murder. Yet despite a national warrant for his arrest, the police and CIB had not managed to track him down.

I ran. My heart pounded as if to beat me down. I ran past the main tram-stop until I reached the next, far enough away to be out of sight. I was shocked. I had all but forgotten the event and had left it behind. I sat in a daze waiting for the tram to arrive. I prayed that he wouldn't be on it. My mind went into a spin. The conflict between compassion and jurisdiction once again broiled inside of me.

By the time I got home I didn't know what was my inner voice of guidance and what was my mind. Mum looked at me, puzzled by my disturbed state.

'I've just seen him,' I said.

'Seen who?' asked Mum.

'Chris ... you know, the man who nearly killed me.' I spoke in bewilderment.

'Oh.' Mum sat down. Her face was a meld of anger, concern and shock. She had become such a dear friend to me that I looked to her for guidance.

'What should I do?' I asked.

She looked at me clearly. 'You know what you should do,' she said.

Those words cleared away all of the scrambling mess in my mind. I did know. I picked up the phone and dialled the number for the Superintendent. When he answered the phone, I gave him clearly the details of my sighting.

Two days later the phone rang. I picked it up.

'Hello, can I speak to Kathryn please.'

'Yes, speaking' I said.

'Oh, hello, this is Superintendent Banner of the CIB. I've been in charge of your case.'

'Yes,' I said.

'Well, we've got some news for you. It's, well, good news – for the rest of your life.'

There was a silent pause. I wondered what that could mean. Had they caught him? Jailed him? So quickly?

'Oh?' I queried.

'Yes. We managed to track Chris to a factory. He's been going under a false ID. But the amazing thing is, when we got to the factory we were told he died the day before. He dropped dead on the factory floor. A tumour. His ID is confirmed. You don't have to worry any more.'

I paused in a silence that seemed to stretch out like a wide blank page.

'Oh. Ummm ... Oh. Thanks for letting me know,' I said softly.

'That's okay, love,' he said. 'Hope you can live in a bit more peace now.'

'Thanks.'

'Okay. Goodbye. All the best now love. Bye.' Click. That was the end of that chapter.

I sat there for a full minute before I could even speak. When I finally did, I cried. I cried for the relief of his soul. I cried for him to be taken to peace. I cried for the tragedy of his life.

For days I puzzled over the mystery in it all. Despite what my soul had been shown between worlds, I still felt touched by the emotions of our world. Somehow I couldn't help but see a karmic irony at work. His death – an internal explosion from a tumor in his head – was probably not unlike the force of destruction he had wrought upon my own. I saw the circle, as we sow, so we reap.

With the completion of that experience came a deepening of insight. I began to see that the consequences of all our actions are held in life's law of compensation. Beyond the mind's judgments, it is in divine law that all acts are accounted for.

In this light, justice and integrity could be seen as the measures of harmonic order and the wisdom of balance – karma.[1] It is the intelligent nature of the universe working in our soul that knows creation as our one Self and all that occurs as a play of cause and effect. What we do, we do to our self. Our actions result in outcomes.

And on our quest from the unconscious state to consciousness we learn about our power to create. We learn from the consequences of our actions. For, whatever we have done to another, be it loving or cruel, is visited upon us. From this direct experience we come to know what such an experience is like and therefore have the choice to either continue or give away such actions.

There is an exchange and synthesis of all energy which keeps the cosmic order of life. This occurs between the finite (the manifestation of form – our little self, the ego) and the infinite (the eternal life source and power of creation – the one Self, the greater whole).

As I connected to the Divine law of Justice, I could see how necessary it is, how it assists our growth. It awakens us to the seat of morality deep in our soul and brings light to our awareness. It lifts us up to live our life in integrity. And I knew the Divine law's discerning power is within the heart's innate intelligence. It is beyond the dictation of the mind or desires – the egoic game of manipulation, beyond our human fears or prejudices which seek revenge for a judgment. It is a power of truth and compassion leading the way for our higher attainment. So justice and integrity are the dictates of the soul.

Such is the power of Love that it shall impart all circumstances necessary for life to ultimately actualise the true nature of love and respect in all beings. Love does not always appear in gentle ways. It can also penetrate with arrows of truth.

I knew then that it is only when we hear and obey the dictates of

[1] The law of cause and effect which manifests in life experience.

the soul that we begin to forge a path that is clear and unfaltering. So, by understanding the effect of all causes, I could see my life as a conscious dedication to the Divine Will: to live in the integrity of truth, respect and love for all.

As I reflected upon all of my life's challenges – the moments of abuse, trauma, rejection and violation – I felt a profound sense of gratitude. Each of those moments had provided me with an immeasurable insight. They were tools in my growth that I knew would serve me further. I could not see the people who had been a part of those experiences as enemies. I saw them as my teachers. And I saw them as fellow travellers in my shared journey and destiny. From them I had gained a deeper understanding about human nature, the pains and trials of life, and the soul's quest to reach greater heights, to be freed of illusion.

Mum's friend, Marjorie had said: 'The greater the soul, the greater the test.'

Mum agreed: 'You must have a big purpose.'

It seemed that I had reached the end of a stage in my journey and that I was ready to move on. And so, as with all endings, one door closes and another opens.

•

Next came a flourishing of creativity. Playing the piano was one of my favourite pastimes to release and express the many degrees of my emotions. I had climbed up to play the dear old family pianola when I was only four years old. The first note I struck sent such ecstasy through my whole being that I wanted to play the entire song of life there and then. Thus began my sojourns with life's melodies upon the black and white keys.

In my first composition I played the deep chords and tickled the high notes, to depict a bear in a dark forest watching a butterfly as she danced in the light above the treetops. Of course, in my childhood fantasy, it was an exquisite symphony. To the rest of the family, it was probably torture.

However, I was so persistent in my pursuits that by the time I was eight, I was granted piano lessons. By the time I was thirteen I had completed and passed all my grades. And by the last and fourteenth grade, I was chosen to play at a concert.

My teacher selected one of the less-played pieces of Mozart. It was a piece I loved, yet found challenging. When the night finally arrived I thought I was prepared but as soon as I sat at the stool on stage my confidence evaporated. I started to shake from the feet up. My knees were wobbling so much I just began to pray. Pleeeeease, hands, don't shake, please hands, don't shake. But then they shook.

Somehow I forgot to breathe until the deadly silence of the hall suddenly jolted me into the realisation that everyone was waiting for me. So with a gasp of breath I started to play. I don't really know if it was good or bad. In fact I didn't even know how I got from the beginning to the end. But next thing I knew the hall resounded with clapping.

I leapt up and without even a bow, ran off the stage. The clapping suddenly stopped and was replaced with a few chuckles. My face went hot as I blushed. I wasn't sure whether the chuckles were because I had bungled the playing or if it was because I forgot to bow. But one thing I was sure of was that it was over. I was glad I could breathe again.

It was by chance that, one day, as I sat playing a grand piano in a hotel lounge, the manager overheard me. I'd taken to searching for these exquisite instruments as I found them superior to our family pianola. And it seemed that the staff in cocktail lounges were more than happy for me to sit and play. So when he asked if I could play for the Royal Hotel, I couldn't help but quake at first. Since the concert I'd only played in minor public displays. But somehow my impetuous habit of enthusiasm and confidence spoke before my fearful mind could shut it up. Next thing I knew I was playing a large repertoire of easy listening pieces for easy listeners. I was applauded and gifted in gratitude with everything from 'mocktails' to laughter and tears.

A sweet old man once asked me to play *Für Elise*.

'Oh, I'd love it if you could play that,' he said with a soft and sentimental voice. 'My wife used to play it all the time.'

His eyes went smoky and distant. So I played it. By the time I finished and looked over to him he had tears rolling down his cheeks. He looked at me tenderly, smiled, and in a sweetly soft and shaky voice said, 'Thank you.'

That was the first moment that I felt the real bliss of being able to touch another. To see those tears was a picture of such beauty that I felt an overwhelming gratitude: gratitude for life, gratitude for love and gratitude for the gift of being able to touch another's heart. It was the joy of Self giving to Self.

That moment was so significant to me. It was filled with a realisation, a far-reaching insight. I realised that all that is significant and beautiful in life flows from emotion, from feeling. I had heard many people playing music as a display of intellect and achievement. I had listened to people play in this way and had played piano for those people too. But it was dry – dry as an old sun-bleached bone. There had been no satisfaction in it. Despite all the efforts and all the aggrandisements, it left the soul empty. And yet there in a hotel, in one simple moment, I felt the significance of satisfaction: the satisfaction of soulful communion.

It's true that the greatest moments in our life are measured by such simple events that words can never truly explain. Yet I knew that was a taste of what I had longed for all my life: a pure open stream, giving and receiving without obstruction.

I realised then where my true wealth lay. Sure, I took home a big envelope of money. My life was moving ahead, with one achievement after the next. But it was the power of spirit shared so humbly that filled me with a wealth beyond measure.

That awoke in me an even greater aspiration to give. I had already received a lot in life. It wasn't out of a lack of gratitude for everything received that I still felt a gap. But in that moment I realised the real joy in life was in being able to give. I felt so filled by this joy and love that I wanted to give everything to all. So I played, with all my heart and soul, and that was the gift that kept on touching other hearts.

About a month later I received a letter stating I had been selected for the position I'd applied for at Flinders University. I was filled with anticipation. The position as Assistant to the Manager in Visual Arts was a six-month contract and meant an enormous opportunity to me. I hadn't really pursued art since High School. Although I had already had an exhibition whilst still in school, it seemed to be a very tough field in which to progress. Competition was strong, with very few options, and I didn't really want to take the route of further study.

I threw myself at the opportunity. Before long I was working on private and government educational requests. Posters, murals, portraits. The diversity suited my insatiable thirst for change and variety. But as fast as the job came, it finished and despite my skills and experience I found my hopes of progress met many dead ends. So art became again an expression for self-fulfilment.

Nonetheless by the time I was eighteen my achievements in natural health gave me the ground to be self-employed with my own practice in diagnosis and body therapy. I was soon flooded with regular clients and a steady stream of newcomers. Finally, I had a valid reason to officially change my surname. 'Cocks' on the business card of a masseuse was definitely asking for trouble. In my challenge to understand our surname I had come to know a little more of its origins and our family heritage. It was apparent that there was both Welsh and Germanic ancestry. So my first change of name came. I chose something that was still connected by pronunciation. 'Coe' had no undesirable connotations yet was a derivative of the German 'Koch.'

Again I experienced the joy of fulfilling service. The practice became so successful that some days I was booked from 8 am to 8 pm with half an hour for lunch.

After four months I burned out. I was left with more questions. My life seemed to be moving so quickly in unseen ways, yet moved by something that already knew the bigger plan.

Turning eighteen had proven to be a milestone in many ways. I was faced with all of the big questions about life, my future and what it all meant to me. That was amplified by my Granny's death. Her departure brought closure to my childhood chapters. She had represented the cheery embrace of simplicity, of love, of a warm home filled with delicious delights.

Then the family decided to sell our seaside shack. That was terribly traumatic for me. It had been my sanctuary and the most significant place of sacredness to me. It had connected me to the land and ancestors. It was my sacred home and place of my birth spirit as a child born onto Kaurna[1] land. It was the spirit of the Kaurna dreaming[2] that had filled me with such peace and beauty. I begged my parents to keep our shack, so that I could live there and look after it. But it seemed the decision had already been made and finalised. Hidden Valley had always filled me with a sense of 'rightness', as if, on that land, my soul was in the place of its true purpose. The freedom of my spirit was nourished by the rolling hills and the glistening oceans.

Suddenly I was faced with a void. I would no longer have the privilege of the freedom to wake up in that wonderful sanctuary. The one place where I truly felt a sense of belonging could no longer house me. I felt lost and lonely. I cried deeply. I fell into the hole of those tears. But there in that deep hole was a surprising light, and my inner God-voice of wisdom. It was as if I could see from a great height, like the eagle soaring over the ocean. From that height I glimpsed, I sensed, and felt the bigger purpose of my journey. I breathed into it.

In the middle of that breath was an unquestionable 'knowing'. My life was for humanity, for earth. In that moment I made a solid vow: to live my life as a gift for all, to uncover the lamp of wisdom, to shine the light of love for everyone and everything, big and small. I didn't know or care how I would do that. All I knew was that I was here to serve for the higher good of all. With that vow in my heart I stood in front of the mirror in my bedroom.

I looked at the ordinariness of my face, my clothes and the room,

---

1 Aboriginal people indigenous to the Adelaide Plains of South Australia.

2 The conscious connection to the ancestors and creation realms weaving all life together through past, present and future.

and sighed. I felt the sameness that was in me and everything. I didn't feel special, yet knew how special life itself is. And I wanted others to be able to feel that too, to know that in this ordinariness is something extraordinary – something immeasurably beautiful, and that we are all that. So I stretched out my arms, closed my eyes and said,

> 'I give this body for the will of love.
> I give this mind for the will of truth.
> I give this soul for the will of one eternal life in all.
> I give all that I am for the love and freedom of all.'

I opened my eyes, took a deep breath and smiling, looked myself in the face and said,

'Right. On with it.'

And so I stepped forward again, not knowing where my feet would land yet sure of my heart's intent.

The 6th Attainment

The Message Man had shown me the gift of growth and higher understanding. Through the joy and pain of all experiences, ordinary and extraordinary, we are birthed into the light. From a greater height of awareness we can see the bigger picture, that all things are threads in God's perfect plan.

Unmistakably I was on a path, a destiny already chosen.

KEY 6.

The Lovers

KEY 6.

The Lovers

The dance of life is a demonstration of love: the delight of Self discovering, embracing, expressing, encountering Self. Unity is sought.

I felt pulled by a magnetic force, attracted to that with which I wished to merge.

Oh great Lover, who are you?
Man and woman?
Yin and Yang, within and without?
Divine Marriage to Self?
The Holy atonement of Self and God?

18. *A Quest of Love*

Rumi knocked on his lover's door.
'Who is there?' asked his beloved.
'It is I, Rumi,' he responded.
'Go away,' her voice came back to him, 'for there
is not enough room for the two of us here.'
Rumi went away to meditate and pray. Returning later,
he knocked on his lover's door.
'Who is there?' she asked
'It is you,' Rumi answered.
The door was thrown open,
and the lovers passionately embraced.

Rumi

I was ready to explore love again. Oddly enough I chose a relationship with a guy who liked to drink beer and smoke dope (as did most young people). I struggled to feel at peace with such a strong difference in our state of being. Yet I had thought it to be part of the play in the lovers' dance: the discovery of unity in diversity. The thing that did unite us so deeply was our love of the ocean. We surfed and swam, ran on the beach and played ball in the late afternoon sun. We had a lot of fun. We trained a lot together at the surf club and lazed around on hot, sunny afternoons. After about a year of being together, his parents started to ask if we were getting married.

My mum seemed to like the idea of it too. She seemed to think it would be good for me to be settled down and she really liked Ben, her nickname for him being 'the little sunshine butter-ball'. He always made her chuckle. He was such a happy spirit. But we felt too young and just brushed the whole marriage thing aside. Then there was humanity's history. It was simply expected that getting married was the thing to do. But we didn't care for what the world wanted of us. So the topic slid into silence – until one day, out of the blue, Ben popped the question. I was so taken by surprise and delighted that I said 'Yes,' but then quickly retracted with ...

'Oh ... ummm ... I'll think about it.'

I *had* to think about it.

What did marriage really mean to me? It seemed like an enormous commitment that I couldn't be sure of. How could I possibly make a promise, 'Till death do us part', when I had no guarantee of what tomorrow would bring?

I worried about our differences. His simplicity was sweet but I simply didn't feel satisfied with a surface lifestyle tainted by beer and dope.

I thought deeply about life and what it meant, and the closer I looked the starker was the truth that stared back at me. I had been struggling with the agendas of normal expectations for most of my life. Somehow I had attempted to repress it through my deepest longing not to remain as some misunderstood outcast on the fringes. Yet I saw the shallowness and the futility in it all.

I couldn't do the treadmill any more. It angered and pained me to think of conforming and my life being reduced to a maddening turbine of grinding need, greed and vanity driven by the gaping hole in the soul. As I observed the game of society, I could see its sickening dissatisfaction. I felt I had been wading through cement for most of my life, trying to find a point of some light, some fluidity that was connected to the essence and presence of spirit – the true wealth and fulfilment of life.

I didn't understand the mentality of excess for superficial gains. I didn't want the futility of running around in the maze: have sex, party, find the perfect mate, climb the career ladder, dress in vogue, drink for the sake of fun and wake up the next day just to keep the whole game alive. All of it is caught in the other maze of the mind's ignorance born of a deep, lonely emptiness – the separation from the God-Self. I could see that all these things are simply a distraction and avoidance of the true presence of life's simplicity and beauty.

I went home that night and meditated, thinking God might give me some sign of what to do. I thought of Ben's proposal and what that meant to my life direction. Was it right or wrong? Maybe my angel would give me an answer. I heard nothing, only silence and emptiness. Yet somehow I sensed that I was knocking on a different door – a door that could only be entered as one, by my Self, as love. The next morning I sat vaguely in some kind of tranced blankness. I closed my eyes.

Instantaneously I was engulfed by bright light. Then within the vast field a minute sparkling dewdrop appeared. I watched it ... glistening ... so bright. And as I watched, it grew. It became a lake and from within the lake there arose a garden of paradise, which then magically encompassed it. On the opposite bank I watched a tree rise up. At first it was barren. It was completely bare. Then a crow landed in it and cawed. It was a messenger from another world.

A sudden bolt of lightning flashed and hit me directly in the third eye. It was momentarily blinding. Then, where the lightning had also struck the tree it began to unfurl with brilliant growth, and beneath it was the presence of the Tibetan yogi I had been meeting consistently over the years. This time he was dressed in full regalia. The instrument he held in his right hand was tall like a spear but it had a different form on top. It looked like a curved blade that arose out of three skulls. He wore a tall golden hat, curved up at the sides and stood draped in gold and maroon robes, looking like the most glorious Hierophant[1] imaginable. His eyes were penetrating. Then a beam of light shot out of his third eye into mine. The words came loud and clear.

[1] The Hierophant of the Tarot deck is a symbol of wisdom, a teacher, and can be seen as message man.

'Prepare you this Divine vessel, for your time has come.'

And in a flash the whole scene disappeared and I was engulfed in a void.

I sat motionless.

Twenty minutes later I opened my eyes and knew that my life was about to change. I didn't know how, just that that was the truth.

That afternoon Mum's friend visited. I told her about the visions of masters and yogis I had been experiencing.

'Oh, that sounds Tibetan or Indian or something. You should go to Buddha House, she said.'

In the instant that she uttered those words I felt a bolt of energy rush from head to toe. My hair stood on end and my whole body prickled with 'God-bumps'[1] (a bit like goose bumps except much more electric!).

It was a giant YES in every fibre of my being.

I stood up instantly. The chair flew backwards in my excitement.

'Yes!' I exclaimed and opened the buffet drawer.

I got out the phone book and opened it. The pages fell open in exactness and my eyes landed straight upon the words in black and white print, 'Buddha House'!

'Oh, my God' I uttered.

I shook. I picked up the phone. My heart doubled its pace and my whole body vibrated. I dialled the number.

A man's voice answered at the other end. It was gentle, accented and willing.

I almost fell over myself. The words started tumbling in a cascade as I recounted my experiences. I didn't think. I just spoke and he listened. I could hear his gentle 'yes' acknowledging my excited outpouring.

When I finally slowed down he said, 'Mmm, yes. I understand. I think you must come in. Very important you come. You must be meeting ... the lamas are coming soon.'

---

[1] A communication of the soul; a strong rush of energy, indicating the recognition of spiritual truth.

I didn't comprehend what he meant on a mental level but on a soul level I knew exactly what he was saying. So I jumped in the car and drove.

I arrived at about two in the afternoon. The gates were arched with brightly coloured sculptures, hanging flags and the words: Buddha House.

The garden was peaceful and inside the centre there was an air of serenity. The man and I walked through a passage with pictures and information. I could see monks and yogis dressed just like the ones in my 'inner world' of experiences. He showed me the meditation room. Inside were statues and huge tangkhas.[1] These images were not new to me. And yet it was the first time I had physically seen any such thing in this life.

We sat down and I told him about my life – the spontaneous yoga, meditation, chanting, visions and inter-dimensional journeys. He listened enthusiastically.

He informed me that two Tibetan lamas were coming in about two to three weeks and that I must be there to meet them. Well, he didn't have to twist my arm! We were still sitting talking at two in the morning. From that day I virtually lived at the centre.

The two lamas were going to arrive about a week apart, due to their event schedules. And soon, the first lama arrived. I could hardly believe it. He had stepped out of my spirit sojourns and into the physical! This was the lama who had often sat diagonally opposite me in the circle. He was 'The Laughing Lama' and always bore a wide grin.

His eyes twinkled with the most mischievous love. We bowed to each other instantly and then looked into each other's eyes with a mutual greeting.

'Hello, again!' We were two old friends meeting. What a delightful joy!

He took me under his arm and chuckling, walked me down the passage to a private room.

---

[1] Work of art on cloth depicting geometrical designs (mandalas), deities and historic figures to convey Buddhist teachings.

We sat communicating, mostly through the light in our eyes, the love in our hearts and the open capacity of telepathy. He kept chuckling and every now and then would pat my leg and say 'Lama's coming ... hee hee hee, Lama's coming,' with his infectiously cheeky grin. It spun me around again in another one of those 'I don't know but I know' states.

Then *he* arrived.

We met on the doorstep. Our eyes locked – such knowing, such presence, was there. He greeted me in Tibetan, and I responded, 'Lama Zopa, Rinpoche'. It was so natural, so profound, so timeless. We were finally here, but brought together in the seamlessness of that which is so beyond 'here'.

We embraced. Tears spilled from my soul. I finally felt at home. We melted into each other's arms.

From that moment I hardly left his side.

Within days I could understand and converse fairly generally in Tibetan (which, strangely enough, was some kind of gift that later on disappeared again). I realised this was the coming of my time. My spiritual journey of destiny had now truly begun.

Over the following days I talked to other Buddhist monks and lay people about my direction. I knew I was ready to renounce the world, take vows, shave my hair, don robes and dedicate to an ascetic life. I felt amazed and amused at the questions that were supposedly meant to determine how solid my conviction was.

'But what about sex?' asked Lisa, an 'unrobed' Buddhist friend.

'Take it or leave it,' I laughed.

'What about a career?' asked another.

'This is my career. It is my life path to serve the Divine.'

'Don't you want to get married'?

'Yes,' I said after a pause, but I knew I wanted the ultimate Lover. I wanted a love where what had been two dissolved into one. 'To my true Self ... to God.'

'But what about your beautiful golden hair?' asked Tenzin.

I laughed, remembering how I had already involuntarily given up my hair when I was a little girl. I had certainly come to realise that my values were held deeper within and that the body is a passing, changing phenomena that does not bring any lasting fulfilment.

But then, just when I thought everyone was trying to dampen my spirit, along came Alma. With her raven black hair and striking features she whirled into the scene like a gypsy sent from heaven. She offered me a tarot reading, which, of course, I accepted with great enthusiasm.

She shuffled the cards then handed them to me.

'Shuffle them till you feel it's enough,' she said.

I shuffled well, and then I placed them down on the cloth. She spread them out.

'Now choose ten cards,' she said. I pulled them out, feeling from my heart, feeling guided to each card.

She placed them into a spread then started turning them over one by one as she began to speak. Her voice was deep and clear.

'The central card indicates a major decision or action that is destined. The Judgment card is a sign that this is the right path, judged by God. The second card indicates a concern of support – whether others on the earthly plane will be able to fully understand or support you – but this is already taken care of by the higher planes. This is a Divine plan.

'The third card indicates travel. This could be both overseas and to higher consciousness, represented by the Chariot. At the bottom here, is the Magician. This reveals the deep purpose. I see this as initiation; that you are on a path of initiation and that it is a continuation of a past life. This suggests that you will be shown the power you have within you, that you will come to understand it more and that it will be acknowledged.

'The immediate past shows you have to let go of attachment to the worldly, perhaps your family, and the immediate future shows a relationship with the higher mind of enlightenment.

'The Hierophant also indicates a relationship with a teacher. Your seventh card says this path is born of the truth in your heart and the eighth card, the Hermit, suggests there is higher guidance, connecting to your inner awareness – an increase of psychic awareness and a journey into solitude or retreat.

'The ninth card, the High Priestess, suggests you are both hopeful and fearful of who you really are. Yet in the mystery you will unveil the great secret of life. I sense that you already know your destiny but that you struggle to embrace the magnitude of your purpose. This suggests that some things are still hidden, but in due time will be revealed.

'The tenth card signifies the outcome: the Universe. It indicates an awakening. I see that there is a great purpose and destiny in your journey. It is destined to be shared with the world.'

She sighed and paused.

'I feel your path is a destined one. You must trust and know that you are being guided, that this is the work of the Divine. Do not let others cast shadows of doubt upon your way – not now, not ever.'

She looked over her glasses with deep sincerity, and then smiled. Her words had spoken directly to my soul. I felt the knowing that this was the spoken word of truth.

I left her, feeling both strengthened and nervous. I felt grateful for such clear guidance yet I still felt the impeding waves of reactions that were sure to arise from others. Finally, I felt there was nothing left for me to do but to face and reveal this life-changing decision.

I told Ben I had to leave. I was now clear that my quest of love was to be fufilled in my spiritual journey. I was seeking a higher dimension of love, something that couldn't be found in the usual game of romance where man and woman wanted to find love fulfilled in their 'other half'. I wanted to know the wholeness of love within myself – the wholeness of the God-self. When I explained this to Ben, both he and his whole family were shocked. The wave rippled through our friends. They all concluded I had gone mad.

Explaining it all to my family was similar. My Nanna thought it was ridiculous and unacceptable. My dad shrugged his shoulders and shook his head. My brother said it was a waste of a pretty young woman. My sister looked bemused yet not surprised and Mum looked at me with loving awe. I simply knew it was what I must do. So I had my hair shaved off and took to robes and a road of renunciation, initiation and retreat.

The week before I was due to go I visited my Nanna to say goodbye.

'Dear,' she said. 'Why don't you think about it for another week? Don't be so rash.'

'I don't think,' I said. 'I *see*. One week, one year, another lifetime. It won't make any difference. I don't have a choice. I am following my destiny. It just is what is to be. It is my choiceless responsibility.'

I turned my back and made my way along my path.

Lama sized me up. He looked straight into my soul. In the private moments of our shared time he looked closely at my long palms and pointed out certain signs that confirmed I was a reincarnation of a 'prominent' kind, which also explained all of my visions and way of looking at things. He asked direct questions and nodded at my responses with approval. He affirmed my path was to walk with him, to take the road of the ascetic. I gave away all of my belongings except a couple of books and bare essentials. I sold my car and cashed in my savings. I was ready to give up everything in this world to know and serve truth for liberated being.

Our first schedule was a series of visits to other centres around Australia.

The 7th Attainment

Every part of my being now yearned to be fully reunited with the Self, at one with God: to be God's Lover, Loved, Beloved.

The dance between the male and female aspects is the play of complementary parts, seeking balance and wholeness.

In LOVE, duality dissolves.

I had experienced that profound Self before. Yet I wanted to remember, to experience that beyond all doubt, and to never leave it again. More than anything I wanted the tools that would come from such certainty so that I may be able to help the world remember too, to embrace eternal love. For that love could unite the whole world.

KEY 7.

The Walking Spirit

KEY 7.

The Walking Spirit

Our body carries our spirit through life.

The world of form is the vehicle moved by spirit.

The self must be transformed in order to reveal and fulfil the true purpose of form.

There was no more turning back. I was moved by the power of spirit.

19. A New Old Journey

What can be gained by sailing to the moon
If we are not able to cross the abyss
That separates us from ourselves?

Thomas Merton

It was late in the morning when we arrived at the remote camp site on the banks of the River Murray. The sky stretched out over giant gum trees shimmering in the heatwaves.

It was hot and windy with the temperatures soaring at around 39–42°C. I realised I was about to dive in the deep end. I was at the dock. The sign read:

WARNING: PRICE OF ENTRY – YOUR MIND.

We had come for a five-day retreat and were preparing for Nyung Nye,[1] a four-day fast. This culminated in an abstinence from food, drinks and even bodily fluids – the saliva that we normally swallowed every few seconds. I had fasted before so it wasn't entirely new. But this took it to another level.

We entered the ceremony space at 4 am. Prayers, offerings and purifications opened the door to our journey into silence and abstinence. We meditated on the symbols within each of our energy centres and anointed each chakra with special oils and scented water. Lama shook the sweet water over my head. Then dipping a

[1] A Buddhist retreat of fasting, ceremony and meditation.

flower into the ornate silver vessel, he flicked it, scattering drops with incantations. I watched his graceful hands adorned with prayer beads. He was the image of a radiant deity, a shining Buddha, with serene eyes and full lips curled into a faint smile. I was mesmerised, moved by his natural yet profound enactment of ritual.

We then sat with our hands in the prayer mudra[1] and recited mantras. The space dripped with the vibration of deep soulful droning.

Over the following hours my mind began to melt – and not just from the heat. The concentration and stillness consumed me. By the end of the first day's mantras and meditation I felt light-headed, having not eaten anything since 5 pm the day before. But I was grateful for water. A part of my mind reacted at the thought of no fluids the next day – but the shaman in me welcomed the challenge.

By the second day's end I was glad to lie down when midnight came. I felt my organs and pulses slowing down as my body reduced its output. With no water to quench my parched mouth, I savoured every salivary swallow. I knew that by 1 pm the next day we would not have even this gratification: our saliva was to be expelled.

By the end of our morning prayers the next day, the mantras had become not more than a raspy whisper, merging with the sound of swirling gum leaves outside. We dissolved in the silence that held all the whispering words of nature.

By the middle of the afternoon we wandered off for self-time and contemplation. I strolled down the dry path. Long reeds and grasses swayed on either side and giant gum trees stood like ancient keepers upon the riverbanks.

The wind was slightly cooler by the water's edge. It swept across the river and brushed across my face. I took a dip in the water. Beneath the warm surface it was slightly cool and refreshing to my hot, dry body. For half an hour I soaked my body, feeling deep gratitude for this vein of mother earth, the great old Murray.

Once out, I lazed upon the grassy bank. The scene entranced me.

---

[1] A sacred gesture.

The constant motion of life shimmered, scintillating within stillness. Dragonflies danced and darted, their wings glistening in the bright light. I watched the breeze blowing across the river, rippling its way to the reeds, which danced and swayed at its touch. And it blew upon my mind. The cobwebs were swept away.

I saw how entangled the mind could be, and how it could wrap itself around a grandiose ego identity. It entwined the world to revolve around the 'me' of a transient body and personality and considered itself so all-important. But what was *it* in the scheme of an eternally moving, unfolding, dissolving cosmos?

So I cast the webs to the wind. I beckoned it to carry them all away. There in the bright light I rested. My mind was brushed bare – left stark and aware in the glaring light.

In a moment I blinked and the moment was gone. Everything danced around me, moved by a power far beyond this self. Vast and limitless it moved all. I realised I was nothing more than dust in the wind.

And, in the openness of awareness, freed of the webs, I felt the power of eternal life ... love ... peace.

But by the time we sat for evening chants my body felt heavy and sour. It was as if I had dropped into its deep storehouse of unconscious *merde*.[1] I could barely sit up.

Yet a deep conviction to transcend pinned me to my post. A back-wash of bitterness bubbled up from the depths. I watched it, stunned by its ugliness. And there, simply in watching, it came and went. It arose ... it dropped away.

The next morning I felt suddenly renewed and invigorated. My body and mind were light and clear and my energy was soft and flowing. The power of being the witness, present to the moment, had captured me. I now knew its liberating power.

We closed the ceremony with more mantras and offerings. At noon we broke fast. I realised the joy of the senses, what a gift it

---

1 (slang) The French word for 'crap' or 'shit'.

was to experience the body. And so I took an even deeper vow of consecration. My body was a temple, to be worshipped as a sacred vehicle.

At twenty I took my first level initiation and vows as a nun. Since I had already realised my devotion to serving humanity and life at the age of eighteen, it was the most natural thing I could do. I dived ever more deeply into meditation.

I was flung from ecstatic heights of boundless release to the deep caverns of my mind's conditions where the samskaras[1] were dark and terrifying. I saw the demons of fear, hate, desire and greed, all grappling to hold on with their last hooks of egoic control. They were the noise of humanity's collective mind – the illusion. I watched: gripped, stunned, silent, cracking, falling, screaming, crying, empty, and unmoved. I watched them all dancing, flittering and struggling uselessly for a place of permanence, while the searchlight of awareness was relentlessly exposing.

We travelled from Adelaide to Melbourne, New South Wales and on to Queensland. My attention was fully engaged with the meditations and self-enquiry. I watched ruthlessly. In moments I almost caved into the trickery of the wretched mind that wanted to convince me that I was mad – that this whole thing was mad.

But then suddenly I was confronted by a Kali-like[2] demon. Her body was dripping black with blood. Her eyes bulged red in wrathful rage and her jaws gaped open in an all-consuming roar of Truth – of life: the consumer, consuming and consumed. I, this idea, this identity of 'me', was a transient play and was destined for dissolution ... into the vast eternal space that lay waiting beyond the gate of her dripping fangs.

In one great swoop I watched her slice off my head with her steely blade. With the other hand she held my head by its hair. Blood spurted like a fountain from the neck. She laughed into the universe

---

1 Seeds of illusion, false perceptions that cause suffering.

2 A Hindu Deity that represents the destruction of all illusions and therefore grants true, unobstructed power.

and threw my head into her gaping mouth. Then, in that instant, I realised I was she who consumed this form of 'me'. I swallowed in ecstatic laughing, blood-curdling delight!

The play of consumer, consuming and consumed dissolved into sweet, vast, empty bliss. No one remained – no this, no that – only vast, formless, endless being. It was as if I had been sucked into a black hole. But not a place of absolute void. It was a dark womb that I was about to be birthed from. It was a place in which the old disappeared and the new could be reborn.

Whilst this account may seem morbid or strange to some people, to me it was a profound state of an egoic death. It was an ultimate confrontation of the false identity of the self. I recalled how Buddha had also experienced similar phenomena. His experiences were the inspiration of powerful Buddhist practices in which initiates used such visualisations to propel the ego death.

In fact, any practice that brings the mind to focus on death, in any aspect, ultimately creates an alchemical field. Remaining fears, attachments and fixed identity perceptions are pushed to the surface – into the light of conscious awareness. If one is able to remain present as the observer, holding the attention on these feelings and images as the witness (rather than the emotional interpreter), all ideas about death and the fear of them are accepted. With this comes transcendence – an incredible calm. Within this is a presence of pure awareness – the state of oneness with all existence, with eternal life.

When we accept death we accept life. When we accept life we are present to the Self that is eternal and forever whole. Whatever appeared as death is then nothing more than a comma in the ongoing story of life. It is no longer a full-stop.

A less confronting meditation that can prepare us for this rather intense shift is to simply imagine living without a head, for a day, then a week at a time. When we follow this 'imaging' we actually live more in the presence of what is actually happening – connected with life rather than having our mind filter everything that is happening.

I had emerged from that field in a profoundly transcended state.

I realised then why I had felt such futility in life's games – why I had seen the promises of freedom in the circumstances of life as nothing more than phantoms in the opera of false hopes. And I saw the futile plight of humanity, how, in such delusion, nearly every being searches in a kitchen for food that can never end our hunger. I saw how the fear of death keeps people trapped in the fear of life.

The compassion in me was so full it was excruciating. It was only then that I truly understood and felt the power of my vows for Truth in the way of the Bodhisattva to awaken for the sake of all beings.

I saw how most of humanity is still caught in limited beliefs and that the conditions of 'duality perception' means that disempowerment seems real and is accompanied by constant doubt. These limited beliefs and duality perceptions are born of the one illusion: the belief in separation from the God-self. As a consequence the mind grasps onto form and identity in the hope of some belonging or security.

And so, the fixation and identification with form diverts our attention from the wisdom and power of love. Then we only see disconnectedness, weakness and suffering. We doubt the power of love, of ourselves and each other. In those moments we perpetuate the vibration of the belief in weakness and so our field remains the manifestation, the very reflection, of such weakness.

As we think, so we feel; as we feel, so we act; and as we act, so we have.[1]

As long as one is held in this doubt there can never truly be the certainty of love and wisdom that is the radiant transmission of compassion. I saw that most people call their behaviour compassion whilst still believing in an inherent weakness and in the delusion of being less than love and wisdom. This can only mean that compassion is just another word for pity – a perception that is not empowering, but actually demeaning to the true nature of our soul.

It suddenly became starkly clear to me that compassion is not something we have to make, but the fruit of the true nature of our

---

[1] Isira.

being. Compassion is the gift of consciously actualising our true nature – our potential made real in form. Only as we consciously embrace the truth of ourselves as love and wisdom, can we become the embodied state of compassion.

As long as we identify with the false perception of self and with the external events as the reality, we can not possibly be in this place of true power. A state of utterly gentle, embracing invincibility, which extends the power of love and wisdom: this is compassion. The act of compassion is the art of reminding another of their own true nature.

It is the art of reminding them that beyond a moment of suffering they are the limitless power of love and within them lies the wisdom of eternal life. This is who they are – not the fleeting event of fear.

An unshakable knowing gripped every particle of my being. It was as if this knowing had consumed any last part of the 'me' that had questioned what my path in life was about. And then I knew it was not 'my' path. I knew simply, powerfully, humbly and unmistakably: it was the path my being was here to serve. It was not 'my' truth, but eternally *the* Truth.

Then, a trail of visions from past lives flickered like an old cinema reel across the screen of my mind. This was my journey. I saw my soul's contract: the 'unchosen' commitment I had made to reincarnate again to serve this awakening. It was in that moment I realised this path was my destiny – there was no question in my soul. I chose to take full vows and dedicate my entire life to serve Divine Will. Yet it was beyond choice. Then, I prayed. I prayed that I could awaken to Divine Will and that I would serve that alone.

Later that night, Lama told me to prepare for initiation in the morning. We were going to invoke the aspect of Green Tara – The Buddha Mother of Compassion. The synchronicity of this with my fresh realisation seemed to affirm my process. When I walked outside I gasped in wonderment. Before me were three complete rainbows arched all the way across the horizon. I knew all was in perfect order.

The next morning I woke from a vivid dream. Lama, the Green Tara and I were holding hands in a vortex of light. And, while we were individual aspects, we were also the same ONE being.

It was pre-dawn. I washed and then started to prepare the offerings. We entered the gompa[1] at dawn. The ritual chanting, offerings and meditation swept me up in a river of tears. The compassion rose in me like a swollen, endless river, its banks about to burst. The dorje[2] (a ceremonial bell) rang deep in my soul, the sound of compassion. Its form represents emptiness, indicating that true love-compassion is not in form or mind, but lies in the infinite space beyond.

At the height of the ceremony, it struck me fully: this was entirely why I existed. Then the banks burst and I cried a flood of tears. I realised I was there, not to ask for compassion from the Deity, but to realise it in myself. It was the gift I wished to give to the world.

After the initiation I sat in my room silently. It was not the rituals, the images or the utterances that held me so powerfully but the burning passion for self-realisation in my soul that ached and prayed from the depths of my being.

'May I have true compassion. May I be all-consumed in compassion. May I be free of any impostor of my ego. May I be pure compassion.'

I burned and yearned to know it in me, to own it absolutely. I sat there crying, rocking, aching. I was baring my soul, surrendering my will to the Divine Will of compassion. I wanted it more than my body wanted its next breath.

Suddenly, I realised everything was turning to light. Although my eyes were closed this lucid light was shining vividly as if my eyes were open. Out of amazement I opened them to see if it really were happening physically. It was. The room was filled with scintillating beams of green, pink and white light. And, as I looked, a beautiful leaf-green butterfly suddenly appeared out of thin air. It fluttered and danced in the light. Its wings were vivid green, the exact green as the Tara deity. I watched in amazement as it danced above me. Then it

---

1 A temple for Buddhist teaching and ceremony.

2 Tibetan word, meaning diamond, referring to a ritual bell in Buddhist practice which represents eternal, immutable knowledge or the heart of knowledge.

fluttered its way gently down the shining rays until it alighted upon my open palms resting in my lap.

I sat absolutely still – amazed. Its fluttering stopped and its wings opened as if in slow motion, then stopped with perfect poise. Then the words swirled in the wonderment of this scene: 'You are Compassion. Mother of Compassion'. I sat in a humbled quiet disbelief yet unable to deny the Divine gift of this message. What followed was the greatest struggle – not to overcome my weakness, but to accept my greatness.

I wept further tears, tears of bliss, tears of gratitude. I felt satiated to overflowing.

Within that outpouring I felt my heart chakra open. It opened so wide that I felt the whole universe was inside it. Sweet tendrils of radiant light unfurled like the petals of a lotus. Beams of light burst in every direction. My whole being blossomed in radiance and, there in the centre, was a pure point of light like a brilliant star of Divinity. It shone and glistened, flickering like the brightest blue-violet flame. It hung in the open space of endless love.

And then I saw that it was an all-consuming Divine point in which all life is connected. Layers of consciousness overlapped in a field of timelessness. I saw images of past lives and then I merged in the play of Divine lokas.[1] I found myself seated upon an open lotus, with my left leg up in a half-lotus pose. My right heel rested on the base petals. The third eye shone and my adorned body sat gloriously poised in a display of loving compassion for every being. Radiant green, rose and white light shone in every direction, offering a healing presence for all life.

I watched the field of memories, seeing I had walked on earth before in incarnations for service and I saw how everything in every moment, whether large or small, beautiful or ugly, spiritual or not, is ultimately all in service of the one eternal life. I had never been anything but this creation play of serving life. The only difference was that I

---

1 Heavenly realms.

was now conscious and aligned to the harmony of Divine Will.

I witnessed the awakenings, the healings, the miracles and the sacrifices. I saw the followers, the seekers and the finders. I saw the persecutions and the torturings. Then it all converged with my present incarnation. I saw the contract I had chosen. And I saw that it was really ALL beyond choice. For in love, there was no longer a matter of choice. There was only the truth of being with life as love. It was destiny.

I found myself seated in a circle of Ascended Masters and Light Angels. There we discussed the evolution of humanity and the qualities of embodiment I could manifest in order to best serve. I saw the sufferings of many under the influence of dogma and hierarchical, secular views. So it was that I vowed to incarnate for Universal Love. The details revealed to me are beyond my ability to describe here. But, in essence, my destiny in service to a vast plan was intentional and of the Divine Will *for* Divine Will. I saw the whole of humanity embraced in this great intent, lit by the lamp of Enlightened Consciousness.

As I contemplated what I had just experienced and witnessed, I saw my life's journey in an even deeper perspective. More than ever I realised how perfect it all had been. Every event was a source of experience, a tool from which I could draw to continue evolving and be of guidance for others. And I saw how, just by circumstance alone, I had entered already the lives of so many as a catalyst for Love and Truth.

But a very deep part of me was wary. I had also observed the immense capacity of the ego's trickery. And to think that any of my self-awareness or reference was for the ego's gratification made me feel sick to the core. So a very large part of me hung back. I clung to a space of non-acknowledgement. I shrouded my being in a dull shabby cloak of 'normality'. Over the following weeks I observed myself struggling to embrace the inner truth of Self – the being that I AM.

I was aware of the perception of humanity that such a powerful truth was almost impossible and exclusive to one Son of God. Yet, within, I knew the truth. I knew it as the inner truth and potential of *every* human born. That it was not a separate claim of being exclusive or 'special'. And I knew that the embodiment of such divine knowing of eternal life had only arrived from previous conscious effort. I yearned to bring the truth to those who seek; to humanity. For in being such love I do not claim, nor ever will, to be a Special Being created of God, separate from the rest of humanity. The I AM, the Divine presence, is within every human. And each one as a spark of the One is destined to return and, in such truth, to know the power in our destiny ...

The things that I have done shall you do also and even greater things shall you do.[1]

And still my mind tried to cling to the little pauper identity. Yet the more I clung the more I dissolved into unmistakeable states of ascended awareness. And I saw the game of humanity and its denial. Many interpreted a voice of ascended awareness as egoic delusion. Yet it was the illusion of the ego to deny such divinity in oneself, in all. In truth, I wanted to sing and shout to the world:

Love never comes to you to say it is more than you, it comes to you to say you are more than your fears.

I was visited by masters, yogis and light-beings that constantly revealed the divinity of previous and present incarnations. And it didn't just come from the inner planes.

Lama talked of the past incarnations and continually reminded me that I was embodied female Buddha consciousness. He continually engaged me in ritual and initiating duties and pushed me towards the role of guide and teacher. I was asked to lead the meditations regularly.

I struggled with the duty. Not because I didn't want to serve, but because I didn't think I was worthy. After all, who was I, a young twenty-year-old Australian girl? Of what benefit could I be next to

---

1 References to John 14:12

these wizened Masters? And yet it was even stranger that a deeper part of me knew the ancient eternal awareness within, transcended all times, ages, levels and places.

I watched with fascination how the pecking order within the Buddhist structure made a perfect mirror to validate my self-doubts. Wisdom was attributed by age, gender, the rungs of attainment, ordination and, on rare occasions, the open recognition of reincarnations. Women, and therefore nuns, were considered the least likely prospect for enlightenment – young women, the lowest of the low.

This became evident from the scowls and whispers when I was favoured with unusual respect, recognition and requests by Lama. Competition was rife amongst the devotees, lay people and the ordained alike. I found it surprising and a reflection of hidden obstructions within the belief system. In fact, I saw it as a hindrance to enlightenment, not a support.

I thought that perhaps it was more evident in the Australian centres because of the culture of iron egos. Yet I was to discover that ego is not race selective. Even in the most spiritual places such conditioned attitudes are rife – just disguised more cleverly!

The next day Lama told me to prepare for another initiation, Vajra Yogini, and asked me to be in the gompa early to set out the Tsog[1] offerings (ritual offerings of oils, lights, incense and foods).

That night I dreamed that Lama took me to a room filled with incense. He appeared as the dark blue deity, Heruka,[2] and led me into the centre of the room, into the middle of a mandala.[3] I suddenly realised I was naked, standing with my back to him. He took his ritual knife, topped with a skull, and began carving a chogun (a double triangle) into my back. The descending triangle, glistening with red blood over my sacrum, pointed towards the base of my spine. The ascending triangle, glistening with pure white nectar, pointed up to the middle of my back. My body had turned red and suddenly I was garlanded.

---

[1] A gathering for Buddhist ritual practice.

[2] In Tantric philosophy, a male personification of bliss and the state of pure Divinity.

[3] A geometrical depiction of creation or the hierarchy of a Buddha field, (a heavenly realm) often circular, used to focus the mind and raise awareness.

I woke up just in time to wash myself and make my way to the temple.

All of the offerings were nearly set in place when Lama suddenly burst into laughter. The two other helpers and I turned around to see Lama almost crying with belly-shaking laughter, while he pointed at me and the floor.

He then started calling, in between his great guffaws,

'He hee ha ha ha ... Vajra Yogini's here! Vajra Yogini's here!'

We all looked in amused, amazed bewilderment. There on the floor was a trail of red footprints that, clearly, *I* had left. The soles of my feet had turned red! The others looked in disbelief while Lama finished setting the altar. Then with a clap of his hands he turned around and asked for the others to leave and come back at 5 am.

On Lama's request for assistance, I stayed in the room. By the time everyone entered I was in a highly altered state. The room had dissolved and I found myself in a heavenly loka surrounded by Dakas[1] and Dakinis.[2] I re-entered the room, in terms of my human consciousness, when the chanting began.

When we got to the visualisation I realised there was no boundary between my dream states, the lokas and the physical world. We were guided through the red and the white channels within our subtle bodies. I realised that the dream state the night before was part of my initiation, and that my channels had been opened then, with the assistance of Lama, and now they were being awakened and activated.

I moved easily and deeply into the energetic body. A great rush of tingling light moved through my energy body until I started to cry with bliss. I dissolved into an ocean of bliss.

Later in the day Lama called for me. I sat quietly next to his feet.

I shared with him the state that I had dissolved in, the ocean of bliss. He chuckled.

'That is your name, Thubten Dekyil: Awake in the Ocean of Bliss!'

---

[1] In Buddhist Tantra: a male being, a spiritual messenger or sky dancer, who awakens exaltation.

[2] In Buddhist Tantra: a female being, a sky dancer, or spiritual muse who inspires spiritual practice.

Then he continued.

'Can you prepare to go to the Himalayas?'

My heart leapt with glee.

'Of course, Lama,' I said with great enthusiasm.

'Okay, good. So, for now, please watch Lama Osel. Look after him. Make sure you have your spare time with him.'

That wasn't hard to do. This amazing child, who was just three years old, was the recognised reincarnation of Lama Yeshe. I nodded and bowed with my hands at my heart and left the room.

I had already developed a playful relationship with Lama Osel. Apparently he had some quirky fetishes that were exactly the same as his last incarnation, two of them being a love of hats and sunglasses. He would take everyone's hat, put it on his head and break out in a huge grin. And every time he saw my sunglasses, he would take them and put them on.

I found it so extraordinary that most of the time he was just like any other small boy – playing with toy cars and trucks, riding a tricycle as fast as he could, playing hide-and-seek and laughing at the simple pleasures.

But then in the middle of it all he would totally surprise me – especially if I was worrying or praying. He would stop what he was doing and come and stand next to me whilst I sat on the ground. He would look straight into my eyes, then put his hands in prayer. Sometimes he would put his hand on my crown and one day he even put his forehead to mine. Just like a Lama meeting another Lama.

The days passed quickly between discourses, ceremonies, initiations, practices and play. Then the day of departure finally arrived. So, after months (a lifetime!) of intensive preparations and eventful journeying in Australia, I was finally destined for the Himalayas, this time in body.

I travelled in the plane with Lama Lhundrup, as Lama Zopa was due to follow two weeks later. And, in keeping with Lama Lhundrup's reputation, we chuckled and laughed most of the way.

We were to land in Delhi. I watched in shock as the plane started descending towards a thick blanket of smog hanging over the land. It looked like mud. I realised I was going to have to breathe in it for four days. The first wave of 'culture shock' slapped my mind.

We stepped off the aeroplane and left behind the last remnants of clean air and ordered society. The chaos hit me instantly. My senses were in overload. The density of the population swamped me and the severity of the militia surprised me. Beggars' hands tugged and weapon-loaded police commanded. My view of life's realities blew to pieces in a quantum shift. We were shunted through inspections.

Once passed, Lama Lhundrup hailed a tri-wheeled motor rickshaw. Its black metal cabin was a tight space with open sides to view all along our way. The air was hot and thick with pollution. I wrapped my shawl around my face trying to filter the air.

The traffic was unbelievable. A jammed, non-stop throng of cars, taxis, bemos,[1] trucks, rickshaws, motorbikes, cycles, runner carts, cows, dogs, chooks, and buses. All seemed to move in any which way each chose to go – beeping, yelling, cussing, barking, flapping and ringing. And in all of the chaos was a supremely surreal order. There was not a single accident.

We finally arrived at a small guest-house in New Delhi. We were greeted by Naresh and his wife, Mr and Mrs Mittal, a lovely Indian couple. Once we were through the front gate, the noise seemed to disappear as if it had all been a dream. We entered another world. The garden was immaculate. Great splashes of colour fell from pots and clung to arching branches of exotic flowers. Birds flitted to and fro and a rich fragrance filled the air.

We were ushered inside and shown our rooms and bathrooms. Mrs Mittal gently encouraged me to take my time.

'You may take a wash, then join everyone in the tearoom. Please, do not rush dear.'

I watched blackish-brown water drain down the basin as the soot washed away from my body.

---

[1] Three-wheeled motor transport with a small carriage capacity for two people.

The house was simple yet exotic. The wide, open rooms echoed. My feet felt cool upon the marble floor. We then sat quietly before tea was served. It was a natural grace that, without a word, we shared in common heart-full silence. Once the tea was poured the silence ended. I answered what seemed like a never-ending stream of questions. I didn't get a chance to ask any myself. Mrs Mittal did most of the talking while their boy, Atisha, sat wide-eyed.

'You are very special to have powerful visions and connections at your age,' she said. 'Not many western women are like you.'

I thought it was less than special (different maybe, but not special) yet for some reason it seemed to be a constant remark.

I shrugged my shoulders.

And so, once left to our own retreat time, I took to exploring. The ambience was ancient. And despite my apparent arrival in a 'new world' I felt a deep stirring of familiarity. I tried to grab hold of its place in my mind, yet was left with nothing more than a feeling.

The next morning I woke to a distant sound of hustle and bustle. I could hear whistles echoing through the expanse of the outside world.

I got up and wandered out the front gate. Mist hung low to the ground and filled the atmosphere like a great ghost. The sky was glowing in a soft violet hue. The first tinges of light beckoned the crow of a rooster. A paperboy called and blew his whistle in the long, wide street. I strolled to the corner of the block.

On the other side of the road were rows of cardboard sheets propped into makeshift shelters. Women, men, children and beggars, huddled in and around them, busying themselves with morning affairs. People with missing limbs sat on hessian bags. Cows wandered in a slow gait along the paths, each with their single large bell donging in a muted tone.

My eyes swept across the entire scene. In one full glance I understood more of this country than I could have ever imagined and yet less than I could comprehend. The fact that I had walked out of an abode that gracefully housed servants and beauty made a stark contrast. It instantly exposed this country's very real extremes of wealth and poverty, living side by side. And as much as I saw it, I could not understand it.

I walked back inside and made my way to the sitting hall. Naresh was sitting cross-legged on a bench seat with eyes closed. He was wrapped in nothing more than a loincloth. His face was soft and peaceful and his neatly trimmed beard seemed even whiter than before. He was no longer Mr Mittal to me. In this transformed scene he sat as a yogi before my eyes.

I took a seat on the floor, drew a deep breath and entered the shared space of silence within.

When I finally opened my eyes the body of the yogi was no longer in front of me. I looked at the wall where a giant fan was hanging. I stared, wondering whether I had been sitting with a phantom. And as I had considered before, I wondered about the notion that everything is a phantom. What is real, after all?

I chuckled to myself, watching it all like a dream, and stood up.

The smell of breakfast wafted in from the back of the guest-house. I wondered why the place seemed so silent and empty. So far I had only seen the couple, their boy and the servants. I followed the aroma.

The great long hall led to a veranda that opened out into a garden. And there, to my surprise, lit up by shafts of light, was Mr Mittal sitting at a garden table, dressed in a suit, reading a newspaper and sipping a cup of tea. It only added more weight to my theory that everything was just a dream.

As I approached he looked up from his paper and glanced over the rim of his glasses. He looked straight into me as if he read my mind, then grinned, winked and resumed his reading.

I watched a pair of butterflies dance in a drunken flight around each other next to the vibrant bougainvilleas. Then, just as suddenly as they had arrived, they disappeared.

I sat down next to Naresh.

'All of life's like that,' I said dreamily.

'What?' he asked.

'Just like the fleeting presence of a butterfly. Everything comes and goes in the flash of the moment of now. How can it be real when it is never remaining the same?'

He looked at me deeply. I saw eternity gazing at me, a vast deep space in those eyes.

'Mmmm ...' he sighed. 'Isn't it a dream?'

His question didn't need an answer. We sat again in silence.

Later that afternoon, I was shown the way to the rooftop. And there again was another surprise. To the right of me was an endless maze of rooftops that dissolved into the horizon. They reached out to meet the foggy blue-grey sky. As I took it all in, I was amazed by the great buzz of activity.

I had never seen so many kites in the sky. They darted to and fro in the air like hawks chasing each other. Huge black ravens held their post on aerials, children laughed and brightly coloured cloths lay on the rooftops like long fat ribbons. I leaned on the wall and took it all in.

I began to realise that this place never fully rested. There seemed to be a never-ending parade of games, work, ceremony, song, dance and play. It fully engaged my attention. The sky started to turn pink and the atmosphere took on another vibration. I could hear the call of prayers echoing over the vast patchwork of rooftops. It seemed like a timely prompt to make my way back downstairs. Incense wafted up to meet me. I followed its scent. The sitting room glowed with candlelight. The Mittals sat at the altar making offerings and Lama Lhundrup sat quietly chanting rounds on his mala.

I bowed with my hands in prayer mudra, offering myself to the Divine, to the moment, to eternity.

I chanted with all my heart in the silence within. Gratitude swelled up from a bottomless well in me. I felt so blessed, so overwhelmed. I was so glad to finally be in company with which I felt such belonging. Tears spilled from my eyes. I watched one fall from my cheek. It glistened, like a golden dewdrop as it fell in slow motion timelessness. It landed on my palm. Then it dissolved.

That night I dreamed.

I was walking along a path that was lit up like gold. And along the way I began to meet the most beautiful souls: yogis, monks, lamas, divine women, old crones and awakened madmen. As we exchanged smiles, hugs, joy, respect and blessing, I realised that each one was a long-lost friend. They each then farewelled me with the distinct words, 'Keep going. Everyone is waiting for you.' They pointed ahead on the path. And in the distance I could see a great golden mountain that looked like a pyramid temple. Its golden steps blazed in the light and people stood waving, beckoning me to come. Great crowds stood waiting.

When I woke in the morning I realised that I was guided, that in every moment I was being watched and that I was heading towards an ordained destiny. I also realised that, as much as I had craved the beauty of belonging and sharing communion with the divine beings I knew so well, I was not going to be granted the indulgence of restful stay in their company. I saw that some meetings would be for longer moments and some shorter, but that each one would pass. And it was my duty to keep going. Not to linger, not to stray nor try to stay. A deep stirring emotion quaked in the pit of my gut. It was a dropping feeling. I sensed the aloneness on my path.

Yet I also knew I was held in an ever-present love of a far greater dimension. What then followed was a deep intuition that my current journey was only a fleeting passage. I realised that I was destined for something beyond the gatherings in Buddhism. I felt a strange sense of contradiction. My choice of vows was meant to be a lifetime commitment. And despite this inner realisation, I felt no less dedication. I simply knew it was what I must do. With whatever was due to unfold, I threw myself into the space of surrendering, not knowing how long or what for. Yet knowing, with unbending trust, it would be taken care of. And so I stepped off the cliff edge of controlled confinement into the space of Divine detachment.

That afternoon we boarded our flight – next stop: Kathmandu.

The plane was so small and tattered that I began to wonder whether we would actually make it. The engine grumbled and the seats rattled. I stared out of the window. The scene engulfed me.

To my great wonder, yet no surprise, I saw a view that was not at all new. This was where I had astral-travelled many times. This was where I had journeyed with Lama to caves. This was the place of my many visions and recurring dreams. And it was a scene that was painted on the background of past-life memories.

As the sun began to set, the great snow-capped peaks below reflected sheets of vibrant colours. Violet, pink, gold and coral.

I sighed deeply. I finally felt I was coming home.

Then the plane began a steep descent and I saw the airstrip we were due to land on, nestled in a valley. It wasn't even a flat space.

As the plane groaned and shuddered, it seemed an entertaining notion that I might die this way – crashed upon the face of the Himalayas. But, in a matter of blinks, we were soon on the ground, safely.

We were greeted at the tiny airport by a small group of monks. Their faces lit up the moment they saw us and, in a great flurry of giggling and bowing, we somehow managed to collect our baggage and get swept up into a jeep that waited outside.

The air was icy crisp and intensely fresh. This was another new sensation that my lungs stretched to meet – this time, gratefully.

I was ushered into the back of the jeep with the three young monks. The hard benches proved tough on my already weary backside, the bumps only adding greater emphasis. I reached into my backpack for another jumper, and gloves and hat. With them gratefully donned I looked up to see the young monks grinning at me, their right arm stuck out nakedly unwrapped, and their freshly shaved heads seemed to glow in the darkness as much as their sparkly eyes. I wondered how my body was ever going to adapt.

The jeep made its way up the valley, bumping and rattling. By the time we reached the Monastery of Kopan the sky was pitch black and scattered with bright stars.

Monks ran and opened the gates to a well-lit courtyard. The buildings' white walls glared under the lights and brightly coloured flags swayed, rising up into the darkness. Bells rang in added pomp, to the great excitement of about thirty monks. Lama Lhundrup disappeared amongst the hugging and greetings and I was led to a room.

I was given a candle, a box of matches and a quick bow – then left, just as suddenly, all to myself. I closed the door thinking I might keep the room warm but in the glowing light of the candle, I soon thought differently. A great gap under the door made a good passage for the blustery wind and the window didn't close properly. The concrete and brick floor was bare, except for two thin straw mats, two almost-as-thin mattresses and one small, low stone platform.

There was a sudden knock on the door. I opened it to see one of the monks standing before me holding a lantern. He beckoned me to follow him, speaking in a mix of Tibetan and broken English. I followed him down the path. The courtyard had become a procession line of monks collecting a bowl of rice and soupy vegetables.

My stomach grumbled with instant approval. As each monk sat, the bowl was placed in the lap, hands were held together and bodies rocked to and fro in a lilting chant, all in wonderfully choreographed rhythm. It was followed by a startling moment of silence, which was quickly pursued by the sounds of clanging spoons and slurping soup.

Despite the intensity of the chilli, I was grateful to eat it. However the next morning, for my poor backside, it proved rather different! So I discovered the legendary 'burning ring of fire' had nothing to do with any esoteric mystical sect. And it wasn't just the encroaching growls and gurgling gripes that drilled their way through my intestines that kept me awake. An incessant pricking of tiny bites ensured my sleep was quite disturbed. The tiny pink dots were evidence that I was not in bed alone.

After another disturbing night I tore my bed into wreckage, desperate to unveil my night-time predators. When I thought I had been masterfully outdone, I stood back with hot flushed cheeks, heaving breath and hands on hips and let out a sigh. Then in a flash it came, like an arrow to its mark. I lifted up the straw mat.

My eyes took in what my mind found shocking, stunning, amazing and strangely beautiful. There, startled by the exposure as the straw mat was whipped up, was a colony of fleas.

There was a hundred thousand, maybe a million – no, a million million! I couldn't comprehend how many were there. And they were already leaping, leaping in every direction imaginable, desperate to find a hideout.

What followed for me was an interesting exercise that highlighted my vows of non-violence, as I did all I could to relocate my bedmates as lovingly as I could. Following that, I felt a falling away of my notion that all the mystical head shaving was motivated by the willingness to renounce vanity. Historically, its use was predominantly a practical measure to control the conditions for head-lice and the likes of my miraculous flea colony!

I was informed that evening prayers would start at 8 pm in the main gompa and morning prayers at 4 am and that I should wash before entering.

I discovered over a course of days that the 4 am start was the first round for the 'keener' ascetics and that 6 am prayers had a far greater attendance.

For me it wasn't a question of keenness or qualifications as a more serious practitioner. It was the simple truth that I felt I had no choice. I had taken the dive. And I wanted to give myself to the practice as fully as possible. I entered at 4 am. To me it was a matter of the power in each moment. I knew that each one was the open door and that to think of practising in anyway other than to the fullest was as good as a door still closed. I didn't want to waste a single precious moment.

So I found myself walking in the blackness along the garden path at 3.45 am. With teeth brushed and my body shocked by a bucket of cold water, I was wide awake.

When I entered the gompa I stepped into another zone. Great rows of butter lamps flickered and shed a golden incandescence upon ornate pillars, scriptures, statues and the serene faces of monks. All was in a riot of colour. I was pointed to my place, towards the side and back with the nuns. Men and women were kept separate. Men were given the higher place at the front, starting with those who had achieved the most and were most highly ordained.

When the geshe[1] came in everyone bowed and prostrated with head to the floor and tails in the air. I felt obliged to follow suit yet also noticed the rebel in me that wanted to spontaneously throw my hands in the air with joy and gratitude. Nonetheless I sensed this behaviour would cause great objections, so I simply observed my inner play. And as I watched I became quite amused at the game of suppression. It seemed that a great amount of seriousness was expected of the practitioners. Somehow the gift of spontaneity was lost in the importance of ritual. The constant quirky comedian in me wanted to burst out with a few jokes of irreverence just to release the air of stiffness in this scene of spiritual identity. I chose to stay silent rather than impose my jokes on others. But I knew it wouldn't be long before the joker in me would break out again.

Then Lama Lhundrup entered. He looked straight at me and gestured for me to move forward, to the front near the lamas. I looked back at him in surprise and puzzlement. But again he gestured with a look of 'yes, now come on, hurry up' as he flapped his hand at me.

So, trying to keep my head as low as possible I half crawled to the front.

Some stirring murmurs rippled their way around the room indicating surprise and questioning from the rest of the group. The few ordained westerners turned their heads. I felt their eyes boring

---

1 A lama (like an abbot) who has attained a high degree of knowledge of Tibetan Buddhist teaching, comparable to a western doctorate.

into me. I sat down, wrapped my robe around my shoulders and stared to the front not daring to catch the eye of anyone else.

The geshe who sat in the master seat looked across and stared blankly at me. It occurred to me that in that moment I saw straight into him. I saw behind his eyes. There was something deeply unsatisfied in his being. It seemed heavy and almost depressed as if the bright light of his spirit had gone dim a long time ago. I caught myself and rechecked my observation. Perhaps I was just imagining things. It seemed strange that depression would exist in someone who was supposed to inspire the light of spirit in others. However, over the following weeks and months it became startlingly evident that this geshe was indeed a zone of flat, sombre expression. In fact he displayed a range of expressions from boredom, nothingness, impatience and anger to a disregarding offhandedness.

I was determined to try and provoke a different response, to somehow ignite his flame. But in all the months I gave joy, lightness, and laughter, I saw only one tiny little flicker. It rose up, as if in an unguarded moment, only to be quickly reprimanded and shut down in its darkness again, in the very moment the geshe realised it was about to burst forth. One fleeting little spark, then it was lost again in a sea of suppression.

A wave of alertness swept across me. I didn't want to become like that. I began to see a suffocating seriousness that pervaded in the great plethora of rules, regulations and intellectual enlightenment concepts. All the great efforts to acquire 'higher' knowledge and all the power of spiritual debate did not guarantee joyous freedom, love, aliveness or simplicity of being. Yet I craved those great powers of discrimination. My mind was hungry for a deeper understanding. And so far, the Buddhist principles and concepts were the clearest maps I had encountered.

And yet ... something felt askew.

So I watched the whole thing as if it was a movie: the events, the states and responses of others and my responses. I found it amusing that there seemed to be as much internal debate in my head as there was amongst the initiates in their training.

I watched a group of young monks in the courtyard engaged in the dynamic practice. First, scriptures would be chanted and then a topic or line of teaching would be presented for debate. Each monk in turn would leap up, give a great flurry of loud statements in exploration of the topic and finish with his arms wide, swinging into a loud clap of his hands as if to say 'my word is highest, now beat that!'

So every time I heard an internal exclamation mark in my own mind, I couldn't help but laugh. I began to see how ironic it was that such intense, apparent intellectual pursuit could prove to be not much more than my mind's egoic arrogance. I began to trust my mind less and less. Albeit I knew it was a tool of great power and importance. I sensed even more deeply, that what I really wanted to 'know' – to realise – was completely beyond my mind and that really my mind was a servant to 'it'. My mind was not the master but it certainly could serve the master. I felt as if I was teetering on the edge of a great divide and that it was the difference between insanity and sanctity.

And so I found myself in a strange juxtaposition. I had to surrender my mind's ideas, everything I thought I knew. I ceased to own it and simply watched it. And the more I did so the more I could leave no stone unturned. I took to an exhaustive process of enquiry. I sat in for every discourse, discussion, practice and initiation. With every initiation came an additional commitment of practice, involving mantras, offerings and visualisations. And, of course, all of this added up to more and more time each day. It seemed that the more I gave away the old, the more I was filled with the new.

During my spare time I particularly enjoyed to just sit and chant AUM[1] (OM) repeatedly. After many weeks of constant practice I discovered the effect it had on the energy centres was a bit like the shift of energy when water comes to the boil.

One OM was like one degree. The more I OM'd the more the energy increased. I discovered that anything less than twenty-seven OM's was like stopping short of boiling point. Seven OM's created

---

[1] The originating and all pervasive sound of creation. Repeated as a mantra in spiritual practice.

a momentary pause, slowing down of thoughts and slight energy balance in the chakras. Twelve OM's began to raise the energy vibration of the whole subtle body. Twenty-seven OM's became a point at which the self was still in awareness whilst the kundalini would begin to surge – like the first bubbling of water. At that point if I continued toning the energy would get stronger and stronger. If I stopped and sustained awareness the energy would gradually carry me into an expanded, interconnected state that swirled like liquid silk. My days continued mostly with the same routine.

Then, early one morning, Lama informed me we were going to go to a cave up in the mountains. I felt an instant rush of God-bumps running up the back of my arms and neck. It was almost as if this was the moment I had been waiting for.

'Where is it'? I asked.

But Lama did not reply with words, he simply stared into me deeply. It was quite some time before he did say,

'Some things are not to be spoken, only to be remembered.'

My body jiggled with a sense of excitement and mystery as his words echoed around in my mind.

Before long we were high up the mountain pass. The jeep rattled and bumped profusely over rough tracks until the path seemed to vanish into the forested terrain.

As we leapt out of the vehicle Lama indicated for me to follow him. He took to a faint, steep path that led relentlessly up the mountain. I began to breathe heavily as the thin atmosphere squeezed at my lungs. As I took in the surroundings a potent sense of deja vu engulfed me in the colours and smells of the great mountainous escarpments. The landscape of trees and rocky mountain ledges was like a scene of homecoming. It swelled up from deep in my soul, threatening to drown me in glee.

Then Lama stopped and stood silently, pointing to a small, almost invisible ledge. That scene almost took my breath away. It was the ledge that I had seen in my astral travels throughout all my earlier years. It was the ledge to the cave in which I had sat as a yogi, transfixed by an all-pervasive samadhi[1] in a previous life, and to which I had returned to write the memoirs of conscious awakening. It was the cave to which I had travelled with Lama in my inner visions and astral journeys.

I stood in a sense of absolute knowing yet gripping, mind-boggling disbelief that this was really happening. And yes, in that moment I pinched myself!

Then Lama turned around and ushered me forward. We climbed up to the ledge and stood in the bright light. The sky above was a glaring azure blue – deep and stark. It seemed to reflect the vast stillness and timelessness in which I was consumed.

My trance was suddenly broken as Lama spoke.

'Go inside,' he said.

I raised my eyebrows in surprise.

There in the wall was the only entrance: a very small hole, not much more than twelve inches square. For some strange reason, I now felt unsure about my ability to get inside. The hole looked much smaller than my body. But then an inner voice assured me, 'It is your cave, it will let you in ... you *know* how to enter it.'

And, I nodded to myself, it was true, I did.

I stepped up to the edge of the small opening. I had to surrender my usual perception of my body and focus on its manoeuverability. I had to soften stiff boundaries into a more fluid form in a way that would challenge even a well-practised contortionist. Gently and deeply I breathed myself into a deep presence of shift and within moments I had popped through the little window.

Inside it was dark. My eyes struggled as if suddenly blinded. Instinctively my hands moved over the walls, feeling their cool smooth form. As I felt my way to the back of the cave I turned around and sat down.

My body rested into a smooth dip beneath my legs and buttocks. And as I sensed that the hollow was shaped exactly to my body, I

---

1 A state of undisturbed bliss in which the perception of a separate self as 'I' dissolves into pure awareness of infinite life-love source, at which moment it is known as Nirvikalpa Samadhi.

shuffled slightly and the stone beneath me embraced my form. Over all those years and centuries, the stone had moulded into the smooth form of a lotus posture, worn away by the dedicated sitting of yogis. Without a doubt, I knew I had been there before. And so I sat, and was taken again into the womb of creation, into the vastness of no- mind, no-form, infinite being.

It was as if Brahma[1] had come again to consume all the boundaries, from which I would emerge again as the one and all, undivided Self in everything, everywhere, always, simultaneously. There was the sweet, deep, endless ocean of silent stillness forever.

It seemed like an endless stream of eternity before I came back to my body again. I took in a deep breath and stood up. Golden light poured in through the hole. The sun was setting low, casting its amber liquid across the mountain peaks. As I looked out the vast valley stretched before my eyes, my prayer beads lay smooth in my hand's grasp, and I gave thanks for the blessing of this sacred land.

---

[1] A Hindu deity: the essence of all creation that consumes the boundaries of the false perception of separateness.

20. Pulled by an Invisible Cord

> Your vision will become clear only
> when you can look into your own heart.
> Who looks outside, dreams; who looks
> inside, awakes.
>
> *Carl Jung*

Time passed quickly and I discovered my visa had expired. That meant I had to travel over the border again, from Nepal to India. This time I would be by myself. I had heard a great deal about Varanasi; mostly, of course, because of the accounts of Buddha's awakening under the Bodhi Tree[1] and the discourses at Sarnath. I felt pulled as if by an invisible elastic umbilical cord.

I chose to fly to Delhi and from there to make my way by train.

I had heard all sorts of travellers' nightmares so I was determined to assure myself some comfort on the long train ride. I joined a great line of Indian people all jostling to push their way forward to the ticket office. A man suddenly appeared by my side, bowed to me and took me by the elbow. With great utterances of respect he led me towards the start of the line. Not a single soul looked in question. He stayed by my side until I reached the ticket window. Then he disappeared as quickly as he had appeared.

In an instant I had purchased a two-tier air-conditioned ticket, a cabin with a bed and air-conditioning, for that coming Saturday. Next I had to find a room for the night. I decided to try for something

---

[1] The tree under which Buddha entered into enlightenment.

a little more on the outskirts.

A voice called at me from the side of the road. 'Transport?'

A young Indian boy called. He stood upright on his pedals offering me his 'very comfortable, madam, rickshaw.' Above the small open carriage with its large spoked wheels fluttered a parasol of bright red and white paisley cloth, fringed with tassels. I looked at him half enthusiastically, half cautiously. By now I knew how far Indians could take bribing, bargaining and outright rip-offs. He saw the question in my eyes.

'No worry, madam,' he said with a sincere waggle of his head. He put his hand to his heart. 'I'm good boy. I look after you. Take you to good place, not much money.'

We smiled at each other. And, thinking of nothing but adventure and an encounter with another dear soul, I put my backpack in the carriage and jumped in. I watched this race of people with great wonderment. Thin bodies working hard, pushing stacks, pulling carts, carrying loads, running, walking, begging, all with an intensity, an urgency. The colours of the village stalls and marketplaces worked upon my eyes. They were great vibrant patches amongst dark bodies and soiled roads. Smells tugged at my senses, both enticing and repulsing.

Then on the side of the road I saw the most extraordinary scene. It summed up human life in one fleeting glance.

A woman leaned back against the wall and holding her baby close to her full, brown breast, took a mouthful of rice with her free hand; two men stood spitting red betel-nut juice between words; a wrinkled old woman stared blankly down the road; a little boy chased away a dog; and a corpse lay in the gutter. Here were birth, life and death. My eyes were so transfixed with the scene that I turned my head as we passed by. As I watched behind me I saw a scurry of people as they parted way for two men carting a stretcher. They laid it down on the path, picked up the corpse, placed it on the cloth stretched between two poles and then trotted down the road. Everything seemed to happen easily and naturally. I contemplated the play of life ... birth, youth, middle age, old age and death. All of it was a fleeting happening, nothing more than a passing dream.

Lama's words echoed in my mind. 'Death arrives unpredictably but is certain to come. Any moment it could come. Don't waste time.' The words rolled around and around in my mind. What then would I rather do than live each moment as if it were my last? I thought of the many times I had been selfish, impatient or insensitive to another. I felt a loss for those moments and realised that it could have been the last thing I gave to the world. The stirring of emotions, the contemplation of the death of the ego and self-disgust were somehow demanded by the circumstances. I wanted to cry. Instead, I responded to the words of the boy giving every ounce of his energy to transport my body to a room. It was the least I could do. I realised then that, actually, more than anything, I wanted to give whatever I could in every moment I lived.

The rickshaw boy pointed to many of the sights, explaining the surroundings. Sprawling plains, rice fields, palm trees and small groves were broken up by tin sheds, rough dirt roads, barren land, workshops and makeshift housing clumped together like miniature shanty-towns.

'Not far, now,' he said as we passed by a large bridge that spanned a river. The narrow streets had parted into wide open fields bordered with occasional shelters. Finally we arrived at a few more streets fronted by hostels with welcome signs.

I was happy for something simple. One bed, in a small room and a cold bucket of water to wash in the morning was enough. My nose was grateful to have a rest from the use of public 'squat' toilets. The smell of accumulated urine and faecal matter in unscrubbed amenities was almost noxious. The young boy bowed to me and shook my hand. 'My name is Rohan,' he said. 'I will come in the morning to take you wherever you need.'

I shrugged my shoulders not really thinking that far ahead, yet he said, 'I insist.' I gazed at his small frame. His thin body seemed to make his limbs look long and brittle as they poked out of old tatty clothes. His face was framed by thick eyebrows and a fringe of floppy dark brown hair, slightly bleached by the sun. His dark eyes looked out at me with a look of longing, almost desperate.

So I grinned, shrugged my shoulders again and said okay. I gave him some rupees. He took them very thankfully and then rode away.

Inside the grounds I discovered a lovely open garden with tables for outdoor dining. The garden and decorations had a strange Mexican flair. With cactus plants and thorny flowers, pebbled paths wove between low-lying whitewashed buildings and arches painted black and pale blue. I was ready for an early meal and ordered vegetable chapattis.[1] The food came out quickly for my solitary meal. Little sparrows flitted to and fro. I was surprised that these birds were as common in India as in Australia. I went to bed that night after my prayers, feeling a funny sense of connectedness brought to me by the presence of a common sparrow.

Then, all in the shift of a night's sleep I found myself, the next day, thrown again into the bizarre setting of India. The train station was a cacophonous tumult of jostling men, women, children, beggars, chai wallahs,[2] goats and chooks. The train was due to arrive within fifteen minutes. There was great pushing and shoving as each person with baggage and cargo (some of which was boxed and some, alive) tried to secure a place close to the boarding line. And above it all, came the distinct wailing call of the chai wallahs. All I could think of was how glad I was to have my two-tier air-conditioned tickets. It was hot, smelly and like a human sardine factory on the platform. I couldn't imagine how everyone and everything was going to fit on the train. And by now it was already running forty minutes late, which was apparently quite normal.

The train arrived two hours late. The rust-brown carriages seemed to roll past like a taunting mirage before finally squealing to a halt in the station. I didn't think it was possible for the noise to exceed its already blaring medley. But exceed it, it did. The platform suddenly

---

[1] Indian traditional flat breads made of flour, sometimes stuffed with vegetables and spices.

[2] Traditional hawkers who sell spicy milk tea.

heaved into frantic activity ... pushing, shoving, yelling and clambering. I didn't know which way to go. And before I could even try I was swept up in the pressing, shoving, and struggling crowds. A great wave of Indians spilled from the train and an even greater wave swelled its way, in a funnel effect, in through the doors.

I tried desperately to keep my head above it all. My eyes searched frantically for a conductor. All the cabins seemed to be without doors. And before I knew it I was picked up by the squeeze of bodies and found myself in the economy carriage. I had never seen so many people in one carriage before. Bodies hung from the doors, out of the windows and jam-packed each of the benches lined up three deep from floor to ceiling. Every last gap seemed to be filled. I looked at my position. There was no train guard in sight.

And then, to my horror, I realised the state of things was worse than I could have imagined. The toilet was leaking its matter. It made a steady, putrid trail from the toilet down the aisle. And the only place left for me was right next to it, a dry patch against the wall. I put my backpack down and sat on top of it. The three benches next to me were filled with men. They stared down at me with leering eyes. In that moment I felt as if I were in the furthest place from the spiritually devoted. I suddenly realised how naive I could be. All my life I had tended to assume that everyone in some way had a similar outlook on life to mine. I had come to accept spiritual lack in the West. But to suddenly face the stark reality of spiritual absence in India was a jolt to my soul.

I waited, passing my time hoping for the train guard's arrival. I watched men, watching me, watching them – picking noses, spitting, sleeping. I pondered old men sighing, women gazing, children sleeping.

My previous disillusionment, which had temporarily settled, was about to leap into shocked horror. I looked up, feeling the men's eyes eating into my flesh. Somehow I couldn't stop myself even though it was the last thing I wanted to do. Curiosity gripped me. My senses were drawn. My eyes ached to see what it was that pressed itself with such intensity upon my aura.

There, leering down at me was a man with eyes like a maddened bull. Suddenly, in one swift move, he pulled out his penis and began to do what most men would only do in the privacy of their own bedroom. I felt sickened as his mouth foamed at the corners, then suddenly I realised I had been so shocked that I hadn't removed my eyes yet. I flinched as I grappled to regain my centre and disconnect the line of energy caught in the field of attention as he lusted over me.

It was one of those moments that saturated my senses, darkly etching its way onto my mind as if with ink that refused to dry or fade. Yet there, in the brightness of the inner witness, shafts of light cast sparkles of compassion and understanding upon those lines, turning them into a passing dream.

Nearly two hours had passed without a sign of the ticket collector. Suddenly the carriage door flew open and in came the guard, dressed in a dark suit and a cap. I leapt up, holding my ticket forward. 'Please, sir,' I said, 'I have a two-tier air-conditioned ticket. Can you please take me to my cabin?'

'Oh no, madam,' he replied with a head waggle. 'No, sorry madam, all full, we do not have.'

'But it can't be,' I stammered. 'I bought a ticket. Look, I've paid for my cabin. Someone else must be in by mistake.'

'Oh no, madam, sorry. Not so. Nothing left,' he said, ignoring my pleading eyes and continuing down the aisle.

I slumped on my backpack. But unready to accept defeat, and quite sure my cabin was still available, I was determined to get it. The air was hot, steamy and pungent with human excrement and sweating bodies that spoke of diets heavy with meat and spices. This odour served as an even greater incentive to muster the determination to resolve my seating arrangement.

Another hour had passed when finally the conductor returned. I leapt up again, this time with well-brewed assertiveness. 'Look,' I said, 'I have paid for my cabin and I want it now. I know it's there because I have booked.'

'Let me look at your ticket,' he mumbled. Then after turning it over front and back a few times, he said, 'Mmm. Well maybe, but you haven't paid enough. Baksheesh, madam, baksheesh,' he said with a look like an old, heavy-set pudding. 'You give me more rupees and maybe I can help you.'

I looked at him, bewildered. I couldn't believe the extent of bribery and corruption in this country. I finally gave in and handed over a hundred rupees. Then in my cabin, exhausted, I slept.

The train finally arrived at Pathankot and I transferred to another transport nightmare. This time it was the heated fumes in one of the backseats of a bus where a young, ragged village girl had just vomited.

I was extremely grateful to arrive in Varanasi without losing my own stomach's contents. When the bus pulled to a stop I stepped out into a hazy purple atmosphere, the last light of the day before lamps and candles began to blaze. I found my way to a room in the heart of Varanasi. The whole atmosphere was startlingly familiar to me. I felt like I was walking in a timeless zone of deja vu.

I stepped off the cobbled street into a corridor. The bright green paint bore a patina of grime and corrosion. A little old man took the price of my lodging and then led me up the stairs to my room. The same green paint greeted my eyes. He handed me the key, bowed and turned away. The room was absolutely basic. I felt a deep gratitude. It was more than many people could hope for.

I unrolled my sleeping bag and lay down on the wooden slatted bed. I was just beginning to enjoy the stillness of the hard surface when my attention was drawn to the sound of an approaching procession in the street below. I looked at my watch: 3 am. I listened intently.

Bicycle bells, blaring horns, moaning cows, yelling Hindus. There, in the heart of Varanasi, I lay listening to the beat of this ancient mother's people preparing holy ceremony. It suddenly struck me how profoundly vast, yet particular, the whole encounter was. There I lay awake, hearing the spiritual observance of a city at a point in the eternity of time, while all the separated minds observed their own spot on the vast map of life. It was 'here and now'. Then I thought: I'm in it!

I sat my body up on the wooden bed. My sleeping bag barely softened the solid experience of conceptual reality. This is a hard bed that really exists, says the mind, at least it probably did for most of the people who had rested on it. Yet, in some fathomless field of awareness, I managed to experience it as the vast, endless softness of space.

I stepped down onto the cement floor, cool beneath my feet. I breathed in the cool mist of the pre-morning awakening. A frame flashed through my mind of a blanketed city, mist hanging in near-empty pockets, chilling the bones of the wasting homeless who have only thin skin to shelter their bodies. The first murmurings of the morning wafted eerily through the fog-filled streets. It sounded dreamlike and I knew in a few years' time it would all be nothing more than that.

The day ahead would be duly hot but the morning was still frigid after the black night. The new moon stared at me through the bars on the glassless window. The bare light bulb glared at me rudely as if indignant to be woken at this early hour and I wondered at my sanity. I brushed it aside with an uplifting sigh. I'm glad I'm here, I said to myself.

I dressed quickly with a few layers of light cloths, put on my socks, opened the heavy door and stepped out into the cool stairwell, into my slip-ons. I passed a small boy wearing nothing more than a singlet and small loose grimy shorts, sleeping in the corner of the first floor. Not a stir. He's probably in another dimension oblivious to discomfort, I thought. I couldn't help but sigh at the thought of my own great fortune.

Outside, the crowds were thickening in the streets and the sounds were growing louder. People were running, whistles were blowing and excitement was creeping, touching everyone present. Even the cows picked up pace. I watched as bright gold and orange marigold flowers started to shower through the air and the first glowing pinks of aurora filled the sky. I found myself swept up by the crowd and tossed in a sea of joy and celebration. What a wonder to see such elevation at a funeral! I thought. These people really know how to see a soul off. What a party! I felt excitement as I recognised that this was the true way to celebrate death, which is nothing more than a passing of the soul into eternal life: the release of a body that can no longer serve for a fruitful life.

Vision in the early morning was still not at its best, yet my eyes were filled with the amazing colours of saris as women swirled past in a frenzy. The whole atmosphere was thick and rich. I felt it sneaking into my cells and then I was suddenly reminded of the earthly realm we live in. My foot landed in a huge puddle of wet, sloppy cow manure. I thought about the Buddhist concept of the pervasive wheel of suffering but laughed at its transitory nature and stepped onwards with soggy, shitty socks.

The procession swung into full pomp as we neared the Ganges. I decided to avoid the jostling chaos of human bodies and cows dancing to the rhythm of uncoordinated music, chanting and screaming. I took a few side-streets, and stepped into another world – 3,000 years old. Tall buildings and remarkably narrow passages rose up on each side, giving me the feeling that I was walking through a maze of tunnels. The air was cool and contained.

The walls, with their ancient knowledge of the generations that had passed by, seemed to demand respect. I felt the pavement beneath my feet, polished from all those centuries of passing feet, human and cow alike. I felt the wealth and the poverty, the richness of the holy and the weight of the culture steeped in their old, cold stones. And I felt my unmistakable familiarity with the place. My deep thoughts were broken by the sound of a distant cowbell. Then, close by, came the clop of hooves and snort of breath as a cow turned the corner of an unseen corridor ahead.

'Oh, shit!' I said out loud. I had stepped in a puddle of it and now one of these holy beasts was heading straight towards me! I wasn't going to turn back so I figured I'd better start climbing fast.

So, planting my back against the wall, I stretched my legs to the other side, braced my feet and pushed my way up the wall, just in time to have the cow pass under me. It didn't even take a second look at this strange human wedged between the walls above. It ambled on down the corridor, its bell clanging with an echoing drone.

I released my brace and continued on my way. Set in the ancient walls, small shrines, arrayed in flowers, paints and dyes, mixed in rivers of wax and puffs of ash, boasted of the millions of splattered prayers thrown at the invoked deities. I thought of the thousands who had made their prayers to these ancient idols, the gods presiding over this holy city. Each one of the thousands was another one, living in the world of 'I'. The air hung thickly with the vibration of such percolated prayers. The whole place stood deeply in assumed power. It sent shivers up my spine. I stared in wonder as I contemplated the prayers rippling out into the universe touching the infinity of one great, all-pervading soul.

Then, the trance of the dim dampness of the walls was broken by a full stream of light as I stepped out into the open domain of the riverfront. I took in the awesome beauty and splendour of the view before me. A strange stirring moved in the blueprint of my soul. Memories. The smells, sounds and sights were a tumbling experience that drew me into the familiarity of this world. The feeling of being home, of belonging, flooded my being. I stood there as if I'd never been anywhere else. It felt as if it were just another usual day; as if I was doing what I would do in the place I had been born, right there in the heart of Varanasi.

I knew it all so well, as if I'd never been away, and yet somehow, my DNA had a firmer grip on my psychic identity than I realised. So I stood swaying in limbo, somewhere between the doubtful reality of two different worlds, neither Australian nor Indian, but – a being of timeless, boundless life – at home on distant shores. Then, as if reflecting my 'nobody' state, it seemed that I was unobserved, although I was the only westerner in sight. I thought that, maybe my shaved head and robes were a camouflage amongst all the other yogis and sadhus.[1] So I stood in timelessness, watching the whole scene being illumined by a purple sky as the sun rose like a glowing hot-pink peach over the river. As I watched the sadhus around me, I felt a raking compulsion to join them in their nakedness, wearing only ashes, ochres and beads. It seemed like the most natural thing to my soul. But instead I wrapped my robes more tightly around my shoulders and turned my head toward the sound of the arriving procession.

In a flurry, bodies rushed into the holy water, chanting and praying. Men in loincloths plunged themselves full-bodied into the water, other yogis remained still and silent on their floating houses, posed in full lotus, oblivious to the wailing Indians who were creating waves on the previously still waters. Women squatted daintily at the river's edge with bowls, plates of flowers and pots for collecting holy water. Others scrubbed vigorously at outstretched lengths of silk saris and cloths, painting the pavement with bright colours. They sang melodically while a huge blue-bodied deity watched over his flock. His smile seemed to emanate both a quiet peace and a powerful protective authority.

Then a boatman broke my trance. He invited me to ride in his long sleek boat. I stepped in without a second thought and with a long pole he shunted us from the steps at the bank. We glided along the river with silent ease. The bow met the dark glossy waters, parting them in a cleavage of smooth fine lines. Streaming sheaths of purple, pink and gold reflected from the sky, and flowed out in the wake behind the boat like luminous waves of light. In contrast to the scenes of constant activity along the banks, here the stillness was pervasive. In that stillness a marvel of God's creation was visible: a synthesis of the omnipresent poise of absolute stillness, passivity, and the constantly re-forming manifestation, activity.

In that seeing was the caress of a liberating insight. I saw that the bow upon the waters of life gives rise to the inevitable ripples,

[1] Spiritual wanderers and practitioners.

and that their passing is also inevitable. I saw how the struggle of the mind and ego to work it out, to cling to, to change or to run from, is nothing more than another ripple: simply a dynamic of tension in a process of change. Whatever appears as conflict is nothing more than a natural dynamic of life's evolution. And the essence of life itself remains indifferent. Like the river, it matters not whether the ripples come or go, be they large or small. They all effortlessly dissolve again into the field of life, which remains forever still and unaffected. And so I watched the ripples passing – the ripples of my mind, the ripples of life – effortlessly passing.

We slowed to a halt. The boatman pointed to the scene on the bank. We had reached the cremation ghats.[1] I watched with fascination. I wondered if the preparations were for the departed one that I had seen being carried along in the procession. The remains of another had already been wrapped and were now being set to float on the river. I couldn't help but wonder at the condition of the water that carried a history of uncountable deposits of more than one kind. And, despite my thoughts, I could do nothing less than dip my hands, arms, and feet into the waters of this great flowing river. I knew her so well, this great Holy River. And she knew me. I cried, filled with fathomless love as I watched my tears fall – to where they had been born so long ago.

I spent my days dissolving in the golden atmosphere of the great Holy City, drawn to the Ganga[2] by the invisible, indivisible force of belonging. Its radiance was constant. Candles, oil lamps, shimmering offerings, and spectacular sunrises – all were in non-stop celebration, fitting for this place known as 'Kashi', City of Light.

I roamed the streets and the ghats, watching, taking in the constant activity of sacred rituals. Lining the streets were stalls and stands purveying lacquer jars, bright vermilion powder, bangles, brocades and bottled Ganges water. Piles of flowers and garlands, yellow and orange, were in abundant display. There were copper pots,

---

[1] Landings on riverbank where the deceased are placed on cremation platforms and set afloat.

[2] The holy river Ganges.

brass bowls, silver plates and offering trays. People were begging, squatting, eating handfuls of rice; yogis were sitting, chanting, posturing; sadhus were praying, blessing and lecturing. Everywhere Kashi's children were bathing, cleansing and offering.

It seemed as if there was no single breath or movement that was lacking respect for the Holy. All was a devotion to the power of this great Mother Ganga, who could wash away all earthly sins and bestow instant salvation: moksha.[1]

To be immersed in such fullness of the Divine all around me was already, in itself, liberating. Relief lightened my soul to see so many living in devotion to the essence of life. And although it was simultaneously obvious, I wondered why I had chosen to reincarnate into the West where life seemed so devoid of essential truth and where most people chose worldly gratifications above spiritual fulfilment. Deep inside I knew why. Although I just wanted to disappear into this great Holy land, I knew that one day, soon enough, I would be destined to return to the West.

So I could do nothing but live each moment of this journey to its fullest.

The next day I took a bus to the ancient Mahabodhi Temple, the monolithic site for the worship of Buddha's place of enlightenment. It was there, under the Bodhi Tree, that Prince Siddhartha – the man, became the Buddha – the Enlightened One. On arrival I wandered slowly all the way round the temple. It was too much to take in the endless details of stone sculptures and rows of deities rising in countless tiers.

I eventually found a place to sit and meditate on a yoga board dedicated to prayers and prostrations. I sat down in the quiet of the garden. Arching branches and flowers created a private space. Dark leaves silhouetted against the powder-blue sky. Gazing dreamily, I began to chant.

Before long I was swaying in a state of deep joy. Then, from the

---

1 Liberation; the final state of enlightenment. Some define this as a final release from the cycle of death and birth.

bushes, three little children appeared. Their eyes twinkled and their sweet faces shone with innocent, delighted smiles. I smiled back. They came close. Each of them had a flower. The tallest girl stood in front of me and dropped her chin coyly. She twirled the flower's stem between her fingers then offered it to me. That brief, simple gesture hit me so powerfully. It was the motion of love unfolding – as pure as the opening of the petals of the flower.

'Oh, how beautiful,' I said.

Then the other two girls offered me theirs as well.

'What you doing?' asked the tall girl.

'Meditating and chanting,' I said.

'Please teach us,' she replied. They all nodded and sat down next to me. Their bodies were so petite they looked like dolls, dressed in pink, yellow and green skirts.

We all chuckled in delight, then I started to chant in melody, with the three little girls chiming in – grinning and echoing me. Then more children came skipping through the garden. They ran straight up to us and joined in.

Before I knew it I was surrounded by nine brown-bodied 'imps', now a group of five girls and four boys. Their dark eyes shone with laughter and joy. They touched me and snuggled closer until we were one great big swaying hug. And so we chanted, laughed, swayed and played until the sun started sinking low. Then, bowing and giggling, we blessed each other farewell. As the children left, the sacred grounds took on another dimension. Thousands of oil lamps bathed the temple in golden light and the chanting of Buddhist prayers began to fill the air, emanating, echoing in every direction. And watching over it all sat the giant gilded stone Buddha, shining with an aura of great serenity.

The following day I returned to Saranath, the ruins of the great stupa[1] that honoured Buddha. It was there that the discourses had been uttered to the seekers of truth, under the Bodhi Tree.

---

[1] A large structure of worship most often a place where the burial remains of Lamas or Masters were stored.

How wondrous it felt to once again be in this place. How strange that the mind could perceive a gap, called a passage of time, over 2,500 years, when the conscious presence knew no time. I looked in amazement at the paradox – this place was different, yet the same.

I sat down quietly in lotus posture. It was as if the place were once again mine. Not another person was in sight. It was all me, my Self, in the blades of grass, the great stone walls, the gentle breeze, the swaying leaves. As I watched, I felt. As I felt I saw. There, within the play of the flux of life, that which appeared as constant change, was the formless ground of all creation, still, empty, unchanged. This ... always this. And so I knew of this Self, that which did not come or go, that which always remained, the eternal presence of now.

I closed my eyes and dissolved into eternal stillness. Life's force echoed infinitely in me. I followed it in ... and in ... and in. Not a thing remained outside of me. And, in the bliss of knowing Self as all, came the shower. The showering that had already fallen. The showering that would fall again and again ... for those with eyes to see, with ears to hear and a heart to feel.

A great raining of golden Bodhi leaves fell upon me, in me, all around me, until I myself was falling upon me. And so I fell, I danced, freely. Falling, showering, illumined being ... golden Bodhi leaves followed by golden teardrops.

Then, there upon the ground, I saw a perfect seed. It was as if it had waited there patiently for this moment ... waiting for these tears, waiting for this showering. It glistened, glowing wet. It shimmered and seemed to shake from deep within. Then it split – revealing a bright green shoot. I sat blinking, staring in awe. I saw it as a sign, a message of the perfect unfolding of every moment. I had fulfilled what I had come for.

I looked down. In my lap lay a perfect golden Bodhi leaf. And so I placed it in my book and stood, knowing I was carrying a leaf of the past, which blessed the present, and in which the future would flourish. All were one, the same, in the endless generosity of life.

The pilgrimage continued. I spent my hours and days in the sacred places until I felt the calling to travel north again to Nepal.

By the time I reached Kathmandu there was nothing extraordinary about the coming and going of so many deeply moving moments. I realised that everything remained essentially normal. There was nothing inherently great or small about my sense of self, being the journey that I was. In fact it was all incredibly ordinary. I could see how, despite the uniqueness and rarity of such experiences, I was still simply *being;* as was everything else. I felt enormous gratitude for such simplicity. How magnificent and grand it was to be freed from the idea of something being important *or* insignificant. What joy to feel the greatness of life without claiming it as my own personality.

I stood in the square of Kathmandu watching all the people coming and going. The village centre was a constant buzz of activity: trading, shopping, and children playing. People were praying, sweeping, chanting and greeting. All was a shuffling of bodies, colours and swirling dust amongst ancient buildings, stalls, temples and the occasional new, western style shop. I could see how, in truth, underneath the scurrying mind, we are all essentially the same beautiful quality – no-ego, simple greatness. How sweet and innocent life really is, I thought. Beneath the masks of fear and arrogance, life remains the same, a shuffling of God particles in a dance of creative manifestation upon a vast, endless canvas of stillness.

My thoughts were suddenly broken as a man and woman approached and stood in front of me. They stared soulfully. Their eyes implored, filled with hope and thanksgiving. Suddenly the woman bent forward, touched my knees then dropped to hers and put her head on my feet. She wept. Her body shook. From the vastness of being, I felt my love enfold her. It was like a mother for a child; like a child for a mother; like a lover for the beloved; like a beloved for the lover. Aching, quaking, deeper than deep, higher than high, this was love reaching love in the stillness of one all-pervasive point. She lifted her head, her hands in prayer and smiled through her tears. Her eyes shone. It was the same love. And so, what could

I do but bow too – bow to the feet of my child, my mother, my lover, my Beloved, my Self.

Then, there we sat, kneeling to each other and laughing. When the moment came for us to stand, her husband reached out his hands. Gently he took our elbows. Then, embracing his wife, he looked deeply into my eyes. It was as if his tension had completely melted. His face was soft like a young boy.

'Thank you,' he whispered.

And silently we farewelled each other.

I made my way to the prayer house, a central temple with giant prayer wheels lining each wall. I moved around it, spinning each of the wheels as I chanted 'Om Mani Padme Hum:'[1] the eternal truth, the Jewel in the Lotus.

Then with a few supplies collected, I made my way to the outskirts of the village. There, the dusty streets were lined with simple mudbrick abodes. Each one was mostly a single room that housed an entire family. That meant mum, dad, the children, the chickens, goats and cows! As I wandered along the street, children waved and women smiled.

The air was hot and dusty. The path began to narrow as it wound its way up the side of the valley. Even though the path was remote, the long ascent was always full of interesting events. An occasional farmer would pass by with a goat in tow; boys would laugh and tease each other, chasing up and down the hillside; and aged women would pass me bearing great basket loads of supplies strapped to their heads and backs.

And there was also the breeze that stirred the old spirit-tree. Every time I neared it, it would seem to come to life. I would stop at the shrine resting between its great roots, dedicated to the guardian nature spirits. I wondered how many people who passed actually saw the spirits or recognised the reality of the connection of the nature-spirits in our lives.

---

[1] The eternal conscious sound and presence that remains central to existence.

As I stood contemplating I looked up at the tree's great, outstretched limbs. There, moving in the breeze, they seemed to bend and lower as if in an attempt to embrace me. And so I stood my body closer, leaned up against its trunk and stretched my arms around it in a hug. I felt the unmistakable response of a high vibration moving into me. It was an unquestionable moment of communion. I stepped back and looked up again giving thanks for the blessing.

As I turned around I saw a villager standing to the side of the path looking close to terrified. It seemed to confirm the superstition that the spirit living under this tree should be feared and respected, mostly from a distance. He stood there staring, fixed to the spot – perhaps in disbelief and bewilderment that a western woman, turned Buddhist nun, could behave in such an unexpected manner. Only his head turned, holding me in a gaze of utter disbelief, as I made my way up the path again. I was back up at the monastery by mid-afternoon and gratefully took to my room for silent meditation.

The days passed, filled with prayer, chanting, rituals, meditation and spiritual discourses. I felt myself entering more and more deeply into the gaps that dissolved the boundaries of body, mind and spirit. Lama started asking more questions and sending people to see me for what he called scrying: the skill of prophecy and clairvoyance. The news also spread of my healing abilities and before long I was being taken to give consultation and healing to lamas.

Then came my time to ask the question that I wanted fulfilled. I wanted to take the next stage of initiation and full ordination. I trusted Lama to hold the space for me to walk through that doorway.

But his answer came as a surprise. He didn't think he should do it.

'I think you must now see the Dalai Lama. His Holiness is waiting for you. He will ordain you.'

'But ...' my re-questioning was stopped definitively by Lama. He insisted this was the right way and the right time, and that I should prepare to leave for Dharamsala by the end of the month. I had ten days to go.

The 8th Attainment

The body is governed by the soul, not the mind.

Through the journey of entering through the body and surrendering even more deeply into my inner self, I found my life was being profoundly carried by a greater power.

The journey of spirit is not exclusively linear or sequential. It is spatial, instant and eternal.

KEY 8.

The Serpent

KEY 8.

The Serpent

To renounce the ego, the darkness of our mind, requires strength. Yet to embrace our Divinity and accept it requires even greater strength. It requires us to reach into our inherent power, our Kundalini. Like a snake we must shed old patterns to keep growing.

From our struggles we consolidate our true power. From the darkest folds and the greatest pressures of earth, brilliant diamonds are born.

21. *Initiation and Ordination*

Seek the wisdom that will untie your knot,
Seek the path that demands your whole being.

Rumi

The bus made its way up the mountain pass. I looked out in amazement as we passed by great forests of eucalyptus trees. The scenery took on an uncanny resemblance to parts of Australia until I spotted long pastures of marijuana. At first I was surprised, then I remembered reports of these fields carrying crops of a strain that contained very little or no THC – the ingredient required for the intoxicant effect. The plants in these pastures were probably destined for rope factories. I couldn't help but chuckle at the thought of naive and excited travellers making their way to the plots, on a quest for an altered state that would end up as nothing more than a headache.

Before long we were in a vastly different atmosphere. The bus careered up the narrow winding road, driven by a madman who seemed totally unwilling to move for any oncoming traffic – until the last moment, when he would suddenly swerve, spinning the tyres dangerously close to the cliff's edge. I shuddered as I wondered how many buses had plunged on a death ride into that deep valley's crevices.

At my designated drop-off point I stepped out, with great relief, into the thin air of clear blue skies above. As I strolled amongst the fir trees, shadows danced with the light around me. I took a path leading up the side of the mountain, past a quaint church that sat in solemn, silent solitude among great forests of deodar and oak trees. I was to make my way to Tushita first and then to a little hut nestled on the side of the mountain at the top of Himachal Pradesh. Lama would be arriving also within days. Once all duties were fulfilled for the initiation, we were set to go into retreat for three months of solitude, silence, meditation and practices. I would be by myself, in a hut high up on the mountain; Lama, by himself, would be in his 'spring retreat' home below me.

Not long after Lama arrived, he called for me.

I sat down quietly on the ground next to his chair. There seemed to be a different air of energy surrounding him. It was deep and sombre. I sat quietly, waiting.

Then he spoke softly, but with great emphasis.

'It is best you go to see His Holiness before ordination. He wishes to see you privately. A time is arranged for you tomorrow. Follow the pilgrimage and then wait for the blessings at the gate to finish. You will be ushered into the grounds.'

My stomach turned upside down. I wondered if I had done something wrong. Yet my heart pounded with a sense of joy.

'Why?' I asked.

'It is time,' said Lama.

I knew that meant there was nothing more to ask and that I would have to find out in the event.

So in the morning I made my way across the valley to the great pass that led to the McLeod Ganj, home of His Holiness. A stream of Tibetan pilgrims lined the road beneath long strings of prayer flags alive in the crisp mountain air. From a distance it looked like a great snake slowly winding up the mountain. They walked, prostrated and chanted, spinning prayer wheels and counting malas. The great line swayed and curved all the way up to the palace gates. As we neared I could see the shaved head of the Dalai Lama bowing to each passing pilgrim.

Then as the line snaked again, I realised I was actually only about fifteen metres away from this great man, who is revered world-wide for his dedication to spiritual truth and to non-violence, even in the face of those who had expelled him from his own country. I stared in wonderment. I felt such deep love, respect and honour for this man and could only pray that I might be able to serve humanity in even a shadow of such immensity.

In that instant he looked up and directly across to me. He looked straight into my eyes and smiled. His face lit up and he nodded at me. In that penetrating moment I felt an acknowledgment. It was as if he already knew me and I knew him. Then he chuckled, nodded again and went back to his blessings. Within moments, the Tibetans in front of me were being touched by the Dalai Lama.

And then there I was, right in front of him. I bowed, put my hands in prayer mudra and then looked in his eyes. It was a moment of eternity. Then he bowed too, and took my hands and put his forehead to mine. The vibration[1] that moved through my body was profound. In fact, it stayed with me for about a week. I stepped on. Even if that was to be my whole meeting it was more than I could have imagined. But it wasn't. I was ushered to the side and asked to wait for an hour.

I watched, filled with wonder, filled with peace – and immeasurably moved. An endless river of pilgrims flowed past the gates; all in the dedication of love, compassion, prayer, gratitude and above all, faith. I watched the trail of people with fascination, taking in their distinctive Tibetan features. Their golden-brown skin, leathery and wrinkled from the harshness of their environment. Their twinkling eyes, evidence of warm, innocent, embracing hearts. Their soiled hands and faces, the signs of frugal measures and meagre basic supplies. Their bright beads of coral, silver and turquoise, standing out against the simple black yak wool garments: a display of beauty, elegance and pride. I was so engrossed in the encounter that I lost the sense of my own purpose in being there.

Yet soon I was approached by one of the palace assistants. My attention was immediately caught again. His Holiness had disappeared, but the crowd continued to wait with dedicated

---

[1] I later came to understand this powerful energy was a transmission – a shaktipat – which is a pure current of Divine energy capable of blessing, healing and awakening the consciousness.

patience. Some of them had travelled hundreds of miles to visit their leader – the incarnate Buddha. It meant nothing for them to wait a few more hours now while His Holiness attended to other matters. I felt a rush of nervous hesitation swirling up through my stomach as I recalled my own purpose for waiting. I shuffled my feet to compose my self; I threw my hands behind my back to lift my shoulders and prepared myself for whatever would happen next.

The small man in black pants ushered me towards the gates where he exchanged a few words with the guards and another man and then motioned for me to follow. I was led through a great open temple watched over by a giant statue, and then down a hall and into a room. There on a lounge sat His Holiness, The Dalai Lama. I was surprised by the simplicity of the room and the normality of what seemed a very informal introduction. I bowed, feeling overwhelmed with respect and bewilderment as to why I was sitting there, by myself with His Holiness. He chuckled.

'Ani' he said.

I didn't look up.

He chuckled again.

'Anila' he said with respect, calling me a nun.

I looked up.

'So, Thubten Dekyila ... Ocean of Bliss ... mmm.'

He played with my name: 'Awake in the Ocean of Bliss. Is that your name?'

'Well, it's a name,' I said.

He seemed amused at my answer.

'So, what do you want?' he asked.

'Nothing,' I said.

'Nothing?' he asked with an amused glint in his eyes.

'No, I don't want anything,' I repeated. 'I'd just like to serve as best I can. I mean really serve, not my ego's idea, just pure service of being.' I said.

'So you can heal, can you?' he asked.

'Well, sometimes, when I touch points on the body, healing happens.'

I said. 'But I don't know if "I" heal.'

'But you are the one who touches and then the patient's body is better, aren't you?' he persisted.

'I suppose so. I mean ... well, yes, I'm present.'

'So please show me,' he said with a gentle smile.

'You?' I was shocked.

'Yes please.' He spoke definitely. 'Why not me? You were sent to the other lamas, weren't you? And you help the people in the streets ...?'

'Yes, but ...' I stammered. I was stunned at his matter-of-factness, his human to human air of sharing.

'But what?' His eyes penetrated me. 'You want to serve, don't you?' His voice had become firm.

I nodded.

'Without your ego?'

I nodded again. I gazed at his smiling, penetrating eyes. Then, without a spoken word I heard him 'speak' directly to my soul.

'Then you must be willing to see that you are good enough to help even the one you thought was most above you, as much as you are willing to stay behind for the ones whom others told you were behind you. You see them as equal. Now you must see yourself as equal.'

I looked down at my hands in my lap.

These words struck deeply at a tight knot in my mind. I wasn't sure I was good enough. But then, I thought, if I am not, how can I really serve as I wish? I felt a deep twisting grip. I struggled to find my inner strength. The knot was being pulled. He was right. I knew it deep in my soul. The knot had to be undone. I had to embrace my own inner greatness if I was to serve for the greatness in others. If I could do that in the presence of the Dalai Lama, then I could do it in the presence of anyone.

So, drawing in a deep breath, I prayed for only truth and love to flow in my touch. Then, with a sigh, I stood up and stepped towards His Holiness.

I started by looking at his eyes and ears. I could tell a lot about the body's energies by observing certain signs and qualities.

'You are going to have a good strong, long life,' I said, 'but you could eat less salt and your liver could be clearer. You carry a lot of energy for your people.'

I touched points along his arms, shoulders, neck and ears. I could feel a strong surge of energy moving though my body and hands. It was powerful and grounding. His body seemed to soften and ease into deep relaxation.

He breathed with a sigh and I sat down again.

'Ahh ... very good,' he said nodding. 'Thank you.'

There was a silent pause for a few moments then he touched me lightly on the head and said,

'Tomorrow you come to the Nagoya Gompa and I will initiate you and give you ordination.'

'Thank you,' I said, bowing deeply.

Then the door opened as if on some psychic cue and I was ushered to the front gate.

The next day at the gompa I was stunned to find myself amongst a group of about a hundred and fifty young Tibetan and Nepalese women who were also attending for the initiation and ordination. It was February 29, 1988, a leap year. I wondered what significance it had. Perhaps it was auspicious, a mark of a rare opportunity. Or maybe it was going to become something almost unreal?

We filed into the court room and took up our position with sitting space only.

The vows were preceded by mantras and offerings of initiation. It all happened so quickly and before I knew it I was handed another name, this time on a piece of paper: *Tenzin Norzin.*

It was tradition to be given another name from the lama who was ordaining. I found out later that it meant Tathagata Wisdom.[1] As much as it represented some aspect of my soul's expression, I couldn't help but chuckle at myself over this chameleon trait that seemed to pop

---

[1] The wisdom of an Enlightened One.

up with new names as I changed the colours of my life. Some women are renowned for the number of shoes in their closet. Mine would have to be the name file.

From a very young age the name Kathryn didn't feel right to me. Its sound and vibration felt in discord to my soul – like I was a round peg that some wanted to put in a square hole. It wasn't that I didn't like the name itself (which meant 'pure one', followed by Rae, as in of light), it was just that I felt it wasn't really mine. This had been very challenging for my parents, especially my father. I could see it was natural that he felt that this was a rejection of them, an insult as they had chosen my name. But it wasn't about a lack of appreciation or acceptance of them. It was something beyond them, beyond this world.

Over the years, I tried on different hats just as others threw a few at me too. Kathy, Kate, Katie, Gypsy, the gazelle, Bo, Katja, Thubten Dekyil, Tenzin Norzin ...

To me it was a bit of a game, a bit of fun – like being on a stage and changing costumes while remaining the same being. And, I knew that none of these were really the right vibration or whole reflection of the being I am. It was as if I was still being dressed in this world, by this world, and yet I was so rapidly casting off the 'flesh' of this world, that it was like trying to tell a blossom its name was still a seed.

My thoughts returned to the palace and the name I had just been handed. Of course we weren't obliged to take on the name but could equally receive it as an inner name. For the moment I was happy with Thubten Dekyil. I left the palace and made my way back across the valley. I felt strangely different, yet the same.

I could see through a lens of awareness, like a moviegoer, watching it all as if it were happening yet less real.

Over the following week I attended daily discourses presented by His Holiness. I cried at the depth of Truth that moved me beyond question. The simplicity of his words seemed to wrap up everything that was complex about life and put it into a meaning that was so clear, so simple, and so profound. 'Human desires are endless. It is like the thirst of a man who drinks salt water, he gets no satisfaction and his thirst is only increased.'

I knew it as my own truth. It is the Truth that lives free of time and place but gives all time and place its real purpose. Beyond all the distractions of desires is the endless river of life itself: free of mortality, free of attachment, free of suffering. It is in that awareness, which is the destiny of all, that the drop is consumed by the infinite ocean.

I cried for the release of whatever remained hidden in me – pockets of fear, doubt, remorse and coldness remained in me towards life. A fire burned deep inside me. It seemed the more I let go of the heaviness, the dampness of all those tears of grief, the more the fire within raged. This fire was raging with determination, raging with dedication, raging with surrender to the Divine, and raging with willingness to be of service. It seemed there was nothing more essential than to be consumed completely in Divine Awareness.

•

As I wandered back across the valley to my hut I took in the environment. There seemed to be a whole new quality to life, as if suddenly there were even more dimensions to see, to feel, to hear, to breathe. The landscape swirled out around me like a scintillating soup of light vibrations. Every pebble was like a mountain and every mountain like a pebble, the self so miniscule in an infinite scape, the Self of all so vast and all within it so transient, a passing slipstream dream.

Then, in the middle of the rhododendron forest, I stopped – still. I had completely forgotten myself, what I was there for. I had forgotten the 'quest', the search for freedom or enlightenment. I was just *being*. I was suddenly in an all-pervading space of utter stillness and immobility. It was the presence of eternity. And within this stillness, this silence, this essence of my real being, was the peaceful, unobstructed flow of life dancing, moving and singing. I saw the perfection in it all. Free of judgments, free of mind, life was simply being. There, in the middle of the forest, nature had revealed my true nature, life's true nature.

For the first time I was able to comprehend with lucid awareness what I had always experienced, what I had always known, but somehow could not touch even with a single thought. Suddenly I saw the boundary between mind, awareness and experiencing dissolve. The scene before me was a dance of effulgent light particles ... the smallest, most irreducible points of love, of creation. I saw that they are the very bridging moment between the formless infinite eternal life potential and the ecstatic display of love in action ... the manifestation of life in form ... its patterns a constant unmistakable reshaping, the working of Divinity itself.

Then a perfect rainbow appeared above the treetops. It reached from the beyond, and above it danced the radiant light-body of a great ornate Buddha. His body radiated rainbow light and his third eye looked right into me. In his right hand was a flaming sword and in his left an open book of pages that scattered golden words in every direction. The symbols flew out touching every corner of my consciousness and I suddenly realised they were all inside of me, inside of awareness and in all of life. They were a divine gift within life to be given to all of life.

This Buddha was Manjushri, the sign of awakened wisdom. It is this wisdom that is honoured and symbolised by the vajra, the ceremonial instrument that was held by the right hand of Buddha.

After all the prayers, holding the vajra to my heart, asking that I see only with the eye of conscious wisdom, there I was, being shown it from above, that it is in life itself, in the light, in the dark, in the leaves, in the trees, in every breath of life – wisdom is all around.

I fell on my back to the ground and shook with joyous laughter and gratitude. And as I laughed I felt the earth and the trees, the flowers and the sky laughing with me. Then suddenly above my head, monkeys had flocked to the branches and their great chattering turned to echoing screams of laughter. And in the treetops, the birds called. I felt as if I was with everything and everything was with me.

'Yes!' I sang out. 'Yes. Yes. Yes!'

When I returned to my room I went straight to my altar. My eyes took in the simple beauty of my small, one-roomed hut. The earthen walls steadily and consistently leached their damp, earthy smell into the air. I breathed it in like incense smoke. Golden light shone through the solitary window and the sound of an afternoon breeze whistled softly upon the pane. The wooden bed rested sturdily next to the wall, my only place of warmth. A few photos, candles and ceremonial instruments sat on a little ledge – my things of prayer, devotion and beauty. I picked up the dorje and vajra:[1] the bell and thunderbolt. I stared at them ... objects: symbols of compassion and wisdom. They represented the play of formless and form, the unity of which was said to equal enlightenment. In a fleeting, all-pervading instant I saw the truth that these symbols reduced the eyes' vision to the objects – a view of duality. These symbols were only a reminder of the truth within us and all around us. Life itself is the play of wisdom and compassion. It is in every living thing. Life is itself, form and formlessness, revealed in every moment!

The following day I felt raw and sensitive. I was fascinated by the degree of shifts in my being. As the layers of mind's illusions fell away, the brilliance of Truth was revealed and, in the settling, I would move deeper to another layer, waiting for it, in turn, to be brought to the light.

As I sat amongst the crowds in the Tsuglagkhang Temple, the Dalai Lama's voice seemed to drown into a soup as my body-mind field began to dissolve. I broke into tears. My body ached. It felt like I was being taken to the last grain of my strength and that somehow in order to gain my true power I had to be stripped bare of my false strength. The facade was falling apart. My head pounded, heavy, dark and deep in some twisted corner of a knot. My emotions quaked. I felt like a puddle of mental madness reduced to blithering mush. My devious mind darted to and fro scurrying like a creature trying to save itself in a hideout. Paradoxically, in the middle of it all was the presence of self-awareness, untouched, amused, clear and witnessing.

---

[1] Ritual instrument and emblem of power and penetrating wisdom.

The tears poured until my nose also began to pour. The people around me seemed to be getting agitated. But there was nothing I could do. The moment had come. I was unplugged. The body, mind and emotions were no longer under my ego's control. So all I could do was pull my robe over my head and give myself to my own private meltdown in the middle of a temple filled with people.

Then the tears stopped. The downpour ceased. I sat still, engulfed in a silence that not a thing of this world could touch.

I left the gompa feeling like a child, like I was just beginning life, like I was an open page ready to be written anew.

I made my way back across the valley. As I was making my way up the mountain pass I could hear the tromp, tromp of footsteps. They were strong, heavy, determined and steadfast. Not too many people took this route except the locals, so I figured it was a villager with a load, eager to get over the pass.

I breathed in the clear, crisp, blue atmosphere. To the left of me the forest stretched up, deep, dark and cool. The birds sang in sweet lilting melodies – and the footsteps came ever closer. They were catching up behind me and almost at my heels. I sensed the person was actually making an approach to me and so I turned to look. Then there, right beside me, was a sturdy, well-built American man.

'Hey,' he said. 'How you doin'?'

I looked at him with surprise.

'Hello,' I responded. 'I'm good, how about you?'

'Yeah, good,' he said.

I looked at him intently. His face seemed incredibly familiar.

'Don't I know you from somewhere?' I queried.

He grinned and shrugged his shoulders.

'Were you at the talks – the Dalai Lama's?' he asked.

'Mmm,' I replied.

'Yeah, me too. Isn't it fantastic!'

'Profound,' I stated. Then I looked at him again, puzzled, trying to place his face.

'Are you sure I don't know you? Haven't we met somewhere before?' I asked again.

Then just as he cocked his head on the side with a cheeky, wry grin, it hit me.

'Oh, oh my goodness …' I said with a shake of my head in a sense of embarrassed stupidity. 'You're Richard Gere.'

'Yep!' he said. 'I am.'

'Oh wow,' I responded, totally amazed that there I was walking up a remote mountain pass in the Himalayas and Richard Gere was walking alongside chatting with me. Hmm! I thought to myself, of all the funny things, the way our life weaves us together.

'What are you doing here?' I asked, totally curious.

'Well,' he said, 'I'm really interested in Buddhism. What about you, a young … Australian … woman?'

'Mmm … it's a long story. But right now I'm going back to my hut over there,' I pointed up the mountain, 'above Tushita. When the discourse is finished, I'll be going into retreat for three months.'

'Well,' he said with raised eyebrows, 'that's impressive.'

'It's not meant to impress,' I said.

The conversation took another turn as we continued responding to each other's curiosities. It eventuated in a goodbye and another memory of two familiar spirits meeting as passing ships.

The next day, when the finishing ceremony was complete, I made my way into the village to collect supplies for my ensuing retreat.

With my supplies well stocked and my commitment set, I closed the door to my hut and entered my private abode of silent solitude, ready for a three-month retreat.

I went over my schedule of practice:

4 am Meditation for an hour
5 am Mantras for an hour
6 am Pranayama, yoga, and one thousand full body prostrations for an hour

7 am Wash and breakfast
8 am Offerings and chants to invoke deity consciousness
9 am Prayers of illumination for all beings
10 am Meditation
11.30 am Stretching and breathing outside
12 pm Mantras with offerings and purification
1 pm Lunch, last meal
2 pm Chanting to the Deities
3 pm Purifying the field of body, mind and spirit
4 pm Breathing, pranayama
5 pm Stretch, walk
6 pm Mantras
7 pm Prayers
9 pm Meditation
1 am Rest

I set my determination to hold to my schedule every day. So, resolute, I entered a phase that took me deeper, higher, into blessedly blissful dimensions ... and into terror. Three weeks into retreat I suddenly hit another breaking point. The burning light of my inner awareness revealed a grave full of ghosts and demons, and some voice wanted to claim they were mine. They were lurking in the depths of my mind but no longer hidden. With the mechanistic blindfold of my mind pulled from its hinges there was nowhere left to hide.

I started screaming, horrified by what I saw. Blood-curdling murderous thoughts of self-hatred and disgust stormed through me on a demonic rampage. A hatred of the world and all its ugliness of greed, desires, shallow idols and delusions engulfed me. Terror struck at the thought that this was possibly my real self and all this spiritual bravery was just a delusional trick to keep myself well camouflaged.

And then came a disgust at my disgust. I leapt up in horror. What was I? What had become of me? Was I going insane? I threw myself outside, screaming, wailing and crying. It was as if I was no longer an individual anymore, but a screaming cauldron of demonic monsters. I threw myself onto the ground, onto my knees, beating my fists on the earth and my body, screaming for freedom, screaming for release.

I screamed and I cried. My body shook and convulsed uncontrollably. I ached with deep remorse and beat myself with my mind's disgust. 'Why?' I cried. 'Why?' I screamed. 'Why?' I hollered to the universe. I demanded to know why I should be so taunted by such delusions. I demanded that I be released to the power of Divinity. And still I cried. The great trail of life's conditions all seemed to be unravelling inside of me until I didn't even know if I, or it, was even me anymore. It seemed there was not even one real point upon which my mind could stand to make sense of any of it.

I cried and screamed for two weeks. I surrendered into the madness. And in that two weeks all I heard was the echo of madness resounding all around me in the great lonely void of life. There was no one to answer. No God with a light, no angel-cum-saviour, no one but my great pantheon of parading phantoms spewing forth endless torment.

Until suddenly, there was nothing left – nothing but silence, emptiness.

My mind went blank.

Blankness followed for a week. The body moved only when it had to. I was no longer I/me, only presence – void, an un-created presence. Whatever was before was demolished. It was probably now the dirt beneath my feet.

Then within the nothingness was a shimmering pulse of light – energy. It was a sharpness, a freshness, a clarity of consciousness, of presence. It was a strength I had never felt before – soft, sturdy, light and wholesome. A strength that I knew had somehow been lost in the hidden folds of my being. It was the very fabric of my soul.

The darkness of the ego had seemed so real, so black and foreboding. But it was the light at the end of it, that was real. In that reality I saw the inextinguishable Self that can never be snuffed out by any degree of the mind's darkness. Cloaking ourself in the ego's armour we fight our way through the darkness, trying desperately to escape the void of the unknown. We feel trapped, imprisoned, by the events of life. Yet in the moment of surrender, the moment of stopping in all that madness, we enter into stillness.

Be still and know that I AM God.[1]

In that stillness, in the depths of that darkness, is the place where we meet the eternal truth that our soul already knows. That is the diamond. The diamond awareness. The Jewel in the Lotus.[2]

I opened my eyes and looked at my surroundings. Everything was still, but moving. I could see and feel the unchanged, all-pervading life source – and within it everything moved, no longer a labelled, fixed reality but a dancing play of life's cosmic flux. Then my awareness became a focused point of concentration. I sat in alert presence of existence, dissolved yet all-present in the timeless point of now. I sat still, unmoved. Days rolled into nights within pure, one-pointed now-being.

•

Two weeks later, I was chanting again.

Aaauummm Aaahhhhhhh Huuunngggg ... Each sound vibrated long and deep. As the sound resonated through me, I became the audience listening. Then, right in the middle of an Aaahh, it struck me that I was listening to the same pulse that vibrated through every being.

During the period of my release there had been one consistent sound making its way from deep inside, like a primordial chord that strummed, wending through all of time, connecting every person on the planet. And it was a sound that was integral to so many mantras.

AH. It is a sound that every human makes. AH when we cry, AH HA HAAAH when we laugh, AH when we sigh, AAAAHHHHH when we scream, AHHH when we orgasm, AH when we understand.

---

[1] Psalm 46:10

[2] This is the translation of the Tibetan chant: Aum Mani Padme Hum.

It is a sound that transcends language and washes away our differences. AH comes from the forgotten space of our sameness.

The more I became absorbed in this universal sound, the wider the gaps became between the words and thoughts. And I began to realise that the space between the sound and thoughts was so vast and all encompassing. When I rested in that space, everything made sense. There was nothing to ask, nothing to answer, nothing to name, nothing to own. Everything was simply the perfect presence of creation, requiring nothing more.

•

I had lost any certain sense of time until I found my little clock under my robes, displaying the date. Six weeks had passed. My supplies were getting low. I looked at the sky. It was still clear. I conceded the aptness of a trip to the village the following day.

The morning air was sharp, clear and fresh as I stepped outside. I went to collect my water from the spring in the little cliff face at the back of my hut. It was crystal clear and icy cold. The water certainly woke my senses up. In fact it was so cold that my fingers had started to crack around the tips, yet somehow I managed to endure and adapt to the harshness of the environment.

I washed, ate a small bowl of rice, then put on my jumper, coat and backpack ready to make my way down the mountain to the valley. I was looking forward to some fresh vegetables and fruit again.

Once down the mountain pass I took the road past the Tibetan library. The view further along opened out into a sprawling splendour: the Kangra, a vast valley of rolling tree-clad hills, all tinkling with golden leaves like shimmering coins. I finally reached Dharamkot, a quaint little village set out like a square mandala of shops and stalls around a central temple, a shrine of Buddhist prayer.

Large prayer wheels lined each side. I made my way straight to it and began to walk clockwise whilst spinning each wheel and offering my prayers and blessings to the villagers. Then I continued on to the left, ambling my way slowly from stall to stall, collecting fresh produce, stopping for a hot lemon ginger tea, collecting candles and incense and handing out a few rupees to beggars. By the time I had made my way around to the opposite side of the stalls, it had just turned three o'clock. The sun was still warm and the air was light and bright.

Then from the distance I heard a deep rumble. I felt a presence of energy approaching fast. I turned around to see, coming from behind me, a billowing sky full of grey-black clouds, rushing towards the village. A wind lashed in, whipping up from the valley, speeding the ominous clouds towards the village.

The sleepy village suddenly leapt into a scurrying frenzy of bells ringing, shopkeepers calling out, doors sliding and slamming and shops being shut up tight. As if set to fast-forward, the whole village closed up before my eyes. I looked around me. There was nowhere left for shelter and I figured I needed to get back to my hut before dark. So I decided to make a brisk trek back up the mountain. I felt a little concerned, as it was usually about a good hour and a half's walk at a fast pace. Just as I watched that thought pass, the sun was engulfed by the clouds.

The scene was transformed in an instant from the brightness of the middle of the day to a darkness that was like night. I shivered. I went to put on my jumper but discovered that it had disappeared. Hmm. I thought to myself, someone must have needed it more than me. I imagined some skinny brown body now nicely snuggled up in my beautiful soft, red woollen jumper and smiled. Just the thought of another's comfort nourished me deep inside. Luckily, my coat was still there; at least it might keep me dry, if not warm. Without a second thought, I started striding quickly.

I was not far up the mountain when the clouds completely engulfed the valley. Heralded by a frightening clap of thunder, they broke open. The rain poured down in a great torrent. It rained so hard that in a matter of minutes the mountain pass was rapidly becoming a river. Thunder boomed and growled. It felt like I was about to be swallowed up. But I pressed on.

Then there was a giant CRACK! I jumped, startled. A bolt of

lightning struck a tree only three metres away from me. I stopped in my tracks. Another bolt flashed down up ahead. I looked around me for shelter. I couldn't see anything protective in the immediate surroundings but I could just make out what looked like a cluster of rocks about twenty feet away. An unexpected lull descended. The rain slowed down, only to be whipped a moment later into slicing sheets of icy wind and a barrage of hail. I couldn't believe it – I was being pelted by rocks of hail the size of golf balls! I started running almost blindly, stumbling frantically, praying for shelter.

I finally noticed a rocky ledge jutting out with just enough space for me to crouch under it. I huddled next to my backpack, trying to block the wind and hail as much as possible. My body began shivering profusely, my lower half drenched, my shaved head feeling vulnerably cold.

I stared out into the darkness in disbelief. Only an hour ago it was a bright sunny day. Now bolts of lightning were cracking, jagged chords of blue-white electricity were all around. Hail pummelled the trees, rocks and ground with the noise of a thousand mad drummers. Water gushed in streams down the slopes, carrying rocks and pebbles with it. I was inside the storm, completely engulfed.

I sat under the ledge, shivering, hugging my knees, waiting. The hail finally ceased, then more rain poured down and the storm continued noisily. Just when I was beginning to think I might be there all night, the rain finally slowed down. It withdrew into a fine thick mist. The last of the giant drops were falling from the drenched forest canopy. An eerie lull fell upon the mountain, broken by the sporadic rhythm of ploink! plop plip ... drip, drip, drip, as the last drops fell into swollen pools and puddles of water.

I breathed in the cold damp air. It was so fresh, clean and full of the forest's ionic vapours that it filled me with a sense of sweet, drunken nourishment. I smiled, amazed at the symphony of the experience. I wondered whether it might be safe now to move on again. Then, just as I looked out through the fine drizzling mist, a wolf suddenly appeared. It stood between two trees shrouded in mist.

I wasn't sure if it was an apparition or real. Nonetheless, it was there before me.

It looked into me with a deep, intelligent presence and, as it tilted its head, I telepathically heard it saying:

'You are safe to go now. I am watching over you.'

Its deep voice touched my inner awareness gently. As I nodded with loving acknowledgment, he lowered his head, then turned and disappeared into the mist.

I climbed out from under my shelter, rising up with a big stretch. As I went to put my backpack on, I realised my fingers and toes had gone numb. So I clapped my hands and stamped my feet vigorously and marched on. Once back at my hut I turned on my little kerosene burner to make tea and warm my hands. I changed my clothing, putting on every layer I could find, then wrapped myself in my sleeping bag. And still I shivered.

By the time morning came I felt more normal again but I noticed my body struggled to regain warmth. I found myself being challenged to attain strength in more ways than one. As I stepped outside I realised the atmosphere was considerably colder than it had been. The mountain peaks on the next ridge were covered with snow. It felt like a cold spell was settling in. My resources were low and my mind quickly recognised a desired escape route. I noticed how the mind thought it far easier to run when challenged than to find the source of strength that reveals a solution.

Later in the morning I changed my focused, steady breathing to bhastrika pranayam[1] in an effort to regain body warmth. I felt somewhat disconcerted at my novice attempt, recognising a lack of confidence in my ability to achieve much. I had heard of great yogis whose powers of inner-heat were put to the test in extremely rigorous conditions. They would sit on the ice with a wet sheet around them until the sheet would dry and the ice had melted in a metre radius around their body! Nonetheless, despite my uncertainty, I was up to

---

1 Bellow breathing: the practice of rhythmical breathing that stimulates internal fire.

the challenge.

I was quite surprised to find the breathing worked. Heat began swirling through me, from the tip of my spine to the top of my head. Then it started trickling through my arms and legs until my hands were hot and my toes were warm.

After weeks of the intense breathing practice I realised how powerful such a simple thing as breath could be. The effect of the deep flow of oxygen and energy through the body is extraordinary. With this simple and normal physical function we can unleash dormant energy, release stagnant energy and emotions and access the formless state of our Self. Breath is literally the bridging current between spirit and form. Therefore the more regularly and deeply we breathe, the more vital we become and the greater our connection to our essential Self. I felt excited at the notion that it is accessible to every single person – we *all* breathe!

Over the following weeks I maintained a steady inner focus. Seeing clear skies again I decided to wash my robes. Well, the next morning it was interesting to find that my maroon cloths had frozen to slabs of ice! I stood there laughing, shaking my head in amused surprise.

Then, just ten minutes later, Lama's Tibetan Shih Tzu dogs came running up the mountain slope from his retreat down below. As they reached the plateau in front of my hut the shining scene turned into a comedy sketch. Their paws hit the flat landing that had turned to ice overnight and instantly they started slipping and sliding unstoppably, their little legs spinning rapidly, unable to wind back the momentum with which they had entered. And if that wasn't enough, they finally slid on their backsides to a sliding stop – thump, thump – one behind the other, straight into my front step. But it did nothing to dampen their spirits. They leapt straight up onto the veranda, shaking and waggling their tails and bodies, greeting me with unbounded joy!

After their surprise visit, I was left by myself again in silent solitude.

The 9th Attainment

I was relieved to discover that strength does not require effort. On the contrary it is when we give up our struggle, when we accept our position that we are able to unite with the deeper presence of strength within. The vulnerability in this surrendering is the hinge on the gate to our true power. When we stop focusing on the product and give our full presence to the process of creation we discover a deeper dimension of strength – faith.

Reunited with this strength I felt ready to meet my destiny.

KEY 9.

The Fire Spirit

KEY 9.

The Fire Spirit

She holds the fire stick for all to see. She is one who carries the light of consciousness; the message of the fire within.

The light and love we seek outside ourself is not on the road ahead of us but in the presence deep within us.

The one who appears as the guide on our road is but the mirror for the light within. She is a crone bearing a lamp in the darkness.

The light-bearer cannot avoid her role.

22. *Truth's Command*

It is only by forgetting yourself that you draw near to God.

Henry David Thoreau

The days and nights passed, one into each other. In the deepening of one-pointedness, all perceptions of form and sound settled again into the unmanifest. There, in that stillness, arose a hearing of all sounds as they really are.

As I entered deeper, the sounds merged with the inky void of silence. Then suddenly and spontaneously, the field of expansive awareness was filled with a great sonorous roar. It was as if the forces of the entire cosmos were rushing and roaring through my whole being, so that I was the cosmos in everything in every direction.

It was not the first time I had experienced this sound. I had encountered it many times in my youthful days of meditation. But then it had been a more localised perception – the experience of the infinite was relative to my form or to an object. The cosmic Self was on the inside whilst being perceived everywhere outside, from event to event.

In this passage the experience of the infinite cosmos, everything of creation and every aspect of being had converged into the one whole Self as a simultaneous experience of the infinite ... everything occurring in the same moment, as everything, everywhere, always ... eternally.

In moments my consciousness would be consumed in a pervading humming and buzzing; in other moments, like an infinite ecstatic vibration of all life, like the sound of a thousand million bees vibrating every particle. Its pulse would accelerate so potently that it would be almost unbearable. It was unspeakably ecstatic. Then in a given moment, it would suddenly ascend into the vast sweeping of celestial winds like a thousand million angels singing and whispering. The Self was the consuming breath of all creation, breathing as all existence in everything, everywhere, infinitely. Simultaneously, all was hanging in the instant of one immortal moment where the in and the out breath were but one.

Then in yet other moments, the cosmic AUM of all creation would rise to carry me again from the all-pervading sound of life into the source ... silence.

Over those days, wherein past, present and future were lived in the eternal moment, I saw and realised the blueprints of all creation: the undivided sound vibrations underlying all phenomena and objects alike, remaining and sustaining as the unending natural law.

What I saw and experienced as 'That/This' was more real than any experience of waking or dreaming yet remains impossible to convey or define in words alone.

In this ongoing stream of exalted consciousness, all awareness and perception was filled with the supernal beauty and radiance of all life dancing in joy and love.

In the final two weeks I maintained an awakened conscious presence in a constant stream. Day turned into night turned into day; every shade of light, every breath of wind, every drop of darkness hanging ... unfurled within the moment.

I also kept up my prayers, purifications, mantras, chanting and breathing until the last five days when all of a sudden I was called – moved – to move. I couldn't sit. I couldn't chant. I couldn't ignore the calling. I didn't know why or what it was, except that it was a magnetic force I could no longer resist.

I stepped outside, wrapped my thick robe around my shoulders, put on my boots and started to walk. I followed the path behind the hut.

It led up the mountain, past a little tin shelter; a place of meeting for the neighbouring mountain locals. To the left the rhododendron forest displayed its masses of bright pink flowers. I could hear the monkeys delighting, feasting on the sweet pink delicacies in the branches of these blossoming giants. To the right the path led into a forest of pines, tall and regal in their bearing. A gentle breeze stirred through their needles, sending waves of a distinctive whispering song to my ears.

After a while I broke out of the forest into an open glade studded with flowers; bright yellow and white buttons, flung amongst the stunningly lush grass. I noticed the remnants of an old ruin, what must have once been a residence of some sort. I sat in the middle of it enjoying the warm rays of sunlight on my face. I had just begun to dissolve and melt into the surroundings when again I felt the calling. It tugged at me even more deeply.

I stood up. I could hear a distant humming, rumbling sound. It seemed to be pulling me to walk further up the mountain, drawn by its calling from over the next ridge. I walked on as if it were a command I could only obey.

After some time I broke above the tree line into a scene of rock and shale. The next ridge seemed to loom closely, its snowy peaks glaring starkly in the thin atmosphere. The land looked arid and moon-like. The rumbling seemed to be even louder, and closer.

I started walking up the steep slope, slipping and struggling to keep a steady pace on the broken splints of shale, slithering upon the slate like a sliding treadmill. Still I was pulled. It was as if it were getting more powerful with every step. Suddenly, as I peaked the top of the ridge, the great rumbling sound was a roar that echoed, bouncing its way to my ears through the pass. At first I had wondered if it was an avalanche, and if some devious spirit had led me there in an attempt to dispose of me. But I could see no signs of moving snow anywhere.

Gripped with curiosity I made my way down the ridge and into the pass. The sound was consuming. Then as the pass took a turn it opened out into a small, tight valley – and there was a waterfall: roaring, tumbling, crashing into a lake.

The round body of water glistened under the vivid sky. I walked up to the water's edge. Flat, round polished stones disappeared into the depths. From crystal clarity the water gradually descended into greater and greater depths of turquoise, sapphire and emerald hues.

I sat down, my breath taken by the beauty. I had never seen anything so pure. Instant stillness engulfed me and flooded me simultaneously with exquisite vibrant energy. I breathed deeply, allowing myself to be fully touched by the whole field of the moment. I closed my eyes, letting the sound and the scents penetrate me. And the more deeply I welcomed the sound, the more deeply it carried me into the silent depths of the lake.

After some time I opened my eyes and blinked, almost in disbelief. It was as if I were in a dream. There, around the edges of the falling water, flying and dancing in the mist, were water spirits. Their light bodies sparkled and twinkled in a joyful laughing melody.

Then suddenly out of the mist of the waterfall appeared an old woman. A shining light. I blinked and rubbed my eyes, wondering if I was hallucinating. But as much as I blinked she stood there. Her long white hair fell in matted tassles over her shoulders, dropping all the way to her hands that hung at her sides. Her long woollen clothes hung loosely on her small frame, in shades of grey like the surrounding mountain scape. Bright piercing eyes looked out from her weathered face and from her chest a ray of light flashed, straight into my eyes.

I blinked with a startle and rubbed my eyes again. When I opened them she was suddenly there, sitting right in front of me.

I gasped.

She smiled.

Her eyes, so bright with ageless light, shone at me like silvery-blue planets, and upon her chest hung the crystal pendant from which the light must have reflected.

'Where did you come from?' I asked.

'Where I come from is of no importance,' she said. 'Where you are going is my concern.'

I looked at her intently, ready to listen.

'You are too attached to these spiritual places and things. Here, India, Buddhism, the robes,' she said, swaying her arms wide and nodding as if holding it all in front of her.

'All these things are just symbols of what you are. You didn't come here for them. You came to be reminded that you *are* the source and the light. *You* are a daughter of God, the Goddess that is Love, you are from the source of love, come to touch all through your embodiment of love. You are a gateway to limitless consciousness and you are here to guide those who seek to know it. You cannot do this in far-off places. The far-off places are fine without you. You have fulfilled your work here before and you have finished it now. You must go to where you are called. You have work to do.'

As she spoke I saw the vivid images of what she described. I saw my path in the West, amongst those who hungered for spirit, who prayed and called for an answer and who ached for freedom and love.

'But who am I to claim a thing so great?' I beseeched. I still felt plagued by doubt. Her eyes flashed at me.

'Who are you to deny what you are, a God-Being created to serve Love? How dare you deny the truth of the Divine?' she commanded with such authority. Her words whipped my pathetic little mind straight into the centre of Divine Will.

I sat straight upright, breathed in and closed my eyes.

'So then,' I spoke quietly, 'so be it.'

'It is so,' she affirmed.

And with that the old crone stood, bowed, turned and walked away, disappearing behind the pass. I lay back upon the flat stones beneath me and stared up into the vast blue expanse. I was empty. Void of comprehension of it all. Yet I was also filled – filled with a deep knowing: Truth.

Trust, I thought. All I can do is trust.

◈

My retreat finished and by the time I made my way back to my monastery room at Kopan, I had started to lose the sense of trust in my journey, and what all of this meant; and asking, most of all, was it truly real?

I ambled along in a daze, attending to the basics. The words of the old white-haired crone spun around and around in my mind and the inner knowing stirred deeply in the pit of my stomach. But what would Lama think and say? I thought to myself, and what about my vows? How can I go back now? I felt tugged and pulled, to and fro. My inner knowing pulled me unstoppably, but my mind resisted.

I tried asking for answers hoping I would get some contrary message. I went and sat on the cliff edge and looked out at the Himalayas. The sun was just setting and the sky was glowing pink and purple. The snow-capped peaks were flooded with colour – gold, coral, lavender and hot pink. Then, from behind them the moon began to rise, full and gigantic, glowing deep crimson. It slowly turned to a hot pink, then gradually metamorphosed its way through orange to peach to gold and silver until it hung like a brilliant white neon ball in the darkened purple sky.

I watched, mesmerised, for two hours. My questions had left me. That was, until I heard the echo of voices in the far-off distance again. I stared at the moon and cried.

I felt chords of fear working their way around a deep and powerful knowing. The fear of uncertainty was pushing against a rock of destiny. Was I capable? Was it really the truth? How could I truly serve such greatness for so many? Why couldn't I be where I loved to be? Was it just delusion that I felt my truth was a life of solitude? Then why did visions of children come to me? How could I fulfil anything when I was so uncertain of myself?

But the more I tried to grab at these fears – floating, passing mental mirages, the more the truth pulsed in my soul. Why then did a part of me try so hard to deny, to procrastinate, to annihilate a truth that was so destined it was unavoidable?

Why ...?

Thankfully, I understood the power of the Divine beyond my mind and so I surrendered again to Trust. All I could do was take one step at a time. So I asked to be given the power to surrender my doubts and to allow destiny to reveal itself.

I watched my mind's constant attempts either to degrade and disown the sovereign power within or to gain some acknowledgment for it. I swung from sickening self-disgust at the ego to outrageous amusement. And still there was a deep sincere yearning in me to know the Truth. All I wanted to know was that the love I had, the compassion and the burning desire to serve humanity – by revealing love and truth, was coming from pure being and not from some delusion of the ego. It was obvious that the love within was so great that I could not bear to carry it for my own benefit. Why then was it so difficult to believe in it?

So I sank down on my knees and I prayed to be shown.

'All I want is to serve for the highest of Love. If I am not in the Love of God I want to know, because I only want to serve God's Love. Please show me. May I be only Love and Truth.'

By the time I stood up I felt exhausted. I had reached saturation point. I couldn't give myself another moment of contemplation. I took some lunch and sat on the wall looking over the valley onto rolling hills, rice paddies and swaying stands of bamboo – scenery like a patchwork of jade. I loved the way the sprawling valley was in constant change.

Early in the morning I would sit on a grassy ledge and breathe in the fresh dewy air, gazing at the thick blankets of mist that had closed in overnight. I often fancied myself as Bilbo Baggins.[1] As he would be, I was enraptured by the beauty of giant trees and bamboo standing tall, poking their tips above the swooning clouds that moved around them like a lover obsessed. And in the rising heat the clouds would retreat, consumed by another lover, the sun. Under those great reaching rays of light, the fields below would glow and sparkle like

---

[1] A leading character in *The Hobbit* by JRR Tolkien.

jade and neon green gems. By late afternoon the fields would turn, like an artist's palette in use, from gold to pink and lilac to purple and hazy blue, to finally being wrapped up in night's dark womb like the blackened heart of a cave.

After eating I contemplated taking a walk to the valley, but instead found a quiet spot to sit under a tree. I moved easily into meditation, a sweet swaying stillness. There beneath the mind was a vast presence – a beauty so rich it washed away the last remnants of struggle. I dissolved so deeply that I felt no boundaries: body, no body; mind, no mind; hearing, no hearing; everything, nothing.

Suddenly I found myself walking, transported in a halo of light. As I entered the village I watched all the people. I felt the love in me rising. It rose from somewhere so deep it seemed to have no beginning and I reached with it, touching everything I could see. It reached so far it had no end. As I watched everyone I felt wonderment at the beauty, the gift of every soul and the miracle that it was all the same Self – the one Being that I am, that all is.

Just as I felt this, a man appeared from the side of a building. He was a leper. His body was rotten and full of puss; large chunks of skin were missing; his eyes and mouth were deformed and his hands reached out like demonic hooks. In plain human terms he had the most grotesque and ugly form imaginable. Yet, I watched in such fascination. For as he came closer all I could see was the Divine – the shining divinity of his being. It was so magnificent, so beautiful, that I felt I was in the presence of God ... the Buddha-Self. In that instant he looked up. We looked into each other's eyes. The five metres of dust between us disappeared and as we looked there was such a presence of love that it was an irresistible force. We moved towards each other, drawn by the power of love.

Our bodies embraced so deeply, we dissolved into one great field of golden light. Energy spiralled in every direction. It was a union that was beyond this world. Nothing but love existed – no longer two bodies, but one field of love.

From within the timelessness of love, I suddenly sensed my form again. I could feel my form embracing this other form. But as we drew back and opened our eyes, there before me was not a leper, but the gentle smiling form of Lama, looking into me with love, gratitude and acknowledgment. And from within his eyes came the words,

'Even as you know the ugliest to be Divine, it is Buddha you see in all. It is you that is Buddha, seeing Buddha. It is you that is Love giving Love. Your love is pure. Now go and doubt no more.'

I closed my eyes and looked up to the heavens and cried. I cried with gratitude and with such wonderment that I had been given this gift of knowing love.

The next day I tried to see Lama. I wanted to know if the experience had really happened or if it was just a vision. But he wouldn't make himself available. In fact it was two weeks before he would come anywhere near me. By then I worked out that it was his way of making sure I understood it from within – through faith. How many more times did I need to be told?

When I did finally see Lama all he would talk about was my going back to Australia. I thought maybe that would happen later in the year but he kept talking in shorter terms.

My attachments were exposed. The old crone had hit the nail right on the head. I was attached to my spiritual home. It had become obvious that whether it was my worldly home or my spiritual home, it made no difference. Attachment was attachment. And soon enough it became painfully obvious that any attachment was the cause of great obstructions for me – even illness.

Just when I thought I was going to weasel in for another six months, I was presented with the inevitable.

Being up early one morning, I passed the kitchen at the back of the monastery to get some water. The big urn was already out on the bench. Gee, I thought to myself, that was a lucky coincidence. And I gulped the water down with gratitude. But, just as I turned around, one of the young monks from the kitchen came out hastily and grabbed the urn. I had a sudden sinking feeling that meant that the water hadn't yet been boiled. I wandered back to my room, hoping I was wrong.

But later that afternoon my stomach started to rumble with terribly suspicious gripes. By early morning I was gripped by violent cramps, nausea, vomiting and diarrhoea. My body heaved in great expulsions. I couldn't take any food or keep anything down. After two week's of constant discharge my body was beginning to feel seriously defeated. Lama sent for special pills. They seemed to enhance my altered state of consciousness more than alter my body. I started drifting in and out of my body. I couldn't even lift my head any more. My body had been reduced to sparse skin on bones, stripped of every last flutter of energy, stripped of any last expulsion. Lama started talking about hospital but indicated the local hospitals were too much of a risk – he didn't like my chances of survival. So instead I discovered emergency flight arrangements were being made for me ... back to Australia!

After another week of Tibetan pills I had stabilised somewhat and I was able to think more clearly. After deliberating over the confused thought that Lama was somehow disappointed in me, I discarded the notion that he was rejecting me and accepted my destiny.

I remembered the dream I had been shown, the golden path and the passing friends, all encouraging me to keep moving. I gave thanks for the little time of stopping I had been given and I knew that Lama had done his part by giving me the physical confirmation of my path.

So I spent the last two weeks as close to him as possible. I watched the others struggling to keep their sense of importance, terrified I was going to somehow displace their important roles of serving Lama in one way or another. I didn't care for an important role. I just wanted to do something, give something, anything, in return for all that he had done for me. So I kept asking if there was something I could do. Finally, one morning Roger, Lama's personal assistant came out with a little bundle. 'Lama Zopa asked if you could wash these for him,' he said. I held out my hands. There, neatly wrapped up were a bundle of his handkerchiefs. 'With great joy!' I said and walked away.

I chuckled to myself. Lama must have gone through at least three a day. For some reason he seemed afflicted with a mucousy throat that meant he would cough up at varying intervals, in between chanting, prayers and blessing the endless stream of dedicated pilgrims.

To another it may have been the smallest, least important job, but to me it didn't matter. To me it was enough to be able to do even such a little thing, for my gratitude was so great.

I spent my last few days with Lama Osel. He seemed to be so aware of my inner turmoil. As much as I had accepted my destiny, I could not deny my sorrow at the thought of having to leave the ones who so deeply understood and embraced me. Lama Osel played with me gently, lovingly. He sat quietly next to me, looked in my eyes and held my hand. And without a single spoken word he comforted me and assured me that everything was going to be okay.

Everything seemed to be so dream-like, as if nothing was really real. I watched it all with distanced fascination. Somehow I had lost a sense of passion, yet rested in calmness.

When I went to sign my papers at the office I suddenly realised the date: the twenty-fifth of May. Hmm, I thought to myself, fancy that! – I had completely missed my birthday. I laughed with delight and gratitude that I could be so present to life, being simply in the moment, that I had forgotten my own birthday. And what was more delightful was that I had spent it in peaceful solitude in the Himalayas, deeply engrossed in prayer and the spiritual practices of dedication for all beings – not in some smoky hotel with a whole lot of drunkenness, like most twenty-one-year olds I knew. Not that I felt judgment towards this – just that I was glad to be where I was. After all, I thought, a birthday was just an automatic ritual that seemed to validate the identity through the freeze-frames of time.

To me it was a far greater celebration to realise that every moment is a birth. The only significance I could relate to anymore was that it was a reminder that on that day, twenty-one years ago, my mother gave herself for my life, my parents took on a great dedication to serve my life and the universe gave me the opportunity to experience this life, that I may serve for the love of all. So, when I returned to my room, I lit a candle and gave thanks.

My birthday was not the only thing I forgot. Gradually I was losing my old self. I forgot my age. I forgot the century. I forgot what I was doing, where I was, what I was. On the middle of the path I would forget where I was going. I had to focus with all my attention to know where I was. It seemed like everything was disappearing. It felt like I was saying goodbye to everything, everything that had ever been.

I walked around the Temple grounds slowly, giving thanks and prayers as I said my goodbyes. Somehow I managed to find myself again at Lama's feet.

Lama held my hands and closed his eyes. Suddenly, the unexpected happened. I burst into tears. A deep awareness in me watched, stunned. I thought I was totally at peace but there in that moment those tears belied such a resolute thought. Then through my sobbing I looked up, Lama opened his eyes.

'I'm going to miss you,' I said. And with stillness and such poise he responded.

'There is no missing in truth. You, me, Vajra Yogini, are ONE. No missing.' There was a silent pause then he looked into me deeply and said, 'Soon you will know this and you will never forget it again.'

I bowed my head.

'Oh Lama,' I said. 'May it be true, not for me, but for the sake of all beings. Please watch over me, guide me when I am blind. I only want to serve.'

With that he put his hand upon my head. 'You are service. It is you who will guide others to see. Bless you.'

We then invoked our mantra of consecration and dedication. When we finished I bowed with my head to the floor. I couldn't even begin to utter a word of gratitude. It was beyond all words yet I knew Lama would know. When I sat up we smiled into each other's eyes and laughed as I turned to leave.

The 10th Attainment

A lamp is not made to be hidden.

Now with ignited light I could do nought but let it shine.

KEY 10.

The Spinning Galaxy

KEY 10.

The Spinning Galaxy

Like a spinning wheel, life turns, allowing the coming and going, all held in the central, unmoving presence of the Now.

All fate changes: what goes up comes down. As life moves in cycles, every season comes to pass.

One must rest in the centre, accepting change, to remain balanced through all that turns. To resist the turning nature of life results in suffering.

Our Liberation from the wheel of life is not in escaping it, but in understanding it.

23. *Back to Australia*

Any path is just a path, and there is no affront,
to oneself or to others, in dropping it
If that is what your heart tells you.

Carlos Castaneda

The mood of my flight home was subdued compared with the outward flight. My body was still extremely ill and weak, filled with pain and toxins. People stared at me as if I was an alien. I started to feel loneliness creeping in again. How was I going to serve people if they could not accept me? I watched the play of the mind's attachment to appearance. How could it be beneficial to appear in a way which provoked such non-identification and rejection? What use was it if I was in a framework of 'us' and 'them'?

For many people, an appearance so out of the ordinary provoked suspicion and was a reason not to engage. In fact, most people seemed so uncomfortable with my shaved head and robes that they couldn't even look me in the eyes. Of course, at that time (1988), many people in the West weren't even aware of Tibetans or Buddhists, let alone the possibility of reincarnation that was beginning to transform attitudes about the apparently fixed state of race and culture.

I began to contemplate the widespread tendency to exclude in the name of religion. I could see the polar extremes mapped out in the minds of 'us' and 'them'. This polarisation exists as: for and against, black and white, right and wrong, good and bad, better and worse. We are either Buddhist *or* Muslim, Catholic *or* Anglican; each one professes to be superior. Yet the religion, the teaching *itself,* holds no prejudice, judgment or malice. The philosophy is pure and all-embracing. Yet through fear, humanity has learned to project intolerance and hatred onto the teaching. Humanity obsessively seeks to identify *us* and *them*; and to possess, in order to gain greater 'power'. In defending our own position, we have no option but to oppose. That is what leads to the creation of bombs.

But when will we learn that we do not have to possess that which is already all-embracing? When will we simply celebrate the gift of diversity? When will we see that the rivers require no religion, that the planet needs no patent? When will we understand that we are here for fleeting moments and that no matter what our colour we are one human family? When will we embrace our sameness and the things that unite us, instead of the differences that appear to divide us? When will we remember that we all come from no-skin and to no-skin we return?

John Lennon's song came into my head:

'I'm just sitting here watching the wheels go round and round,
I really love to watch them roll,
No longer on the merry go round,
I just had to let it go.'

That summed up how I felt. I was watching the wheel of life spinning and spinning; watching how we are all souls getting on and off, encountering every different aspect imaginable. The Buddhists referred to it as samsara, the wheel of suffering: the constant struggle between good and bad, up and down, life and death, and so on. And all the judgments, arising from the ego's position in any moment, were what caused the mind to spin. But that was not a merry-go-round; it was a *moody-go-round.* Now I was just sitting back and watching it. I wasn't on the moody-go-round any more. And I knew I was about to let it go.

By the time the plane landed in Adelaide I felt so weak again that I could barely walk. Finally, after collecting my backpack, I went to wait for a taxi. I hadn't even rung my parents, as I wanted to surprise them. As I stood waiting, people frowned and stared at this thin ghost-like form wrapped in maroon and saffron robes and with barely a quarter-inch of hair. A middle-aged couple nearby began speaking to each other in German, half looking at me with an air of contempt. I caught words '*Sehen sie auf* (Look at that). *Vas ist das* (What is she)?' asked the wife. '*Ein dum Hare Krishna* (A stupid Hare Krishna),' said the husband. Judging by the volume of their voices, there was no consideration that I might understand German. I recognised that I would probably experience a lot more of these attitudes. It provoked the question: Was this the sign that I would be better off disrobing, or was it to test my faith and commitment?

I felt a deep stir within as I recognised the wheel of life was turning. I sensed the coming to an end of a cycle and the stirring of a new season.

The taxi pulled up at the front of the house.

It was like a time warp. Nothing seemed to have changed at all. I walked through the carport and opened the back gate with a 'clink' as the gate-catch opened and closed.

'Ryan,' I heard Mum calling inside. It was early morning and she probably wanted Dad to check on who had come through the gate. Then the kitchen curtain briefly flashed open. Mum was still in her nightgown.

The back door swung open and Mum stepped outside with a fleeting look of uncertainty before she realised it was me.

'Oh, oh darling! You're home!' She was delighted. I smiled. 'Ryan!' She called out. 'Kathryn's home!'

By the time I stepped inside, Dad was in the back door hall. 'Well,' he said with a half chuckle and a twinkle in his eye, 'welcome home, love.' He stepped forward and gave me a stiff half-arm embrace. Expressing emotions was still hard for Dad, but I knew what he felt inside. Next came Mum's flurry of concern about how sick and thin I looked.

'How long are you staying?' she asked.

'Well, I don't know,' I said, 'I'm meant to have a room at Buddha House but I don't know if it's ready yet. And anyway, I feel too sick to be there yet without a car. I think I need to see a doctor.'

It only took the slightest mention of needing help and my mother was in immediate action doing whatever she could. It was strange that people often got annoyed by her so-called over-helpfulness. What an irony, I thought. In this world there are so many people who really need help. My mother only wanted to help, yet the people around her most of the time didn't want her help. What a strange mix-up.

Doctor's tests finally confirmed that I had severe *Giardia Shigellosis;* and not just in my intestines, but apparently also causing damage to my liver. This made treatment and recovery a tricky and drawn-out process.

The orthodox medical treatment made me feel worse, so I resorted to Naturopathic care. I began an intensive cleansing and de-toxing program to eradicate the bug and clear the liver and spleen.

Three weeks later I moved into the room at Buddha House. However, over the following months, it became very evident that there was little willingness to support this 'young nun'. I was keen to fulfil my offering of duty as had been requested by Lama. He had asked me to present meditations and teachings but this was met with disregard and derision, as if I were not capable compared with the older monks. Instead it was suggested I should be happy with house-cleaning duties and that I should leave the teachings to the knowledgeable ones – in particular to the men, as they were considered to be more intelligent and closer to enlightenment.

I wasn't sure if I was responding from ego or if it was genuinely a deeper knowing in me that I was being denied an ordained duty. Was the truth of consciousness, beyond gender or age, also being denied? Whether it was one or both, it provoked an even deeper question in me. I felt frustrated that the truth of Buddha consciousness was constricted by controlling attitudes. And, furthermore, that many beings were being guided and influenced by such attitudes, under the guise of Buddha's words. I felt surprise at a sense of wrath that arose in me at the thought of this injustice. Again, I wondered at the possibility of my own arrogance.

Feeling there was nothing else I could do, I sought my mother's counsel. Her thoughts and feelings only added more weight to my questions.

'Well, it doesn't make sense to me,' she said, 'I think it's ridiculous. No one seems to consider your value or needs at all – what is 'Buddhist' about that?' she demanded. 'And don't they know who you are?'

I looked at her, startled.

'Well,' she said, 'you're not just *anyone*. Alma came to me after you'd gone. I went to Buddha House a few times and she came to speak to me. She told me what Lama Lhundrup had said ...' Her voice became low and quiet. 'They came to get you. They knew before they came here that they were coming to find you, because you are an important reincarnation. Because you are born with a destiny.'

I cringed at the word 'important'.

'Oh well, everyone is a reincarnation with a destiny. We've all lived before and we're all going somewhere,' I said, trying to brush it off.

'Yes, but you are different,' she said.

I closed my eyes and started to cry.

The feeling inside was unmistakable. This was the truth, yet I couldn't stand the thought of any ego identification. And still somehow I knew I had to get over it and get on with it. I sighed deeply.

'I know,' I cried, 'I do know. I wish it wasn't true. Why can't I just be like everyone else?' I looked at her with my hands open, then dropped my head onto them and stared at the lace cloth on the kitchen table. How bizarre, I observed. There I was, in a normal kitchen, in a normal house, with a normal mother, seeing how totally not-normal this whole experience was.

Mum put her hand on my shoulder. 'Because you are you,' she said.

Her words trailed off into a silence. Stillness enfolded us. We sat staring blankly. Outside the trees swayed, the blue sky shone and a crow cawed. It called, as if from another world, calling me to walk tall, between two worlds.

That was the beginning of a new-found level of love for Mum and me. It was a time of tender unfolding, like two delicate buds, blooming next to each other, the faint new scent mingling in the sun.

I had been through my own passage of great unveiling. There was nothing secret any more. And as I contemplated that it gave rise to a natural inclination to reveal the hidden past to my mother. Until that moment I had never told another soul of my first encounter of sexual violation.

I looked at my mother sitting next to me at the kitchen table. Her face bore a sense of defeat. Yet simultaneously I could see a soft new light of hope in her open, questioning eyes.

'Mum,' I said gently. 'There's something I want to tell you.'

'Oh?' her eyes looked forlorn as if she already sensed my secret.

'Do you remember how I cried so much in America? How I was so moody and strange?'

'Oh dear, I suppose ... but you know I don't remember much at all. I was too unconscious, stuck in my own problems,' she said. I sensed her guilt.

'Well, I think you should know that something devastating happened to me then.'

The knowledge of that dark violation wrenched her heart open.

Mum's face turned from bewilderment, to shock, to anger, to howling tears.

'Why didn't you tell us? Oh God! Oh my God.'

'Mum, he threatened to kill me. I was only eight. I was terrified. What could I do but keep it secret?'

My mother sat there heaving with tears, her face buried in her hands, shaking her head.

When her tears finally settled she looked at me with a light of understanding that I had never seen in her eyes before. There, in that light, was an outpouring of compassion.

'Now I understand. So much makes sense to me now.'

It took her many months to overcome her sense of helplessness about what had happened to me and to understand how I had found peace, forgiveness and compassion in my heart. And then came an even greater opening, an opening to the light of the soul.

So I moved to and fro, between the spiritual seekers at Buddha House and the dining-room sojourns with my mother.

I lasted another month at Buddha House before deciding to find my own place to live. I had to be sure it was for the Divine Truth that my choice was made and not just some egotistic excuse. So I sat and meditated upon it. In the sacred darkness of night I listened to my heart. There, within, was a voice whispering over and over.

Blessed are the simple of spirit, for theirs is the kingdom of Heaven.[1]

With that voice came powerful insights.

My heart told me to avoid complexities and hierarchy in the spiritual world. I saw that those who followed these things were limiting and controlling their approach to the God-Self. I could see that Liberation (Heaven) had nothing to do with these rules of hierarchy. If I were to submit to these rules for ascension I would have to do so according to the protocols or permissions of another. My heart knew that these rules were man-made. They were not of God. If I kept myself tied to these requirements I would be closing the door on Heaven within. Why should any one of us need permission to experience that which we already are? Why was it beyond a woman? Why need it be exclusive? Each of us in our simplicity is already the perfection of God's creation.

Immediately the Tower of Babel sprang to mind. The religion of Babylon was ruled by a hierarchy of priests who assumed the right to control the people's rise to heaven. There it was: above and below, right and wrong, the same polarisation in the name of religion. Such an elite policy of ascension is nothing more than a set of stairs in the mind. My heart could see the consequences. To follow these stairs is to separate out parts of God, parts of the whole. With this comes rejection. Such a kingdom is then divided against itself. Any religion, city or people divided against itself cannot endure, nor can it inherit heaven: for there is only one spirit. On the contrary, to honour and accept diversity, to acknowledge and allow for our differences results in greater harmony.

Heaven is in our embrace of our whole Self and all life as one.

---

[1] Reference to Matthew 5:3

We cannot divide it. No one person belongs more to the one spirit than another. There is only one true authority: the power of our ONE God-Self within and all around. Our embrace is in our acceptance of life as it is in its totality. It is in the end of polarisation, the end of duality. And it is an innocent mind that seeks not to judge or define anything as better or worse.

I knew then that all my heart was asking of me was to live one simple step at a time: to be present in each moment as that which I am.

The next day I made the decision. I followed my inner voice. It said clearly: 'Now is the step, today is the day, follow the truth within you.'

I went to the newsagent and collected a local newspaper. There, in the accommodation section, was an advertisement for a self-contained granny flat. The next day I moved in. I was glad because it was close to the centre and I still wanted to attend pujas[1] and services. And I knew it would also give me the space I needed without the projections of other people's beliefs and thoughts of what I 'should' do or what was 'right or wrong' for me. I knew those answers could only truly come from God deep within me, in the silence beneath the mind, in the space between 'this or that'.

The more I withdrew, the more I saw a deeper calling to somehow integrate my life more holistically again. I saw that my path could not be fulfilled by surrounding myself with walls and conditions in the name of renunciation; on the contrary, I had to embrace life and the world. Indeed I understood the importance of spiritual commitment and guidelines that are able to support higher awareness. Yet I found some of the principles and structures were no longer of service to me. I could no longer believe that life is something that had to be escaped. Suffering in the world is not because of its turning, changing nature but because of resistance to it and lack of understanding of the turning wheel. Only through understanding can we be free of the ego's moody-go-round. I wanted to reach and touch people; and in order to do that I needed to be reachable and touchable myself. I had to embrace the nature of life in all its mystery and wonder. I saw that life is aching to be honoured and met – not to be rejected. Of what benefit is it to renounce or be without *attachment*, if on the other side there is *aversion?* I recognised that my concerns were exposing my own process and stage of growth. I had valued the teachings I received, and understood that I had come to integrate those over many lifetimes. Now I felt called to surrender the structures. I knew I was being called to embrace my whole self, my authentic self in totality. That meant in the form I expressed in the world *now,* the way I lived and related with life. I wanted to come down 'off the mountain', to walk as myself in body, mind and spirit. Despite profound insights and the awareness of the essential Self I saw how the process of integrating that in form has its own dance. What had appeared as previous states of knowing was recurring in different degrees which meant that some 'lessons' appeared over and over, in different settings. Each time the experience led to a deeper and deeper integration. I was only now beginning to understand how this looked and felt. It was evident that attachment and aversion were so relative.

As I contemplated moving on from Buddhism it was not at all about a judgment or an aversion. It was about a deep knowing that it had served me well, and that it was simply time for me to move onto other experiences. There were many things that gave me the opportunity to reflect.

I thought about the faces of those whose self-indulgence was hidden beneath robes worn in the name of renunciation, a path supposed to bring Liberation. Too many times I had seen desire – the desire for union, the natural pulse of attraction and sensuality from which we were given the gift of life – lurking, banished to a dark and devious corner, morally condemned. I had seen also the result – and inevitable breakout. True freedom could only arrive with the completion of natural desires. What man could truly turn his back on a glass of water when he is thirsty? It may be a motion of the body but it will live on in the mind. It is only a matter of time before one will reach for the glass. Yet if the mind believes this to be a sin then the act will be done in secrecy and guilt and will be riddled with poison.

I felt compassion and understanding for a struggle that could not always be ended by an assumed vow that promised liberation. I knew that our freedom, somehow, does not lie in our renunciation of certain acts but within the consciousness of our actions – free of attachment and aversion, free of judgment and fear. I saw that as long as there is denial or repulsion of a desire, there is bondage to the mind.

I looked into my being. I looked into the play of life, being. I saw the gift in life's diversity – that life itself is a constant intimate fusion of attractive forces appearing as the play of birth and death, form and space, male and female, polarities, uniting and separating. I saw that every part is a natural expression of God, the wholeness of God.

And when I looked honestly, I saw that there was still that most natural yearning within my humanness: that longing for communion, friendship, companionship and a deep meeting of self meeting self, uniting as consciousness. I knew that what I yearned for was beyond the desire of physical satisfaction and yet that physical union represented the possibility of the sacredness of love expressed on earth. So began my process of vigilantly unsheathing myself from any fixed point to life. I opened myself willingly to know the Divine within it all – with or without a partner, in a cave or in a city. I chose to embrace the Truth of God in it all.

At the time I was grateful to have Lisa, my friend within the Buddhist fraternity who was not 'robed'. She was a wild exemplar of dedication to the philosophy within an uncloistered life.

After months in silent self-reflection, I could no longer hold it in. So there, in my friend's presence, I began to talk.

'Lisa,' I said, 'I just can't believe any more that liberation is something separate from life – from love, intimacy, singing and playing, in the cities, in the gardens and on the dance floor.'

'Oh,' she sighed, 'thank God for that!'

'I mean,' I continued, 'as far as I'm aware, liberation is a state of awareness *freed* from the illusion of life's conditions, not a place or a set of rules *separate* from life's conditions. And I think it's about being fully home in myself ... being at peace and accepting myself as I am:

not trying to become something better or purer or elsewhere.'

'Sounds good to me,' she responded.

'So why, then, if life itself is already the play of liberated elements, would we be condemned to the realms of Hell if we got on with it and danced with life?' I quipped.

'Hmmm ... good question. You tell me.'

'Well, I don't know about you, but I'm not here to fear life – or to see it as a jail sentence, I'm here to wake up and dance – fully alive!'

'Well, yeehaah!' she exclaimed. 'Shakti's[1] come out to play!'

We broke into belly-aching laughter.

When the laughter finally settled, she said, 'So, my favourite little nun, do you wanna put on some dancing shoes and hit the disco?'

I looked at her wide-eyed, surprised and yet not, and giggled.

'Sure,' I said. 'Let's take the love of life to the city.'

I watched my mind doing back-flips as I did what was highly questionable for one who was robed. My mind struggled to move without a tug from the conditioned factory of shoulds and shouldn'ts. I was aware that behind me was a prison warden's rules of some liberation lost if I indulged in such a 'worldly' act. For that fact alone I figured it was of great benefit that I make it to the dance floor. I wanted to experience for myself the deep liberation of life that moved beneath every event. I was ready to dance as the simple spirit.

I came out of the bathroom laughing. The image in the mirror was a hilarious display of contrasts. My hair was still cropped short – a giveaway of the 'nun' in me, yet my body was dressed in the clothes of any other 'worldly' person about to engage in the play of what was usually vanity. The short, tight denim skirt hugged my hips. An off-the-shoulder blouse emphasised my breasts. A pair of bright pink stilettos added even more height to my long slender legs. And my blonde hair – now an inch long – was jelled and spiky. I topped it off with a touch of makeup ... pink lipstick. I laughed. I looked like a Parisian punk!

---

[1] In Bali, 'shakti' often refers to spiritual power. In Hinduism, it is the female power of creation.

I laughed, but in my mind I saw a clashing play of two identities – a nun and a modern young woman. I was no longer interested in either identity. I was interested in experiencing the play of life in all its diversity.

We arrived at the dance club to discover a room full of people, laughing, drinking, smoking, kissing and dancing. I watched the dichotomy as my mind observed the shallow play of people's futile grasping for joy in the senses. Yet I saw the 'is-ness' of it all – life unfolding for each one in their own mysterious way. I felt a deep sense of peace swirling in me as I embraced the perfect beingness of it all. It seemed to swirl and entwine its way through me until I felt it coming back at me in the music and the lights.

I began swaying until my body moved, unstoppably, onto the dance floor. I dissolved into the rhythm of the music, becoming the music, the dancer and the dancing – all an undivided play of life. The joy that moved in me and through me was ecstatic. All I could feel was love and gratitude for life – for every beat, for every being. I spun ecstatically, laughing and flinging my arms with infinite joy and gratitude – flinging love to everyone and to everything in every direction.

And deep in my heart sat the stillness of Self, the Buddha in a cave; silent, within the play of every particle of creation. I was revelling in being both the silence from which the beats arose and also the beats. I was consumed by the scintillating dance of life in my body; swaying and swooning in the ecstatic bliss of emptiness in which the dance floor had manifested. The space was no longer a room with four walls and drunkenness, but the leela[1] of God in an all-connected play with every particle of creation in every direction held in the embrace of pure love. It was the centre of the wheel, celebrating the direction of every spoke, celebrating its eternal spin.

When I opened my eyes all I could see was a perfect field of love. Light flowed in every direction – it spiralled out from my heart, from my hands, from every pore as I stood swooning, crying in tears of laughter

---

[1] Divine play.

and bliss. All around me I saw the perfection of form and space, everything in the perfect place in the ever-flowing moment, a divine orchestration. Everything spiralled in a perfect field of all-united harmony: life in every direction.

When the music began to change I realised that people around me were watching with fascination. Then a young woman came up to me.

'Wow!' she exclaimed. 'That was amazing – you're an amazing dancer. What are you on? Can I get some of that?'

I looked at her and laughed. 'Everyone can get some of this,' I said.

She looked at me wide-eyed and curious.

'It's called love. It's inside you, me and everyone.'

'Oh, wow ...' she said, and smoothed her skirt self-consciously. She stood in a daze for a moment before walking away, then turned and smiled – like a little girl.

Later on I was sitting near the bar drinking a soda when a young man approached me.

'Hey,' he said, 'What's with the short hair? You're not gay, are ya?'

I chuckled. 'No,' I said.

'Why so short then?'

'Well, there's more to life than hair,' I said. 'Hair comes, hair goes, but life keeps going.'

'Oh wow,' he exclaimed. 'Yeah! That's pretty cool.' He looked at my near empty glass. 'Hey, can I buy you a drink?'

'Sure, a soda would be nice,' I replied.

'What! Nah, come on, have a real drink.'

'No thanks, I don't drink,' I replied.

'What! Why not?'

'Well ... I don't say it's wrong for you or anyone else,' I said, 'just that alcohol is inebriating to the mind and body. And – well – I choose life and I respect my body.'

'God, what are you thinking?'

'Clearly!' I responded.

He looked at me as if I were mad, and persisted: 'Yeah sure, come on, one drink's not going to hurt you.'

'No thanks. I'm only alive in this moment. That one drink could be the last moment of my life and I'd rather go out seeing it clearly.'

'Oh, far out,' he said. 'That's pretty deep.' And he walked away.

Lisa looked at me and chuckled. 'Ha ha. You could bring a new revelation to the world yet. *Dharma in the Disco* brought to you by *Girl on the Dance Floor!*'

'Ha, ha, ha! Here's to life in the light lane!' I threw my arms into the air. And with that we laughed and danced our way through the night.

•

So began my strange journey of touching people's awareness with something from beyond: everyday people, people in the parks, people on the buses, people in the streets, people on the dance floor, people everywhere. Even in my dreams.

For the first time in three years I slept soundly, for seven hours. One night after meditating I lay down to rest. I was still in a clear meditative awareness and found myself leaving my body as a light form. Within the etheric body I had the ability to transport myself instantaneously to the other side of the world.

I found myself hovering near a train line in London. When I saw a train approach I knew I was meant to board it. It rolled into the station like a silvery bullet pulled into slow motion. I passed straight through its walls and sat down. The train started to travel out of the city. Two stops later it came to a halt. I watched the people getting on and off.

In the distance, I saw a girl boarding at the other end of the next carriage. With a vision that could see through form, I clairvoyantly watched her walk through the carriage; she was ignoring the few spare seats. Then the connecting door opened and she walked into the carriage where I sat. Seeing the spare seat opposite me she sat down and gazed out of the window. Then she turned with a start when she realised I was sitting there, a body of light.

'Oh, my God!' She was awestruck.

'An angel! You're an angel!' She stared at her hands in her lap for a few moments then looked up with eyes full of bewilderment, uncertainty and hope.

'I prayed,' she whispered as she turned to stare out of the window, her mind flashing over the stream of her thoughts in the last few weeks. Her voice was distant. 'I've been praying so hard.'

She turned suddenly and looked directly at me. 'Did you hear me pray?' Her words fell out in excited possibility, reflected in her wide eyes.

I smiled and spoke telepathically: 'I am here.'

'Oh my God, I can't believe this. There's so much I need to ask you. Please help me,' she implored. 'Why am I here? What's happening to me? What am I meant to do? I don't know how to handle this life, this world. What am I meant to do? Oh, please help me.'

I held her in love, deep in the all-connected divine light of Love, and without a spoken word, I talked to her soul.

'You need not worry, you will be guided and all your questions will be answered. Know that you are watched over, that there is a higher power at work in your life. Soon it will be clear. We will meet again soon.'

I touched her mind with the light of love and truth and smoothed her soul with peace, then, with a soft out-breath and a glow of light, I left.

When I woke up, the garden was fresh with drops of rain. I smiled. No matter what we do, I thought, the rain still falls, the sun still shines and life moves on, day in, day out.

•

By the time I was twenty-three I was ready to make a more definite shift, away from the umbrella of Buddhism. The wheel had turned.

I began to experience a greater frequency of visions, linking dreams and events of different lifetimes, different cultural experiences and different dimensions, all to the same source – to the Divine I AM. Within each expression, whether that of a beggar or a saint, a shaman or a mother, a prophet or a carpenter, I could see the all-connected flow of the one soul of life, shining through so many changing points.

I realised more and more clearly that one Self shines through all beings as well as every 'body' I had ever been. And it is this same one Self shining in all places and times, regardless of any outer appearances. Here, in this awareness, was the seeing, the breathing, the hearing of the one immortal unchanged moment, the now, in which all phenomena appear to rise and fall. Seeing that unity resulted in the knowledge of universal innocence, and of the purity and perfection where judgment can no longer exist.

In seeing the perfection of the Divine shining clearly inside all, I could no longer live for exclusive identities, beliefs or philosophies. I could no longer live to belong, to own or be 'something', for I saw that all life is forever being as it is, perfect, moment to moment. I felt the egoic world of boxes slide into oblivion.

Three months after the dream in which I met the girl on the train I found myself watching dreams becoming reality again. Without fail, the next day everything would happen exactly as it had happened in the dream state. In fact it left a big suspicion hanging over the definitions of 'dream' and 'awake' realities as separate things – the unreal and the real. And in amongst this would be the occasional connection from something months or years before.

One afternoon I ventured to the beach. As I walked down Jetty Road I felt a sudden shift as if I were about to experience another 'event'. I looked at the tram tracks that ran down the length of the road to the beach. The light seemed to reflect off the steel like the bright awareness that shone on my inner mind, alerting me to the rising sensation that made its way up my back. I felt my aura open and shoot out wide and the light became brighter.

Suddenly a young man turned and stared from across the road. Without taking his eyes off me he crossed over quickly and walked straight up to me.

'Hey!' He spoke in a broad English accent. 'I couldn't help but notice you. I dunno why,' he said, 'but I felt I had to meet you and talk to you, or something.'

I smiled and chuckled.

'Do you do yoga? You look like you do,' he asked, looking at my broad shoulders.

'Actually, yes,' I said.

'Wow, that's great. My name's Martin, what's yours?'

'Oh ... just call me Katja,' I said, not wanting to complicate the conversation.

'I want to learn yoga and meditation. Can you teach me some things?' He was very matter of fact, very direct, and very unabashed.

'Sure.' (What else could I say? I thought).

He followed me to the beach and proceeded to ask me about yoga, the mind and spirituality. After about an hour he sat quietly shaking his head in amazement. 'Wow,' he said. 'I can't thank you enough. This is so amazing.' Then he looked up with a sudden look of wide-eyed awe. The light bulb switched on.

'Hey! You've got to meet Sally. I mean, she's got to meet you. She really needs help, y'know. She's really looking for answers,' he said. And with that he leapt up, asking me to come with him.

'Come on, she's back at the lodge. I know she's got to meet you.'

I joined him without another thought.

We turned off Jetty Road and walked down the steps of the backpackers' lodge. I followed behind Martin. His tall body seemed to take on an even greater power from the anticipation in his determined stride. We went down another set of steps. I could see into the lounge room below. His broad shoulders acted as a wall that kept me hidden from the others in the room, yet I could see just past his sandy blonde head. There, sitting on the couch, was the girl from the train in the dream three months ago! I stepped out from behind Martin just as he spoke.

'Hey Sal, you've got to meet ...' His words dropped away. Martin's excited eyes turned to concern and puzzlement as he took in Sally's frozen, wide-eyed face.

I watched her jaw fall open. Sally sat staring at me, breathless and speechless. And then came a stuttering and stammering of disbelief, trapped in the presence of Truth; for seeing is believing.

'Oh, oh, oh my God! Oh, my God! I can't believe it! You're ... you're ... you're the angel ... from my dream. You were the angel on the train. Oh my God! You said we'd meet. I can't believe it! Is this really happening?'

I smiled, knelt beside her and took her hand.

'What is a dream and what is real?' I asked her.

She looked at me blankly. Then after a long silent pause she sighed.

'Oh, thank God,' she said, 'there's so much I have to ask you.'

After three hours of questions and insights, she sat back and cried. No longer tears of pain, but tears of relief. I looked at her and gently spoke.

'Blessed are those who suffer for love's sake for they shall inherit the kingdom of Heaven.'[1]

She looked at me, puzzled. So I continued, lovingly.

'When we reach for our soul that is Love, we discover a greater power beyond our suffering. In surviving our suffering we are able to go beyond the life we have been conditioned to, to experience the love of God in a greater way. We can never know God, love or heaven in the limitation of our conditions. Our suffering is in our attachment to our small poor-me story. But as we start to let it go, as we let the wheel of life turn, our suffering becomes a mourning. It becomes a release, and opens the space for us to see the bigger picture of God. We can only have a truly sacred journey filled with love and peace when we can open to this greater presence. So your suffering brings the gift of your growth.'

Finally she could understand that all of her struggles had a higher meaning and were leading her to something beyond the confusion. She was on her path of awakening: waking up from fear; waking up from the lies; waking up from her little story and spreading her wings to take flight.

---

[1] Reference to Matthew 5:10

24. *The Medicine Wheel Keeps Turning*

It is good to have an end to journey towards,
But it is the journey that matters in the end.

Ursula Le Guin

Tucked away silently in my lovely little self-contained granny-flat, I continued to embrace each moment. Once again I felt so graced by the immeasurable beauty in the simple things: the dappled light dancing in the leaves; the colour of the sky, open and blue or filled with soft grey clouds; the flitter of a leaf in the wind, the sound of a bird in the morning; the warmth of my little home. It was a wonderful place to live. Nestled in a cottage garden amongst old gum trees, I felt a sense of belonging embracing me softly. The sounds of suburbia in the outside streets disappeared beneath the whisper of leaves swaying in the wind and rustling against the window.

As I sat meditating I 'heard' a distinct call within. The same soulful flute that had haunted me when I was young was lilting its way through my inner ear. Then a sudden flash vision of an eagle. Then the deep voice of a Native American '... don't forget the medicine wheel ... you carry a message for us all.'

That night I dreamed.

I was walking through a dark valley, lit by a full moon glowing in the blanket of a deep violet sky. In the distance I heard a wolf call. I knew it was bringing me a message, so I stood still. Within a moment it was standing by my side, its coat silver in the moonlight, its eyes sparkling like the stars overhead. It walked with me to a tree at the top of a cliff, where an owl sat on a low branch.

Below the tree was a medicine wheel: its directions were marked clearly by coloured stones. We entered from the south, next to a black stone.

'The womb,' I said.

'Innocence,' replied the wolf.

'Birth and death,' said the owl.

I saw images of women – young, old, maidens, mothers, crones, grandmothers – all sacred. They all emerged from the void and gave birth to the void, inviting life to return to void. I entered in, into stillness and silence: nothing, pure emptiness of being. And in that pure emptiness I was as a child, an innocent, infinite child of eternal life.

Then a deep rumbling moved around me and rain began to fall. I looked to the southwest, at the green stone. I saw life all around it, green grass and shimmering leaves, nature pure and incorruptible.

'From absolute innocence, all life is born,' I said.

'And in the heart innocence remains,' said the wolf.

'Eternal life,' said the owl.

I walked across the field of life, savouring the beauty of life's gift. In the west I stood at a red stone.

'The place of the setting sun,' I said.

'All that is born in the world comes to an end,' said the wolf.

'Introspection brings freedom from attachments,' said the owl.

I sat quietly and closed my eyes. I could see the image of

a bear entering a cave, a shaman entering a lodge and then I saw myself like a Buddha, in a cave. I felt the deep stillness within. It was in that stillness, the letting go of the outer, that I knew the connection to the eternal life. I gave thanks for the cave.

I opened my eyes and walked again around the circle. I stood at the northwest – an orange stone.

'Creativity,' I said.

'Pure intelligence,' said the wolf.

'Diverse potential,' said the owl.

My heart began to burn with fire – inspiration. I spiralled and danced, feeling the joy of creative force moving through every cell of my body until I stopped at the northern point.

There at my feet was a white stone, luminous like the moon.

'As above ...' I said.

'So below,' said the wolf.

'Infinitely,' said the owl.

I looked up and felt a *whoosh* as I left my body. From high in space I saw the earth and all the galaxies spiralling in infinite space. Life rolled out before me, in me, all around me ... only being ... ONE endless being ... Great Spirit. I looked down and saw my body looking up at me with open arms. And within an instant I was in my body again.

I looked to the northeast. The sky glowed with the light of thousands of spirits. The ancestors smiled – great spirits of every race. I saw the history of my love affair with life on earth. Looking over me were the golden lights of the east – Tibet and India; the warm red of the West – American Indians; the rich ebony of the south – Aboriginal and African Dream-time; the ancient white galactic light of the north – Egypt and Machu Picchu; the doorways to my stellar homes. Within and around each one I could see a radiant blue light – undivided.

'The light of the soul,' I said.

'The light within all,' said the wolf.

'The light of ONE,' said the owl.

I bowed to the ground in gratitude.

When I opened my eyes I looked to the east. The sun was beginning to rise. I walked around to the next stone, yellow like the sun.

'Source of life,' I said.

'Eye of the eagle,' said the wolf.

'Power of spirit,' said the owl. As I stood breathing in the golden light an eagle rose up from the horizon. Its cry echoed across the valley. I watched it flying high to the sun and then, from that great distance, it viewed me and I viewed it. Then I saw the play of life; how all the little events are fleeting, held within a bigger picture, a much bigger picture. From the height of this seeing I looked back to my feet, knowing they are guided for a purpose far bigger than each small step.

And so I walked on again, around the circle to the south-east and stood next to the violet stone.

'Wisdom and compassion,' I said.

'Trust in the Divine Will,' said the wolf.

'Serving the Divine,' said the owl.

I knelt upon the grass. 'This body belongs to Great Spirit, serves Great Spirit and lives for Great Spirit,' I said. 'Let the Divine Will be done in me.'

'So it is,' said the wolf. 'It is so,' said the owl.

When I opened my eyes I found myself sitting in the centre next to the old grandfather. His long grey hair fell in braids over his shoulders. His ancient eyes of wisdom stared into my soul.

'You have journeyed far, Daughter of Great Spirit. We are watching over you, for you have more to complete. You were called to the south entrance first because it is where your soul is journeying now. You will be meeting your husband soon and take the passage and rite as mother. You must fulfil this for two souls before you can enter the west and give your life away fully as flesh. Then you will enter the western gate where you will die and be born again through the north before you will enter the eastern threshold to serve as the eye of the sky, guiding others with your all-illuminating light.'

'Thank you Grandfather,' I said. 'May I fulfil all as it is required.' There was a deep sense of peace and knowing in what had been shared in truth.

•

Yet when I awoke I felt puzzled and disturbed by the last message in my dream ... Children? I thought to myself. It was baffling. I had remembered having visions of a boy and a girl when I was younger but I had put that down to the motherhood fantasy syndrome that is common to most girls. Since then I had fleetingly considered such a thing in my dizzying attempt to understand a life of love in this world. But I had cast all of that aside when I realised my life's purpose was to serve all of humanity. I couldn't possibly imagine how being a mother exclusively to two children was going to fit into my journeys around the world. I wondered whether the message was perhaps a metaphor pointing to something else. And surely that was what the message of dying was about too?

That afternoon I was inspired to draw. I didn't know what was going to come from inside the creative energy but when I finished I looked at the image in wonder. It was as if it were drawn *through* me, not *by* me. The collage of images was clearly a depiction of the powers of Native American spirit medicine working through me: the medicine wheel – a twelve-pointed star enfolding my face as the sun and moon, both as grandfather spirit and daughter of spirit; the eagle's eye, the falcon's wing, the rainbow of creation, the creatures, the plait of time and forces; past, present, future; the Father, Son and Holy Spirit.

I stared at it in wonder. I 'knew' what every colour and symbol represented. It spoke to me of wisdom that came from beyond time and place, yet wove its way through all times and places.

I pondered upon the dream and its messages for many days until it seemed to dissolve again into the stream of life in which I moved.

The 11th Attainment

I made peace with the wheel of life. It was now my quest to be in Mastery with the turning, established in the ever-present centre.

KEY 11.

The Boomerang

KEY 11.

The Boomerang

Whatsoever we have chosen, be it unconscious, conscious or super-conscious, is what we come to experience. What we put out comes back. This is our karma.

As we sow, so we reap. We are the cause and effect of our own wheel of life.

The thoughts and actions of the past had led me to my present. I was ready to undergo whatever karmic adjustments my soul needed to complete.

25. *Along the Way*

> Adventure is something you seek for pleasure ...
> but experience is what really happens to you
> in the long run; the truth that finally overtakes you.
>
> *Katherine Anne Porter*

There were other things that now called my attention: survival and responsibility in the world. No matter how dedicated I was to the spiritual, it became very evident I still had to survive and make my way in life. It was the karma I had to face for choosing to be in the world.

Unlike in the East – where yogis and ascetics are given alms, donations and such support – I was now in the West, where such things were less common. Hence I was faced with the inevitable: get a job.

So I left my robes behind and took to the world again, weaving my way between the world beyond and the one beneath my feet. I was highly aware that what I chose in my life now would impact on my future. I understood that what I chose to think and act upon was the fuel that energised the outcomes of my life. So I spent time discerning my direction.

I conceded that if I had to work in the world then I wanted it to be creative – a gift of joy for others – or of some purpose and service to the higher good of others.

So I picked up my studies of herbal medicine again: acupuncture, body therapies and a new one – iridology. While studying I worked as a cook and kitchen hand in the only organic, vegan-vegetarian café at that time in Adelaide – the Clear Light Café. Even that seemed to be a perfect orchestration of spirit. The owner had a deep and long-time love of Buddhism, having met Lama Yeshe. Lama Yeshe reincarnated as Lama Osel; Osel means 'clear light' in Tibetan. It also happened that her business partner was my naturopath who had helped me through my body's recovery. It was evident to me that I was being embraced by a fusion of spiritual connection and worldly living. I felt very blessed by the deep love we all shared for a common journey.

It also happened that, after many months in a relationship, I found myself suddenly estranged. There was a tug between, on one side, a soul connection and his desire to take it further and, on the other side, my 'knowing' that it wasn't 'right'. My ability to be beyond emotional attachments triggered great anguish for him. I struggled to find a way to explain my transcendence in a manner that could be understood humanly. Instead I was interpreted as cold, aloof and uncaring.

This concerned me deeply because I knew in my soul that I cared infinitely. I was still trying to understand the whole dynamic when a month later, in a public toilet, I came across a Taoist poem scrawled in faded red texta pen on the back of the door; it read:

Thus it is said ...
The path into light seems dark;
the path forward seems to go back;
the direct path seems long;
true power seems weak;
true purity seems tarnished;
true steadfastness seems changeable;
true clarity seems obscure;
the greatest art seems unsophisticated;
the greatest love seems indifferent;
the greatest wisdom seems childish.[1]

[1] Lao-tzu.

I felt great relief that there were words of wisdom that conveyed clearly and simply the truth of life as I experienced it.

And I came to accept that this understanding could only arrive in its own time within each heart. No matter how much I could want this for another, it would not bring it any closer. It would happen only in the timing of their experience.

And I had to learn to let go even more because it meant I had to accept disappointing another to be true to myself.

So, picking myself up and moving on, I threw myself again onto a path of healing services. I had acquired enough accreditation in natural therapies to set up my own room. It wasn't long before my practice was booming. I seemed to move in my own unique way with the therapies, combining acupressure, massage, reflexology, energy work and auric clearing. I even pulled out my crystals again.

It was an extraordinary thing to feel such immense joy from another human being's transformation. And if I hadn't experienced suffering, I couldn't possibly have felt this incredible gift.

I watched with wonder at the limitless power of the universe as it worked through me. It brought relief to people who had experienced sciatica for years, it brought emotional liberation to heavy souls, it brought confidence to the timid and it brought joy to lonely hearts. I felt so fulfilled with this that I just wanted to give more and more.

But once again I discovered that eleven hours of hands-on therapy per day, solidly for three months, was more than my body could manage. I wasn't giving back to myself. Before I knew it I was burnt out again. And I was ready for a change.

It was in a dance club where I was once again celebrating in life's pulsing rhythm that a chance encounter brought me into the presence of a big-hearted truck driver. A week later I was on the road to Sydney.

At first I didn't really know what I'd run into. The pace was three times faster than Adelaide and greatly different from the caves and temples I had occupied not so long ago. The motivations of people and the lifestyles seemed diametrically opposed to the life of spiritual service. And yet there was an air of excitement, creativity and adventure to it all. I opted to take the ride of adventure for a while. Somehow I knew that my path of Mastery was not attainable in seclusion. I also sensed that it could not be found in old patterns. I knew I had to break apart everything associated with the past. Whatever was supposed to be the 'way' of liberation remained a condition that I saw as something to break. It was that pattern that kept the cord of karma alive in the mind. I sensed that I was yet to fully understand and transcend this karma and that it would be revealed to me equally in the world of form as it had been in the world of spirit.

I began to notice that karma is often thought of as a power above us. Although I had encountered teachings that highlighted the importance of discrimination, there is still a notion that the world and its events are being 'done to' us. This results in limited perceptions and various degrees of disempowerment.

Having made myself available again for healing and spiritual guidance I noticed a recurring issue amongst the people who came to me. They felt trapped and limited by the circumstances of their life and were looking for ways to be healed, for their pain and worries to be removed, or to receive some miracle from existence (or from me!) that would make it all go away.

And common to them all was the disbelief in their Self, in their own inner guidance and source of creative power. It seemed very difficult for these people to believe that they could change their own circumstances, that they were the creator of their own experience and could therefore resolve their karma consciously.

As the people opened their hearts to me I could see patterns in many ways. No matter whether the issues were about doubt, loneliness, a lack of faith, creative blocks, health matters, relationship issues, career direction or life purpose, each circumstance related to a sense of disconnection. That disconnection was primary to the constant feeling of disempowerment, failure, and disappointments.

And the disconnection was both the result of, and exacerbated, by limited perceptions. The individual did not seem to know how to find another solution and would unconsciously refer back to the same limited programs of behaviour.

I could now see why I had felt so rebellious towards education. I realised that most of our learning is based on *what* to think, rather than *how* to think. As a consequence the full capacity to access our own innate knowing has remained dormant and trapped in beliefs and models of thought that do not necessarily serve us or align with natural progression. It also creates a dependency on external solutions, resulting in greater frustration and a sense of self-defeat.

The feelings that arise from this, whether slight or extreme, created greater states of discomfort, and the individual often becomes emotionally reactive or suppresses the feelings with a quick 'feel good' fix. If the underlying issue is not resolved these behaviours can often become addictive.

I saw everything from chocolate and sugar addicts, workaholics and shop-aholics, to sex and drug addicts. I was amazed at how many people were really very unhappy despite wealth or health. And I was fascinated by how many 'ordinary' people were hooked on marijuana.

But I could see how it was a smoke-screen over their pains, frustrations and disappointments. I began to realise how my own previous experiences had been teachings in disguise. I had come to understand through direct experience that any dependency on an external source of happiness, insight, freedom or joy was subject to great limitation.

I had witnessed the use of marijuana in a sacred context or for creative inspiration. It could temporarily alter perceptions and even for some, give moments of insight. But for most, those moments remained fleeting and the insights, superficial. I had also learned that through yogic and meditative practises, the divine powers were developed with far greater clarity and that our inner consciousness takes us to the limitless, whilst the drug only takes one to a certain level.

I also saw how, out of impatience, and a desire for a fast route to higher experience, many individuals developed a dependence on drugs. Paradoxically, the feeling of freedom it created resulted in a dependence on the substance to *get* the feeling of freedom. That bondage was far from true freedom. The user then spiralled into a fog – the mind became deluded, emotions were suppressed and the system became toxic, which sometimes catalysed extreme symptoms typical of bipolar patients. In other words, dependent users would be fluctuating between the happy open 'high' and deep violent anger, with diminished self-esteem and a contraction of communication – the exact opposite of what the individual was really seeking.

True freedom requires a significant shift from the addictive and dependant behaviours. And to be able to break out of such behaviours requires great vigilance. It requires the ability to be constantly watchful. As the person becomes more aware of the destructive elements of their behaviour it often triggers self-judgment which only compounds the underlying limited belief – the belief that they are not good enough or whole enough already. Sadly, the focus remains fixed on what is 'wrong' and on a sense of defeat and failure.

Unless we change the workings of our mind we continue to be pulled again by the habit of conditioned beliefs. In my interactions and experiences with clients, I also became aware that it was not helpful to stay fixated on reviewing one's thoughts, feelings and beliefs nor was it enough for an individual to just 'surrender' to the Divine (while it is still considered something other than what we are). There is a need for balance between investigation of thoughts and release from thinking into pure awareness. I could see that this related to any process of transformation.

For true transformation we must be able to enter the space between the thoughts to reconnect with our true essence. As we embrace this again we uncover our deeper, inherent power of consciousness. This consciousness is without limitation and is the source of true Self awareness.

It is because of the immense power of the essential Self that even the smallest of connection with it can begin to change our whole life.

In this open state of awareness, our limited beliefs and behaviours begin to fall away. Provided we also transform the workings of our mind. This process can seem incredibly contradictory as we move between illumining realisations and the struggle to connect them within a world that is still mostly viewed through limited perceptions.

Reflecting over my own life I could see this paradox playing out through my own encounters. And I often wondered how it was that, even though I had experienced profound states of the God-Self, I still had my moments of doubt or denial. Now I was beginning to understand more deeply that the process of *integrating* awareness within life is multi-layered, appearing to go around in loops. With each cycle the physical events provide the field through which the expression and essence of higher awareness can be lived. To me, that was the ultimate dance of liberation, the game of God.

I became aware that it was that quest, to merge higher consciousness with life, that drew me towards other people. I entered that dance somewhat naively, without truly understanding that the higher states of consciousness do not guarantee a compatibility with all people. In fact I discovered that it often highlights what appears as the opposite.

Whilst I experienced the beauty of the all-oneness, the true essence of the Self, those around me were still deeply associated with their own perceived disconnection from the Source. Consequently, they were still dealing with their own limited perceptions and the effects of that. And, paradoxically, the vast difference in perceptions made it seem like we were worlds apart.

Yet it has nothing to do with judgment or separation. It is simply the effect of two very different dimensions and degrees of awareness. It is like a bird trying to describe how to fly to a tiger. The tiger has within himself no point of reference to the wings. It is very easy for the tiger to feel as if he is being judged whilst actually the bird can simply see he is stuck on the ground, in the forest, and cannot see the way out.

I felt like the bird. I understood the soaring heights of conscious awareness. And I understood the frustration of the tigers who were trapped in the forest, unable to see the way forward. What I didn't realise yet was that I tended to misinterpret the compassion I felt. It resulted in the notion that something was unfair. Why should I keep flying when the tiger is crying at me, complaining I am too far away? So I often traded my wings and pretended to wear stripes again. Of course that had its own consequences that I was yet to fully resolve. And it wasn't until my marriage that I would truly understand that.

•

So I continued my journey, integrating all of my experiences into the world. Whilst I moved between jobs, artistic adventures and creative enterprises, I continued my spiritual practices. Having had so many experiences of expanded consciousness I was now finding it of great benefit to be more focused on my body again. So I took up a regime that included more yoga.

At dawn I sat for an hour, breathing in cyclic rhythms. Not only did this breathing continue to sustain the calm inner stillness, it also generated a wonderful current of clear vibrant energy through my body. Sometimes I found my awareness naturally following that to a deeper level.

My attention would move into the base chakra and flow upwards with the in-breath to the crown where, with the out-breath, it would spill into the whole field of my aura. The energy flowed around and through my body, vitalising it, filling it with warm tingles. And with the next in-breath the energy would flow up my central channel again. This breath and energy flowed, looping around and around, giving a distinct shift of energy. It seemed to allow a deeper connection between the more expanded awareness and the field of my body, allowing me to be clear and light, yet grounded.

After the seated breathing I would stand with my feet slightly apart and feel this same flow of energy moving through me, except that I breathed from the earth and connected the energy with my feet on the ground.

This energised me so much that I couldn't help but leap and skip with the joyous energy that filled my body. My yoga routine often came after a run to the beach, a swim in the ocean and a dance in the sun.

During this time I was living at Whale Beach: a wonderful bay on the northern beaches of Sydney. It was the perfect setting for me to find a balance between work and my spiritual life; and my body and higher consciousness.

It also proved to be interesting in other ways.

Liesel, who owned the house, was an artist, eccentric and performer. She was well known for her support of tantric masters, yogic madmen and ecstatic shamans, all of whom she loved to welcome into her home. So she was very happy to have me living in the lower half of the house.

After I had moved in she informed me of the impending arrival of a 'friend' of hers – a wild shaman of Native American Cherokee blood who lived most of the time in Bali performing ceremonies and rites. My body rushed with 'God-bumps' when she told me. I was deep in the middle of asanas when the shaman arrived.

'Katja!' Liesel called to me. 'Katja, Shankara's here. Come in and meet him.'

I was struck immediately by the power of his presence. His wild spiralling black-brown hair spilled around his face and gleaming eyes of deep ocean-blue looked back at me. It was the first time since the lamas that I saw clear conscious presence looking back at me with vivid telepathic awareness.

We simultaneously put our hands at our hearts and bowed respectfully to each other. Liesel seemed a little unnerved by our obvious and immediate deep connection.

So this was the 'mad yogi', I thought to myself. I was interested to see how 'mad' he was, or whether he was more refined and matured. It seemed evident from the potency in his energy and aura that he was quite evolved.

We decided to sit and meditate together.

Silence descended upon the house. Not even the insects could be heard. We sat in deep presence for two hours. As we started to come out of the meditation I had a clear vision that I was being called to a sacred journey with Shankara and that I would be travelling to Bali.

The next morning Shankara and I sat on the cliff top. The words that followed seemed only to be a confirmation of what we had already understood telepathically.

Shankara spoke. 'You have travelled far already in spirit and I see that you are ready for another journey. It is good that we can meet again after so many lifetimes. It is good that we meet now at this time. I invite you to Bali. My valley home will grace you, just as you will grace it – with your conscious presence.'

'Thank you,' I said. 'I will prepare.'

'Very good, we will discuss arrangements later. My divine consort Parva will help with the arrangements.'

I paused, intrigued by the way he described his partner. I had never heard a person refer to their lover as a divine consort. It was something usually found in the practices of Buddhist or Hindu tantra. I knew this was not going to be ordinary!

I knew that my savings could sustain me for my periods of retreat intensives, but it wouldn't be enough to take a trip overseas.

'Okay,' I replied. 'I need three months. I have an inner practice to fulfil and to create what is necessary first before I come. The results of this will determine if I can come,' I said, leaving space for the uncertain ... life's own great mystery.

'You will come,' intoned Shankara. His voice stood in the centre of my awareness, stable as a pillar; its certainty pushed aside my doubts.

•

Over the following three months I entered into the depths of inner practice and set the intent that the way would also open to create the money I needed. I had very little contact with the outside world other than the occasional sound of Liesel's car coming or going and the odd fleeting moment of our passing bodies.

I sat from 4 am till 1 am, only resting my body for three hours. I chanted, meditated and set my body into deep trances of postures. I held my awareness in the focus of the creative power within Self, within the infinite life force. I focused every thought upon the inner creative energy. I moved between mantras and visualisation. Sometimes I would simply repeat over and over: *I am the source of creation.* I would align this thought vibration with the mantra AUM AH HUM[1] and then sound that repeatedly until I experienced its vibration as the total Self. Likewise I would hold the vision of my self aligned in total connection with creation. In these visions I was able to hold the image of abundant flow in my life. It took me to the place where there was no separate perception between the 'self' and creation.

Interspersing these visions were flashbacks to various circumstances and situations in my life. I began to witness the connections that lay between the various levels of my conscious field and the creative power of the universe. I could see how the thoughts I had given most attention to created the strongest vibration. And it was the movement of these vibrations that shaped the events that unfolded in my life. They were literally like a magnetic resonance attracting the form that matched the thought!

I began to see myself as the cause and the events in my life as the effect. I was entering the ultimate witnessing and understanding of karma. I also noticed that the universe did not edit the thoughts that were preceded by 'don't want'. What it responded to was the image that was most focused upon. So if a thought was: 'I don't want to be poor', the focus was actually on the image of *being poor.* This was an extraordinary insight. *Ask and ye shall receive*[2] could be reinterpreted as *focus* and ye shall receive!

Throughout this experience I also remained very open. I had no attachment to outcome and remained in a state of open suspension. This openness was a vibrant field, free of any interruptions. It was

---

1 This intonation is a self affirmation: creation is the Self I AM in all.

2 Matthew 7:7

a space that was totally available for the universal energy that was free of the mind. In this space I was able to see how non-attachment allowed the room for the higher will to take form. It was like dropping a pebble into a still lake. The effect was one of direct movement between the pebble and the lake. On the other hand I could see that attachment created many ripples and the effect of the pebble was then interrupted by the ripples already existing in the lake. So I allowed myself to rest ever more deeply into the space that was between the visions and sounds.

After two months I entered a luminous field in which the all-pervading creative force spiralled up from deep within the Self as vast space. Its radiant pulse vibrated in one ceaseless ever-present force. I felt it move into the form of mantras and mudras. Each appearing form of energy arose from the consciousness that directed them. It was like one giant, all-connected mandala of light and sound, as a divinely awake dance of creation. I felt myself in its every fibre and it within my every fibre. I was it and it was me.

Then one afternoon, as I moved within this fluid pulse, I went upstairs to fill up my water jug. Liesel was in the kitchen in a great fluster.

'Oh, Katja, please can you help,' she implored. 'I have dinner guests and I'm running late.' She spoke while flapping her hands around. 'Can you chop the parsley for me, really fine, you know? Soft and moist.' I did know – like in the restaurants. Liesel was renowned as a connoisseur of fine cooking.

'Here.' She handed me a ten-inch hunting knife with a razor sharp blade. I watched the whole scene in amazement. Everything was happening within the creative field of light intelligence while the mantra swirled in and around it all, deep in my awareness.

'The parsley's in the fridge.' She pointed. 'Here's a board. Now chop. Chop, chop – really fine,' she said, determined to make sure I had really understood.

I nodded while taking the parsley from the fridge. The vivid green seemed starkly contrasting in my hands from which I could see deep golden, orange and rose light radiating.

And then, to the rhythm of mantra, I chopped.

I chopped until it was really fine – moist and powdery fine. I looked at the dark green mound of fine powder. Its scent wafted through the air. With my left hand I picked up a pinch in my two fingers and thumb. I held it up feeling the beauty of its sweet cool softness and admiring the creative play unfolding in a field of light.

I felt a strange electric tingling between my fingertips. Liesel turned to see what I was so mesmerised by. And then, before our eyes, a fat red ladybird manifested – it popped out of my fingertips! Its body was as big as a sweet pea and bright red. I counted eight black dots on its back. Liesel stared, speechless.

We watched it crawl down my fingers onto my palm. It sat there on my open palm for another fifteen minutes. I looked at it intently. That manifestation confirmed my alignment with the creative source. I knew then that I was ready for the next stage of my journey and that the creative forces were supporting me. Some might say: luck was on my side. Yet I knew that I had merged with the power of karma itself. It was no longer an unconscious experience of life being done to me, but rather I, being life, was playing it consciously. I had begun to tap into the field of intentional creation.

I walked outside into the bright light of a full moon. I gave thanks for the gift, the sign of conscious creation and abundant creative force. I raised my hand and the ladybird flew into the moonlight, taking my prayer of intent into the universe.

The following day I found myself on the phone to one of the organisers of the Mind Body Spirit Festival. He asked me to be a clairvoyant reader in the tarot section for the Sydney and Melbourne fairs. I had been recommended to him by the Psychic Association of Sydney, for whom I had worked.

I accepted gratefully, figuring it might get me closer to the $3,000 target I required to cover my costs for a three-month trip to Bali. A stir of excitement moved in me as I felt a mix of belief suspended in the beauty of non-attachment.

The following weekend I saw people end-to-end for four days. The same thing happened the next weekend in Melbourne. I counted my takings at the end of the festival – $3,000! The three months were up.

Two weeks later I was off to Bali.

The 12th Attainment

My world of events was revealing a greater play of consciousness. Whatever had appeared as a karmic law outside myself was revealed as the power arising from within my very being.

I now knew that what I chose with deep belief was the power of cause and that non-attachment was the space in which the effect would take form.

We either remain an unconscious target in the game of the boomerang or we become aware of what we set in motion.

... We remember ourself as the Master and creator of our own fate.

KEY 12.

The Chrysalis

KEY 12.

The Chrysalis

Old ways of knowing must die in order for the new to emerge.

When we are free of social conditioning, our true purpose can emerge.

The Chrysalis waits in the passage before her next stage.

In patient suspension, surrendered of mind, I hung like a chrysalis, dormant, waiting for the emergence of my purpose in metamorphosis.

26. *Scorpion Medicine*

And I have felt ... a sense sublime
Of something far more deeply interfused,
Whose dwelling is the light of setting suns,
And the round ocean and the living air,
And the blue sky, and in the mind of man:
A motion and a spirit, that impels
All thinking things, all objects of all thought,
And rolls through all things.

William Wordsworth

The plane landed in Denpasar in the late afternoon. I stepped outside to find Shankara standing right in front of my view. He smiled with bright eyes and outstretched arms.

An hour later we were high up in the lush mountains, pulling in through open gates to a large, open-plan Balinese house. Statues of Ganesh and Shiva[1] greeted us at every corner and giant tangkhas[2] of Kali,[3] sacred yantras[4] and mandalas hung on the walls.

Shankara rang a large bell and lit incense. I stood beside him feeling gratitude that I had been welcomed into such a sacred space. Within moments, Shankara's partner entered the room, a petite young East Indian woman with thick black lustrous hair that fell down the length of her back. We bowed and greeted each other.

---

1 The central and highest Hindu deity representing God – the male principle of creation.
2 A work of art on cloth depicting Buddhist teachings.
3 A female aspect of Divinity.
4 A diagrammatic symbol for a field of energy.

'Namaste,'[1] I said.

'Om swasti astu,'[2] she replied.

'This is Parva,' said Shankara, 'and this is Katja,' introducing us.

Parva showed me around the house, then down to my room which overlooked – as did the upper lounge area – a vast deep valley in which the great Ayung River roared. I stood on the cool dark-red floor, taking in the simple yet beautiful decorations of batik cloths, bamboo lamps and a sheer cloth that enclosed a single hanging bed.

To the side of my room a large open veranda nestled into the hillside, a riot of lush green plants, ferns and exotic flowers. Further along, the path led down to a natural spring that flowed from the cliff face. The cascade of crystal water, under the skies, surrounded by the lush valley, was the most exquisite shower I had ever encountered. The water was sweet, cool and refreshing, a welcome rejuvenation from the heat.

The river below, a great rushing body of water, was visible gushing over rocks and caressing the roots of ancient giant banyan trees. I could see a few villagers bathing and washing clothes at the water's edge.

I walked back up the path and stood on a private ledge, feeling blessed to be in such a natural environment as my bare body drip-dried.

Once back in my room I dressed in a light sarong, set up my space and then started to explore the rest of the house. Such beauty, imagination and simplicity of design appealed deeply to my spirit. Every ledge and corner was a place of worship. Shankara seemed to have as many (if not more) statues and pieces of sacred ceremony than I did. Tibetan bells, vajras, drums, incense pots, conch shells, oil lamps, water bowls, flower garlands, sacred ash, crystals, power stones, feathers, bones and staffs. It was as if I was surrounded by an extension of my own eclectic journey.

We ate a simple meal of rice and vegetables before joining to sit

---

1 An Indian spiritual greeting which means: the God within me sees the God within you.

2 Balinese greeting, honouring the Divine within.

in a circle. By then another three people had joined us: a virile young man, a wide-eyed twenty-year-old girl and an elegant American woman. It was clear that we were all on a spiritual quest that had brought us together in that moment.

Shankara offered his intentions and insights for the journey we were going to take together over the following month. Our days would be spent in yoga, meditation, ceremony and the study of ancient texts and creative projects. I felt immediately inspired by the suggestion of a sri yantra[1] being painted on the wall for the lower practice/study room. However, it was the next thing he said that grabbed my soul.

'I come from a great line of medicine men of the Cherokee. Our medicine has been passed on from shaman to shaman for hundreds of years. Our medicines are from deep communion with mother earth, nature and her creatures.'

He pulled out an ancient looking vessel which had coloured threads and beads hanging from it. 'In this bottle is a medicine tonic that has been used since the beginning of our medicine men. Every batch that is made contains a specific ratio of the previous batch – that means that each potion holds within it the ancient power and tonic of the very first ceremonial creation. It is believed to bring instant connection to Great Spirit through the ancestors and the healing powers of earth. Together we will prepare a tonic starting this new moon and take it to completion by the full moon.'

We all looked into the fire in the centre, potently aware of how sacred and rare this experience was. We all sat silently for another fifteen minutes.

'May I speak?' I asked. Shankara and the others nodded with invitation. 'I feel it will be of great benefit if we could look deeply within at this point and clarify our intent as we now join together for this vision quest.[2]' There was unanimous agreement.

'Then let us first clear the field,' said Shankara. He stood up and

---

[1] Considered to be the supreme yantra. It represents the process and field of creation – like a diagram of Genesis.

[2] A meditation or spiritual gathering for the purpose of connecting with the soul awareness.

took a bundle of sage off the ledge and collected his hand drum. He lit the sage, then 'smudged' each of us, clearing our auras, by sweeping smoke over and around us and then around himself. Then he picked up his drum and began beating. Its deep, full sound resonated throughout my body. Then he began chanting. It struck every chord in my soul. It was ancient and familiar.

When he sat down he began to speak again.

'Oh, Great Spirit, may we be as children, open, and ready to receive the Will from above. Let us open our hearts to the Truth within.'

The afternoon finished with preparations to start the medicine wheel the following night. The plan was to have everything ready for the ceremony to start at ten o'clock under the new moon.

Thirty-three medicinal herbs were lined up for preparation. Some had to be boiled, some only simmered, some rubbed, some crushed and some ground. Each move was made in a clockwise circle 108 times, with a mantra for every herb. When each was ready it was added to a pot holding a base of 152 herbs and the source ratio of the founding tonic. The pot was then placed under the moonlight and kept in the dark during the day.

Every day was an unfolding of profound spiritual insights, practices and celebrations. We moved together, with and around each other in unison, experiencing a deep harmony and ease of flow. With each day the medicine tonic was watched over, each stage fulfilled with prayers, mantra and thanksgiving. The fourteen days passed quickly and brought us together again into the circle.

The moon shone brightly, large and full over our heads as we gathered together. With the medicine pot in the middle we began our prayers and mantras. Finally the tonic was presented. A small coconut cup was half-filled, then passed around the circle with further prayers. We sat quietly and entered into a deep meditative trance. From within the stillness a vision arose. It was as if I were watching from the sky.

I was a young Indian woman walking across the field towards tepees. I walked in deep peace and power, embracing the earth's love with every footstep and creation's beauty with every breath.

I lived, growing and maturing at one with my family tribe. As a wife, I watched my husband leaving with other warriors, leaving me with one child and another in the womb. The children grew, loved by aunties, uncles and elders and I became an elder – the seer and oracle of the tribe. My hair, turned white, fell in great long plaits over my shoulders, and in a great circle I sat listening to my fellow brother playing a flute – a song like the soul of all creation. Tears of love and joy streamed from my eyes as the deep flow of love for eternal life, for earth, for creation, spilled from my soul.

•

When I came into my body again I realised I had been given greater clarity about a past life. It was from there that the song of the flute had journeyed with me, held deeply in the heart of my inner being.

Over the following days I regained even greater clarity about the wisdom and lore that was so deeply woven into my life as an American Indian. It was so magical to see and know presence as something still deeply alive in my soul in the present, and to meet another from the past in the ongoing journey of now – Shankara, my brother – same being, different body.

He and I spent hours talking and sharing our experiences that unmistakably confirmed the connectedness of a shared past life, which still held us in a deep bond in this life. We discovered also how many parallel roads we had travelled in the journey of sacredness on which we both still moved. It tied us together across the lands and cultures of the West, the North, the East and the South. How intimately our lifetimes are woven together, I thought, as I watched my inner awareness flicker across the Native American, Egyptian, Indian and Aboriginal civilisations.

Then, unexpectedly, he looked at me and said:

'You will be a mother – you will bring two children to this world – two special souls.'

I looked at him, half screwing up my face. 'We'll see. If that's meant to be ...' I shrugged my shoulders, surrendering to the unknown. I couldn't even begin to imagine how such a thing could happen. 'I'm not even ready yet,' I said.

And despite my puzzlement, I was open to the possibility of an unseen plan. 'Three years,' he said, then stood up and walked away.

That night I dreamed. A girl and a boy spirit both called to me from the stars. And then I saw their sweet faces smiling with joy. It was a vision that I suddenly remembered from many years ago, a vision of love and destiny.

The next day Shankara asked to speak with me.

We sat next to his main altar beside the statue of Shiva.

'Katja,' he said. 'Sun Woman. You have great power. It is a power through which you will serve many but it is not fully awake yet. You must be purified more in order to hold the energy in your body. And, you must be able to endure forces of great challenge. It is important you take another rite of passage before you enter the next level.'

I looked at him intently.

'I would like to take you through the passage of scorpion medicine. It will help you purify the psychic powers you have that caused you distress, and open you to the eye that is even higher, above the events, the bigger view, the all-seeing.'

I looked at him, startled, entranced. It was exactly twelve years ago that a scorpion had bitten me.

'Twelve years ago,' I said, 'I was bitten by one.'

'I know,' he said. There was a pause before he reflected more deeply. 'Twelve is the cycle of solar fire/consciousness. That was your first passage to raise your psychic powers. You are now ready for the next level.'

I looked at him, not knowing what would follow, yet trusting, knowing it was truth.

'Tomorrow is the dark moon. We will enter ceremony at midnight. Do not eat anything from now. And spend your hours only meditating.'

I bowed and walked away.

•

The sun rose behind the distant mountains. The air filled with the morning sounds of birds, rushing river and distant villagers calling each other along the rivers banks, all echoing through the valley. I prepared myself. I prayed and meditated. I felt I was rapidly approaching an exit from a cocoon.

In the afternoon I washed under the spring in the late afternoon sun. When I went back to my room I pulled back the covers of my bed, intending to sit. I didn't realise why I would even be taking off the covers, it just happened. But in an instant it became very clear. There, in the middle of my bed was a large black-brown scorpion. Its stinger tail flicked up and curled. I gasped. Surprise, shock, disbelief and amazement engulfed my mind.

I knew instantly that I had been graced with a sign. I was on the right path. I was ready for initiation.

Nonetheless a flicker of suspicion toyed at my mind. I wondered whether Shankara had put it there. Yet he had left the house earlier when I was still sitting on the bed and wasn't even back yet. When he returned I approached him.

'Shankara!' I called out. 'Have a look in my room,' I said. He followed me with a look of elated curiosity ignited by my own excitement. We entered the room. There on my bed was the scorpion, trapped under the glass which I had placed over it. Shankara's eyes opened wide and his face lit up.

'Oh, ho, ho!' he exclaimed. 'Om Namah Shivaya![1] Wow, you still got the medicine workin' through you!' He began to laugh. 'Huh!' We

[1] A celebration and invocation of Shiva, the central Hindu deity, God.

stood there laughing in amazement.

Then he left the room. I sat on the bed next to the scorpion until Shankara blew the conch. Five minutes to midnight. I walked to the fire pit.

There stood Shankara, dressed in a suede shawl with two giant malas hanging around his neck, one carved from bones and the other made of Shiva rudraksha beads.[1] We 'smudged' each other with sage smoke and started prayers and chants. Without needing to confer with each other we moved into deep ceremony in perfect synchronicity.

After a round of drumming we sat down opposite each other. I felt we were not alone. I sensed the presence of many spirits. The flames flickered and then Shankara uncovered a glass bottle filled with a translucent liquid. There, in the bottom of it, floated twelve scorpions! He began to swirl it, holding it over the flames while chanting and calling in a crescendo. Right at the peak of his heightened calls he began to flick some tonic into the fire and the flames began to leap into the sky like giant dancing spirits. Then with a final call he took a mouthful and passed the bottle to me. Taking a single mouthful, I swallowed. One great gulp.

Like molten fire it moved down my throat and into my belly. Its acrid smell stung my nostrils. Intense heated energy began to rush through my veins like a molten volcanic river. My body shook and trembled and threw me into a transcendental surge of body movements beyond my mind's direction. My body twisted, stretched and leapt, spinning and careering around the fire.

Soon Shankara was spinning and dancing wildly too, and we began calling in great wails of shamanic tones. Suddenly we were surrounded by ten dancing spirits. We became a spiralling dance of twelve threads as if thrown into a wheel of fire.

It pulled me in, deeper and deeper, until there was nothing but fire, inside me, and all around me. I was consumed, transformed into all-pervading fire. Within the burning light I could see the ecstatic

---

[1] The seeds from a sacred tree that was linked to Shiva. Hence the seeds are specifically used for malas for Shiva worship.

collision of particles and gases in space, all dancing in exquisite form. I could see galaxies and stars spiralling, birthing and erupting. The macrocosm and the microcosm of fire breathed in every direction.

And within it all was an exquisite formulation of codes, like helixes of interlinked intelligence of sequences and keys. I felt the pure force of radiant energy igniting every cell of my body. My body was ablaze. I saw myself as blazing spirit, earth-fire body, galactic firestar, cosmic fire of creation and destruction. I felt my heat expanding and reaching into all life and all life reaching into me. I watched the mind of God, the all-cosmic force, dancing in every spark – each one born of the One. Then my body fell down and I dissolved into infinite light.

From within an eternity I soon realised I was watching my body on earth from space. I saw a great series of events unfolding. I watched the events of earth and humanity entering a passage of great purging, and I saw beyond, the bigger picture ... into the evolution beyond.

I entered into a series of visions and dreams that formed a collage with those I had experienced previously.

The dreaming and visionary states were consistent, always vivid, and ranged from dramatic to ecstatic and were often portraying events of terror and disturbing events for humanity. I saw pestilence, war, famine, terrorism and great disruptions upon earth. I saw dark waters, dead rivers, acidic skies and oceans, burned lands and seas of blood staining barren land. I saw great earthquakes, flash-floods and death-boding droughts. And I saw ghost cities.

All of the dreams left me with a penetrating awareness that life on earth would be faced with cataclysmic changes. It isn't a question of *if*, but *when*. From what I could see I knew these affairs would be a matter of reality within my/our lifetime, perhaps between 2000 and 2020: I didn't know when for sure. From previous premonitions I knew defining the time was beyond the scope of prophecy, yet such foresight did know what would be revealed in due course by the master of time itself – Life.

And I knew that these weren't just bad dreams that we would wake up from, but that it is a reality we will all be facing one day as a reckoning – and that reckoning will be the real 'wake-up'. It will expose, once and for all, that what humanity has thought to be real is really a deluded dream leading us to the decimation of the world we have created. Our ignorance of our precious earth will leave us with very little that is truly precious. According to the Cree Indian proverb:

Only when the last tree has died will we realise we cannot eat money.

I cried. How could I not?

Within the visions was a consistent witnessing of mankind's arrogance, greed and vanity; and also the awareness that scientific genius and so-called intelligent materialism were unconscious, diabolic forces of destruction. From my witnessing window of life I watched the crossing over of my visions and 'awakeful' dreams.[1]

What I had already seen in the field of conscious awareness was the preceding cause of what would inevitably occur in the physical dimension. Each new day I was witnessing the causative forces of humanity's self-inflicted, self-fulfilling catastrophe. For these things have been prophesied. I could see that each person within the collective whole of humanity is determining our global fate – where our way of life is taking us – and that our thoughts and beliefs are bringing the prophecies to fulfilment. For we are the creator. I witnessed more greed, more war, more consumerism, more divisions, more tragedies and a larger and larger retreat from the essential nature of life. I watched in real time – in real life – these forces unfolding in the world around me.

I looked on in bewilderment, puzzled by my part in it all. I shuddered, looking upon the face of a barbaric 'civilisation', wilfully driven, wantonly raping the earth. I shivered, questioning the purpose then of even living. What was the point, I thought, if somehow, I too,

---

[1] The state in which my body is at rest yet I am in an awake, conscious state of awareness. These are not normal dreams in which events seem to occur on the unconscious plane. Within this awareness I am directly experiencing past, present or future events: in what humanity has, does, or will refer to as 'reality'! In a state of vision I experience a temporary shift of consciousness to events that are outside the environment of my body. Sometimes this is a state of awareness of events occurring in another part of the world. Even though my body is resting elsewhere, I will experience the situation as fully as others in the real event.

am a cog in this perpetual turbine of destructive fate? And the answer returned from deeper within: for Life, for Love, for eternal Life.

What I saw ceasing, ending in great chaos and human tragedy were the forms and attachments of greed: the maps or mental patterns of fear and destruction and the world as we know it – but never Life, which is eternal. I saw that depression or grief at such an ending could only exist when life was seen as being only the mortal form and impermanent events. It was evident that humanity must go through a death of old beliefs in order to emerge in a new form. Beyond it all is the purity, the love of creation that continues, free of the heavy burden of the rapacious greed of mankind.

In letting go of old, limited beliefs, we naturally return to knowing our very being as the eternal life itself, in true liberation. In this knowing, death and birth dissolve into the eternal play of constant transformation, the very motion of eternal life. And, therein, I saw the greater fate of creation, the metamorphosis after the crushing forces of destructive reckoning – the meek shall inherit the earth and it is as children that they shall enter heaven and realise it upon earth, in the gift of Eternal Life.

❁

And so I declared my life, as I had before, for this Truth, for this Love. Just as I have died in the name of Love and Truth before, so too shall I serve again, for the Truth, the Love, the Eternal Life to be remembered.

What more could I do? It was no longer a question of praying for love and peace. It was a question of being. As Mahatma Gandhi said: *Be the change you want to see.* I could see how traditional prayer often keeps the mind tied to the image of the limited event, which only continues to perpetuate the same issue. The conscious energy remains stuck on the perception of *lack* rather than aligning with what *is*. When we are full of gratitude we uphold the energy of connectedness and fullness and we discover the power of peace that is already within us. Naturally then we feel, see, think and act in peace. We BEcome peace.

And so my prayers ceased as the *wants* and were reborn as the gratitude and the dedication to be at one with life, to hold all in *gratitude*, in love. I handed myself back to Life, knowing that Life itself is the master knowing when to give form and when to take it away. In such perfection does the master call the sun to rise, the eagle to soar, the stars to shine and the leaves to fall, yet to unfurl again and again and again. And this body, this mind, is deepest in peace when returned to the command of Love – Life's divine intelligence.

•

When I came to, the sun was just beginning to rise. I stared out across the valley. Somehow I felt different. A deep sense of peace filled me as I sat in a state of detached knowing; knowing that whatever happens is a play, whatever happens is a gift in the evolution of eternal life.

By the following week I felt it was time to go. I gave thanks to Shankara, knowing that I could never thank him enough, for he had the courage to walk with me through the alchemist's kiln.

I wasn't sure where I was going to go, except I knew that I still had more sacred work to fulfil.

Shankara held his closed fist out to me in an offering. I held out my hand with my eyes closed. The cool form felt fascinating. I opened my eyes to see a beautifully ornate ceramic medicine pot about three inches long, turquoise enamel with carved stone and coral beads. And hanging from the bottom swung a little skull and a baby, carved from bone. I received it with deep gratitude, recognising its symbol of death and rebirth – metamorphosis.

'The resins inside are especially for ceremony. You are an alchemist. See you in the eternal fire.'

With that I bowed and said goodbye.

Although I had journeyed through a great chamber of metamorphosis, I knew that another was calling me.

27. Raining

> Whosoever will save his life shall lose it and
> whosoever will lose his life shall find it.
>
> *Matthew 16:25*

The ageing blue bus careered along the road. It wound its way through mountain passes, open fields, black smog, village scenes and coastal plains until we pulled up in a large parking lot at a shipping port. I was looking for somewhere more remote and relatively untouched by tourism.

I was in what I called 'the flow'. I had learned at an early age that there is a constant attunement to life's passage as it unfolds moment by moment and that it makes itself clear in my feeling body, sometimes even as a strong yet gentle and quiet inner voice. It is the intuition that lies within us all but few people trust or acknowledge it. I discovered that if I simply responded to these inner cues, without getting into my mind's debate, I would meet an effortless flow of synchronicities as everything I needed unfolded spontaneously all around me.

So when a young local suggested I take the ferry across to Lombok, from where I could try to get to a smaller island, I felt a familiar vibration in my body. Feeling a 'yes', I simply responded, and without effort I was soon boarding the ferry. I was in the flow again. One thing led to another and before I knew it, I was being swept across the ocean by a fisherman in his long boat. Like a large canoe with giant arms that arched out on either side, it skipped along over the turquoise waters, propelled by a small motor.

I was helped ashore and welcomed to the island of Gilli Air. Immediately a young teenage boy approached me. His dark eyes sparkled and his wide smile revealed a mouth full of perfect white teeth. His young body looked strong and developed from hard work. He bowed deeply. Then he looked at me with a deep gaze and said, 'I've been waiting for you. I'm here to help you. Please let me serve you.'

I put my hands together at my heart. He did the same.

'My name is Ludi, what's yours?' he asked.

'Katja' I said.

'Oh, Dewi Katja Yani!' he exclaimed. 'White Goddess! You are great Shakti.' He bowed again. 'Please come with me.' Along the way, Ludi explained to me that he was a Brahman and that he had been praying for a teacher. He said a month ago he had had a vision that a white woman with long golden hair would come to teach him yoga, meditation and higher awareness and that he was not surprised to see me step off the boat.

'Well,' I said, 'I'll do whatever I can to help you.' He smiled, and then I added, 'I would also like to focus on ceremony and prayers of unity with God creation.'

'I'll do my best to help you, too,' he said. 'You can come and stay at my friend's. They have a few bungalows, very cheap, just five dollars a day for everything, meals included.'

It sounded just right for me – simple and right next to the ocean.

The family welcomed me. I felt like I had come home. I made myself comfortable in the bungalow and before long Ludi came with a lamp, a bowl of water and a bowl of flowers. I lit a candle and some incense and then offered the water and the flowers to the divine presence of life.

Ludi was highly intrigued by my Tibetan bell and vajra, yet held a respectful distance. He sat quietly in lotus posture taking it all in and then closed his eyes, as did I. We sat for an hour until it was time for dinner.

The next morning I prayed for the sign of where and when to start my practice. I had already received the awareness that I was to create yantras at specific points to make the whole island into a sacred mandala field.

I walked out on the beach, across a mass of sun-bleached, broken, sea-washed coral. Each footstep sounded with a soft crunch. I breathed in the salt air with deep satisfaction. The atmosphere, rich and humid, wrapped itself around my body. It wouldn't be long before my skin would be moist. As I walked along I prayed to be guided and shown the way. Like a child, I called to the father-mother source. As I called, I felt a deep humbled presence in my being, as if life were so great, so magnificent and divine that I couldn't possibly give enough thanks or service to repay my gratitude. I sighed with utter willingness to give my whole being to the Divine. I wanted nothing else but to serve Life, to serve Divinity. I sat down feeling completely surrendered to the Divine Will.

There, at the very spot at which I sat, I could feel something hard, cool and smooth right on my perineum. I lifted my bottom and reached under me. In my hand was a perfect cowry shell. I picked it up just as it had sat under me. Its underside was upright displaying a pure white body, opening down the middle. Its shape was exactly like a yoni, the sacred form of the female genitalia; the manifesting symbol of Shakti-Goddess.

In that instant I heard the words, 'This is the birthplace of your ceremony.' I sighed with deep gratitude and sat the cowry shell in front of me. I prayed to be held in the source awareness of Goddess in the womb beyond the mind. As I prayed, I felt my whole being become engulfed in stillness.

For days I returned to the same place, making offerings and prayers and yantras in the coral sand. I knew I was to stay in the same location until I received the sign of completion. More days passed until I felt my whole being taken into the deep; beyond the mind, beyond the created. It was as if I lost myself and dissolved into vast nothingness.

Suddenly, from within the void there was a heaving and I felt my being pushed by a pulse of pure creative force. When I opened my eyes, the sun was just coming up and Ludi was curled up like a baby two feet away from me. As I shifted, he stirred and opened his eyes.

'Today is the beginning of forever,' I said. 'This is the dawn of the new.'

I stood up. A new radiance swirled through my base chakra[1] into my second chakra. I felt the pulse of creation moving through me.

Over the following days I centred the energy in my body, focusing on yoga postures and pranayama. Ludi followed my every move, always respecting my space. I then recalled an inscribed mandala that I had seen in my meditations. Many times it spiralled around my awareness like a glowing disc. It held me and embraced me as if I was born out of it. As I drew it on a page in my diary, I had the clear knowing that it was intended to be an insignia around my navel; its design being that of a sun-moon lotus encircled by an inscription of dedication:

Self-Born from the Lotus, in love and devotion for all.

Ludi looked on in great interest asking me what it meant and what it was for. When I explained it to him he took a deep breath in and then simply nodded.

I felt ready to take the next step. So I walked and I prayed again moving around the island in an anti-clockwise circle.

At the ripening of each moment I was shown signs, through nature, visions and messages. I felt my self, moving ever more deeply into surrender, strung up like a chrysalis in a cocoon. Everything I had been before had to die in order for the Self to emerge.

I prayed for God's power and the work of Shiva to transform me. I prayed that the next layers of my mind and ego could be laid down, taken by Shiva, the destroyer, revealing Divine Intelligence, in order that I could truly be a vehicle of the Divine Will. As I stood watching the sun setting in the west, I called and implored the power of Shiva to be worked in me. I walked into the water with my arms stretched

---

1 Energy centre of the subtle body.

wide as I called, 'Om Namah Shivaya, Om Namah Shivaya, Om Namah Shivaya'.

I chanted over and over as I scooped the water into a shower upon my body and mind. 'Oh, Lord God of all creation, forgive me for all my acts of false allegiance,' I cried. 'Take from me the arrogance, the stupidity of my mind and ego, take from me this darkness. Strip me of all conditions. Let me die to this world that I may serve you alone in the glory of Eternal Life! Take from me this belief in 'me', 'my body', make it yours. Oh Lord, Shiva, consume me. God, I am yours.'

I cried and I shook with every inch of my body, mind and soul as I continued to chant: 'Om Namah Shivaya'.

Finally, I walked out of the water feeling empty – I couldn't give another inch of prayer.

Then as I walked up the beach, I heard a giant crack. The clear sky was momentarily transformed. A massive flash of lightning bolted across the sky, a great shining trident! Shiva's three-pronged staff represents the three tattvas[1] of existence: that which is the uncreated, pre-created and created. It was as if Shiva himself had filled the sky in a vast body of blue-black clouds.

At the same moment my toe kicked something. I bent down to pick it up. My eyes opened wide as I saw in my hand a pure white piece of coral, perfectly formed as a trident! I fell to my knees and cried:

'Oh Shiva, Shiva, Shiva! You are with me and in me! Thank you.' I fell face down with my body laid out in salutation.

Thunder boomed and shook through my whole being, consuming and chasing away the darkness of my mind.

When I finally sat up, the sky was clear again. I felt saturated in the truth that there is nothing but the power and love of God's work in me.

I am God's body, mind and soul, I said to myself deeply. God, I am yours: use me as you will.

I closed my eyes and breathed into deep, silent stillness. There

---

[1] Levels of creation or consciousness.

within was a space so vast that there was no longer an identity of a 'me'. All that remained was pure consciousness. It was so vast and all-present; nothing existed outside of it. It was like an endless hall with no boundaries. Just pure, luminous awareness. I was it. It was me. It was endless.

And therein was the rise and fall of all things. All that appeared to come and go was an eternal presence of the one same instant. Birth was death. Death was birth. The strike of thunder was the empty silence. Within that pure presence was an infinite depth of truth, knowing, being. And that being was bliss without end, stillness without motion, a space in which all creation unfurled in liberated delight.

Somehow, within that eternity I became present to my body again. Slowly I opened my eyes. All I could feel was a vastness of joyous delight. I sat in awe and wonder as I realised that I had entered what the great Sages of Shaivism had philosophised about for aeons. I had entered Chitsabhā.[1] I cried in humbled, ecstatic gratitude. I had prayed to be consumed, to be nothing but the presence of God, of Shiva. And, indeed, I had been consumed, returned to the very source of Self.

I continued offering prayers, making yantras and invoking the aspects of Divinity within and without. I gave thanks to all directions and offered my allegiance to serve in every direction for the life in all. 'Brahma, Vishnu, Shiva, Buddha, Christ, Devi, Laksmi, Kali, Tara, Goddess, God,[2] I called to every aspect of the one great Divinity.

The days passed in one constant stream of now.

•

It was in the middle of the afternoon when Ludi came to join me. He kneeled quietly with his eyes cast down. Something was on his mind. 'What is it Ludi?' I asked him.

He faltered as he struggled to find the way to speak.

---

[1] The hall of consciousness, the very presence of Shiva; that which is known to be the infinite one Self, the source of all creation in which form/formlessness are the one eternal dance.

[2] Refer to Glossary.

'Dewi,'[1] he spoke quietly, 'You have been here for over a month now and you see how dry it is. Our people are so worried. The rains have not come. No rain now for so long. Our village gardens are dying,' he paused and took a deep breath. 'Please can you help us? You have great Shakti. You can make prayers to bring the rain.' He looked at me with imploring eyes. In his eyes was the pain he felt for every person on the island.

'I will do a ceremony,' I said. 'If it is God's will it will rain.'

I asked Ludi to gather more flowers, offerings and water to prepare for the ceremony.

As he walked away he turned and stopped again. 'If you make it rain, I will take you to get your body inscribed,' he said. 'I will take you to a shaman. He can make good tattoo. He will do it for you.'

I didn't care so much for that. I just prayed that God's work could be done. Deep inside I knew it was absolutely possible, in the power of Love; the Divine Will could be manifest on earth.

Just after sunset, I drew a giant mandala and sat in the middle of it. I gave thanks to all the directions, the elements and the source. I drew my conscious awareness deeply into the vital elements of the sky, the ocean and clouds. I breathed deeply, feeling my being expanding beyond the body, expanding into the elements themselves. There, driven by love, I summoned the forces to unite in the name of God. I saw it as done.

The atmosphere began to fill with electric vibrancy. A rush of magnetic forces began to ripple through the elements. Clouds began to gather, hastened by the wind's divine breath. Within half an hour, the sky was full of dark rumbling clouds, their bodies heaving and filling up in great billowing pillows. The energy became so full that it bellowed.

Then from a moment of deep stillness a fat rain drop fell and landed atop my head, right on the crown chakra. Ludi looked up in wide-eyed amazement. Splat! A drop landed right on his forehead.

---

1 'Dewi' means the same as 'Devi', the goddess principle.

Within moments giant drops were falling all around us, quickening into a great torrential downpour.

The earth steamed, puddles formed and bells rang. The villagers were singing and dancing in the rain.

Ludi and I looked at each other and began jumping around with laughter.

It rained all night and half the next day.

Ludi came with extra offerings of fruits, oils and water.

He bowed down and knelt next to me as I sat on my bed, meditating. 'Thank you, Dewi. We can't thank you enough. We know the Great Spirits will bless you.'

'Don't thank me,' I said. 'It is the work of God, the Divine.'

'But you are Divine,' he said. 'You are from the Divine. I thank you for that,' he replied. Then as he stood to leave he said, 'And don't forget my promise. When you are ready I will take you to the shaman!' He smiled with a child-like enthusiasm.

Over the following days, I reached a point of dissolving so deeply that I could no longer move. I sat in undisturbed samadhi for four days and four nights. And in that sitting I journeyed into the infinite heart of God. I felt such love, such incomprehensible love, that no thing continued to exist as separate. All was inside this love, as this love embraced all. I dissolved into the love-light of all existence.

Four days passed by, submerged in vast realms of the soul. Then I found myself enfolded in a luminous field of rainbow light. From within the light I could hear a symphony of the most angelic orchestra of flutes and harps, instruments and choirs of God's angels; it was beyond anything of earth. It filled my entire being with radiant bliss.

And within the bliss the light burst forth with even greater unfolding beauty. All around me flowers were blossoming, spiralling up the walls of my bungalow, crystal gems sparkled, butterflies and birds danced and creatures all began to gather. Everything was an unfolding beauty of life's magnitude. Then I realised the walls were translucent, everything had turned to etheric light.

Across the yard came a young white brahman bull. His body

was luminous and swaying. He came to the veranda and gently clip-clopped his way up the steps, then put his head around the door. His lush brown eyes, like pools of infinite beauty, gazed deeply into me as he lowed his declaration of love. Then he entered the bungalow and lay down beside me.

'Oh beloved, oh my beloved,' I cried as I gazed at the white bull beside me. 'Oh, beloved creation.'

I sighed in bliss, knowing nothing but love for every speck of creation. I cried rivers of bliss, streaming light rivers of bliss.

From that moment, all of life took on an even greater lustre. It was as if a dark, damp veil had been lifted.

28. *Lotus Born*

To be a King in the heart, be a servant to the maid.

Isira

The day was bright. Flowers shone like coloured lamps in the sun. Palm leaves swayed, dancing between shadows and shafts of light. Ludi came to my door. He smiled at me serenely and joyfully. Today he was to take me to the shaman. And I knew I had completed my time on the island, so returning to Bali via Lombok was in good order. I turned with one last little sense of hesitation before boarding the fishing boat. I had become a part of the island and its people. I smiled with my heart full of gratitude. I knew I would never see these people again and wondered at the mystery that would continue to gently nurture their lives.

We travelled together in silence, until we arrived at a tiny hut on stilts and climbed up the ladder to an open loft.

A small man with long black hair and intense eyes was sitting against the wall in lotus posture wearing nothing but a Balinese sarong. Incense smoke wafted in the warm steamy air. He smiled upon our arrival, greeting us with a welcome blessing. He looked at my neck, impressed by my mala beads. Then he looked into my eyes.

'Hmm,' he said, 'powerful peace, great shakti. Welcome.'

He signalled for us to sit near him.

'So,' he said. 'Ludi tells me you would like an inscription on your body. Please show me. I will be honoured to help you.'

I took out my diary and opened to the page on which I had drawn the mandala.

'Oh, beautiful,' he said. 'Did you design it? What does it mean?'

'It's a sun-moon lotus. The script says *Self-Born from the Lotus, in love and devotion for all*. It is the consecration of this body to the work of the Divine: the truth beyond duality. That's why it is the sun-moon lotus; it is the united force of male-female polarities,' I said.

'Oh, very good, very good,' he nodded. 'So are you ready then?' he asked.

I nodded.

He showed me to the mattress upon which he placed a fresh yellow sarong. I lay down and breathed into stillness. Instantly I expanded beyond the body and watched with peace as he began the work. Within a few moments he stopped and looked at me with a puzzled look of wonder, while the tattoo needle still buzzed and whirred.

'You don't even blink!' he said with amazement. 'No heart racing, no blinking, no pain?' he asked.

I smiled peacefully.

He shook his head in wonder. 'This is most unusual!' he said. 'You have very powerful shakti, oh, great shakti! Unbelievable, the navel is a very painful place, usually.' He continued to shake his head and mutter in amazement. 'Thank you for letting me do this work for you.'

'Oh,' I said with a sigh. 'I thank *you*. Thank you.'

He worked for about an hour, the tattoo needle etching the design deeply into my skin. By the time he had finished I was so deep in meditation, it took me some time to return.

When I did, he put his hands together at his heart.

'Dewi,' he spoke in a deep tone of sincerity, 'our people believe that there is a White Golden Goddess and that She will come to bless the earth with Love and Light. You are great, I am sure you are filled with Her,' he said with wide deep eyes.

I looked at him, breathed, and then chuckled.

'Well,' I said, 'creation is a blessing; she is the goddess. And me, well, really I'm just a child; an infinitely blessed child.'

Nothing more was said.

We bowed to each other, then held each other in a long embrace. Ludi and I departed.

Ludi ushered me into a small motor cart, destined for his home. I had been invited as a guest for the night. From the moment I arrived I was treated like royalty. Ludi's mother could barely stop offering me different foods and drinks, greatly impressed that I was also vegetarian.

The depth of humility, generosity and hospitality of the Balinese people touched my soul, but in this case it became almost embarrassing. I was not used to receiving so much attention and felt less comfortable being served than I did serving. Nonetheless I endeavoured to remain present, understanding it would have been taken as an insult if I did not accept all offerings.

However, by the end of dinner, I could not sit still any more. I stood up and started collecting all of the dishes. There was a great flurry, as the tiny woman, Ludi and others in his family chased around after me trying to take all the dishes back. But I just couldn't let them. The gratitude in me was too great. I wanted to serve and give thanks.

It was clearly a great shock to the family that their guest was serving them. It took them a long time to settle down while I stood at the sink washing dishes.

Then Ludi came up to me. 'You know this is not necessary,' he said. 'You don't need to.'

'Of course, I don't need to,' I said. 'I want to.'

'Why?' he asked.

'Because I feel such gratitude and I know that no one is higher – as above, so below – no one lower. We are all together in the One life.' I said. 'I do this because of love.'

He stood silently with deep love and gratitude in his eyes. When he finally answered his mother, who wanted to know what I had said, she put her hands to her face and burst into tears. 'Tank you,' she cried. 'Tank you.' I took her in my arms and tears spilled from my eyes too.

Finally I made my way back to Bali, ready to return to Australia.

The 13th Attainment

Having made my way through the chrysalis' chamber I found myself flung into the course of my life's unfolding purpose.

The next stage of my destiny beckoned me.

KEY 13.

Death

KEY 13.
Death

All life involves stages of major transformation ... passages between the cycles of an eternal flow of creation.

Death of thoughts, experience or form is but a passage of renewal.

Dawn follows our darkest hour.

29. *What It Takes*

> Life's fulfilment finds constant contradictions in its path;
> But those are necessary for the sake of advance.
> The stream is saved from the sluggishness of its current
> By the perpetual opposition of its soil
> Through which it must cut its way.
> It is the soil which forms its banks.
> The spirit of fight belongs to the genius of life.
>
> *Rabindranath Tagore*

My spiritual experiences continued to nourish me and I found it an interesting dance to make my way through the world. It appeared as if I was going through a series of mini-deaths relating to work, friends, home and relationships. Over a period of two years I moved house several times, eventually ending up back in Adelaide. So I continued to discover that most of life reflects a paradox. Whilst the awareness of all-connected life filled me with great love and a state of unity, there appeared to be contradictions in my life, particularly around relationships. The state of unity and love amplified the states of others around me who still felt disconnected from their own true nature. Therefore it was common for their issues whether moral, spiritual or material to be stirred by our meeting and this often resulted in them reacting with judgment and opposition.

I was fascinated at how the contradictions could be so obvious yet unrecognised. Some of them became very apparent in my work. In a state of unity there can be no division in life between the spiritual and the material, yet humanity seemed to perpetuate this division. Many people often challenged me about receiving money for my 'spiritual' services. Yet modern life in Australia meant earning a living was essential, as was the need to sustain a balance between the spiritual and physical elements of my life.

Whilst I moved through different jobs I found an increased desire to be able to give to others. The ocean of love and awareness was becoming so deep within me that I was naturally overflowing and wanting to share it for the benefit of all. Although I was only twenty-six years old my reputation as a spiritual guide was growing. The news about my psychic abilities was spreading rapidly which meant that I could provide a service that supported both my purpose and my financial needs. It also fulfilled my immense desire to assist others in connecting with their own higher insight.

During this busy time I had many worldly matters to deal with and found it necessary to create the space for inner stillness. So when I was not in appointments with people I spent quiet time by myself. My commitments also involved a lot of concentration which increased my mental activity. This meant it was important for me to balance this activity with self time and quiet reflection.

I began to understand even more deeply the necessity for meditation. Meditation is not only essential for spiritual growth. It is essential for peace, calm and harmony in the body, mind and emotions. With meditation we can put aside the pace and noise of life. We can let go of the impulses that drive us to distraction and regain a place of stillness. Stillness is as essential to the mind as sleep is to the body. And, in that stillness, we discover the space in which all things are connected. This releases us from the compulsion of always trying to get something or to get to somewhere else. The never-ending chase! We can finally slow down and enjoy the moment. We can even discover how life is already so fulfilling in each moment that we don't seek the distractions any more.

I enjoyed my own company in many different ways. And whilst I reflected on the necessity for stillness I became aware that this stillness is always occurring, beneath all things. Even in activity, if we are still in mind, we experience a calm presence no matter where we are or what is happening. Whatever we give our dominant attention to creates our dominant experience. Hence, if our dominant attention is in the busy mind and busy body we have very little calm, whilst if our dominant attention is centred in the stillness of the awareness our dominant experience is one of peace. So whatever I was doing, whether walking, working, gardening, sitting or shopping, I made it a practice to simply watch my mind. That brought me another insight.

I could see how the mind is a miniature universe whilst the universe is the expansion of the mind. With limited perception – being engaged with small identifying thoughts – we only experience a confined aspect of life. With expansive perception – simply witnessing or resting in pure awareness – we can experience the boundless universe.

So I learned to witness more and more consistently, simply observing rather than following the stimulus of the thoughts. Through this practice I was also able to see the unreal nature of the thoughts and see that, if I just witnessed, the thoughts themselves would dissolve. They were just like waves, rising and falling, whilst the awareness was like the ocean. It remained unchanged no matter what waves came and went, big or small. Then, if I kept following the backdrop of awareness in and further in, I came into contact with my innermost being ... vast light, vast presence. Truly, it was and is beyond description ...

30. A Child of Destiny

Fate is what we find on the path we forgot
we had already paved.

Isira

Within a matter of months I found myself in contract work with private and government educational institutions. Recognising a gap in educational courses, I began developing and writing programs for life skills, personal development, conflict resolution, stress management and communication skills. The programs were welcomed with great enthusiasm, particularly in TAFE (Technical and Further Education) colleges and Centrelink job programs.

And, to my great joy, I was offered a position at Wanora on the mid-coast of the Peninsula, in a centre which a friend, Jilly, was managing. We had met many years ago on a bus ride to Melbourne. It had been evident right from the start that we had a soul connection. In many ways our lives have seemed to flow in parallel, so it was a great joy to be able to work alongside each other again. Also, I had the joy of driving along my favourite coastline, in the hills, valleys and beaches of my childhood. I felt greatly blessed that I was able to find work in the ordinary world and still breathe in the spirit of the land.

Then one day, while driving over the rise into Wanora, I suddenly saw the landscape shift in a time warp. The familiar sandhills rolled out in gentle slopes to the western shoreline, yet I was aware that the landscape I was watching was untouched by white man's buildings.

Stretched out in the river plain below was a trail of wurlies and families meeting, working, eating and living. Little eddies of smoke swirled up from campfires and disappeared into the pale blue sky. The estuary was hugged by bushes and children chased each other along the water's edge. It was a scene of great beauty, simplicity and innocence. The people were all moving as if in total harmony, laughing and playing as they carried out their tasks. It appeared that this was a meeting, perhaps for trading, between tribes from two different regions.

It came and went in a flash but I knew I had seen the place as it had been before white settlement. My heart ached with a deeper recognition of the detrimental changes that had transformed the sacred meeting place.

It awoke in me a deep ache, a longing for the ancient lore and a way to help humanity restore our sacred relationship with mother earth. It also highlighted the part of me that felt so at odds with modern life. I felt the core of my being as a living native spirit. And I knew that that spirit felt dissociated, felt the yearning for connection with my ancestors, and felt the common pain of all my Aboriginal relations.

Over the following months I continued having visions and experienced communication with the ancestor spirits of the land. I heard their voices warbling in a song-like rhythm, awakening a deep knowing in me of the ancient language.

I spent hours walking along the dreaming trails and sitting at sacred sites that the spirits guided me to. They conveyed such great love, power and wisdom that it left me with a longing for the communion of spirit in this world again.

Then I received the direct message that it wouldn't be long before I would meet my ancestors, that it was time to awaken the ancient grandmother spirit in my soul and sit with my bloodline. It sent great waves of excitement and confusion through me. I thought back to my unanswered questions, my granddad's long dark limbs, his message from spirit and my 'Auntie' in the park. But, as I thought of my blonde hair and fair complexion, I felt a tug of doubt. I had heard of many 'white Aboriginals' due to mixed blood yet also knew that it was controversial. It was common for Aboriginals to argue that Aboriginal identity should be based on darkness of skin. A part of me felt almost afraid to even consider myself as (part) Aboriginal. I knew that it would raise questions; not just from other Aboriginal people, but from my family. And despite such disputes I knew there was evidence in unspoken secrets.

Even deeper within was a knowing that the power of spirit, the gifts of the ancestors and the dreaming of any land could never be owned, could ultimately never be the right of one person more than another. I knew that we had all traversed the world and walked as the different races. I knew that we were all connected to each place and time in the power of our spirit. More than anything I knew that we all remained the same: from no-skin we come and to no-skin we return. In that moment it felt as if God's hand brushed me – a sense of deja vu rippled through my mind. I knew that there were many more things that remained a question. All I could do was surrender to my journey, whatever it did or did not reveal.

Despite these things being a great source of contemplation for me, I continued to revel in the satisfaction of my work programs. One day, following an afternoon seminar at Jilly's centre, we decided to catch up.

'So, what's been happening? Found a nice man yet?' asked Jilly.

'Pff!' I dismissed the idea. 'No, very happy by myself, thank you very much.'

'Oh, come on Katie,' she exclaimed. 'You're beautiful, don't you feel lonely?' I looked at her soft eyes, imploring with love and friendship. The wind blew her wispy brown curls of hair around her face and the scene around her seemed to swirl in slow motion. That moment drew me inside, reminding me that I was already in communion with life. Such beauty in nature alone, displayed in every thing in every moment, could fill me with great joy and fulfilment.

'No, not at all. I have peace in my heart. Besides, life is really entertaining as it is and I feel such freedom now that I'm past the

Marcus journey. (I had had a fleeting, uneventful relationship with a wealthy Greek Orthodox man.) You know, if ever I was to meet another guy, I hope he's just a free spirit who drives a Kombi or something!'

'Oh, I'm so glad about that,' she said. 'I really couldn't see it working with him. I think all that money jammed up his head. I think you need a SNAG (sensitive new age guy).'

The next day after work, Jilly pulled me aside excitedly.

'Hey! Katie, you've got to meet Jake, this guy who's working with the youth in town. Guy and I asked him to look after our yacht for us, so he's living on it for a while. And guess what – he is a SNAG! I just know you two should meet.'

I looked at her suspiciously. 'Now hold on a minute,' I said. 'Don't you go getting any match-making ideas. I'm not interested in anything. I'm happy by myself.'

'Oh, come on,' she cajoled. 'Just friends. You know you could do with a bit more fun, meet some more people. You've become such a hermit again.'

I looked at her and thought over what she had said. It's probably true, I thought to myself. I had become a little recluse again. It would be good to get out a bit and have some fun.

'Why don't you come to the yacht this weekend? I reckon we would all get on great.'

'Ummm ... Oh, all right,' I said.

When I pulled up at the dock I couldn't believe my eyes. Jilly's car was there and next to it was a gold Kombivan. No other cars in sight. Oh no, I said to myself. What have I done? I thought about my comment a few days ago and contemplated the bizarre connection between 'what we ask for', and 'what we get'.

I stepped up onto the jetty. Jilly and Guy were sitting on the benches and a tall man with dark hair stood near the helm.

I stepped on board. Jilly grabbed me straight away.

'Isn't he gorgeous?' she whispered in my ear. I rolled my eyes at her. Actually, I didn't recognise any particularly strong attraction to him, despite the fact that most people would have described him as 'tall, dark and handsome'. Yet as I looked more closely there was something rather captivating about his pale blue eyes and his cheeky grin. And – standing at six foot, four inches tall with long legs and broad shoulders – he certainly struck a pose.

Once all introductions were covered, I put my question to Jake.

'Is that your Kombivan?' I asked.

'Yeah it is,' he said with a dimply grin.

Oh great! I thought to myself with a sense of wariness. I still couldn't believe what I had just said a matter of days before was somehow appearing right before me.

The afternoon passed quickly as we discussed many topics. We discovered that we all had common interests, especially to do with nature and adventure. The day ended with Jake asking me if I'd go bike-riding with him sometime.

I hesitated at first, concerned with what I might be getting myself into. But after a long pause I thought, well why not, he's a nice enough guy, he'd make a good friend. 'Okay,' I said.

'How about next weekend?'

'Oh, *(so soon?)* um, well how 'bout you give me a call first? ' I said, hesitating to fully commit.

The next weekend came and I found myself having a great time. We rode through bush tracks, laughed a lot and then drove to a market to eat. He enthusiastically joined me in a vegetarian roll, saying he wanted to get healthy. Hmm, I thought to myself, another interesting common point.

The following weekend was my twenty-seventh birthday and he asked if I wanted to go out again on the weekend. We'd had such a great time and got along so well that this time I didn't hesitate.

After some lunch, we were strolling through the markets when I suddenly felt an opening of energy in my heart chakra and a vividly audible voice deep inside that spoke: 'You should be holding this man's hand; he is your husband-to-be.'

I shook my head in shock and stared up at Jake. Oh, God! I thought to myself. That's a bit too intense; where did that come from?

His clear eyes looked down into mine and he smiled. In that instant I felt an energy swirl between our hearts and before I knew it, he took my hand in his. My heart pounded and my face flushed red, while my mind flapped around, totally flummoxed. We walked hand-in-hand without saying a word. I watched, as if from above; watched us being worked by fate.

Over the following month we spiralled into an extraordinary depth of connection. Suddenly I realised a profound love had consumed us in an all-powerful, attractive force. Every spare moment we had was spent together. Next, along with his recognition of my obvious psychic awareness, came a fast-track of Jake's 'initiation' into the world of spirit. In awe and great enthusiasm he seemed to lap it all up, intrigued by the timing of our meeting, as he had planned to take a trip to the Himalayas before we met. It was coming up in September and he hoped I would go with him. I wished I could, but I already had contracts for the programs I was managing and lecturing at three different TAFE institutions. And besides, I knew he was meant to go by himself.

In the month before his departure, I saw a series of vivid visions. I realised he was the reincarnation of the warrior in the Native American life who had left me with our child and babe in womb, never to return. I had watched him, a young warrior, ride off with others to meet a neighbouring tribe who were threatening to claim our homeland. And, as I had watched him disappear over the horizon, beyond the great stretch of long golden grasses, my heart sank. I knew he would not come home. That was the last time I saw him. I had pined for the rest of my life praying for him to come home, but he never did ... until now.

Then I heard 'them' again. The spirits of the children were calling me from the heavens above, 'Mum ... we want to come soon.'

I responded to them with my soul awareness that my destiny meant I couldn't be a normal mother ... that I might not always be with them. My soul knew I had other things to fulfil and that it might take me away from my children for many months at a time. And yet they revealed their knowing of this too, and that it was all perfect in the predestined order of our co-created journey. They were powerful souls in themselves, with a purpose for which I was the perfect vehicle to bring them to earth.

'Don't worry,' they spoke, 'all will be well.'

Then, one morning as we lay in deep embrace, Jake stared down into my eyes. And there, in that same instant, I realised I was him, staring down at me, holding me in strong tender arms. As I looked I was the complete experience of Jake – his feelings, his thoughts, his deep love. And in his thoughts were the words ... 'Oh, dear beautiful, beautiful woman. You are the one I want to marry. You are the one I want to be with. But how do I ask you – will you marry me?'

In a flash, I was in my body again. I looked up into his shining eyes of love.

'Yes,' I said.

He started and pulled back, staring at me in disbelief.

'Hey? What? Did ... did you hear what I was thinking?' he asked with mystified excitement.

'Well I said yes, didn't I?' I grinned, giggling.

'Yes?' he repeated. 'Yes! You will marry me?' he asked excitedly.

'Yes,' I said, 'solemnly.'

We laughed and cried, squeezing each other tight.

Over the following weeks, I guided Jake in ceremonial prayer, an opening of his spirit to the higher consciousness so that we could be journeying together in deeper awareness.

He sat in ceremony with enthusiasm and naivety. He hadn't experienced the spirit world in such a way before and struggled to integrate the sacred laws that were spoken into his everyday life, especially in such matters as non-violence and respect for all creatures great and small. (He had a propensity for killing spiders and squashing any bug that came in sight and couldn't understand my demands and insistence on taking them out to the garden.)

One day I found him cursing a trail of ants that were evidently setting up home in the kitchen. He still didn't seem to understand when I expressed my concern for the little creatures that humanity constantly killed or misplaced. 'Who says they don't have the same right to live where they choose?' I enquired. 'We humans keep building our homes on top of theirs! Maybe they should be throwing us out!' Jake just looked at me as if I was mad.

So one day I sat down with him and asked him to open his heart to spirit that he might truly hear what I had to say.

'All of life is connected,' I began. 'I know my oneness with life, with you and everything in it. The creatures, the insects, the spiders are another part of me,' I said, patting my heart. 'They are my friends and allies in the spirit world.'

'What do you mean?' he asked.

'As a Native American, in past lives, I learned the art of "shape-shifting". This is the ability to translocate the conscious self into the form of other living creatures. They can help us to be in places where as a human we cannot be. I have a deep relationship with certain animals and creatures, one of which is the spider. The spider has the power to create from within itself and move between the higher and lower dimensions,' I said, stretching one hand to the sky and the other to the earth.

He looked at me with a stare of amazement overlaid by a slight glaze of cynicism.

'When you are away,' I said, pinning him sharply with my eyes, 'don't kill any spiders. I will come to visit you. If you see a spider, know that I am there.'

Jake couldn't hold himself any longer. 'Pff!' he half started to laugh, but when he saw my look he drew it back in.

'Don't mock the power of spirit,' I said, and left the room. I walked out into the sunlight and gazed at the blue sky ... the same blue sky I had looked to over so many aeons. Soon Jake came outside.

'Sorry,' he said. 'I wasn't meaning to disrespect what you say. Just that it's ... well, it's sort of "out there"!' He put his arm around my shoulder.

'Yeah, well, you better get used to it,' I said. 'That ain't even the half of it yet.'

We looked at each other and chuckled, realising the adventure we were both in for together.

The following week, Jake was due to leave for the Himalayas. I gave him a journal suggesting it might come in handy to document his experiences.

Three weeks after he had gone I was digging in the garden when I felt myself dissolve into deep consciousness and suddenly re-form in another place. I was a spider sitting on a rock on a ledge overlooking a great valley of the Himalayas. I looked up and saw Jake standing on the ledge with his hands over his heart. He was so taken by the beauty of the landscape.

Then, in that moment, he felt his overwhelming love for me and happened to look down. At his feet he saw the spider. A rush of electric God-bumps flashed from head to toe. He sighed and breathed in, overtaken by a deep knowing that I was there with him. He threw his arms out wide with joy and tears welled up in his eyes. His realisation of our profound connection in spirit flooded his heart with love.

Then, just as suddenly, I was back in my body, squatting next to the garden. I went and wrote down the time and the experience in my diary. When Jake got back we compared notes – he had had that experience at exactly the same time! It had moved him so deeply that he too wrote it down in his journal, dated the same day.

On his return we resumed plans to marry. Neither of us wanted a church wedding so we opted for a garden ceremony, a reflection of our love of nature. Both our families were so full of joy – everyone felt we were the 'perfect match'.

The night of our wedding was a strange experience for me. I had thought I married someone who wanted to take a conscious and sacred journey with me, that we were going to grow together in deep presence and higher awareness. But that night I looked on with my first sense of disillusionment as I watched Jake wipe himself out with alcohol. He fell asleep in a drunken stupor without even a kiss goodnight. It filled me with a strange sense of discord. I watched my mind, with acceptance and non-judgmental reason, tuck away the feeling. It went into a neat little storage box labelled: 'It's okay, we can make it work'.

Then I dreamed. I saw the face of our little girl, her shining spirit looking over me. She showed me she would be here soon. I was still unsure of my capacity to even conceive as I had had a history of ovarian problems, polycystic ovaries and amenorrhoea.[1] In fact the specialist had indicated that it was 'highly unlikely' that I would be able to fall pregnant.

Yet destiny proved its own certainty. The next night, as Jake and I were deeply united in sacred union I saw our etheric bodies completely fuse. The light vibration was incredible – like a spiralling vortex. Then it opened from above our crowns and a brilliant rush of light entered into our field. An explosive rush of creative force spiralled in, and sent out an exquisite burst of light in the same instant. In that moment I knew without a doubt that our first child had entered. I had conceived.

We left the next morning for our honeymoon, a trip in the Kombivan to Eyre Peninsula. We camped by the beach beside a grove of young she-oak trees; the long dangling needles whispered a delightful song in the breeze and clouds gathered along the horizon. My soul drank in the peace of nature; my heart felt alive as we delighted in the simple beauty of our surroundings. We spent our days enjoying the sound of waves as we skipped around and chased each other, lay under passing clouds and played in the sand. It was a bit too cool to swim but not too cold to laze around on the beach.

After a week we drove to a small cove called Shelley Beach. We walked along its peaceful stretch, not another soul in sight. At the other end of the bay I climbed on the rocks, enjoying the beauty of the rising and falling tide as it flowed into little waterfalls and rock pools.

Suddenly I felt a strong, familiar presence. Dolphins! I thought.

---

1 Absence of menstruation.

I stood up and scanned the bay. Sure enough, not far out, a pod of six dolphins was entering the bay. I started running across the beach, pointing and yelling. 'Dolphins!'

Jake watched on and then chased after me. 'What are you doing?' he asked, looking totally bewildered as a I stripped off.

'I'm going to swim with them! Aren't you?' I asked.

'What, are you crazy? That's a bit dangerous isn't it?' he replied.

'No!' I yelled, and dived off the edge of the reef.

I swam towards them and stopped at a respectful distance. Then they were all swimming up to me and around me. I dived underwater, playing with them. My whole body was filled with ecstatic glee.

A young female took particular interest in me. She swam right up, making whirring giggling noises, eyed my stomach, nodded her head then did a swoop back around and swam on her side, rubbing her tummy next to mine and flapping her dorsals. She was telling me she knew I had a baby in my womb! She was so full of joy. As I watched I saw a field of rainbow light surrounding us. They played with me for about half an hour before moving on to feed.

When I finally came out of the water I was so ecstatic that Jake was disappointed in himself.

The next week we returned home. I dreamed I lost a tooth and then woke up craving green apples. I was so convinced I was pregnant that I bought a pregnancy test from the chemist. As soon as I got home I followed the instructions and waited ... it turned up negative! I was stunned. It must be wrong.

I told Jake. He said, 'Ah well, apparently a lot of women get "phantom" pregnancies.' But something inside me was still sure it was a real little spirit.

A week later I still could only eat green apples first thing in the morning; and certain smells, like coffee, made me nauseous. I finally decided to go to the doctor. The test came up positive. Jake was over the moon with delight.

Over the following months we decided to build a home, closer to the beach and the coast of my childhood. I had saved enough for a deposit and the extra money for furnishings. With my savings and his reliable job we managed to secure our home. We hoped to have the house built before the baby arrived. We opted for a small cottage-style design with old red bricks, lime mortar and book-leaf stacked slate. The block wasn't large but it was enough for a cottage garden, a vegetable patch and a stretch of lawn. And it was close to one of our favourite beaches.

•

I continued to work, finding fulfilment in the courses and lectures I offered. It gave me great joy to see the change in young adults, who had been considered at 'the end of the line'. They had been aggressive, dysfunctional people with no sense of confidence. Now, they were cooperative. They were happy, creative and expressive employed people.

In my self-time I meditated deeply and watched the wonder of a child growing in my womb. The etheric field went through very distinct stages of vibrations and colours over the months. I also watched a small number (usually three or four at a time) of small fine blue spirits who would come and go, helping to integrate our light bodies and keep the vibrations balanced.

At around about seven months, activity increased greatly, with the spirits coming and going a lot and the light field magnified. It had changed from a soft pink and purple with faint rainbow waves to a strong rose and gold colour. At the same time, I started experiencing complications with strong contractions. I had an overwhelming sense that she was going to come early.

I stopped working and focused internally on the baby and my energy field. I sat for hours and took long walks along the beach. I meditated and stretched, feeling deeply peaceful as I breathed in the great open beauty of ocean, earth and sky.

Then one afternoon at about twenty-eight weeks, I felt a huge shift in my field. I was sitting in the little lounge room, sorting out the CDs in the stereo cabinet. The late afternoon sun was filtering through the white lace curtain and an air of stillness was hanging over the cottage. Everything appeared so ordinary yet surreal as deep within me I recognised a surge of conscious awareness. It was followed by a strong wave of vibrating light that swept through my womb. I looked at Jake and said, 'I think she's going to come soon, maybe only another two days.'

He tried to hide his concern, not wanting to bring any stress to the process. Yet I felt deeply at peace in a knowing of simply what 'was'.

That night I had a vividly lucid dream.

I was sitting under the Bodhi Tree in a state of fullness when the moment arrived – I gave birth. As I looked down, it was the most perfect, beautiful white baby elephant, fully adorned. As she arrived the Bodhi leaves turned to gold and showered all upon us. Angels and spirits filled the sky while rainbows and heavenly music caressed us.

I awoke in the morning knowing the birth of a great spirit was about to happen.

The next afternoon my waters broke. Jake was in a flapping frenzy as I sat in a deep state of peace.

We had planned a natural birth at the hospital with a bath available if everything progressed well. We phoned the hospital and were advised to make our way in as soon as possible. Within the hour we had arrived. A deep feeling of calm had totally embraced me so that time disappeared. There was nothing but the energy, the movement of the body, the flow of breath and the pulse of contractions suspended in the timelessness of the now.

As the contractions grew stronger and I surrendered to them in each moment, I entered a deeper and deeper state of bliss and peace. I could see a giant mother angel enfolding me and great pulses of cosmic light flooded us with each contraction. The great waves of rose and golden light swirled all around us, filling up the room with a sweet scent. But despite the consistency of strong pulses, my cervix was not dilating enough for the baby to move through the canal.

After twenty-four hours with not much change the nurses began to worry. They were also surprised by my being blissfully happy and in a deeply peaceful state with no painkillers. At the thirty-hour mark and after no response to a gel for opening the cervix they decided to monitor the baby. I was ushered to the bed and asked to lie down.

Suddenly the room took on an air of distress. The baby was showing signs of stress. I was informed that it was an emergency and that I would have to have a caesarean section.

I responded, still in deep peace ...

'Okay.'

Seconds later a little nurse came into the room with a large needle. The midwife asked me to turn on my side. 'We need to insert a needle now, dear,' she spoke gently.

I felt my heart, still full of light and peace.

'Okay,' I responded calmly.

'Oh,' said the little nurse as she stroked my arm, 'you are so peaceful. Just a little sting now.' And with that she inserted the needle into my lower back.

The spinal tap went in without a flinch, I was rolled into an operating room, and before I knew it, I was shown my new baby girl. On August 23rd, 1995, she was placed on my chest briefly before she was suddenly whisked away.

Jake held my hand, comforting me.

It wasn't long before we were informed that we had to be transferred to A1 emergency paediatrics at Flinders Hospital – there were 'complications'.

My heart leapt to my throat. Our newborn, Lilha, was struggling to live. I watched my dear little 'skinned rabbit' shivering, jaundiced and hooked up to apparatus as she struggled to stay alive. At only twenty-eight weeks her lungs were not properly formed. It was unsure for the first week whether she would live. I barely slept, sitting next to her in her little controlled box, praying, singing to her, showering her with loving light. I wasn't even allowed to hold her, let alone breast-feed, which was terribly uncomfortable for my enormous, productive breasts.

My only consolation was a 'hand hole' that I could reach through to touch her and a mechanical device to relieve and store all of my milk.

I watched Jake's stress levels soar as he kept up with work and tried to visit us as much as possible. My mother, whom I had grown to appreciate so dearly, provided me with great consolation. Over the last few years we had grown together – recognising our deep spiritual bond and our friendship as two souls meeting on the path. And now we had an even deeper unspoken bond – motherhood.

I felt emotionally overwhelmed and incapable as I watched other mothers, next to my room, holding, feeding and bathing their newborns. I ached to hold Lilha in my arms.

Finally, after a month, she turned the corner. When I held her on my chest, she took a deep sigh and wiggled her tiny body as if trying to get even closer. I cried with relief.

It was another month before we could take Lilha home – to our new home.

Things continued to improve as Lilha became ever stronger. Yet along with that came the usual challenges of a new family: sleepless nights, more laundry, financial hurdles, emotional sensitivities and the needs of three different individuals. At times I found my energy was spread too thinly as I tried to sustain and meet all of these needs.

Over the months, I watched my particular care (some called it 'fussiness') with food take a slide as I tried to somehow fit in more with Jake. He had a strong penchant for 'fast food'. And it meant less time spent in the kitchen if we ate the same thing. I preferred to compromise my own standards than endure the conflicts that repeatedly arose over our differences.

His family also had a tendency to enjoy regular meals of fast food such as fish and chips, cakes and pastries. So any mealtimes spent with them were also less than my healthy standard. As Lilha's appetite improved she took breast milk more regularly. Her little golden brown body began to fill out a bit, yet as a result of the extra breastfeeding, I began to lose weight and energy rapidly. So I started eating even more 'unhealthy' food like cream buns, donuts and cakes in a desperate but unsuccessful attempt to put on weight.

Then one night as I sat in bed reading I felt a sudden intense onset of pain in my solar plexus, penetrating from inside to the front and back of my body. It grew rapidly into a seizing, suffocating cramp followed by intense nausea. I ran to the bathroom and began vomiting. The pain was so extreme and gripping that I ended up doubled over on the floor, writhing, groaning and struggling to breathe.

It grew worse over the following hour until Jake reached panic point. He called an ambulance. I was taken immediately to a public hospital. The doctor finally looked at me after two hours of waiting.

'Oh ... you've just got gastro,' he deduced bluntly. 'Go home and rest, you'll be fine.'

I looked at him in utter disbelief. I knew it wasn't gastro, that something was seriously wrong. 'But ... it can't be, it's not!' I exclaimed. 'I know it's something serious.'

Jake stared in disbelief.

'Oh, yes well, gastro can feel really serious. Don't worry you'll be fine,' he said patting me on the arm and walking out.

Jake's words chased after him. 'What are you talking about? This is seriously wrong!'

But his words were just left hanging in the air, of no more meaning or importance. We were abandoned and left alone with the starkness of our trauma.

31. *Life and Death*

> If you stay in your centre and embrace death
> with your whole heart you will endure forever.
>
> *Lao-tzu*

Jake and I looked at each other in disbelief. I was sent home with a common painkiller, which didn't soften the intense pain even by a nudge. I was totally disoriented. I had been able to endure and go beyond the pain of labour yet this was almost unbearable. A few times I even found myself just about ready to give up my body, as the pain was relentless.

Finally, after about three weeks, it settled down and life seemed to get back to normal except that Jake seemed to be increasingly stressed and somewhat disconnected from me. The glow and enthusiasm that initially connected us had fallen away within the first few months of our marriage.

I was feeling exceptionally sensitive and felt the discord as something I needed to address. Yet no matter how I tried to communicate with Jake it was met with growing resistance.

Instead he took to avoidance and suppression. The television would be switched on, a beer opened, and before long he would be asleep. And that's how we would go to bed together, night after night. So many things were left unsaid. Too many things were ignored and avoided. And no matter how much I approached Jake to find a way to understand what was disturbing him, it was met with the same resistance.

Gradually over the weeks and months, this grew into a cyclical pattern: a denial of issues; suppressed emotions erupting in aggression, anger, and impatience; a descent of energy into apathy, forgetfulness and misperceptions; and then a return to the strangely adamant view that there was absolutely nothing wrong.

It seemed that as long as I was willing to ignore the underlying angst, we could go about life as if it were normal. To the world outside, to family and friends, it all seemed like the perfect marriage, the happy family.

I was beginning to feel a deep rift. It was between us – but even more, it was within me. I was no longer feeling the balance between my inner being and my outer life. I held most dear to me the principles of love, growth, communication and openness; in fact, I felt they were absolutely essential for a relationship to work.

However, it was becoming painfully evident that I was moving along a different path to Jake. We had different priorities. It seemed Jake just wanted everything to cruise along as if there was nothing to work on. He was happy for the smiling faces at picnics and adventures in the park, as long as we didn't talk about our feelings or conflicts; whilst I felt all those social niceties were picnics of mediocrity – shallow and meaningless.

To me, the niceties were masks to hide the pain, screens to avoid a deeper uncomfortable reality. I couldn't live a life like that. I wanted a life that was real, even if that meant facing my shadow. And somehow I couldn't imagine a flourishing relationship with someone else who wasn't willing to be just as real.

Everyone would delight in Jake's boundless love for me, and in the belief that he would go to the end of the world for me, to hell and back. But what he wasn't willing to do was face his own darkness. And that was what I longed for most. I knew that that was what would bring a truly liberated presence of love and a real connection that could keep growing.

On occasions I felt the great hazard of a possible loss of my own integrity. I would stand awkwardly in the middle of those social gatherings, feeling that I didn't know what to do any more. When friends and family asked how things were, Jake would smile with his charismatic charm. 'Great! Yeah, it's all good.'

When they looked at me for confirmation, I would cringe inside, feeling I could only join the celebration by being false.

I struggled to find the middle ground of acceptance. I loved all that was wonderful in Jake and in our life, but as long as there were underlying issues, the fake smiles that kept the issues secret, it was all just a shaky facade.

Two weeks after my 'gripping solar plexus' had settled down, it struck again, with even greater intensity. The ambulance took me to the hospital again. And, again, I was sent home with a similar response: 'Well, look, gastro can come and go in waves, sometimes over several weeks. It should settle down soon.'

It took another three weeks to really settle, leaving me feeling quite weak and frighteningly frail.

About a week later it hit again. Because we were in a country location, the same drivers came when we called the ambulance. They were horrified to see me again. They decided to take me to a different hospital – a little further, but still public. To my great disbelief, I was faced with the same diagnosis. Jake, furious, and frustrated at having to watch me suffering so intensely, grudgingly took me home.

Lilha, despite my distress, continued to be exceptionally peaceful and happy. She was catching up quickly, filling out her body even more. Nonetheless, she was like a tiny doll with fine ginger hair and penetrating dark brown eyes, that sparkled and shone. She looked like a little golden fairy. With this striking combination of features she continually attracted attention wherever we went.

Four weeks later the pain hit again and this time it was a devastating blow. I was already still struggling with great frailty and I had very little energy with which to endure. The ambulance drivers were incredulous that I had been sent home the last time.

My pulse was almost off the dial and my body was showing emergency readings. I started losing consciousness just as they asked

Jake if we had private insurance. Fortunately we did, so they decided to take me to Ashford near the city rather than risk a public hospital again. The trip seemed to take forever as my body writhed in pain. Even with the 'gas' given to me, the pain sent unbelievable shock waves through my body.

On arrival I was checked into emergency immediately. I started moving in and out of my body, unable to endure the pain any longer. I moved into a tunnel of blissful light and for a few moments my body ceased breathing. I could see a swirling field of angels in the golden white light but something was stopping me from moving through to the other side. Jake became terrified. It was his fear and his grab at my arm that pulled me back.

The next morning the hospital tests finally revealed that I had acute pylo-nephritis, an infection in the kidneys, and the kidneys had begun to shut down. I was immediately administered fresh blood and antibiotics and after some weeks had settled into a stable condition and was allowed to go home. Thinking things had returned to normal, I busied myself with the ongoing finishing touches to our new home.

But only two weeks later, the same pain struck me again. I was stunned. The ambulance returned me to the hospital. In the early hours of the morning the tests revealed that my gallbladder was so poisonous and swollen that it was on the edge of exploding. The blood tests came back revealing chaos in my liver and pancreas. It was too dangerous to remove the gallbladder in case it exploded and poisoned my whole body.

The only option was to hook me up to fluids and flush; and wait. My poor body heaved up bright green and yellow watery bile every hour or so and trembled and shook.

I dissolved again, this time even further into the field of light. I felt deep peace there in the light, glad to be free of the body. But then I saw my grandfather and grandmother. They smiled at me and then shook their heads.

'Not yet,' they said. 'You can't come yet. But don't worry, we'll help you feel more peace.'

I felt a warm wave of peace wash over me and then a big image like on a movie screen flashed up before me. I saw Lilha waiting for me with her arms out. Suddenly I felt a rush as if I was sliding backwards down the tunnel of light.

With a jolt I landed in my body and breathed.

I opened my eyes.

I was all alone.

Half an hour later a nurse came in.

'Did you get some rest, love?' she asked. I just looked at her. 'Your husband went home. He was glad to see you sleeping.'

Still I just looked at her. I couldn't even talk.

'That painkiller's really knocked you out, I think,' she chuckled as she patted my arm and changed the drip.

An hour later the pain shook my body again. The nurse came in with another needle – apparently I was being administered the highest dose allowable in Australia. I could scarcely believe this, given that the degree of pain was indescribable.

I watched my family come and go while I dissolved in and out of blissful light. I seemed to be moving deeper and deeper into this light, while they displayed greater and greater distress as they watched my body disappearing before their eyes.

Then one morning when a nurse was lifting my body for circulation I happened to turn my head to the left. The room was a stark and sterile cube of grey and white. Against the wall was a cupboard, a sink and a mirror.

As I looked, I saw the image of a grey ghostlike body, skeleton thin, with black hollows under the eyes staring back at me. I was quite startled when I suddenly realised that it was my body.

Oh, my God! I thought. My body! I'm nearly dead. I realised then that it was the death tunnel that I had been through, not just an expanded state of awareness. Oh dear, I thought again. No wonder the family are all so distraught. They were watching the dying of a twenty-eight year old wife, a daughter, who was too young to die. I didn't dare tell Jake what had happened.

I realised then that the dying state of my body reflected a process of major transformation on all levels. Although I was able to view this from a different perspective I could see how traumatic it was for my family. Suddenly their fear and pain hit me even more deeply. I realised that to them, this represented the possibility of an enormous loss, not a passage towards renewal. I knew I had to make it through.

Finally, after months of intense ordeal, my gallbladder was removed and, with my bodyweight down to forty-five kilograms, I slowly recovered enough to go home.

32. *Little Baby, Ancient Soul*

When we forget we are the ocean
we are afraid for the wave that is
approaching its death upon the shore.

Isira

I found immense wonder in the growing delight of Lilha. The depth of her peace, joy and presence was striking. One day, Jake, Lilha and I were in our friend Kane's travelling bus with Mary and Keith. Mary and Keith had become close friends after coming for soul guidance readings. With her long legs and shapely figure beside his boyish frame, they seemed an odd couple. Yet both displayed a depth of personality that took them beyond the usual stereotypes of the physical world.

Kane was an eccentric rune-maker and Celtic shaman whom we had met through a lady who owned a float tank centre. His presence was a great delight to me as it reflected the deep remnants of Celtic mystery and magic that still vibrated in my soul. (I had previously learned that there was Welsh and Scottish Celtic ancestry on my dad's mother's line.) And the fact that he lived in a bus tantalised my spirit even more. It appealed to the gypsy nature within me.

The bus was filled with the mystical and magical: feathers, crystals, talismans, drums, paintings, runes[1] and cloths. The essence

[1] Divination tool using stones inscribed with characters from an ancient alphabet representing archetypes.

of the freedom and authenticity of his soul's expression was something I deeply admired. It also represented great adventure. It wasn't long before Kane invited us all to join him on one of his adventures, a trip along the coast in his bus.

Lilha was about six months old and hadn't yet managed to sit herself up, so she was happily lying back, snuggled into plush velvet cushions. We were heading down the coast to watch the whales. Kane was driving while the rest of us chatted and gazed at the passing green misty scenery.

Suddenly Lilha pulled herself up into lotus posture, put her fingers into mudras and placed them on her knees. We all stopped dead-still and stared. Then, she took a deep breath, and out of her mouth came a pure celestial, 'Om' that seemed to ring for at least a minute. We all dropped to our knees with wide eyes and gaping mouths.

She stayed seated, eyes closed in a serene glow for about twenty minutes. When she finally opened her eyes it was as if the sun were shining out of her whole being. She smiled at us with love, beaming with sparkling light and then closed her eyes, laid back and dissolved into a radiant smiling stillness.

Her magical display only confirmed more deeply that her presence was that of a very evolved soul. When she finally opened her eyes again she uttered one sweet word: 'Mumma'. My heart melted.

Over the following months, my health seemed to gradually stabilise and I started offering readings and soul guidance at fairs. It was the sort of work that I felt was part of my true nature and a way to serve and assist a deeper purpose in people's lives. Soon I was experiencing a consistent flow of people seeking clairvoyant and psychic insight. Most came by word of mouth, and a few came from having seen the occasional flyer I had pinned up around the Peninsula. People even turned up saying Lama Zopa had told them to find me. There was soon a growing reputation that I was renowned for incredible vividness and accuracy. And, before long I was invited to do more readings with the Australian Psychics Association.

Jake managed to accept my 'business' with a degree of distance. We seemed to be growing further apart as my attempts to find common ground with him continued to fail.

I sensed we were heading towards our own death: the death of our journey as husband and wife.

The 14th Attainment

Having accepted that the dark night
of the soul was another passage,
I could see the dawn that awaited,
albeit on a distant horizon.

Every death is but a corridor:
a junction between the stages of our
eternal life.

Death is transformation.

KEY 14.

The Middle Way

KEY 14.

The Middle Way

From a state of apparent fragmentation, we unify each element of our experience:

> Body, emotion, mind, soul.
> Unconscious, sub-conscious,
> conscious, super-conscious.
> Earth, water, air, fire.

Trials, temptations and consequences lead us to integration. Through temperance, we transform extremes, we transcend the illusion of division in duality; we enter the middle way.

In the middle way we find unity and wholeness.

33. *Insight*

> Keep yourself clean and bright.
> You are the window through
> Which you must see the world.
>
> *George Bernard Shaw*

Life appeared to be moving along normally again when, out of the blue, I was gripped again with the identical pain in my solar plexus that had laid me up in hospital before. I was totally bewildered, having thought everything had settled after my gall-bladder was removed, despite a few niggling symptoms.

I was taken to hospital again. This time, the head specialist Tom Wilson was called in. I proved to be a puzzling case. The blood tests came back showing my liver enzymes were totally chaotic again, but the medical team could not work out how or why. Radiology and ultra-sound left them none the wiser, so they decided to do an endoscopy – sending a minute camera down the oesophagus to have a look.

That sent my body into even greater turmoil but revealed nothing further to illumine the cause of it all.

Again my body went into meltdown.

The following afternoon the news came back. Not good. I had an onset of severe pancreatitis. That meant the enzymes were somehow obstructed and had flooded back into the pancreas where they proceeded to consume the organ's tissues. The pancreas was eating itself!

The pain and nausea that wracked my body was unbelievable. This time I really struggled to have the will to live. I slipped in and out of my body, dissolving further and further. And in the space, free of my body, I was able to see more deeply into the cause of such an intense condition.

I observed the ongoing struggle I had, on a deeper level, with the 'physical' realm, perceiving it largely as something intolerably cruel, dark, burdening and caught in the disease of illusion. I felt contempt for being 'trapped' in a world that worshipped the ego, material gain and sense gratification. I longed to be returned to the spirit realm of love, truth and oneness. The barbaric mind-set that drove most people's actions was something that repulsed me.

The primitive nature of the human body, including my own, was a thing of disgust that I deeply yearned to be free of. Despite my highest intent to make my life sacred, I had managed to create a giant rift between being 'Self' and being in a body.

In the expanded state of awareness I saw the remnants of great pain, anger and resentment that were trapped deep in my soul. I saw how a part of my mind had reacted to these deeply stored memories on a human level. I had pushed aside the pain of violation, burying it under the attribute of 'unconditional love' for those who had abused me.

I had lived so deeply in tolerance and compassion that I had denied the value and respect of my being and my body. I had unconsciously condoned such ill-treatment in some dark mental programming that said I did not deserve anything better.

And in doing so, I held onto a sense of injustice, and deep anger, resentment and bitterness at the abuse I had endured. The illness I was experiencing was simply a reflection of my incapacity – body, mind and emotions – to hold onto such self-inflicted violation any more. And so, over those weeks and months my whole being uprooted the very core of it all. In great heaving pulses, my body expelled litres of vile, bitter juices of bile.

And with each great, vomiting expulsion, I felt the release of the bitterness. The deeper I went, the deeper it came from, until I realised I was vomiting up the bitterness of my ancestors, and their ancestors – to the very core of the collective human psyche. I saw the layers of emotions that were entwined through history, from the vitriolic wheel of perpetrator-victim-perpetrator-victim.

Then, right at the very bottom of this pit was a gripping fear.

In the past, in both this life and past lives, I remembered the pain of monstrous abuse, violation and persecution because I had stood against authorities and the power of suppression. I had dared to stand for Truth, and as Truth, claiming my life in the one authority of the Divine. I had suffered and died in flesh for eternal life.

And it was the experience of suffering in flesh that I feared. For I knew I had come for the same Truth again. And already I had suffered greatly in the physical. Already there were those again who wanted to pull me down, believing the presence of such awareness was just some grandiose claim.

Being a bearer of Truth was a threat to their illusory existence – a threat that the lies would be exposed and the masks torn away and they would have to face their shadow-self. Yes, with great compassion I also saw their fear: fear of giving up the illusion, fear of the eternal Truth. Because for the Truth to be embraced, what is false has to die. And what is false has been hailed as the truth for so long, in its well-rooted position, that it has much to fear: the death of itself.

I also saw, through the passage of life, how necessary it had been for me to 'know' this suffering. For only in truly knowing the suffering, where it came from and how it existed, could I then fulfil my calling to show the light *beyond* the suffering.

I saw the misinterpretation that led to my resistance and desire to run from body. I had thought of the body and world as something lower than Truth, somehow something that had to be escaped in order to return to God. But now I was seeing clearly that the world is also God – the creation of God. The words: 'Thou shalt never see me as I am but may know me in the things I have done,' echoed through my mind.

It is only through the free will of our thoughts and the illusion that we are separate that we experience the world in bondage and suffering. I could see that in the very fabric of life's nature is an immeasurable perfection of such beauty that there can be nothing other than innocence – and that is the face of God, the life of God, the gift of God.

In all that immeasurable wonder I could no longer believe that God had made a mistake with my life or the world. I could no longer see it as a place in which we have been imprisoned for some sin. And I saw that, in not being fully at one with God the Divine, in form as much as in spirit, I rejected the power and perfection of life – only to create my own hologram of something 'less than'. It is that which creates the experience of separation and suffering. I, too, could only endure so much suffering.

I knew now that the experience of suffering gave me the light of the way through which the illusion could be transcended. And I saw how deeply rooted the remnants of body identity lay – for I, too, had been born into a world of flesh. Yet I knew I had come in the name of the Divine, and once again I must die to the false mind of flesh to be raised up as the truth of Eternal Life, the power of love beyond the veil.

In that moment I realised that I was at the passage of final reckoning, that I was dying as the seed in order that the tree may rise up to bear fruit; a gift from God that would go on giving for those who hungered, who called and prayed for the return to Truth, to Love, to Eternal Life.

Ecstatic peaceful bliss flooded my whole being. In the face of death I saw the bigger picture – Eternal Life. I saw the truth again, deeply and wholly: that all which is suffering passes away. There is only the journey of God: being, eternally. Whatever had appeared as death was but a process of transformation.

I was ready and willing to undergo whatever it would take. I chose to fully lay down my life, so that I might raise it up as the life of the Divine. In the giving over completely to the Divine so that IT could fully descend into the body, I could be present to the Divine equally in body and in spirit. I wanted the alchemy of Body and Spirit to actualise heaven on earth.

As I lay in the hospital bed I became acutely aware of the history of suffering, that the pain experience of my 'body' and every body, in varying degrees was a product of the illusion of suffering and of unconsciousness.

I felt the vibration of the fears of my parents and grandparents, of their parents and grandparents, living out in my body's cells, something often referred to as genetics. And I felt the vast stream of connectedness between every being on the planet; and saw that no single person's pain is their own, that it lives in all of us.

Suddenly I realised I was feeling the illness and suffering of all humanity, and that it was the calling of God within me to no longer turn my face from it, nor pray that it was any different, but to finally meet it, to love it, to hold it, to see it and be with it.

So I lay there, holding the core of all suffering in my being, holding it in the power of Love and Eternal Life beyond, in the light of consciousness. Simply accepting and embracing.

I realised then that, just as all our fears are connected, so too is our love; and the power of whole presence is not missing in anyone, not even the sickest. The difference between health and disease lies all within our presence: whether we can be fully conscious and present to every moment, or whether we want to turn our face and run, going 'unconscious'.

I began to see that the split between the super-conscious, conscious, sub-conscious and the unconscious was directly in relation to our experience of life, through soul, mind, emotion and body. Now I understood the power of conscious creation. AND why meditation is the key to liberation!

All experience is conducted through the perspective of mind. Our perspective dictates all consequences. Through consequence we enter the first stage of conscious knowing. Conscious knowing widens our perspective. In this wider perspective we may become aware of our greater consciousness.

It is when we re-integrate the conscious realms that we are able to command our body to do what is of our highest reality. It is then that we come to 'know thyself'.[1] In the power of this knowing lies the pure source of faith. It is then that 'with the faith of a grain of mustard we may command the mountain to move'.[2]

What previously seemed immovable is seen as completely attainable. For the Self is the creator and commander of that which is to be commanded. It is totally within our makeup that we have the power to create at the conscious level.

In deep presence I then observed the patterns of the light particles. I was watching the very points of light that are the bridge to the source of all. From within formless potency the love awareness arose and, in its power, moved into life; life as love in action. I saw these adamantine particles – the components of all manifesting life, the irreducible points of God – all being moved by the command of love.

These patterns of light display the formulating substance of our soul: the DNA upon which all of the wisdom of the universe is imprinted. Every living thing contains this divine intelligence. It is fundamental to the system of all life.

I could see then that all wisdom is already a part of us. Perhaps that is why Truth is so familiar to us all. The moment we hear it we know that something deeper inside us already knows it and is in fact the very author of it.

It is why the masters have all said that there is nothing to learn, only that which we are to remember.

Re-member.

That means we are re-orchestrating our awareness from what appears as a split to a state of wholeness again; bringing the parts back together.

I then witnessed with startling clarity that the gaps and loss of cohesiveness to the life force are in the patterns of thought that

---

[1] Inscribed on the Temple of Apollo at Delphi.

[2] Reference to Matthew 17:20.

are devoid of conscious love. It is where the body of life is *rejected* and hence, where we remain unconscious. This was truly a revelation. I continued watching.

The patterns of light began to reveal distinct fibres, like gossamer threads all vibrating at different speeds. The variation of these vibrations is creating all the different physical experiences within the universe. *Everything* is composed of these vibrating threads. The speed and rhythm of movement determines the nature of the form's expression. And what was modulating the speeds?

ME!
Every me in existence.
Yes ... YOU!

We are all constructing our experience through the vibration of every one of our thoughts, words and actions. According to the fluctuation of our vibration, we either manifest disturbances or harmony. And every fluctuation is affecting everything else in existence.

We are literally shaping the field of our experience from each vibration in the Now. Hence, we 'attract' certain experiences in our so-called outer reality.

I began to fully merge with this field, entering a total immersion of Self in creation. Knowing and experience became as one. I was not my body, my mind or my soul. I realised that I am – we are – something much greater, vastly beyond, and encompassing the totality of all energies that created body, mind and soul. I was witnessing the end of a perceived separation of me from ME, me from God.

Submerged in this awareness I felt an instant connection to limitless power, yet it was fleeting. I knew that the secret to holding myself in this all-abiding presence lay in consciously re-uniting with my form. The illness was not because of the form itself but because of the relationship, the lack of love for form.

I saw that either humanity is attached and engrossed in the form, believing our self and life to actually be the body, or we are in rejection of the body, believing it to be some form of lowliness or punishment that we must ascend from.

Now I saw the truth: the form of body IS the Divine play, yet remains but a fleeting speck of what we truly are; and only the mind's perception of the body as anything less than Divine is the delusion – and the creation of its suffering.

I could see that the physical world is the context in which we *experience* our inner being, our God-Self which is of spirit. Our world gives the face, the symphony, the play, the loving touch of, for, to God.

How truly we are 'made in the image of God'.[1]

Now, with such certainty of my experience and witnessing, held so deeply, so humbly in the power of Truth, it was my intent and vow to live in love of body, mind and soul equally.

And so my insights in the hospital bed and beyond continued.

After weeks of waiting for my physical condition to settle, the specialist decided to risk another test. It was finally diagnosed that I had a very rare 'genetic' disorder/abnormality of the 'avoti' sphincter. This small ring of muscle which connects the bile duct to the pancreas was abnormally small and malformed which resulted in spasms and contractions. That meant that every time it had spasms or seized up it was a major block in the digestive system, leading to chaos in the liver, pancreas, blood and kidneys. And food consumption was a major hazard: essentially, it created a terminal condition. And there was very little understood about the condition or its treatment.

Dr Wilson decided the best and necessary approach was to somehow open the ring valve to relieve the spasms and pressure. I consented, feeling it was possibly the most effective immediate response.

The operation seemed to be 'successful' even though in the process it had once again triggered the pancreatitis.

And so, with still plenty of time to do nothing but contemplate, I

---

[1] Genesis 1:27.

took an even closer look at the condition of my body. With fascination I began to see the profound paradox of life in our bodies. Humanity seems to be suspended in a fine balance between an incredible power of resilience and undeniable fragility. Our bodies can endure such harsh treatment and conditions and yet the slightest shift can also become fatal. I also saw how deceptive our physical world can be. Despite everything seeming normal on the surface, the effects of these disturbing shifts are gradually creeping towards a tipping point. And it is only because we aren't paying attention that we overlook all the little signs along the way.

So, as I began to pay greater attention, I could see a direct relationship between the foods I had been eating and my body's reactions. I could see also that it was distinctly the foods for which I had compromised my higher health ideas – sugar, caffeine, chocolate, fried food, wheat and dairy – that caused the great disturbance.

I saw how each of these foods 'scrambled' the cellular communication, causing both agitation and blockage – all of my previous studies in natural health had given me a solid foundation for understanding this. They were examples of extremes: foods that had been processed excessively and were no longer in their simple, natural state. My body-mind was literally saying: no more! I noticed how the desire to consume these foods came from an un-conscious, unbalanced view towards life. To eat such foods was to deny love for my body. With unshakable insight I saw how I had been using these foods to try to hold myself back, to somehow keep myself lesser and not embody the full Divine power that arose within me!

From a physiological perspective, these foods were difficult to digest which required a bigger trigger of bile, which in turn couldn't get through my 'smaller' abnormal avoti ring and caused it to seize up. This body behaviour was a physical reflection of my emotional-spiritual struggle to fully digest my life's purpose! I had believed that what I truly was, and what was asked of me to serve, was too big for the little incarnation I was!

I saw how temperance, the practice of moderation, opens the

door of heaven. I saw that it is the calling of every soul to embrace and accept the perfect balance: the equilibrium between the macrocosm and the microcosm; the Father and the Son. Each of us is in the Alchemist's kiln. And all of our struggles eventually lead us to the heart of the Divine union that already exists: the union of Heaven and Earth, above and below, within and without.

Temperance is the practice of applying our conscious awareness to our experience and feelings in order to achieve balance. There is a synthesis of awareness gained through the physical, emotional, mental and spiritual aspects of our journey. As a result we begin to establish a state of equipoise between the elements of earth, water, air and fire; we walk the middle way.

So it became clearer that each physical crisis was a juncture at which I faced major initiations on the spiritual plane. I was taking steps into greater expansiveness. And with every step I had to confront the fears and resistance in myself and in those around me. It was evident that this occurred in repeated cycles, the learning revealing itself on more than one occasion. The levels of awareness were to be integrated with my living experience and would not necessarily be completed the first time around. The patterns often arose in variations allowing a true shift on all levels to be attained. I had to surrender to, and embrace, the greater Self within my life.

I realised I had been tempted by the 'demons' of the 'lower world' (and that was not actually the world but the dregs of humanity's illusion, where it existed in me). The demons were unconsciousness and fear, which led me to hold on to behaviours that denied the heights of life as Love and Truth. The temptation had been the test that I faced: to stand next to the very things that I knew in my soul were of no service to me and rise above them. Yet I had yielded, tempted by the 'demons'. These are the limitations of the mind, the behaviours and actions that constitute the 'lower world'. I had weakened. Until then I hadn't quite had the strength or courage to stand before those demons and say, 'No. I choose the expression of the Divine.'

Humanly, I was afraid of being too different again, being ostracised and losing relationships. So I compromised my higher Truth! I had gone ninety-five per cent of the way and was trying to hold back – wanting to keep one foot still in the lower world. But my destiny was to go beyond. God wanted me to go all the way! I found it astounding to see how increasingly subtle these remnants were, yet they seemed to have a great power.

So, with every further expansion in consciousness, which was accompanied by an increase in presence of power, energy and awareness, I was confronted by minds that demanded that I not be so puritanical or 'high and mighty'. Once again I was told to 'get real' as I struggled to convey my knowing that it is the world of the 'little me' – the fleeting desires of the ego and personality – that is unreal.

It seemed as if I was trying to explain something about another place in a foreign language. And how could that be 'real' if I, too, was of this flesh? Surely I was being unreal? I also doubted my ability to present the teachings, which I knew I had come to give, for fear they were impossible for others to believe or embrace.

Hence I would contract again, and the effect was, literally, an internal traffic jam causing disintegration. I had experienced increased accelerations of higher vibrations and all my channels needed to be open, not closed. To remain closed meant greater danger. So I began to see that my body had to undergo a recalibration in order to hold the extent of power that was flooding through me. My body, mind and soul had to be tempered. The dense, heavy vibrations could no longer be of service. Nor was it of service to deny the highest Truth any longer for the sake of the lower world of the ego and its illusions.

I committed to the higher Truth and affirmed my intent to release all compromise. I was willing to go all the way and I wondered what that would mean to my relationship with Jake and motherhood. I had a deepening stir of troubling awareness that 'all the way' was beyond my worldly life as it was.

My body finally stabilised and I was able to go home again. But only two months later I was hit again by a massive convulsion.

The ambulance drivers arrived to find me virtually unconscious, with Lilha, screaming and crying, clinging to my body on the floor.

With the body admitted to the hospital again I found myself surrounded by immense fears and concerns of my family and Jake. The previous operation had grown over into scar tissue causing more obstruction.

I dissolved into a deep, deep void.

Now I could only surrender to the powerful forces of nature that carried my soul through its passage of being tempered, to find not compromise but temperance and the perfect balance.

34. *Ascension*

> Man has falsely identified himself with the pseudo-soul or ego.
> When he transfers his sense of identity to his true being,
> The immortal soul, he discovers that all pain is unreal.
> He no longer can even imagine the state of suffering.
>
> *Paramahansa Yogananda*

Over the following days I was barely conscious of the physical dimension at all. I began journeying through vast dimensions of light and space. I found myself being taken to exquisite realms beyond all capacity to describe in terms of this world. I saw myself assuming my pure light-body of the angelic realms, traversing many dimensions.

I was taken to a great chamber beneath Mt Meru in the Himalayas. I was guided by an exquisite Being of such radiant light, it appeared to be unbearable for human eyes; yet, as a light-being, I was able to perceive such splendour with great joy and wonder. This Being appeared to be neither male nor female yet held the authoritative presence of an emperor and the grace and love of a cosmic mother.

As we arrived at a rock face, the Shining Being evoked a pure harmonic chord and emitted a great ray of light that revealed an entrance. We passed through the rock, transmuted as light, into a chamber.

There, in the centre of the chamber, was a great pillar of central light, like a flame. Radiant glowing gems of blue, gold and rose shone in threefold brilliance within it. Around the walls were great sheaves of crystals etched with luminous sacred symbols, guarding precious recessed spaces. I was guided through one on the left side of the chamber. Above its golden alcove was a stone ledge and upon it, watching over the scene, sat a pure white dove. In the light below was a glowing tomb-like crystal capsule, and in it lay the resting light-body of an exquisitely angelic lady. Her shimmering body was robed in scintillating rose and gold light. Upon her heart was a magnificent open rose, exuding heavenly light and fragrance; pure golden hair cascaded around her supremely peaceful, beautiful face. She was an ageless presence and an image of pure innocence.

My Divine guide moved closer to my side.

'It is your very Self that you now look upon,' spoke the Divine Being. 'Upon your ascension[1] you were laid here as an etheric vehicle for earth, for Love. It is time that you awaken again, remember and reunite with your light-body of service. You must now merge once again with your seamless garment. As the feminine embodiment in which you incarnate now it is this form you shall once again serve.' I suddenly saw the overlaying light-body, the seamless garment of Divine Light. I knew it well for I had been with it before. I had encountered both the male and female aspects of Divine Light throughout different passages of other lifetimes. And I recognised the strength of that light that had been celebrated in men

[1] The word ascension is in reference to the raising up of the body/mind into the light-body through the communion with the Divine. Although most often associated with Jesus, it is something that has been documented to have occurred to a number of evolved beings throughout humanity's soul journey. Ascension is also often referred to as Christing. Again, although this has association with Jesus Christ, the word Christ/Christing is a reference to the illumining of consciousness, the light that occurs in atonement with God.

throughout history. Yet this time the masculine aspect stayed in the background while the feminine light began to radiate and vibrate.

Then I was levitating above the glowing form and slowly lowering into the light.

As I merged I felt an exquisite rush of electrical bliss igniting every particle of my being. I felt light exploding in every direction and along with it, Divine Love, Wisdom and Power. 'I' dissolved into a presence of unending magnificence, and unparalleled beauty. It was a state of complete fulfilment, as I merged with this light.

Within that presence was the power of God's command deep inside me. Thus it was spoken:

You are now again Christed as a daughter of God, brought to earth for that which is to be served in and through the awakening feminine. It is this you are sent for and this you know as the truth, to serve the Divine Will of Love within the charter of humanity's awakening. For it is that all souls hold the potential for Christing.

As those words vibrated through me I felt the pure presence of the Christ Self[1] within every soul. I felt the magnitude of power and divinity that is the true nature of every child of creation. I knew the liberated truth that this Self is the true essence of every single being. I also knew that what I was now embodying was the Divine gift that waited to be embraced in every other person. It was this message that all the Masters had come to serve. The Self, the I AM, is the essential truth and presence of us all.

I arose. The triple flame of blue, gold and pink light sparked brightly in my heart chamber, the dove descended upon my right shoulder and I heard the words emanate from my being:

---

1 This reference to Christ is not about the incarnation of the individual as Jesus, but as the pure consciousness of the Divine Self that is the essence of every soul.

'I AM the light of Love, Truth and Peace. I AM as the Divine almighty ONE, serving the way of Eternal Life.'

'Go, and light the way, Beloved Lady,' spoke the radiant Being. 'For now, as you are raised up, shall you also raise up the children who pray.'

As the words were spoken I heard the prayers of humanity echoing all around the world.

•

Suddenly I was watching earth from space. Then above me was a great passage of void. I felt drawn, consumed infinitely. And within the vastness of silent space arose a deep vibration, as deep as deep could be; and within its depths was every tone imaginable, sounding up to the greatest heights, as high as high could be. I was being drawn into the all-pervading vibration of the cosmic OM!

Then above my head appeared a massive, glowing ring of light. As I drew closer I realised I was entering an immense portal of liquid light, its great streaming pillars embedded with radiant crystals. The sound of a celestial orchestra welcomed me.

As I was drawn higher, I suddenly became aware of a circle of great Light Masters, twelve Ascended Masters. As I approached they called to me.

'Isira, we await you, Isira come, return to your rightful place.'

As I approached I saw the space clearly awaiting my presence. I entered in. I then saw the integration of the whole, and the journey of each soul aspect to that moment – relative to earth time – as it approached the turn of the century. It was shown to me that by the turn of the calendar I would be integrated and activated to begin service in Divine contract under the highest Will of I AM, as Isira. With this was the clear conveyance that 'Isira' was the correct name vibration for this incarnation – meaning 'the ocean of light'. It is also the union of Isis and Ra (the Egyptian Goddess and God), signifiying the light of consciousness, the Self that is beyond duality.

I was then shown the passage that followed in body. It was an intensive transition of recalibration and the final tests through which I would pass in order to fulfil the service of Divine order. That service was radiantly clear. It was not a question of any egoic identity. For such a thing was for no acclaim or self-gratification. It was simply the truth of the creation within me as willed by the Divinity of God. As I radiated in the infinite depths and stillness of pure consciousness I simply saw the task ahead. I saw the return to earth as inevitable, as blessed and blessing, for the 'new way' of the eternal life to shine within all. And so it was that this message radiated from my being ...

I have come now for the new way of the eternal life to be known as the light shining within YOU. I walk beside you as that which you are, that which you are to remember as your true Self. I have come that you may take up the staff of power within; that it may be the open channel for love to fill your body, mind and spirit now. For thy rod and thy staff[1] *are within you ... as it always has been ... and are awaiting the moment of opening, the moment of activation for the ripening of your being in love and your blossoming.*

Now is the time to turn over the old: let the fallows be filled with the new seeds of Truth as it is to be, and let them serve that which is the stage of humanity's journey now. For that which is ours eternally is to be brought to life in this which is alive ... in the Holy Grail of the body now ... the mother

---

[1] The rod and the staff here refer to the covenant of God within us. The rod is the bridge between God and each person: it is the energy that is flowing with limitless power when we are directly connected to God. It is the link between our self (as the microcosm) and our higher Self-God (as the macrocosm). The staff is the central internal channel (the sushumna) through which this God energy (the rod) may flow when the staff is open.

which is the form of all life. For Hers is the womb of all creation ... that which is renewal ... that which is alive in every dancing moment on earth.

This is the cup through which life flows in the present, powered by the love of that which is eternal. This cup is forever open in Life's accommodation. Let us set free the old, the tired, the bound; let us release whatever clings to the past into the power of Divine Will. And from its surrender, let us open ourselves to the power of the new, of change, of adaptation – of our very evolution.

Let us hear our voice speak the words of our living hearts. Let us see our homes and communities built upon our living love, not upon the bones of our historical ruins and the maps of what has passed and gone. Let us speak of the sacred presence in our living moment that we may celebrate it in the life we are now, together ... eternally NOW.

The Divine Feminine is an aspect of the Holy Grail. She is the body of all, as the Divine Masculine is the source of all – both are as ONE. She is the Life and the Love made manifest in all, and together they are neither male nor female, for they are the Divine play and manifestation of that which is ONE in all.

So now is this call for you to seek the light of love; the sacred cup of life, within you. Release the belief that it is elsewhere as if separate from your very being; for the Holy Grail is in every grain and in that which you are in every moment. And in the deepest embrace and acclaim of the Divinity that you are, that has made you, that lives in you in the immortal flowing field of Life, in the ever present now, you are to drink of the Eternal Life ... here NOW ... from this which IS Life NOW and forever.

Release yourself NOW, from that which is past, to be at one in the Holy Grail NOW. And mistake not this cup to be fixed in any given moment or form but embrace it as the ever-transforming field and play of manifestation moment to moment. In such flowing embrace lies the power of openness, and in such openness flows the infinite fullness of eternal life. So it is, in the at-one-ment with the sacred life, you shall see that what you have thought of as birth and death is the ever-flowing play of the Mother's gift in the oneness of the Father's infinite presence.

In such conscious embrace the two are one and all, within all that is life ... infinitely forever. And to drink of the ever-present love of the Mother and Father in every creature, every child, every man and woman, every moment, is the realisation of the Promised Land ... the Kingdom of Heaven in the Queendom of Earth.

So it was that the power of Divine Truth flowed in me and through me.

I returned to body again feeling overwhelmed by everything I had experienced in my journeys beyond body. All I could think was ... Is this real? Is this who I really am? Isn't this just some ego delusion? Oh yeah, sure. Everyone says 'I was Cleopatra; I was King Henry; I was this person – that person; I am the chosen one!' Me? Ascended? Oh, no! I don't want to be so foolish.

And yet, despite the flutterings of my mind, I was deeply consumed in a state of power that was nothing less than knowing the truth of what I had experienced; for it was more real than anything I had ever encountered before. It was deeply and humbly real. And, just as I had struggled to accept the Truth and Divinity of Self, I saw it as the very same struggle within every soul, and the very same truth that we are to *all* embrace once again.

The more I flailed with the mind, the more I was taken again and again to the past life events which were the foundations upon which the living presence I was now had been built. In this I was unmistakably the experiencer, the happenings and the events. And, in that witnessing, I saw again the unshakable reality of the truth. In my soul, stirred the most profound state of humility. In tears of amazement and gratitude, I wondered how it could be that I was so blessed by this gift of Divine purpose.

I knew that to question the simple truth of my being was the same as to ask an orange to deny itself as a ripe fruit which God had sent forth to be a sweet gift of golden juice. Slowly but surely, the certainty of such greatness washed away my doubts.

For these works that I have done shall you do, and even greater ...[1]

These words echoed through my awareness. I knew that was a message for every person, not just my self. And I knew that if I could embrace my own purpose and power, as had others, that it would bring greater faith upon greater faith.

Meanwhile, as my body lay in the hospital bed, I 'came to' enough for the specialist to discuss matters with me. It seemed the only option was for more surgery. The first choice was to try a similar cut, different angle than before. The second choice was to fully open me up and reconstruct, which would risk thicker scarring and more obstruction.

I wasn't happy with either choice and decided I wanted to go home. I felt I had finished with the whole experience, I had learned what I needed and now I wanted to go and heal myself. I knew as the power of I AM consciousness that it was within my command. All I needed to do was to direct my thoughts clearly to the image and the completion of what I had chosen to experience.

Yet the doctors, Jake and family were exasperated.

'Are you crazy?' yelled Jake. 'Look, you're still really sick. You've been through the death tunnel, your body is still struggling and you are nowhere near fixed. You can't go home!'

'Yes, I can,' I said. 'I'm going home. I'm tired of all this. No one can fix me now but me.' I looked at him with a look of 'and that's that'!

He sighed and shook his head. Then after a long pause he said, 'okay, in a couple of days, maybe you'll be more settled by then.'

'No,' I replied emphatically. 'Today.'

---

[1] John 14:12

He rolled his eyes and stormed out of the room.

He finally returned, bringing a brooding look.

I asked him to help collect my things and dress me. My body was so frail, weighing only forty-three kilograms.

It wasn't long before we were in the Kombi, puttering down the road. The van began to purr as we rolled along the highway. Neither of us spoke a word. I could see the golden hills in the distance, great undulating bodies like the curves of voluptuous women. How that sight filled me with such spirit, peace, love and joy. They signified my place of peace, my childhood sanctuary, my homeland and the great wilderness of nature that I loved so much.

The car cruised up and down the great slopes, passing through Wanora and Myora.

Suddenly as we neared the cliffs of Moorina, I had an intense knowing that I had to get onto the beach. This particular stretch of coast had been greatly significant to the Aboriginals. Along the cliff edges I had come to know the places of great power and healing as revealed by the ancestors. I had been receiving vivid communication and visions that took me directly into the dreaming. I saw how it was not something altogether lost, just hidden; and that the dreaming was the deep interconnecting force of spirit between all things, time and places, past, present and future.

I looked over at Jake. The sun was starting to sink low over the ocean. I sighed, then spoke.

'Jake, I have to go onto the beach.'

'What?' came his shocked reply, 'What are you talking about? I've just prematurely taken you out of hospital. You're just about dead. And you want to go to the beach? What's wrong with you? I need to get you home,' he said with great exasperation.

'Look,' I said, sighing again. 'I just know it's what I have to do. Spirit is telling me. I have to.'

'Hmpf! Spirit! Most likely the drugs,' Jake mocked, referring to the powerful dose of painkillers I had been administered.

'Please ...' I looked at him pleadingly.

'Oh, alright,' he conceded.

We took the next turn, down the hill and then pulled up in a wide vacant carpark. It was a cool but mild afternoon with not another soul in sight.

Without even thinking I was moved. My body walked down onto the beach, along the stretch of cliffs, then began to undress. With no thought at all, I stripped bare and walked into the water. The sun was low, casting a golden hue as it lowered itself to the horizon. Its golden light stretched out across the flat steel-blue of the ocean and lit up the cliff faces like a queenly palace. I walked into the great sacred waters of earth. As I entered I felt an all-consuming reverence of earth, of life, of God, the greatness of all creation. I began washing myself, offering up my illness, my blindness, my ignorance, my ego. I cried, I prayed to be wholly washed free.

I entered deeper and deeper. I let go of all that had appeared before me and I surrendered utterly into the power and presence of life within me and all around me. The boundaries dissolved. I melted into the ocean, the earth, the sun, the sky. Everything dissolved into an infinite ocean of blissful light. There was nothing but pure love, life being in every direction. Time disappeared. All existence reappeared.

My body presence remained transcended in this state for about twenty minutes. Then within the vast light I felt an electrical current and a returning sense-awareness of the body, yet still in the all connectedness of creation. It was an ecstatic rush that gathered from infinity and began to pour in through the uppermost reaches of my aura.

It was as if I was a thousand, thousand feet tall. As the rush of pure creative light poured into my being I felt I was being entirely consumed by, engulfed in, Love.

I saw in that moment that the body-mind creation is the field that in absolute oneness of the Now is as an open cup through which the Eternal Life can flow in fullness. The Omnipresent, Omniscient One was returning to me, descending as I was ascending, becoming at-one with IT. Every light particle of my body ignited.

Every atom danced in ecstasy. Every cell became whole and radiant. I knew that I was embracing the Holy Grail of myself, of all life.

And from within I spoke, I heard, I cried in joy, in bliss, in love, in power.

I AM the Resurrection and the Life.[1]
I AM Love Eternal ... Limitless energy renewed in form now.
I AM raised up, made as the eternally new.
I AM whole presence, for I AM in God as I AM.

It was with the voice of conscious knowing that I spoke.

Rivers of golden tears poured from my eyes, streaming into the ocean. My cup was overflowing.[2]

In that instant I realised I was completely healed and renewed. Not a flicker of pain or discord remained in my body. Suffering was no longer a reality. I felt the bliss, peace and radiance of illumination in every atom, every cell. My whole being vibrated with a vitality that I had never known in body before.

I finally walked out of the water, up the beach and squatted on the sand. I could not speak. Jake looked at me silently – waiting, confused. When my body had drip-dried, I dressed and walked back towards the car. Jake followed. I still could not speak. It wasn't until we arrived home that I could. The car engine stopped. Silence and stillness descended like a spell. Then I spoke.

'I'm healed,' I whispered in a low voice. 'I'm completely healed.' Slowly, I turned to look at Jake.

His expression of surprise turned to a cynical note that chose to humour me.

'Mmm ... uh huh ... sure.' He got out of the car and opened the front door. I was glad to be home.

Lilha was deeply peaceful. She had stayed silently present through the whole experience, gazing upon it all with an ageless wisdom.

---

1 John 11:25.

2 Reference to Psalm 23:5

I woke up full of alert energy. The bedroom was dim in the pre-dawn light and familiar smells of our household filled the air. Jake lay next to me, still in a deep sleep. A sense of warmth embraced me. The sun hadn't yet risen and during my stay in hospital I had ached to watch it come up over the hills.

It had been months since I had enjoyed such a simple pleasure. As a child, when we weren't in the valley and we were enclosed in suburbia, I had taken to climbing onto the roof of the house for a better view of the sunrise. My parents had forbidden me to do so, but I disobeyed them. What else could I do? The sunrise and sunset couldn't be fully seen or appreciated from the closure of a yard. And those wonderful sky-shows were a thing of great glory to me. As long as I could see that beauty each day I felt I could enjoy at least one thing that was magnificent. So I learned to be as stealthy and silent as a cat.

Now I only had to walk to the field next to our house. I stood and breathed in deeply, slowly. The joy of life, of being alive, filled me with gratitude.

The sky turned luminous pink and brought a soft early morning glow to the long grasses.

As I returned to the yard I felt a rush of inspiration. Potted plants waited against the fence in dormancy, neglected for my own growth.

With a great flood of energy I responded to the vision of their potential – a garden of swaying bushes, trees and flowers. I started digging.

The front yard was nothing more than a hard, barren patch of dirt. I dug it all up in a matter of two hours. I looked at the house. It was still silent. No sign or sound of any other rising bodies. With relentless energy I swung the pick and shovel, laid down compost and straw bails and set all the plants in a cottage garden style.

Suddenly the door swung open. I looked at my watch: 11 am. Jake looked out at the scene in bewilderment.

'What the hell are you doing!' he commanded.

I looked back with a cheeky grin.

'What are you doing?' he repeated. 'Look, you just got out of hospital.' His face was turning red, as his exasperation rose. 'You nearly died! You're still sick and you're meant to be resting!'

I threw my arms in the air with ecstatic joy.

'I'm healed!' I called out. 'I'm fully healed!' I exclaimed. 'Can't you see? I don't have any pain or illness left in me. And I've got the energy of a twelve-year-old! In fact I've got more energy than I can imagine!'

He stared at me silently. A long pause followed before he spoke again. 'Okay ... you might be better than yesterday but you shouldn't exaggerate. You should still rest! What am I meant to do? Nail your foot to the floor?'

I couldn't believe it. He still couldn't really see.

Not wanting to exacerbate his annoyance I looked at him lovingly. 'Okay, okay, I'll just water these plants and I'll come in,' I said quietly.

Lilha was playing happily in the lounge room. Although she was just over a year old, she still looked like a tiny doll and weighed only seven kilograms. I felt nothing but deep joy as I looked at her. She was truly a living wonderment, a delightful kaleidoscope of so many aspects. She had such presence – whether sitting in lotus position with her fingers in mudras and holding the gaze of a wizened sage; smiling and shining like a radiant sun; giggling like a funny little lamb, or delighting in the sun, sand and surf. She loved everyone who came and captured their hearts.

I found great peace and fulfilment spending most of my hours with her. Then in her sleep times I meditated, gardened, painted or took appointments. Gradually, the stream of appointments grew and grew. It seemed to just 'happen', mostly through the rippling word. And amongst the ones who came were a few who didn't want to go. They had found in me an ear and a voice that the soul had ached for.

Jake seemed to mellow again and became more open to the spiritual discussions, having others to kindle his curiosity; and we all felt a certain bond, influenced by the past.

35. *Vision Quest*

> There is but one cause of failure
> And that is man's lack of faith
> in his true Self.
>
> *William James*

Keith and Mary arrived at our front door like excited children. As I opened the door a burst of light followed them in, as eager as they were, filling the house with joy. They had been intimately aware of my 'life and death' experience over the last months and were intensely eager to learn more about the insights I had encountered. Word travelled quickly around the Peninsula as I shared stories of meditation, mystical practices and energy activations that could unlock our deep inner powers. Before long I was asked to hold sacred circles as there was a deep yearning by others to discover the same depth of connection to spirit as I had. I was asked to guide other people through meditative methods to facilitate a conscious shift.

Keith, Mary and Jake were keen for us to sit together in a circle for a vision quest. I had learned ways to create a very specific and direct opening into the source of consciousness. In the right setting this could unlock a door to the higher calibration of consciousness. It was in this state that the timeless dimension of consciousness could be accessed and therefore insights into the true nature of Self and life could be obtained.

I was deeply excited by this request, as I wanted so much to help others open up through a powerful connection to spirit. For most people this connection is nothing more than a concept. It usually remains unseen, unheard and unfelt. And I knew this yearning to connect to the mystery was the natural quest for every soul.

Through my own experience I had discovered profound yet simple doorways of sacredness that could bring the connection into a living experience. I had learned the divine power and clarity of yogic and meditative practices and that our inner consciousness takes us to the limitless. All it requires is a way to pass through and beyond the finite point of the mind. This has often been said to be as difficult as 'passing a camel through the eye of a needle'.[1] Yet in the surrendering of the struggle the way is made immediately effortless.

When the four of us were seated I opened the circle. With closed eyes and an open heart, I prayed for the consecration of the Divine Will. After a meditative pause I invited the others to each speak their heart's intent.

I then prayed for the ancestors and guides of each direction to be with us and asked that our circle be protected. I knew that during such quests the doors were open to many influences, egos and spirits alike, some mischievous and some of darker intent. So I held the firm vision of a pure space for our shared vision quest. I continued to pray and chant, asking that the enlightened presence of the source consciousness would be our highest guide.

Once we had each taken our prayers and intent into our heart we sat quietly, breathed deeply and closed our eyes. I instructed the others in a slow, melodic dialogue, taking their mind deeper and deeper into the source of awareness. Gradually I encouraged each person to shed the mind's limitations, resistance and grasping. With each stage of release came a deeper and deeper surrender into pure presence in the moment. With each breath each person entered into the expansiveness of pure conscious presence. Slowly the words disappeared as each person centred into a stillness.

---

1 Reference to Matthew 19:44.

I simply sat, still, dissolved, expanded, present and aware. It was silent for a period that could have been one second and simultaneously hung in eternity. Then, within the vastness of space there was a sudden distinct vibrational shift. It was as if everything was tingling and vibrating boundlessly. Suddenly Keith opened his eyes and gasped.

'Oh my God! I can see the light around you! Oh wow!' he exclaimed with wide eyes as he looked at each of us. 'I can see soft light shining out from all of you!' he laughed with delight.

Mary suddenly appeared flustered, 'Oh, oh no ... Oh, I think I can feel spirits all around us,' she said.

'Yes,' I spoke softly, 'breathe into the knowing of all as Divine, seat yourself in the love,' I said assuring her.

Then suddenly Jake and Keith were both staring at me.

'Far out!' said Jake. 'You've changed! I can see you, like, you're an old, old American Indian woman.'

'Me too!' exclaimed Keith. 'I can see that too! You've got really long white hair in plaits.'

'Oh, wow' said Jake, 'This is freaky!'

I turned and looked deeply into his eyes.

'Only to the mind that clings to your identity in time and place. You are an eternal spirit. Look into me. Do you not see the same presence you have known before?' I asked.

Tears began to well up in his eyes.

'Oh my God!' he sighed. 'I see. I do see. We have been together before.'

'Yes,' said Keith. 'You are the wise old woman.'

Mary then turned to me and took my hand.

'Oh thank you,' she said. 'White Feather ... it's you!' She paused and took in a deep sigh. 'Thank you for being here again. We'd be lost without you. Well, I know I would. Please help me. Please be my teacher, again.'

'With great pleasure. It will be my deepest honour if I may serve you,' I replied.

I then shared with them in brief the journey I had experienced through the death tunnel and that I had been called the name that was my true vibration now ... Isira.

They listened intently, respectfully and acknowledged my name and admitted it might take time to get used to it.

'Wow' said Keith. 'I knew you were special.'

'No!' I said. 'We are all special. No one is individually special. I am no more special than you or anyone else on the planet. It's just that we all grow at different rates like flowers in the garden. Each one is born, created with the same eternal potential, and is in their own unique passage of growth. In the garden of life there may be a flower that is still yet a seed, a flower that is still a bud, a flower in full fragrant bloom and a flower whose petals have faded and whose spirit is returned to the source, to earth. We are all destined for glory. It may take many lifetimes to reach the zenith. I only look different to you now because I have given up the lie of the illusion whilst most of humanity still lives in its fear.

'But when one does and others have not yet, it does not mean for a moment that the shining one is exclusive to God. I am here as an example to remind you of your own true brilliance and to encourage you also to reach up and grow. I am not here for you to see yourself as lesser. I am here to show you what you really are. I am here to show you your greatness.'

Jake had stood up and moved. It seemed to be too deep for him.

Keith smiled. 'Well, I hope I really grow,' he said. 'And I'd love your help too.'

Jake brought us all some water then sat down again.

'Well,' I said, holding up my glass, 'here's to our growth.'

Everyone followed suit. We then held hands and gave thanks for the loving support we had in each other and the guidance of Great Spirit and prayed that we could continue to grow for the highest good of all life.

❁

Life continued, and along with it my health grew stronger. Although I had arrived at a point of profound transformation in my body, I knew from previous experience that it was still necessary to maintain vigilant attention to the insights that had arisen during my illness. I understood that there was a continuing process to integrate such a powerful shift into my ongoing life.

Hence I resolved to maintain a practice that cultivated a deeper connection of the higher awareness to my body and its connection within the world. I had recognised how the senses were an incredible point of energy, connecting the spiritual dimension, consciousness and form. So I adopted a routine of active meditation to be deeply aligned to these senses. No matter what I was doing, or where I was, my primary focus would be concentrated on one given sense for the whole day.

On Mondays it was sounds. I listened to the constant rise and fall of the sounds, coming and going within silence.

On Tuesdays it was touch and feeling. It was particularly good to move about barefoot seeking out different terrain, such as gravel, then sand, then grass.

On Wednesdays it was smell. This also highlighted a deeper presence to breath and the connection with breath to the environment.

On Thursdays it was sight. I simply watched the constant flow of images, shapes and colours.

On Fridays it was taste. I gave my full attention to eating, drinking and swallowing.

On Saturdays it was witnessing of thoughts. This meant staying present as an observer. And actually I found there were less and less thoughts to even witness!

On Sunday it was inner source of being. I took my awareness into the innermost presence of my being and moved from within that essence. This practice led me to a profound alignment with what I referred to as the Presence. I realised that it is when we are so aligned that we are able to live as our true nature as peace, love, joy and freedom.

No matter which sense I concentrated on I experienced deeper and deeper states of 'innocent' awareness: free of dialogue, interpretation, labelling or defining. I became simply present, *fully* present, in the moment. As I deepened in this awareness I eventually developed a simpler and more direct way to access this state which I call The Presence.

These states also heightened my love of solitude, moments of pure silent communion with nature. So I took to walking along the beach and cliff tops. Spontaneously I felt an opening of such oneness that I would find myself laughing blissfully with the entire ocean, dancing wildly as the wind, sitting deeply still like the rocks and singing with the cosmic symphony.

One afternoon I found myself calling so deeply, it was as if it had arisen from the depths of the ocean itself. Then to my left I could see the form of an Aboriginal spirit – a tall, lean man standing on one leg like a stork and holding a long spear. It was anchored on the rock and pointed heavenward while he stared out to the ocean. I could hear his deep lilting voice communicating to me telepathically.

Somehow it was like a song, woven into the sound of the wind and waves. I could hear the language clearly and in my mind I heard it instantly as complete cognition. I was amazed at the lack of obstruction, it was as if the Aboriginal voice were no different from English in my inner awareness. Such is the truth and clarity of 'consciousness,' I thought.

As I listened he conveyed a message of great wonder.

'Your ancestors are whale-keepers. In your soul is the power to communicate with the dolphins and whales. Your 'grandmother' line is Kukatja – woman of the red rocks, lore of the red roo. Your 'grandfather' line is the Mirning – man of the oceans, love of the galaxies.

'This truth lives in your blood today but it is through the power of your spirit that it will be revealed, for many doors are closed on the surface. Many would choose to deny the truth of your native spirit. But through the power of spirit in you, doors shall be opened. It is the whale calling in you that has brought me to your side now.'

I stood silent, immobilised.

'You will be given several transmissions to help prepare you for your work. First will come the inner, then the outer.

'You will be awoken more fully to your past incarnations as an Aboriginal elder. As a grandmother spirit you are almost as old as the beginning of our time on earth, your love for all things, for earth herself, is unbreakable. As father star you are a keeper of our dreaming, your light still shining the way through vast galaxies.

'And you are a rainbow warrior, for it is true that you serve the Great Spirit of every direction.

'Soon the dolphins and whales will call you to bring others together and hear their message. You are one of their voices. There will be others you meet as well ...

'Now close your eyes.'

I closed my eyes yet continued to 'see'.

Before me was an open space of void, like the night sky, expanding beyond galaxies. As Self, I dissolved and became absorbed into the vastness ... internally awakening to the greatest field of a never-ending macrocosm. As this form became expansive I was transported through a portal. Then I traversed a plane of energy in an instant, like a sonic boom and found myself in the depths of the ocean. I began singing and moaning – a deep drone.

As I sang I realised I was a vast body, floating, swaying through the deep waters of earth. I recognised my form. A mass so large, feeling no separateness, floating in the night-black water ... beautiful floating. I felt no breath and all breath, as my being became one with the great oceans. I could hear my distant companions' calls echoing, vibrating in me.

I was simultaneously aware of being a whale as well as being the water and the bodies of other whales and dolphins. As I called

I began to rise up and in a rush of propelling energy, my mass surfaced and the consciousness of self was transported out of the portal.

I suddenly realised I was seeing and connected with an incredible intergalactic light-matrix. In this moment I realised I could see all of consciousness pinpointed in flashes of intergalactic maps. I saw other star systems, the Pleiades – the bright seven sisters, and the interconnected relationship between them, the whales, dolphins and civilisations of man – the Atlantean, Lemurian, African, Egyptian, Aboriginal and Mayan.

I saw a great matrix of interlinked codes and light patterns that conveyed the evolution story held in the Akashic records.[1] And I felt myself as absolute vibration between light, form and space. It happened in what was like a series of rolling scenes, all in one instantaneous flash. The whole experience was in complete tangible presence.

Then I watched as if flying above the coast, flying over the body of the whale as it showed me the dolphin dreaming trail,[2] the songlines of the whales and dolphins[3] from the great west coast all the way to the southern tip of the Peninsula. I could hear the ancestors calling and singing with the yidaki[4] and clap sticks.

•

Then the warrior spirit spoke again. 'You will be given more signs soon. You must take a journey to meet some of your fellow light-workers.'

He became silent. I thought to myself: How am I meant to know what I've seen is really true?

'Open your eyes and look to your feet. It is a gift for you. It is a sign of the Truth, the one-seeing. Trust.'

I opened my eyes and looked down at my feet. In the sand was a

---

1 The spiritual record of all of history and every soul's lives.

2 This trail is sacred to the Aboriginals and is part of the dreaming and their connection with the dolphins.

3 The routes that the whales and dolphins have been travelling along for thousands of years.

4 An original indigenous word for didgeridoo.

small oval stone with a distinct dark circle in the middle.

As I looked at it more closely I realised it was unmistakably the form of an eye! It stared at me as I stared at it! Then I turned it over and saw that its underside was like a perfect little sole of a foot. I closed my fingers around it, took a deep breath and sighed in amazement. The ancestors' words floated to me, disappearing into the distance ... 'The eye of the soul.'

The spirit had left, but his words remained with me, echoing and reverberating, a message that went to the very core of my soul.

Back at home Jake showed a degree of interest as I conveyed briefly what had happened on the beach. Lilha stared deeply with her penetrating eyes as I spoke, then pointed at my clap sticks that sat in the corner. I looked at her and laughed.

'Thanks, beautiful,' I said. 'Yeah, you know what's happening, don't you, you old spirit.'

She giggled, then smiled.

I walked over to the altar. I then heard an inner voice.

'Now it is time to collect your medicines, into your dilly bag.'

I opened the cupboard door and took out my small suede medicine pouch. I had kept it amongst my sacred things, cherishing it from the day it had come to me in the canyon. Inside I had already placed a crystal, my Tibetan Mala, initiation bands, the medicine pot from Shankara, the coral trident and cowry shell from the island. Now I wrapped up the 'eye' and put it in the pouch.

I sat silently holding the bundle in my lap. Each item represented an aspect of the sacred world and reminded me of my responsibility to walk the path ... the beauty way of love and respect for all.

Then two days later, I felt moved to find out more about Aboriginal Dreamtime and if there was any correlating material to support the visions and messages I had been receiving about the Whale and Dolphin dreaming. As I was researching papers in the library's archive I came across an account of a dreaming story of a different kind. It was as if it jumped out of the file at me. My heart started thumping. Something inside me already knew that I was about to read something deeply significant. And as I began to read, my eyes opened wider and wider, gripped by the story. It was almost an exact account of the recurring dream from when I was a child ... the red roo dreaming! I sat there astonished and speechless as I suddenly realised that the story was clearly of myself, the one in the dreaming who had been prophesised by the ancestors of this land. I felt a strange sense of responsibility creeping up on me and yet I wasn't sure what it was all supposed to mean.

I walked home in a daze, contemplating the bizarre complexity of my life. And yet it all made sense to the higher field of my awareness. In that awareness it was profoundly simple. It was the thread on which all complexity was strung together in a perfectly divine order.

36. *Divine Love*

Love is the open door of eternal enlightenment.

Isira

There was an unexpected knock at the door. Although it was the weekend Jake didn't bother to move. He was used to nearly every person being a visitor or client for me. I opened it to find Kane standing there, looking confidently full of mystical excitement. He strode into the lounge room, took a seat and immediately started talking about the whales and that he dreamed he had seen me riding on a whale's back. I felt the strum of synchronicity striking through the chords of our lives.

I talked to him about the practical vision I was developing since the messages I had received the week before: I wanted to find a venue to create a centre for sacred, spiritual and earth awareness.

We both felt a shared passion for the environment, for protecting the whales and dolphins, and being able to inspire others through spiritual activities such as lore circles, storytelling, meditation and celebrations. I felt a growing excitement whilst Jake sat quietly watching the whole thing from the sideline.

Before he left Kane said: 'Oh, by the way, there's a gathering of whale and dolphin people in Hervey Bay in a few months; we should go.'

The ancestors' words which had been spoken before rose up in me with a rush of God-bumps ... 'You will be given more signs soon.

You must take a journey to meet some of your fellow light-workers.'

'Hey, I'm really interested,' I replied.

'Okay, I'll get more info for you.'

I looked at Jake. He frowned suspiciously. I saw Kane off then came back inside.

'What was that frown for?' I asked.

'I'm not sure about Kane,' said Jake.

'What do you mean?'

'Well, look, c'mon, you're a great looking young chick. He's probably got the hots for you.'

'Oh come on!' I exclaimed. 'We have a spiritual connection! He's a spirit brother to me.'

Deep inside I felt a faint twang as I realised Jake's words had a hint of truth in them, but I quickly pushed it aside not wanting to lose the excitement I was feeling. It was all too synchronised to ignore. It seemed that a higher power was directing and, I thought, I could keep the boundary clear.

Over the following days Kane visited several times. I welcomed all he said, feeling touched and slightly amused. He conveyed such seriousness, yet at the same time had features that reminded me of leprechauns. I found such a mix of presence delightfully entertaining. He showed me his Celtic runes, staffs and sacred drums. He talked about his common dream for something similar to my own. And we talked of so many inner visions we had both experienced that were so linked, it was almost uncanny. In fact, almost too uncanny. We seemed to be linked into the same visionary dimensions of sacred journeys. He even had a strong relationship with the crow, that also came as a messenger of the 'between' worlds to him.

And he seemed to gradually build up a friendship with Jake. Then one afternoon I became tired of talking and instead chose to sit in lotus posture next to the altar in the lounge. I looked at the images of Divine beings on my altar then prayed that I may know the highest Truth; that it could be God's Truth that I serve.

I was used to entering deep states, even in the middle of a busy place, so it wasn't long before I dissolved into deeper inner silence.

The room disappeared.

My body began to vibrate and expand in energy and then I dissolved into vast light.

The light became so bright it was like a blinding flash. In an instant I found myself in another place. I realised I was watching a scene that I knew, as it was my very own experience I gazed upon.

I was looking through a passage between the walls of buildings, into a village square. Buildings of white and golden stone with narrow cobbled streets in between them, all faced into the centre. People dressed from head to toe in long cloths were moving in and out of the square. Some led donkeys; others carried wares upon their heads. The sky above shone stark blue in the dry heat.

I stood watching and waiting ... Then I saw ... myself. I recognised my form as a teacher and man of mastery, of unshakable love and oneness with God. I watched as I walked through one of the corridors, dressed in a long bleached robe, with a knotted cord around the waist, bearing sandals upon my feet. The strangest sensation occurred as I watched my Self in his body, knowing every step as my own, yet I stood also in my place of witnessing as a woman. I could wait no longer, for this was my Love, my Self, the very embodiment I knew of such great love.

As I watched my powerful form, as my Self, walk into the centre, I walked too. We walked towards the well and, at its edge, stopped and sat. We faced each other ... Self meeting Self. We looked into each other's eyes ... Self gazing upon Self. The love, the beauty and divinity were so exquisite, so overwhelming, that we drew into a deep embrace. And, as we held the presence of Self, each other, we dissolved into ONE infinite being of Love.

All that remained was Love... bright, radiant, infinite light of Divine Love. I was returned.

In that oneness was the great and almighty power of eternal love. The knowing of unceasing presence ...

•

For about an hour my body sat at the altar, while I dissolved in light.

When I finally began to reform in the conscious presence of my body, I realised fully the limitless love of my being that is never absent – the pure source of Divine Love.

Slowly I opened my eyes. They still could not fully see boundaries. Everything was engulfed in a hazy glow of golden white light. It took another ten minutes with eyes half cast before I could really focus again.

When I did, I turned to see Jake and Kane staring at me. Instantly Jake exploded into great gasps of bewilderment.

'You! You! ... What happened? You disappeared! You turned into light! ... Where did your body go? You just disappeared before our eyes ... into light!

'Yeah! Whoa! Far out! Just light! ... A glowing orb of light!' chimed in Kane.

I couldn't speak. Tears were flowing down my face. Tears of immeasurable love. Golden tears of bliss. In fact, the words 'love' and 'bliss' were not even close to what I felt and realised. What could I say? There were no words. And besides, who would believe what I had just experienced? I was just a young Australian woman, sitting in a little cottage in South Australia.

The recognition of that particular incarnation served wholly to remind me of that which I AM ... LOVE. It matters not what the form, the name or identity is ... My true identity does not lie in the linear path or physical reality ... it lies in my love. And the knowledge of my previous form, which had mastered the awareness that I am

Love, served to confirm that as the one and only truth.

The body is only an effect, of which Love is the cause. As I realised this I could release myself from the need to validate my being through any body or personality identity. Who or what I had been or am in body is truly an insignificant mirage next to the knowing of myself as Love. Knowing this, and what that love was to do, was the only thing that mattered.

And that pointed me to one place alone. The past, memories of identity, or the searching of future attainments, are all the ego's clinging to that which is not real. The place of love was and remains the being I AM, eternally NOW.

The 15th Attainment

I had discovered the master of all temperance ... the centre of all opposing forces, the meeting place of dark and light. Whatever is extreme or out of balance can only continue whilst we choose one side over the other.

Temperance lives in one place alone ... the ever present NOW. IT forever remains the middle way, all that sustains balance.

KEY 15.

The Shadow

KEY 15.

The Shadow

The closer we are to truth, the more we discover contradiction. Life is a divine paradox.

The shadow reminds us of the stark truth that we are both saint and sinner. Our judgment of the thing we see as wrong is the evidence of our struggle with our own inner darkness.

That which we judge is born in the one perceiving judgment.

We must embrace our shadow in order to transcend it. The only way to free ourself from the prison of that which binds us is to accept that the shadow itself is a passage to the light and that we alone are responsible for our experience.

37. The Sacred Feminine

Not only are you the shadow
That is dancing on the wall
But you are the hand
That shapes that shadow
And the light through which it is cast.

Isira

I left the room and came back to find Kane and Jake drinking beer and 'shooting the breeze'. It was a significant shift of attention. Of course, to many, this would be a normal and even pleasant scene; but to me it was in contrast to the course my soul was following. What had just occurred was miraculous. But only moments later, their amazement and awe were gone, their level of consciousness had plummeted. If a similar drop in temperature had occurred, everyone would have been shocked, concerned and prepared to take action. But a drop in consciousness, especially from an exceptionally high level, which challenged the mind's preconceptions, to an old and familiar, if relatively unconscious level, was not uncomfortable and perhaps even reassuring to the ego that is threatened by the emergence of divine power.

It all seemed so shallow and pointless to me. I saw the veils drawn in by Jake's unconscious habit to escape the fullness of life. I so much wanted to be free from the lifestyle that was happy with surface affairs and dampeners that concealed emotional issues. To me, that supposed life of carefree happiness was very unreal. It was a substitute for true happiness. It provided a smokescreen over the background of deeper sorrows that didn't go away with a few beers. It was only a matter of moments before those hidden issues would be revealed in emotional reactions and moods. I already knew how difficult it was to sustain a level of relating when such differences in states of awareness were occurring. It meant we could not meet each other on equal footing. As a consequence, issues of relating remained unresolved.

Once again it felt like I was unable to explain my position. To others it seemed that I was just 'difficult' and that I should be happy with the life I had. But to me that was like telling a monk he should be happy to do business with an oil company. It was like expecting a land-dweller and an oceanfarer to understand each other. I had come to see and know a very different perspective of life. For me to continue where I was, in the same setting, was like asking me to go backwards. It was like asking a tree to draw itself back down into a seed or an eagle that had soared to great heights to return to its baby wings.

And still I wondered if it were possible to find the middle ground where we could understand each other, where maybe we could live in harmony, as an oceanfarer and a land-dweller. Over the following months I watched Jake continue to deny his own issues and, as I raised my own issues with him, it seemed to trigger him even more. I could see his frustration. I knew that, from his own experience, he was also doing the best he could. Although we were experiencing very different states of perception, we were both feeling the effect that those differences were having on our relationship. It was also evident that our goals in life were quite different, and our paths were slowly but surely heading in different directions.

I began to reflect incessantly on why – although we truly felt love for each other – our relationship was breaking down. And as I thought about each of us as individuals I could see why we were attracted to each other. We both had a genuine desire to love and bring love to life, friends, family and work. Jake was truly a wonderful person. He was everyone's friend, and no man's enemy. He was deeply loyal, fervently committed as a father and, in his heart's intent, meant to be as supporting of me as he could be.

I thought about myself. I had wanted to fit into an ordinary world – to somehow belong in the world as much as in my states of higher awareness. I realised then that I had been afraid of my own magnitude and that if I showed my true power I would be less appealing or even confronting to others. Consequently I boxed my true Self away, compromising for a place where I thought I could fit in. Yet that only meant I was further away from myself. I had felt so isolated for so long by the stark gap that arose between me and other people that I seemed to choose compromise instead. I was trading my wings. Jake represented the perfect partner for a simple, ordinary, wonderful life. Yet I plainly had overlooked the consequences that would continue to arise from the fundamental differences in our perceptions and, even more significantly, the discord of denying my full being and purpose.

Along with that came different likes/dislikes, social needs and lifestyle choices. It was starkly evident now that we weren't just on different pages; we were at opposite ends of the book. Jake liked pubs and the same lifestyle as friends who enjoyed the simplicity of the average family – with working adults, two cars, two-and-a-half kids and a mortgage.

It seemed that there was nothing much more to life than general affairs. Any possibility to move into deeper growth or spiritual development was side-stepped and personal issues swept under the rug. To face personal fears for further growth meant that they first had to be owned, and that was often seen as a weakness. Yet the more Jake avoided his shadow, the more I was compelled to unveil my own. The possibility that facing fears might bring greater depth, freedom and a real connection to limitless love was even laughed at. As a consequence I could see how, through denial, a certain facade was presented to the world.

It bewildered me that two people could love each other so dearly, live under the same roof, go to the same places together, yet be worlds apart. We were a living paradox. I began to wonder if love was really enough to make a relationship work. It seemed to me that it needed more; that as long as two people's minds had vastly different views of love and life it could remain impossible for the connection that was needed for a relationship to endure and flourish – like oil on water.

Two days after that contemplation I happened to open up a diary that had inspirational words on its pages. The words leapt off the page at me. *Life has taught us that love does not consist in gazing at each other, but in looking outward together in the same direction.*[1]

I tried every angle to bridge our communication gap. Yet it became increasingly impossible. I felt caught, trapped between my desire to find resolution and the feeling that I was obstructing my soul's destiny. Yet I continued to try and find a way for a balance between bridging and not compromising.

All I could hear again and again were the words 'unconditional love'. Love is beyond conditions, for love in itself has no opposites.

I tried to understand what this meant for our relationship and for each of us as individuals. I turned in every direction trying to find answers and yet I couldn't turn to those to whom I most wanted to turn, because Jake refused to share our conflicts with his friends, parents or work colleagues. I felt torn between my own needs and the fear of betraying my husband's trust. As Jake's unresolved issues were like shadows behind closed doors, I felt my own true nature was being boxed up, itself becoming a shadow.

•

Despite the challenges for us personally, we both continued with our own directions. My work continued to increase as I focused on developing the dolphin dreaming trail project of PODEM (People Organising Dolphin and Environmental Management), giving spiritual readings and guidance, and presenting at Mind Body Spirit Festivals and workshops.

---

[1] Antoine de Saint-Exupéry.

My work was really beginning to expand and diversify. I took great interest in the land and communities, feeling deeply moved to support in a way that could inspire collective healing and conscious evolution. I was constantly amazed how life seemed to have its own way of connecting people and arranging things effortlessly. All I did was offer myself to serve the highest Will.

Along with my passion to inspire others was a deep desire to participate in the indigenous community. I felt how vital it was to create a connectedness between Aboriginals and 'white' people. I could see how all people are caught in elements of pain and alienation, and that if we look deeply enough it is evident that we have all been divorced from the power of spirit. I could see how most 'white' people are also 'broken': separated from their roots and from connection to their own lands and ancestry. Most of all, nearly all people feel disempowered, denied the right to be fully present and at one with the land on which they were born or on which they live.

I could see how this issue remains a pain of shame, denial and embarrassment. I saw how evident this shame is in the lack of support from the governments, in the anger that Aboriginals hold towards white people and in the fears of white people to really make connection with their indigenous neighbours. It was evident to me that true reconciliation can only begin when each side can both forgive and have compassion towards themselves and each other, and choose to work at healing together. It wasn't long before these contemplations opened doors. Once again I saw life neatly arranging connections with the right people in the right places at the perfect time.

I was involved in the Adelaide Festival when a young Aboriginal man approached and introduced himself as the son of Georgina Williams. The first time I met Georgina, a Kaurna elder, I had felt a strong connection with her. I sensed that I would meet with her again and possibly work with her in some way. Since then we had had a few small interactions and it was evident that she was interested in my clairvoyant abilities and connection with the spirit world. She had also introduced me to one of her cousins, Betty Sumner, at

Warraparinga, the centre for indigenous support in the Peninsula. They had both asked me to look at land and to psychically connect to the ancestors to confirm existing evidence and documentation of sacred sites. These were current issues for land rights and of great significance for the Kaurna people. It seemed that gradually, one by one, I was being connected with my Kaurna relations.

So I wasn't surprised when Karl introduced himself, and said that his mother wanted me to come and do more work with the community. With his carefree spirit he grinned at me, his pale green eyes shining in the sun. And as quickly as he came, he went, moving around chatting and laughing with everyone he greeted. I watched his graceful strength, his athletic body painted ready for a cultural dance, his brown spiralling hair falling around his ochred face. My heart was so full of joy to see that not all Aboriginal hearts were heavy and weighed down by resentment. I was happy to ring Auntie Georgie again and felt excited at the prospect of working together and sharing in loving spirit.

The night before I made the call I had a vision of a sacred circle. I saw it as a council of shared vision, a unifying of hearts in connection with spirit. And I saw that it was to unite the community, people of white and indigenous descent. When I suggested the sacred circle Auntie was excited.

'Oh, that's great, love,' she said. 'That's just what we need. You know there's just so much negativity that people want to dump, that we should do something positive. So how 'bout we do this in three weeks? That'll give us enough time to let everyone know and invite a few more people.'

'Great,' I replied. 'That sounds just right for me too.'

The day before the sacred circle I made gifts for the elders and Aunties. It is traditional to make an offering in the spirit of goodwill, and I felt it as a true heart-giving for the gratitude I felt, to be connected and blessed by the custodians of the land on which I was born.

When I arrived the next day I was delighted to see about forty people milling around. It was so beautiful to see that people of many different skin colours had come to gather. Auntie Georgie came over to me quickly and gave me a hug. We drew back slightly with our hands still embracing each other's shoulders and looked deeply into each other's eyes. Her light golden skin lit up as the sun momentarily burst out from behind a cloud and her face, framed by short silvery hair, shone with a sense of spirit and joy. I loved looking into her pale blue-green eyes. The fact that she was fair in complexion gave me a sense of peace as I still contemplated the controversy of my own story. I knew that she would be one who would not judge by the colour of skin.

The circle was deeply moving and heartfelt for all who were present. It only saddened me that most people would lose sight of the gift received in such gatherings, finding reasons to be busy and not continue connecting in such a powerful way. I saw the strange dance of denial that continues to creep into people's minds, easily diluting faith in the power of healing that could come from the simple measure of connecting. Yet deep in my heart I knew that all was, in perfect time, a journey toward great healing and awakening.

Two months later the news of the day brought a tragic story of a dolphin that had been slaughtered in the Port River. It was horrifying to most people, yet perhaps more horrifying to the indigenous community, as the dolphins are such a significant relation in the family of Kaurna dreaming. So I found myself once again by Georgina Williams' side. With a small group of people we sat at the river's edge, to offer a mourning prayer for peaceful release of the dolphin's spirit in its passage. That one small event seemed to amplify the deep sorrow that nature was feeling for the great violation that was happening to earth. I felt the mourning of the dolphins, of the river, of the earth herself ... mourning for her sacred life.

Over the following weeks I felt a deepening of communion with earth and along with it an increase of insights. My experience of spiritual phenomena was at an all-time high. Every day I was experiencing omniscient states of consciousness and 'downloads' from spirit beings. I had been given another message about more gatherings and told that I was to meet the 'American Bear'.

The next day I felt drawn to a small shop on the beachfront. There on the notice board was a sign for a gathering in Sweat Lodge[1] with a Native American Elder known as 'Running Bear'. God-bumps ran up my arms, back and legs.

Then, just as I was about to leave the shop, I noticed a blue stone dolphin. Without a thought, I purchased it.

When I phoned the Shamanic College, Ruby answered the phone. We both felt an instant connection. The Sweat Lodge was set for the next month so I secured my place.

A few days later I went to the beach again. This time when I stood looking out to the ocean I had the sudden impulse to chant. The tones that came out took on their own form, becoming eventually the powerful resonant sound ... 'I AM Love'. Then the sounds suddenly merged with everything – the entire ocean and the field of earth – and I dissolved into one great field of life.

Then, as I felt the wind on my cheek, I realised that I was the consciousness of the wind. I swirled and rose, spiralling over the spraying waves, the stark cliffs and the grassy hilltops. I felt the journey of each eddy of wind – where it came from and where it went. From the flitting butterfly wings, to the swirling clouds and swaying trees, to the grassy plains and ocean airs, to a hovering bird and the kiss on my cheek. On and on, I journeyed through past, present, future. I was the wind – one ever-flowing wind, spiralling in all directions, dissolving into vast space as all cosmic breath. It was a state of such oneness that all I could feel was a profound presence ... there was nothing but God ... the endless beauty and power of spirit in all.

When I opened my eyes I saw a whale breaching, then a young one next to it. 'Wow!' I called. 'Oh, how beautiful.' Then a spray came up and in a moment I felt a cool dampness on my face. It was as if its breath had blown across the waves to touch me. Everything was

[1] A Native American purification ritual which takes place in a womb-like lodge in intense heat. Prayers and chanting are used to guide the participants into healing and visionary states.

flowing in a timeless presence of pure being. There was no thought ... only awareness. I breathed in the vastness of the scene: grey-green waves danced and swirled, merging with the hazy grey clouds that hung on the horizon. As the clouds floated above me in the cool misty air, so also my feet delighted in the coolness of the sand beneath their soles.

I turned slowly and began to walk but kicked a stone with my toe. I bent down to pick it up. I couldn't believe it! In the stone were distinct markings ... a mother whale, a baby whale and a love-heart! In the top a perfect round hole was worn right through and, jammed in the middle of it, was a tiny flat pebble, which made it look like another eye. I looked back out to sea. The whale and her baby were no longer visible.

I sat down, closed my eyes and gave thanks. I felt so immensely blessed and guided by Life in every moment, and by how God was touching me through all of existence. My heart was full of gratitude. I breathed in the cool damp air, relishing in its vital energy, and slowly opened my eyes. The scene was alight with a soft and eerie glow. And as I took in its beauty I sensed I was not alone.

Suddenly I saw spirits whirling all around me. This time they were all Aboriginal women. They started 'singing' me.[1] The words rose and fell in a lilting play of soft yet powerful notes. I could hear the words clearly ...

Yinar minar, yinar minar, yinar minar. Ngaiya uttara ngamala, yurrawe. Ngaiya uttara ngamala, yurrawe. Ngamalaja ngamalaja ...

They were singing up the earth-woman in me. I knew they were waking up the power of the sacred feminine in me. It was as if they wanted me to dig it up from the very depths of earth. Then I saw a great grandmother's face in the sky and her voice came with the message:

'It is woman's turn now. Our power was buried long ago. Through corrupt powers we had to hide behind the men and bury our lores. But we have kept them deep in Earth, waiting for the right time. Now the time has come. The way of the Spirit-woman must be seen. Earth is in great danger and needs the power of Love to come again. Rise up earth-woman. Do not walk small. We ask you to walk tall.'

I felt my spirit instantly rising up with an ancient power. As she spoke I began to see how her presence was revealing to me the ancient line of my Grandfather's mother's ancestors. Her words continued.

'You will be guided to your ancestors. You must take initiation. You are Sun Woman, Yurrey Wayamay.'

I walked home half in a daze. My life seemed to weave a story in so many different ways that I could really do nothing but accept the mystery of it all. I had already come to realise that for as many answers I could find there were infinitely more questions.

The next morning the phone rang. I answered to hear a young man's voice on the end of the line.

'Are you Katja?' he asked.

'Yes,' I said.

'Are you doing the dolphin dreaming trail?' he asked.

'Yes ... but ...' I said, pausing. I froze. My mind went into a spin. How could anyone have my number or know about it? I hadn't disclosed or passed on any information yet!

'But ... how do you know about this?' I asked in a shocked voice. 'No one has any information yet.'

'Well I do,' came the young man's voice again. 'A copy of your proposal has turned up on my desk this morning.'

'But I don't understand,' I said, feeling rather spooked. 'I've only got one copy and it's right here on my desk.'

'Well then,' he said, 'we're obviously meant to meet, aren't we?'

'What's your name?' I asked.

'Max. Shall we meet? Do you have time today?'

'Sure. How about one o'clock at my place? My daughter will be asleep then.'

'Okay, great.'

I gave him the address, hung up the phone and sat staring at the bookcase in a daze.

At one o'clock sharp, Max turned up.

He was a young, fair-skinned, Aboriginal man with startling green eyes. I invited him in and made a cup of tea.

'So how come you're doing all this stuff?' he asked.

'Because I'm guided to ... by the ancestors,' I said.

'Oh,' he nodded. 'Well, I want to help.'

'Hmm. That's great.' I replied.

'You've got to meet Wiley. He's a shaman and he knows what stuff is going on with the dreaming trails. He's guided straight from the ancestors too, and he's been initiated by the big mob. And,' he said, looking out from under a furrowed brow, 'he's got magic powers.'

A slight shiver ran through me as I sensed that could mean the work of something other than love. I stayed connected to that awareness in the back of my mind as we opened up further conversation.

I felt an instant bond like a brother and sister between us. That bond seemed to draw us together on a daily basis. We spent hours talking on the phone and meeting, either at my place or his. To add to it all his four-year-old son and Lilha seemed to hit it off. They played happily with each other for hours, making castles in the sand, playing 'chasey' through the garden and toying with the keys on the piano. And to the delight of us all they often shared a little kiss and a hug.

It wasn't long before Max and I made a tentative time to take a trip to see Wiley and talk about the proposal. It seemed he would have more information. And I was suspicious, but curious, to know who or 'what' was toying around with the same dreaming trails that I held so deeply in my heart as sacred.

After several weeks I finally got to meet Wiley. He was a middle-aged white man who had clearly studied a great amount of metaphysics and was well-versed in ways to impress and convince others of his authority in matters of spirit. But after about an hour my 'alert antenna' was buzzing on a loud speaker, inside my awareness.

This man was hot with a lot of talk but I felt like I was rapidly being woven into a much darker scheme.

Later that night, I was talking to Max when I felt a sudden rumble in the house. I sensed it was a warning. When I said so, Max brushed it off. But when I continued talking, a black spider suddenly appeared on the floor in front of me and leapt towards me! That was a definite warning sign. I heeded it immediately, saying I had to go.

That night in my dream, I got the clear message that it wasn't yet time for the outer work of the dreaming dolphin trail – that it was meant to show me certain powers, places and connections and that I had to learn the difference between light and dark forces.

I felt increasingly uneasy – as if I was being manipulated and duped from different directions. Then, in confirmation of the warning, Max turned up the next day and vented his full darkness at me, saying how dare I, with barely even a drop of black blood in me, claim the work of songlines; it was his right, not mine! His voice spiralled into such anger and frenzy, I thought he was going to physically attack me. I tried to defend my position but it was like fuel on an already raging fire.

'You don't know anything, you stupid white bitch!' he screamed at me.

At that point I felt myself toppling from the deep calm centre.

Then I heard Lilha wake up – crying. I ran into her room trying to calm her down. Then I went back to the lounge-room.

'Look, Max. I'm sorry. I didn't mean to upset you or anyone. It's best to just close the book on it all. Please go. I can't have this in my house. My daughter is here.'

'Ah yeah! Fucking white ...,' his words trailed off as he spun around frantically, shaking his fists in a crazed frenzy. 'And look at me! I'm stuck with it now – half-white, half-black!'

He was punching his chest. As he was screaming, I suddenly saw a vivid overlay of his past life. He had been a white marshal who had killed and maimed Aboriginals! Oh! ... I thought, as I realised the twisted grip of karma in which he faced his own violations.

'Please go,' I said. 'Please. I just want peace now.'

I prayed for help.

It seemed to work. Suddenly he just stopped and stormed out. I felt deeply saddened that once again I had been manipulated through spiritual deception – his intent had not been wholly pure. Of course I also saw with deep compassion that Max's anger was not really about me at all and that he just wasn't equipped yet with the skill to deal with his pain. His shadow self was screaming. I realised that even though I might have been able to help him heal, it didn't mean he was ready or willing to accept that from me. I was saddened that the baggage he carried interfered with the true gift of spirit that connected us.

I was amazed at how many people could come in the guise of spiritual truth marred by egoic agendas. It seemed that if it wasn't some desire to win me to their bed it was jealousy or utter contempt. But I still hadn't met them all yet. I wondered when the tests would cease.

I was, however, assertive in letting go of anything that was not in the highest integrity. That too provoked enormous contempt in others. I was not willing to submit to their emotional manipulations and efforts to convince me otherwise. Despite their ongoing antagonisms, I would not compromise. And it seemed that I was yet to be put to the highest test.

*

Over the following week it also became unmistakably obvious that Jake's intuition had been right. Kane had a desire to seduce me. He had no chance of that, which I communicated clearly. What I found difficult, however, was allowing an immediate distancing. I really hoped for our friendship to continue, as his spiritual nature was something I so deeply yearned to share. But it became obvious that it was just too tempting for his ego to think that any contact meant he still had some chance.

I began to feel rather perplexed by how many people –

especially men, seemed to gravitate to me wearing a spiritual cloak that camouflaged self-gratifying desires.

Through it all, my mother remained my greatest pillar of love. Over the years we had transcended our shared pains of the first sixteen years of our life together and had developed an unshakable bond of friendship filled with a deep love and respect. With her understanding, support and friendship, she was a greater source of stability than any other person. She was my one and only true confidante. For hours she would console me, listening patiently, advising, encouraging and reassuring me. As my trials, particularly in my marriage, seemed to be increasing, she made herself even more available, spending two or three days a week with me in the house.

Interestingly, for some unexplained reason, Jake felt uncomfortable with my parents, which made it even more complex – especially, when he would arrive home to find mum with me again. However, I refused to reduce my relationship and time with my mother when she was such an intimate ally in spirit.

38. *Giveaway*

The biggest room in the world
Is the room for improvement.

Unknown

I woke up filled with an anticipation of the sacred. Today was the day for the Sweat Lodge and pipe ceremony with 'Running Bear'. I spent my day feeling grateful for the gift that our Native American relations hold. Their love and honour of earth is a thing conveyed in such simple yet powerful ways. That love is something I felt to be so deeply alive in me. It was a love that I knew I had lived, that remained well-ingrained in my soul. It was a love that compelled me to express once again through ceremony and ritual.

As I collected my things, I stepped into my 'reading' room. My eyes landed straight on the blue stone dolphin. I picked it up and wrapped it, knowing it was meant to go to the elder. I felt deeply gladdened as I knew the ability to give something in respect and gratitude was in turn a gift in itself.

I arrived at the Shamanic College and was greeted by Ruby, a short, full-breasted lady with long dark hair and smiling eyes. We looked at each other, feeling an immediate soul-connection. I then went to put in my $20 for registration. A middle-aged woman was debating with the girl on the desk, claiming it was fraud to ask for money for a 'spiritual' service. I was more than happy to give. It was my observation that money is also a gift of creation and when handled with the right intent is a beautiful certificate of exchange – a symbol of gratitude.

I could also see that most people hold onto views that are a product of a different time and place. As far as I could see – in our society in which we are currently living – money is an essential and integral element in everything we live with – including the workings and facilities that are able to support the gift of our spiritual development. I knew it cost money for the teachers to come. And, they came for me to have the experience! So of course I was happy to give money for that.

I looked at the woman's obviously new silk shirt and wondered why she would be happier to give money, without debate, for material objects that did not bring true joy or wealth to anyone, yet was so resistant to support an opportunity that might give her more nourishment than all of her clothes, cakes and coffees. I left the room as I contemplated the thought that I would give every cent I had if it could support the awakening of Divine Awareness.

The ceremony was due to start at 7.30 pm – in about half an hour. Another six people had yet to arrive to complete a circle of eighteen people, and of those only twelve would enter the Sweat Lodge. When the last person arrived, we all sat in the council room. Owl and eagle feathers hung from the walls and a large circular mat marked the four directions.

'Running Bear' sat down in the South. I sat opposite him in the North. He began his prayers, chanting with the drum. Then he gave thanks that he could be here in the land of the South and asked for the ancestors' blessings that he could share his medicine from the West as a token of peace.

'It is a time now for us all to be coming together, all colours, as one family. I bring with me the medicine of my ancestors that each may receive and remember the wisdom in us that has been given by Great Spirit. My prayer is that through this ceremony we will hear Great Spirit's guidance and remember the part that each of us has to play in bringing peace to all people.'

He unwrapped a long pipe. It was beautifully carved with beads and feathers hanging down from the end. Then he took out a small pouch and untied it, opening it up to reveal a mix of herbs and tobacco. 'Before we begin, we will ask for a giveaway. In our tradition there are two types of giveaway. The first is something that is old or doesn't serve us anymore – like negative thoughts. The second is something that we value deeply such as our highest ideals or a prized possession.

'The second is a more powerful giveaway. When we give the thing we want and love most we are really showing our gratitude and true ability to give.' I noticed the woman who had argued about the money shuffling uncomfortably on her cushion. 'We will begin with the first giveaway. If you don't have an object, then think of a thought.'

He looked to the ground then spoke. 'I give away arrogance.' He then looked to his left and nodded for the lady to speak. She looked ruffled but suddenly spoke as she looked up. 'I give away fear,' she said, then looked to her left. 'Anger,' said the next lady ... 'Judgment,' said the man next to her ... 'Greed,' said the next man ... 'Isolation,' said the next ... 'Alcohol,' said a woman ... 'Self pity,' said the next ... 'Prejudice,' said another ... 'Loneliness,' said the woman, and then looked at me ... 'False perception,' I said.

And so it went around the circle until each had spoken.

'Each of you will now receive a pinch of herbs for the second round. As the bowl is passed around you are to speak your intent with which you fill the bowl, what you give to the universe, to life.'

Again Running Bear spoke as he put in his pinch ... 'Gratitude,' he said ... 'Peace.' ... 'Love.' ... 'Togetherness.' ... 'Abundance.' ... 'Strength.' ... 'Truth.' ... 'Unconditional love.' ... 'Innocence.' ... 'Friendship.' ... I closed my eyes and spoke from the depths of my heart: 'My body, my being, and my life as service.' ... When the bowl had passed all the way back around to Running Bear there was a deep stillness that resonated with a sense of becoming.

He filled the bowl of the pipe then told us each to take a small puff and offer the smoke with our inner prayer to Great Spirit. He showed us the way to hold it then tap our right and then left shoulder before offering it to the heavens.

Despite the fact that the herbs were not any mind-altering substances, it seemed that the very ceremony itself had taken everyone into a deep state. We sat with eyes closed and bodies still, until Running Bear finally gave thanks for the circle and called in song with another chant. This time we were invited to join in with rattles and other instruments.

Running Bear then handed around the circle a little pouch for each of us – a piece of cloth which contained a shell, a gift from the west coast of America. He then asked if there were anything else any one wanted to share or speak in closing. Expressions of gratitude were presented. Then I reached into my bag and pulled out my parcel. 'Running Bear,' I said. 'I have a giveaway. I want to pass it to you.' He looked across at me with warm eyes. I handed it to the left to be passed around the circle.

When it reached his hands, he sat quietly holding it silently for a moment. Then he unwrapped it. A great smile stretched across his face. 'Aah!' he said with a slow nod. Then he looked into me with old wise eyes. 'You are dolphin woman!' he said. 'My brother told me to look out for you. He sends his heart to you ... to assure you, you are on the right path. You are well guided.'

He then added, 'Now I have something for you. 'It is from my ancestors for your medicine bag.'

He pulled open his bag and dug deep inside it. He pulled out a tiny blue cloth pouch that was tied with green string.

'These are medicine herbs from our elders and ancestors. It was given to me in my first initiation with the pipe. Now it is for you to carry. The prayers of the elders will be with you ... they will always answer your prayers,' he said.

I received it with profound gratitude, feeling humbled and overjoyed by the ongoing synchronicities of my journey. In that moment I realised even more deeply, how truly we are all woven together in the tapestry of life.

I also knew I was unmistakably being called into the Sweat Lodge.

We stepped outside under the new moon and as I undressed I

gazed up at it. I knew I was being asked to receive a message from spirit and so with implicit faith I stepped forward without a moment's hesitation.

My whole being felt at peace as I entered into the pitch black cavern. I knew not what to expect and yet had a sense that I was about to have a profound experience.

Inside the Sweat Lodge I moved quickly and easily into a state of expansive presence. As the stifling heat increased with each round of fire, rocks and water, I breathed even more deeply into an altered state of awareness. We proceeded through the ceremony with intense heat increasing as we approached the northern gate, the place of spirits entering. My faith in the moment grew stronger. Within seconds the chanting faded into the background and I felt myself leaving my body. A great void lured me into a space of inky black emptiness. My consciousness was clear, my awareness alert. I adjusted my perception to see if I could sense any presence:

I was gazing into the night sky, filled with an infinity of stars. Suddenly from the distant horizon, an owl appeared, flying at an intense speed directly towards me. It seemed as if it were going to fly right into me. My eyes grew wide and the owl's round eyes pierced into my vision. In that same instant I suddenly realised *I* was the owl. Realising this truth, I turned with a rush of power under my wings, swooping towards the stars. I flew through the inky night, up and up, towards the infinite delight above. I heard the stars' song calling me. Old man dreaming was welcoming me. The Milky Way beckoned my embrace.

As I approached, the rainbow serpent shimmered in ecstatic delight ... a splattering course of stars and clusters of cosmic light. I mounted its form, upon its glittering neck, and together we flew towards the distant horizon below.

Soon I could see a large form rising up from the sleeping red desert. Uluru, the heart of warm, red stone, breathed silently in the darkness of night. She beckoned us, calling us to her womb. There, at the side of her still body, was the mouth of a cave. We entered into her darkness and laid ourselves on her cool sandy floor, spiralling into earth's navel. Darkness again engulfed me.

My form disappeared.

•

Within this emptiness a new vision emerged.

I was the expanse of space way above the Earth. I looked at her beautiful shining body. How radiant she looked. Immense love welled up in my being. As the love spread its wave of bliss over me, I felt such connectedness to my Earth-Mother, and all that live upon her, that my waves of love began to enfold her great glowing body.

Soon I noticed I was closer to her form and as I adjusted my vision I realised that the wave of movement I was seeing from the stream of bliss was a river of people moving across the land together, joining hands and weaving a light pattern of love. An immeasurable wave of peace and joy flooded my being. I felt truly blessed.

•

I saw it as my calling and purpose to fulfil the call to honour Life and Love, for the healing and peace of which our people and our planet are so deserving. And so came my prayer and dedication ... to hold the hand of as many people as possible, to touch all in the power of Love, for unity.

39. Chosen

Your children are not your children.
They are the sons and daughters of Life's longing for itself.
They come through you but not from you,
And though they are with you
Yet they belong not to you.

Kahlil Gibran

The house was dark and quiet and the sounds of sleep filled the space with calm. I moved quietly along the corridor and into Lilha's bedroom. Her perfect little body and face were a picture of absolute peace. An overwhelming love flooded my whole being as I saw such vulnerability in her as a baby and yet the undeniable power of a bright and ancient spirit. In her I could see the way of the future and the knowing of the past and the bliss of the present. I could see her strength and wisdom, which would be revealed through her own path. The words of Kahlil Gibran echoed in my mind ...

Your children are not your children. They are the sons and daughters of life's longing for itself. They come through you but not from you, and though they are with you yet they belong not to you ...

As a mother I felt the undeniable bond of love to serve her, to guide her, to nourish her and give to her as best as I could. As a spirit I saw a time coming when things might be different – a destiny we had both chosen.

Over the following weeks I received constant visions of my life as Divine service. I seemed to dive ever more deeply while Jake retreated to the edges again. I lost another degree of faith in the continuation of our shared journey, yet prayed even more deeply for it to work.

There were still things between us that kept some spark of hope alive. I even wondered why the spirit of a boy still kept asking to come into our life if we couldn't make things work.

Contradictions arose in many ways. It didn't help that other 'clairvoyant' people around me kept saying they saw us going in different directions. I continued to respond, 'But we have choice! It doesn't have to be that way.' I didn't want to hear. And yet something in me just knew, deeply, that I was being prepared for a major change. For the response would come: 'It is not a matter of whether something has to be. Sometimes it just is.'

Within the experience of preparation for my service, the interdimensional states of my being continued to expand immensely. It was as if I were in an acceleration chamber.

Sometimes the rushes of energy that coursed through my body felt almost violent – yet at the same time ecstatic. I only had to sit still or close my eyes for a matter of seconds and I would enter into vortexes of light and be charged with such intense energy, it felt like I was a rocket that was about to take off! The body would begin to breathe in fast rhythmic pulses before dissolving into subtle open breath, while I would become an expansive awareness watching it all. I was no longer inside the body but was watching the body inside of me!

I journeyed into dimensions of sacred geometry that revealed the creative constructs of the cosmos: spiralling, intertwining, flowering fields, interlinked matrixes of fractal inclusions, expanding from within to without to within. And within it all, I would breathe and pulse, having the consciousness as creator and created. I entered into a slipstream of ever-present awareness – no more sleep, no more gap, all one constant conscious stream.

One night, not needing to rest, I simply sat in lotus posture on the bed. Jake slept deeply. I entered a field of communion with a circle of lamas. I too, was one of them. They shared with me the current undertakings of service occurring on the planet and my preparation for more extensive work through omnipotent consciousness.

Just as they started to introduce me to a lama who sat quietly in the circle, I felt Jake stir slightly. Lama Zopa had just introduced me to the quiet lama – telling me his soul was preparing to incarnate and that I was asked to be the vehicle for his birth. Then suddenly Jake appeared in the circle. He saw me sitting with the group of lamas.

With great excitement he sat bolt-upright in bed and called out ... 'I can see you! I'm with you – with the lamas!'

His eyes were still closed. His body was still sleeping, yet he had entered into the same dimension and was aware of it. We looked at him and smiled and then dissolved.

With a slight dropping sensation I returned to my body to find Jake sitting up next to me.

He grabbed my arm. Now his eyes were open. 'I was there!' he exclaimed. 'I saw you!'

'Yes, I know, we saw you too,' I replied.

'What were you doing? How did I get there? I don't get it! How did that happen?'

'Don't worry,' I said. 'Some things are beyond the mind.'

'But what was that all about?' he persisted.

'Do you really want to know?' I asked.

Jake stared at me and nodded vigorously. 'Of course I do!' he exclaimed.

'Well, I was being introduced to a soul who wants to be born through us. He is a lama.'

'Oh ... far out! Wow, that's amazing,' said Jake.

Then he lay down and within minutes was fast asleep again. I decided to lie down too.

As I rested I saw a vast sky above me. Then, from in the sky, I heard the voice of a boy calling ... 'Mum ... Mum ... I'm coming soon ...'

There, in the luminous space, I saw the image of his spirit riding on the back of a dragon. Then I heard him speak again. 'Through many bodies have I come, but now on the dragon spirit I ride ... I am the dragon spirit.' His eyes were still ancient like the Lama's but I could clearly see the new form he was choosing as our child – a boy.

40. *Creation Cave*

> Until one is committed, there is hesitancy, the chance to draw back. Concerning all acts of initiative (and creation) ... the moment one definitely commits oneself, then Providence moves too.
>
> *William Hutchinson Murray*

Before long I found myself pregnant again. And I was growing consciously and spiritually at such a rate that it was no longer possible for Jake to keep up. In fact, the more I grew, the greater the gap appeared to be.

I could no longer stretch myself to accommodate 'pub' outings and conversations lubricated by alcohol, smothered in the fog of cigarettes. A sense of resentment towards me grew in Jake, his family and friends as I retreated into Self, choosing quietude in my room and meditating, even when guests were present. Once again I was drawn more and more deeply into a monastic lifestyle.

I was considered somewhat rude, aloof and arrogant for replying honestly when Jake asked about my absence. I simply found it rather boring and disharmonious to my being. I could only find real interest in matters of the heart and the Divine, which arose interactively in only a few individuals who came seeking.

I also lost all interest sexually. Without feeling a connection emotionally or spiritually, I found it impossible to be intimate. Intimacy to me was an act that emerged from a deeper connection. The gap and the pressure of discord continued to grow. Discord arose out of our hopes, expectation, obligation, frustration and disappointment as each of us, in different ways, tried to draw the other closer. We each felt the undeniable gap, the yawning distance that threatened, underneath all the hopes.

After months of prayers and futile efforts, I began to give up. I just couldn't keep any last glimmer of faith alive. It seemed like all the last energy for growth was draining away. I so wanted to 'make' our marriage work yet found it almost unbearable to my inner truth to live with choices of such diminished spirituality. To me, love was a two-way street that could only continue to grow if that flow was equal between two minds, two hearts, *and* two spirits – not just two bodies.

On top of all that, I knew Jake was exhausted. He used up every bit of energy in his work. I knew he was making milestones in his field. He was well-respected and celebrated for all his accomplishments. He put everything that he could into it, but that resulted in exhaustion.

And it became difficult for him to see that as a mother, a wife, a housewife and a spiritual counsellor, my work ran around a twenty-four hour schedule. My day didn't start at the office or finish when I got home. I didn't get a silent lunch or the quiet of my own presence in a drive to work. My work continued all day and very often all night. Jake just didn't comprehend that, by not helping outside of his work hours, I didn't get the rest or support I needed. He was too tired to see or understand.

Thankfully we lived in a landscape of great wonder and beauty that provided a last common thread, the joy of walks and adventures in nature.

As my pregnancy proceeded I sought the support of a doctor who was willing to attend to me with the option of trying for a natural birth again, providing I was at the right hospital in the event of needing another caesarean. After the birth of Lilha, it had been diagnosed that I had a 'flower pot' pelvis, an unusually small pelvic structure that statistically rarely achieved a great enough dilation for the passage of a baby. Hence, despite two days in labour with all final stimulants applied, my cervix did not open wide enough for Lilha.

Nonetheless, the doctor was willing to allow for the possibility that with the second pregnancy, the cervical capacity might improve. Over the months I began to display the same patterns as I had whilst Lilha was in utero. When premature labour started to threaten again at around twenty-five weeks, I was instantly put on medication. I also took natural medicines and spent as much time as possible meditating and breathing into deep trance states.

In the twenty-eighth week I went into a frenzy of clearing and organising the house. Jake started to worry. I had done the same thing the week before Lilha arrived. Then, in the twenty-ninth week, I went to the bathroom one day and I felt a sudden 'pop' in the top of my aura. It was like I was unplugged and the cosmic forces of energetic light rushed in and down through my form. I knew I would be in labour by the next day.

By the following afternoon I felt so deeply consumed in the cosmic waves of energy that engulfed me that I ended up squatting in a yoga posture in the middle of the lounge room.

As I settled inwardly my consciousness shifted and I began to experience myself as a full-blood Aboriginal woman.

I felt the ancientness of the land in me as I squatted on the red earth. Its carnelian sands, soft beneath my feet, stretched into the vast distance. The sun melted into the horizon, casting a gold and pink glow across the field. Leaning trees with thin outstretching branches topped by sparse leaves turned into shadowy silhouettes. Then the full moon began to rise, its light shining on my black skin, and turning the sky to violet.

Tufts of spinifex grass glistened like silver, shimmering under the lunar light, as the moon's full body climbed towards the heavens.

As the moon reached its zenith above my head, I felt a great rush as my energy field opened. Then from the moon poured a great stream of pure liquid white light.

It poured down through my central channel and into the womb, the creation cave. There, it filled the space, surrounding the babe until it was so full that the cave's mouth opened. The gateway opened to the luminous flood. My waters broke!

The great flood of luminous water poured onto the red sand and began streaming, snaking across the land to the horizon like a vast shining, silvery river. And, as it touched the horizon where it met the sky, I saw a great star rising up, filling the sky with brilliance.

•

Jake had been sitting on the couch in the middle of all this, transfixed by my unmoved silence. However, when I had remained like that for more than an hour, he became worried and called my name several times. I was beyond contact, so he sat and waited. Finally the scene dissolved and my conscious awareness merged with my 'now time' body.

From within the great depths I mustered up my voice to speak ... 'My waters have broken.'

Jake leapt up in a flash and came running back with a nappy. There was a great puddle on the carpet.

'I'll call the doctor,' he said.

After twelve hours of labour it soon became evident that the cervix was not going to dilate enough by itself. The doctor gave the order to try the gel and give it another hour.

Then about twenty minutes later Elijah made an unexpected, abrupt shift. His head dropped down into the deeper canal – the cervix had widened another two centimetres. There was great excitement at the prospect that I was going to have Elijah naturally. In the middle of it all I stayed deeply centred and calm ... even when the doctor began to take on a note of grave concern. Despite Eli's having lowered into my birth passage, it was evident that there was no more dilation. No matter how much I 'bore down' with each contraction, he was unable to move any further.

The doctor attempted to keep a calm demeanour yet he couldn't help but radiate an air of panic.

'We have to try the forceps,' he said. 'He's stuck, and his pulse is showing signs of stress.'

My cervix wasn't dilating any further.

The doctor began exerting great force. The baby was too far down to operate – we had gone beyond the moment of a caesarean.

With the forceps not working, the doctor ordered suction. 'With each contraction you have to bear down, push as hard as you can!' he almost yelled. The scene was changing to panic, yet somehow I still stayed centred.

Still, the suction wasn't working. The doctor even had his foot on the end of the bed using his full weight as leverage. Finally he tried the forceps again and I corralled every last degree of strength and focus I could gather. And, with one final great push, Elijah made it into the world, battered and bruised on the way.

It wasn't long after his arrival that again we had to be transferred to intensive care at Flinders Hospital, with the same difficulty as with Lilha.

For days I sat watching Eli's spirit. He hovered over his body, undecided. I prayed for him. I chanted to him. I assured him. I trusted in his great spirit to make it through. And, I consoled him, that if he chose not to stay, I would embrace that too. Then suddenly on the ninth day, he dropped into his body. He wiggled and squirmed as if feeling his way into his skin and then let out a tiny squeak. I knew he was saying, 'Okay, I'm here.'

The following two months were still a great challenge for his little body. The intensive care unit was exceptional with the extent of support and compassion they gave us. They had already supported us previously with Lilha, so there was an even deeper bond of trust.

Jake displayed an amazing depth of devotion as he did all he could to take care of Lilha and nurture me, through a time that was extremely emotional for us all.

At ten weeks, Elijah was finally allowed to come home.

It didn't take him long to make up for lost time. He suckled and nursed with great gulping delight. Before long he was a solid little baby that gave no hint of being born so prematurely.

41. *Wise Old Lama*

A human being is part of the whole, called by the universe. A part limited in time and space. He experiences himself, his thoughts and feelings, as something separate from the rest, a kind of optical delusion of his consciousness. This delusion is a kind of prison for us, restricting us to our personal desires and to affection for a few persons nearest to us. Our task must be to free ourselves from this prison by widening our circle of compassion to embrace all living creatures.

Albert Einstein

The door slammed behind Jake, emphasised by a gust of wind. He rarely seemed to return home from work in a good mood. I was always having to be careful, always trying to rehearse my speech so that it wouldn't spark his temper. I waited until he was settled in the lounge room before broaching dinner plans. My body desperately needed healthy food. Since my time in hospital, my body seemed to be even more finely balanced, and much easier to tip out of order.

'Honey,' I opened my sentence with an air of warmth. 'How about some steamed vegies and brown rice for dinner ... something simple?'

Jake rolled his eyes. 'How about I order pizza?' he grumbled.

I rolled my eyes. 'I could make a nice sauce to go with the vegies,' I implored.

Jake's look had turned to a hard-set suppressed rage.

He stood up, taking large strides that accompanied his angry mood, forcefully opened the fridge and took out a beer.

'Do what you like,' he said. And with that he took four more strides to the phone, grabbed the handset and dialled to order pizza.

I stood in silence, staring at the kitchen bench. Either I was going to relent or I was going to keep taking solitary steps.

Over the following months, Jake seemed to spiral again into deeper states of disconnection. I could see the same patterns of retreat. The renewed glow that had embraced us with the arrival of Elijah began to dissolve. Our relationship grew increasingly tense. It was as though we were trying to communicate from totally different planes. I used all of the communication skills that I had been teaching for months. Yet, in most moments, it was futile energy. I resolved to give him more space and time, praying that it might allow him the time to open up.

I became starkly aware of what I did, what my days and nights consisted of – attend to the cries of the children, listen to Jake snoring, meet the early morning cries for milk, open windows, cook meals, wash dishes, vacuum floors, close doors, wash, iron and fold clothes, shop, chop vegetables, watch Jake watching television and drinking beer, water the garden, walk the pram, change nappies, rock and sing sleepy children to sleep, tidy the house, close windows, listen to Jake snoring, open windows ... Every minute was accounted for in my relentless daily grind.

Of course, this grind is familiar to women all over the planet, and for many of them, to serve their family is the highest duty, the greatest sacrifice and service of their lives. My family was precious to me, and yet I knew I was called by a larger purpose, a plan that was beyond the nucleus of my own little family. That plan, moved by compassion, encompassed all of humanity and creation. This was why I knew my role as a mother to my children would be fulfilled in a different way. Yet I wondered how it could all be possible. Somehow my life didn't appear to be fulfilling that greater vision.

Surely this wasn't all I was asked to do? I felt plagued by doubt and debate. Why had the angels ever come to me? Why had I been given so many signs? Why had I been called as God's emissary if this was all He wanted of me? Why would I be filled with such an infinite ocean of love and spirit if only a few drops could be given? I felt weighed down by the menial tasks that had to be done.

To add further confusion to it all any remnant of intimate communication between us fell away. The last spark between us was gone. I felt so deeply challenged. My life seemed to be losing meaning. I wanted to accept Jake's state and yet felt an undeniable frustration at being 'unmet' on nearly every front. I felt like a flower withering in a desert.

My mother continued to be an unconditional support.

Despite the challenges of everyday living, I also continued to experience further awakenings of consciousness – each encounter becoming more and more vivid, whilst my dreams became completely lucid and conscious.

One night I found myself travelling.

I was on a long beach. Its vast stretch was lit up by the golden light of the late afternoon sun. I looked across the sand and noticed a few people, recognising Don, one of Jake's friends.

As I looked out to the ocean I suddenly realised it was rippling with motion – a great stirring of activity. Hundreds of dolphins were swimming through the waters towards the far end of the bay. I felt them calling me, beckoning me to follow. As I did, I found myself edging around a cliff face that led into a cave. Its mouth opened out to a ledge at the water's edge. I stood inside and stared out at the teeming water, which splashed and sparkled as dolphins leapt from the ocean into the afternoon light.

Then I noticed a large dolphin making its way to the cave. Suddenly it launched itself onto the ledge of the cave.

> It greeted me with delight and then stood up on its tail and proceeded to communicate a series of messages to me. It spoke of the preparations of the emotional body of humanity and the support that the dolphins and whales are offering. It showed me my galactic connection to the dolphins and my ongoing relationship with them in this life. It awoke in me the memory of even deeper sensory awareness through light, sound and consciousness.
>
> Then suddenly its face began to change as it spoke of the ongoing work that would unfold in the future. Instantly I saw the shining face of a man. The dolphin was clearly showing me its human soul incarnation. He smiled deeply as he gave me the message of our future. Then he changed again into the dolphin, slipped back into the water and swam away.

•

The next morning the 'dream' experience played over and over in my mind. It also reminded me of a previous experience I had encountered in the flesh when I was fifteen. I had gone on a surfing trip to Eyre Peninsula and was bodysurfing at Pondelowie Bay when I suddenly found myself surrounded by twenty-five dolphins. They played with me in the waves for an hour. I also experienced vivid 'communication' from them, which led me to understand certain breathing techniques to awaken and clear the subtle channels of the etheric field.

I told Jake about the dream and how I had also seen Don on the beach.

'Huh,' said Jake. 'Wow, that's interesting. Don's coming to visit tomorrow night. He's really into dolphins too. You should tell him about the dream.'

It wasn't long after Don arrived that I raised it; I was too excited to wait a moment longer.

As I spoke Don's eyes lit up wide.

'Far out!' he exclaimed. 'I had that dream too! I mean, not all the same details as you, but I was there ... on the beach! I saw them ... the dolphins! Hundreds of them!' He looked at me in amazement. 'What does it all mean?' he asked. 'I mean, why did we have the same dream?'

'Well, those of us who are connected with the dolphins are being contacted in many ways. The messages are to inspire us to connect even more deeply to the Love and Truth we are. We have to be shown how intimately connected we all are to understand we are a part of each other and that we have to move to the next level if we are going to have a future of harmony. Those of us who are ready to 'see' are being shown so that we can also show others.'

'Yeah, wow ... you're right. I really believe what you say. But how can I become more aware too?' he asked.

'Just love,' I said. 'Embrace and give love to all things in every moment, and you will see.'

'Yes!' he exclaimed. 'You're right. That's what it's all about! Love. Love is all we need ... Ha ha ha ...'

Jake started to laugh: 'Yeah, yeah, yeah ... love, love, love ... and everything'll be sweet ... ha ha ha.'

Don and I looked in surprise at Jake's cynical display, then looked at each other and shrugged.

The next day Kane rang up to tell me that the international whale and dolphin conference was coming up in Hervey Bay in the next month and he just 'knew' that I was meant to be there. The moment he said it, I 'knew' too.

Jake was apprehensive but eventually became more supportive as I prepared with great determination. He decided it would be a nice thing for him to have four days by himself with Lilha while I took Elijah. With Elijah having just turned four months old, he was about to have his first sacred gathering.

I sat in the chair feeling amazement for life's adventure as I prepared to feed Eli. As he took to my breast I looked down at him feeling a great rush of life force. Love consumed me as I felt the wonderment of the circle of life. Then as the love welled up in my being Elijah unexpectedly pulled himself off my nipple and stared up at me. There, in my arms, was the presence of an ancient powerful being. It was no longer the face of a baby but that of a wise old lama looking at me. I suddenly realised how immensely blessed I really was, I couldn't believe it.

'Oh, my God,' I sighed. 'You chose me to be your mother? ... Oh ... thank you. Thank you. Thank you.'

I cried, cradling him in wonderment. He smiled. Then, so deeply, he looked into my eyes. It was a full conscious response that looked into me. Then he blinked, his little face became a baby's again and he happily returned to suckling as if no big thing had happened.

42. *The Dolphin Legend*

Amongst all things there is a deeper communication, of which the source is love.

Isira

August 1997: Elijah slept soundly or gazed at me quietly for the whole flight and trip to Hervey Bay. Once at the venue he immediately caught everyone's attention. He was like a giant people-magnet – a force far bigger than his little body.

It wasn't long before I recognised many familiar souls and knew, without a doubt, that I was in the right place.

Particular 'brothers' and 'sisters' seemed to have an immediate response that was very open and receptive. We shared our common stories of being guided by spirit and finding the whales and dolphins to be intimately woven into our journey. Dr Arpana Gita, also known as 'Dr Didge', was such a kindred spirit to me that I felt overwhelmed with gratitude at being in his company. In fact there was such depth and openness that I could clearly see that he was my self – another aspect of the one Self.

Before long he offered to initiate Elijah with a didge,[1] for a sound healing. He came to our room, which was positioned close to a great lake. The air was thick with nature's stillness and motion and a deep silence seemed to create a prelude in anticipation of something

[1] An abbreviation of didgeridoo – a long hollow ceremonial instrument made from native trees of Australia.

profound that was about to unfold.

I lay Elijah down on his lambskin. He gazed up at us silently and wiggled his toes as he settled into the soft lamb's wool.

Arpana undid the top of a long brightly woven bag and unravelled from within it a large, redwood didgeridoo with a flared bottom.

'It's beautiful,' I said.

'Mmm ...' he nodded. 'This is, at the moment, my favourite yidaki ... that's a true native word for the didge. Didgeridoo is a white fella's word,' he said.

I could feel his deep respect for the Aboriginal people and that being a white fella did not mar him with a lack of true reverence.

'Well, let's welcome Elijah to this world shall we? We can call on the ancestors and ask them to be his guides and protectors. The song of the yidaki is said to be a voice for the elders and spirits. We might even get the whale song for him.'

He put the long hollow trunk to his mouth and with one deep breath began to 'sing' the ancestors.

Eli's eyes lit up. He stared up at the yidaki in total alertness. It was as if he knew the sound, as if somewhere in his mind he was hearing it from a great distant past. The sound resonated – deep, soulful, slow, rhythmic droning. The floor vibrated and everything seemed to be consumed by the 'song'.

Suddenly another sound began to enter into the deep vibration. First a high note that wavered, then it plunged into a deep drone, rising and falling. It was unmistakeable: the whale call. Elijah seemed to enter a trance, as if he was way beyond body.

Without warning, two spirits suddenly appeared, their light-bodies displaying their form as two male elders. I could hear their singing and clapping sticks as they gave Elijah a blessing of guidance, protection and connection to the spirit world of ancestors. Time disappeared as we dissolved into the deep power of spirit's presence.

When the 'singing' was complete Elijah turned his head and arched his back as if he was waking from a dream. I knelt beside him and took his little hand in mine.

Arpana knelt down on the other side of him. Elijah immediately turned his head and gave him a big grin.

We both laughed.

'Thanks, mate,' said Arpana. 'I take it that means thumbs up!'

'I think so,' I chuckled.

We stood up and shared our gratitude for the experience, then wished each other farewell as we prepared ourselves for the leisure of a restful evening.

The next morning we all gathered for the official opening with Uncle Bill and Auntie Pearl (two of the representing elders), and a supporting group of Aboriginal representatives.

We were led through a ceremonial fire of smoke. Its rich scent of gum leaves billowed in grey-blue clouds as gradually, one by one, each person was blessed with the cleansing. The circle was blessed again by key speakers and then transformed into a scene of native dance. Gradually the performances welcomed the greater group into playful dancing and singing.

The crowds began to mingle as a sense of collective destiny drew us into soulful interaction. Young women vied for turns to hold Eli, leaving me hands-free to dance and mingle. Then, in the middle of it all, I felt suddenly drawn to the other side of the group. I simply followed the feeling. I moved through the crowd towards the outer field where only a few people stood near lamps.

I was surprised to see how many people had arrived. There must have been at least two hundred. Amongst the faces were many people I already knew from other places – of this lifetime and others. The air was thick with laughter, music, dancing, friendship, joy and playfulness.

Women danced and played in long dresses and vibrant colours, men strolled barefoot and beat out ecstatic rhythms on the drums, children laughed and ran in and around the crowd, and the inner fire circle grew brighter as the night gradually began to enfold the scene.

As I approached the far side of the grounds, a man with silver hair tied in a ponytail turned around. His face was instantly lit up by a fire torch. There, shining at me, was the face of the man-dolphin I had met in the cave in my dream!

We just stood staring, smiling with radiant joy for what seemed like forever, until someone else approached. It was obvious we were engaged in a deep sharing so we were soon left in the quiet space again.

He introduced himself officially and we began to talk. When I told him about my dream he chuckled saying, 'Yes ... the golden dolphin legend ... that's what I'm here for – to share the legend of our dreaming journey with the dolphins.'

'Mmm, yes, ' I said. 'I 'spose we all are here for that, in one way or another.'

The night continued to be an unfolding of profound synchronicities and connections that left me going to bed knowing there was a lot more to my presence at the conference than I could possibly comprehend. I did know, however, was that I was in the right place, that I had been prepared for this and that I was about to receive further guidance.

Over the following days I discovered a profound connection with many of the presenters. I recognised that these were some of the fellow light-workers that the ancestors had told me I would meet and work with.

It was evident that each person had a significant purpose and was following their calling: Scott Taylor – founder of Cetacean Studies Institute, author and educator; Peter Shenstone – *The Golden Dolphin Legend,* Director of Planet Ark; Kim Kindersley – filmmaker: *The Gathering, Return of the Whale Dreamers;* Drunvalo Melchizedek – Sacred Geometry, teacher of *Flower of Life* and Mer-Ka-Ba meditations; Credo Vusamazolu Mutwa (Awakener of Zulus) – African shaman/spiritual leader and storyteller; Aunty Pearl King – Kamilaroi elder, spiritual inspirer; Joan Ocean – co-founder of Dolphin Connection, author and facilitator of dolphin journeys; Yantra de Vilder, writer for music, film, theatre and multi-media; Dr Kote Lotah and Al Lul Koi – trained A-Tis'win elders of the Chumas

Native American People, head medicine man and woman of their people; John C Lilly, grandfather of dolphin communication research, author of fourteen books and 'explorer' of mind/reality; (Uncle) Bill Smith – representative of New South Wales Aboriginal council in Australia. I felt immense excitement and gratitude that I was there to experience the friendship and insights of each of these extraordinary people. It amplified my sense that it was my time to step forward and really fulfil my own purpose.

And it became evident that our paths would continue to meet in the sharing of a common spiritual purpose. The synchronicities were abundant as I watched a play of parallel lines of life between myself and each of these remarkable people. I watched with fascination as I could see each one as another aspect of myself fulfilling a role from another perspective.

Aunty Pearl King and Uncle Bill reminded me of my roots and my connection with the ancestors. They helped me to see the part I would play in sacred circles with elders and that it was all like a trail of breadcrumbs left by Great Spirit for the awakening from the dream. They reminded me that greatness followed from simple steps and from the perseverance to keep walking, just to keep walking – no matter how hard it seemed in moments.

Joan Ocean reminded me of childlike play. I could see the same innocent child self as I knew in me. And in the lightness and joy of the play came the ease to keep doing whatever I knew I simply had to do. In the face of those who feared one who sang of truth, love and oneness, I could remain light and innocent, committed to love.

Kim Kindersley inspired me to follow my dreams, no matter what. I also had a knowing that along the way our paths would continue to be entwined. The extent of his sacred journeying with elders, shamans and medicine women was another parallel reflection of my own journey. We discovered we were connected to some of the same people and that it was inevitable we would work together on his movie-making ventures. That was an exciting prospect as I was really interested in the sacred events that were being filmed.

It turned out that Credo V. Mutwa was one of the key links in Kim Kindersley's movie and sacred journey. As I sat close to him I could feel his power. This large African man, draped in traditional clothes, held a large talking stick in his hand. As he wove his story, bringing the myth of all the characters including the dolphins and whales into the pinnacle point, he stared at me in wild excitement and pointed his stick at me with great gusto as the words flew from his mouth, '... and all the creatures, all the creations of the One shall You know as yourself!'

I couldn't help but recognise his intense direct message to me. And I gave thanks that it was a confirmation of my prayers.

When he finished I stayed close, sitting next to him on the ground. He looked at me through big round, coke-bottle-thick glasses. 'You already remember this. You just have to give up the moments of doubts in yourself to fulfil your knowing,' he said.

'How do I do that?' I asked.

'You'll be given every opportunity. If you stay committed enough you'll be watching, and when you're handed the keys you'll know which one will open the lock – one at a time.'

I stared at him with a blank mind. My mind didn't get it. But that was okay because I knew it wasn't for my mind to get. Deep inside my heart I knew what he meant, and it was in the heart that I felt the trust.

The whole weekend kept weaving around the same thread of awareness, the same message that those of us who had encounters with dolphins had awoken to.

With some reflection I wrote in my diary:

> LOVE, the essential space of purest being, is all encompassing. Everything is commanded and created by love. It is so simple. The answer is pure love, unconditional love. Dolphins communicate this message to us by helping us to understand the healing process through the ascension of our emotional consciousness – letting go of all reflections

of fear, guilt, and the belief in separation.

The dolphin represents a form that is beyond judgment and fear – it has the ability to totally transmute any 'negative' input (as has been proven through research), which would be the equivalent of our ability to forgive and transcend.

When we interact with dolphins, it is in their environment, the ocean-water that is mother earth's manifestation for the embodiment of humanity's collective emotional consciousness. We are 78% water; mother earth is approximately 70% water. The colour blue (synonymous with water) in ancient medicine traditions refers to the kidneys, the emotional seat of our (appearing) physical being, the storehouse of the genetic coding of our fears.

To be freed of our fears is to be transformed through love, to release the unreal from our belief that it is real, and return to the one and only reality – LOVE.

If we can ride on the rainbow (the complete spectrum of our self in shadow and light) in awake awareness, seeing all as our one Self, then all energies that appeared in conflict will be brought into harmony. The shadow and the light are of the one. In this knowing we release the belief of our limitations and separation into the space of consciousness which knows and creates its own manifestation. Here is the freedom from the perceived prison. The transcendence of our belief in duality is critical to our wholeness and peace.

The one who is dreaming creates the dream that appears to be real yet is only a dream. The dream and the dreamer are one. And in knowing such, we shall awaken beyond duality.

If we can hold our awareness in this truth – that Love is the true state beyond appearing divisions – we will experience the reflection of all life as such. The vision we hold in our minds is what appears as manifestation. On this level of experience, we can and do create our future because the future already exists in the given state of Now!

> The dimension of the ego mind is coursing on towards its own awakening through the reflection upon the symbols and messages of one Truth ... Love is all there is. The dolphins are one such reminder assisting us to let go of fear, separation and judgment and embrace ourselves as the Truth of Love.

As my quest continued I discovered consistent references of accounts in communications connecting dolphins and whales with the ancient cultures and inter-galactic races – everything I had encountered through cosmic vision, journey and messages.

And so I felt inspired to share the message of Love in whatever way I could and affirmed once again that there was no other true or higher purpose in my life but this.

The 16th Attainment

The only way to be free of prisons
is to be free of all conditions.
The conditioned links in the mind
are the bars: good versus bad,
right versus wrong, should versus
shouldn't, saint versus sinner.
I chose to accept the Self in the play
of the light and shadows.

By facing the darkness I opened
the way for the light of truth within it.

The prison only appears real as
long as we own the perspective of
being trapped.

KEY 16.

The Earthquake

KEY 16.

The Earthquake

All structures are eventually outgrown. Whether physical, mental, emotional or spiritual, we must allow the destruction in order to make room for the new form that serves.

Sacrifice brings growth.
Destruction reveals freedom.
The phoenix rises from the ashes.

I would have to give up the conditions of my world in order to gain the destiny of my soul.

43. *Love Without Conditions*

Love is bigger than its looking glass.

Isira

When I returned to South Australia, the connections I had made were kept alive and continued expanding as I shared the vision and message of that which was the one common call – the call of the one in the many – the call of Love.

Naturally I endeavoured to focus on the love within my own relationship. What puzzled me most, however, was that the more I chose love, the more Jake seemed to go in the opposite direction. It was my profound understanding that each of us creates our own experience and can only look to ourselves, to face our fears and transcend them, if we are to have a life of love and fulfilment. Ultimately that choice lies in the power of the individual. I had tried everything to encourage, inspire and support him to look into his fears, so they might be brought to the light of understanding and self-forgiveness, but he remained adamant that it wasn't him that was the creator of his own experience and, to my frustration, that he was totally okay. He left responsibility for his challenges in the ambiguous clutches of 'the other' or 'the world' or 'the system'. In this response, he was hardly unique, and many would see his perspective as reasonable, because this victim stance is so commonly held. On the other hand, I had spent lifetimes refining my relationship with Truth; I had had countless confirmations of my understanding. It was my life's purpose to share that Truth, yet it was missing in my own marriage.

So the gap kept growing. In that widening came an even greater loss of intimate attraction. I also found this puzzling. Whilst I loved Jake dearly, I no longer desired intimacy. It was as if I were realising we were cut out to be friends rather than lifelong lovers. No matter how much I tried to invite that spark again, it just didn't seem to happen. And sadly that didn't help matters.

Jake still felt attraction for me. I even tried to respond and please for the sake of our relationship, but the more I did, the more I felt I was living a lie. My lack of physical interest in him was because of his lack of connection to me emotionally and spiritually. This only increased his emotional withdrawal. Our foundations were crumbling beneath us.

I was tired of trying to meet others on their level and not being met on my own. I seemed to be growing and moving at a lightning pace, leaving Jake further and further behind. Once again I felt like an alien in a strange land. My language and way of approaching things just didn't seem to work in Jake's world.

And still I continued to hear the same message again and again. I was even visited by a spirit who spoke the words clearly: 'Love unconditionally'.

I cried in frustration at myself in the bewilderment: I thought I had given everything I could to be an unconditional love for him. But had I? So the question that remained a puzzle on this level was 'what *is* unconditional love'? How did that look now when I had let go of this world of perceptions, and seen the falsity of the ego? How did that work with my relationship with Jake when any sense of 'togetherness' seemed to be a conflict of our individual 'truth'?

I accepted Jake in his own experience yet I wondered if it meant I would have to accept Jake's truth as my own. But I knew to do so would compromise my own truth, and would leave me without that which I most deeply desired: to live my life wholly in the integrity of liberated consciousness.

Then one afternoon I realised I had been doing all this giving

– for us, the children, for him – because of my attachment. I was attached to wanting him to feel the same, to want the same path: *together,* that was the condition I imposed. And I also wanted him to be free of his own turmoil. Somehow I thought that I could help that happen for him. I now experienced the full realisation that I was not responsible for his happiness. I had assumed my love for him could only be unconditional if I stayed with him. This realisation split me open like a hammer striking a rock! My egoic perception was suddenly cracked open. My desire to stay with him no matter what, was itself the block.

Unconditional love in this instance was to honour both his truth and mine – to set him free to be on his own path and to follow my own was the unconditional love! In that moment of surrender I recognised the far-reaching truth in this message. It felt like my ego mind's idea of 'unconditional love' had been completely cracked open to reveal the brilliant light of the true meaning.

How profound, I thought. To part was not an act of division: it was a change of form that was *inclusive* of the whole truth. I could see how conditioned we are to perceive a separation as an unloving act. Yet life is forever transforming. It is only the moments, the body of events that appear to part. The expression of love simply changes its form whilst we remain forever united in the journey of life.

I saw that it was a conditional idea of love that made me stay with Jake, wanting us to share the same path yet as a result compromising my own path. Unconditional love was without any condition: that is, love for Jake and myself without setting the condition that we must stay together or that he must share my path or that I must walk in his way. It was about acceptance. To love myself unconditionally, I could not compromise my own truth. That meant I had to leave Jake and that, in doing so, I was truly loving him and myself unconditionally. In leaving Jake I would honour and accept his path as true and valid for him and likewise honour my own. In fact as long as I remained with him I was obstructing his own process of growth. To leave him *was* an unconditional act of love. As long as I was with him our views would continue to be pitted against each other, appear to be contradictory and create an unconscious sense of being wrong and guilty.

I wanted to set him free. I wanted him to be fulfilled as his own being, and not be subjected to a path of extreme comparison or conditions, whether they were his or mine. I wanted him to be fulfilled through his own level of choices. And I wanted to fulfil the highest truth of my own path, to share the one Truth, to serve God, the one Eternal Life in all.

And I knew that that Truth could only be a gift for those who wanted to know it.

•

The tears stopped. I sat dumbfounded that it had taken so long for me to see the truth when there had been so many signs.

Yet, despite the knowing, I watched the part of me that wasn't ready to act on the knowing. I was still tempted to see how far I could push it – to see if there could be a different knowing like: Oh no, it was all just a test; now we can really be together. Something in me wanted to cling to my little world of conditioned safety. But the voice in the depths of my heart knew it wasn't like that. The tower was already falling apart. I knew the inevitable. It wasn't 'if' we would go our own ways, it was 'when'.

From that moment, things were not the same. The final curtain was drawn on the fairytale. The prince and princess didn't live happily ever after. I realised the idea of a perfect happily-ever-after love had been, has always been, a myth. Within that realisation was a mix of feelings. The disillusionment seemed even more highlighted, yet at the same time there was a profound sense of having been released from the illusion.

I could see how the desire for the 'perfect' partner is mostly born of a broken identity within the individual. That feeling of brokenness gives rise to the desire either to find the 'other half' to make oneself whole, or to find the 'perfect' person who won't reflect our own 'imperfection' through pain and arguments. The search for perfection becomes externalised and therefore can never result in the fairytale of the perfect romance becoming real. For all the while it is based on the illusion that perfection is somewhere to be made or found outside oneself.

These are still the symptoms of the ego; the false identity of the self as broken and imperfect. That means that the relationship will act as a mirror in which these limited beliefs can be seen. It means that the pain will be under the spotlight. And until individuals can transform the *cause* of the pain within themselves they will continue to attract it in their partner. Yet such pain can also be an invitation to love – to truly love and accept, rather than to validate what is 'wrong'. Through love and acceptance of 'brokenness', we come into wholeness.

It had also become deeply evident to me that when two individuals are at such different stages of their growth, their capacity to be present to each other in love is at great variance. I had continuously witnessed this in my relating with Jake.

It became evident to me that as we return our self to wholeness that such wholeness is then reflected within life itself, the oneness with life, with the all, with God. Within such wholeness is liberation and in liberation we are then free to live that wholeness, whether in our aloneness *or* in relationship. We then no longer seek perfection in the other, but embrace our journey, perhaps alone, perhaps with another. Yet it is still the same journey – the journey of remembering our wholeness as the Self that is united, at-one with God.

I continued to watch the same play of the myth of human love the world over, and I cried with compassion for the pain of the many who continue to believe in the illusion.

The illusion showed up in the antagonisms of our friends who did not hesitate to express their resentments for my decision. I saw that it was a great confrontation: a mirror that was shattering their own hopes and starkly reflecting their own secret fears. It was a cold hard passage of reality for us all. Yet still, deep inside, I ached for a communion in which the state of true love could be shared, free of the mind's projection of fear.

In the light of my freshly magnified awareness I suspected it wouldn't arrive on earth in the form of a relationship. I was beginning to see that relationships are really about returning us to the whole love within our own being, as they unstoppably expose all of our conditions and our belief in the lack of love.

That means we attract to us all the things we need to transform or let go of. The 'other' can never truly fill up what is missing in us, but they will bring it into our full conscious awareness. And that offers the opportunity to find wholeness within our Self. I saw that this is the only reality I could live from that moment on.

I longed to give myself fully to the one true unity – the return to God.

I attempted to communicate my realisation to Jake yet couldn't muster the courage to admit it was really over with him. He seemed to take it as a big enough warning that he decided to try and 'work' on himself. Yet we both knew our relationship had disconnected. He busied himself in an attempt to avoid the truth. I got on with my truth.

I continued working with the Aboriginal elders of the Kaurna people in an endeavour to open up circles between more people – white and black, for sacred affirmations to unite the hearts and minds under one spirit of love, forgiveness and unity. All events combined to mirror intensely that I was being called to follow my path and that I was only procrastinating as long as I put off the final moment of parting with Jake.

I thought of all the reasons why it would be 'wrong' in society's eyes and how I would be judged so harshly. It simply wasn't 'right' to separate once married, you had to stay bound to the vow through thick and thin. And it was the 'worst thing' a mother could do: to move out of the home and 'leave' her children with the father; it was the mother's duty to stay and let the husband go.

Despite recognising a higher plan at work, my mind still worked over these thoughts. Whilst there were many arguments (from others) that supported the usual conditioned idea of what was right, I continued to see the universe's different plan. Jake had even insisted that if we parted, he wanted to be the main carer of the children. And something inside me knew that was part of the higher plan too.

•

Then one day when some of our friends were over, everyone asked me to look at their coffee cups. They loved the clairvoyant messages I was able to see for them. This time Jake also seemed more enthusiastic than usual. I was quite pleased because I wanted to see if I could glimpse what was in store for him when we separated: Would he be okay? Would he be happy?

To my surprise, when I looked in his cup, there in the patterns left by the coffee, I could clearly see the image of a woman, short and voluptuous with short brown hair, naked, waiting in bed for Jake! I blinked as I looked again. My mind flickered to a sense I had felt in the last few months of someone else growing close to Jake.

This feeling kept growing. A week later I found myself looking into Jake's coffee cup again, and there in the patterns was the image of the same woman! This time I had a deepening knowing that there was some growing connection happening in the background of his life. So I put it down to the possibility that it was something that was yet to happen, if not soon.

I withdrew more as I tried to understand the complexity of change that seemed to be looming even closer. Along with the intensity of my constant observations and awareness of life's impermanence, I began to see life dissolving more and more into a dream-like field.

I would enter into states where, for days on end, I couldn't feel solid form but experienced an endless mirage of energy in every direction. It was almost impossible to function humanly. Fortunately, at that time, there were friends constantly visiting who helped around the household.

Everything disappeared into shimmering light and what had seemed like different states between 'awake' and 'asleep' was now one uninterrupted stream of awareness. Within this awareness what had appeared as the world and all its forms 'in time' all converged into an overlapping warp of all events – past, present and future occurring in the same instant. Yet I encountered oscillation between these dimensions, actually experiencing them as they appeared.

Then one evening when Keith and Mary were visiting I found myself entering an overlapping of dimensions between a past interaction of higher life and Egyptian initiations; the present incarnation of living in Buddina; and a state of being in the future that was evolved beyond anything imaginable on earth.

I started talking in a stream of messages that connected the earth evolution story to the ascension beyond the dream – what had been prophesied in many different ways as the 'Golden Age'. The message conveyed specific events of the past and future that were linked to cataclysmic forces and also described heavenly assistance that would activate awakenings for many people. The message also affirmed that I was here to serve in this.

As I spoke I suddenly stood up and went to the bathroom. The overlapping consciousness continued. I stood at the basin and looked at the/my hands – I was so aware of not being the body that it was strange to still see the presence of a body somehow held within the vastness that I experienced; it was all like an awake dream.

I looked in the mirror and saw a massive being of shining blue light enveloping my body. As I looked I saw that it was a being of light that was so evolved in future terms that it resonated way beyond the illusion of the world. Then suddenly as I looked I realised that it was MYSELF! I had returned from the future in order to guide humanity out of its deep sleep! The seeing and knowing was so clear and absolute that it blew away any potential of my appearing earthly body-mind's doubts.

I managed to return to the living room but couldn't say another word.

'Oh my God,' said Mary. 'You're all sparkly – like light!' As she spoke I heard her voice as the voice of myself. It was a bizarre overlapping as I realised I was only with myself – that everything was myself – as the one mind – asleep on the earth level, yet what I really was, was not the body-mind dream, but a field of God's infinite, eternal Love – awake in the dream! I cried with this realisation as everything began to dissolve. An ecstatic rush rippled through my whole being that was so endlessly big, it was bigger than the entire cosmos!

Eventually I found myself sitting in the lounge room again just in time for Mary and Keith to say good night.

The following days continued in one endless stream of dissolved light.

Little did I realise that I was on the very brink of my life's most significant turning point: the central event which would re-sculpt everything that had come before it and everything that would ever follow it.

44. The Disintegration of Illusion

When you have come to the end of
your mind and you must step off the edge
be sure of one of two things:
Either you will find something
firmer to stand on
or you will learn to fly.

Isira

My life, as I had known it, was about to totally disintegrate. I had just passed my twenty-ninth birthday. Late one evening as I sat in lotus posture, the rest of the family slept, while I entered a deep state of no-mind. From within a vast void, I traversed a warping field as if time and place had been donuted[1] into a different dimension.

Suddenly I found myself standing on a tarmac, dressed in a full astronaut suit, looking across at a giant rocket on a raised launching platform. It was totally 'normal' in my state of awareness that that was exactly where I was, in nothing short of 'physical reality'. The entire experience unfolded in completely present-sense awareness, of touch, taste, sound, sight and alive consciousness.

---

[1] An energy shift where I experienced the creation field dissolve into its own centre – zero point – infinite space – and simultaneously emerge, rolling out from its central void like a giant donut ring only to fold right back around on itself in a continuum. Within this field was the awareness that this pattern was repeating itself in the macrocosm and the microcosm.

It was 'normal and real' that I had got up that morning to board a rocket. It was as normal and real as it is for you holding this book in your hands as you read! However, my 'real' physical body remained in a deeply absorbed meditative state.

I was preparing to walk across the bitumen to board the rocket. My headset gave me clear instructions from the control tower.

As I entered the rocket I strapped myself into the reclining pilot seat. Following instructions, I began to set all the instruments in preparation for take-off.

Once all the gauges were set, I heard the clear instructions to 'Prepare for take-off ...

Engage ...

Countdown.

10 ...

9 ...

8 ...

7 ...

6 ...

5 ...

4 ...

3 ...

2 ...

1 ...

BLAST OFF!'

With a massive thrust of energy the rocket left the launching pad. As it accelerated the ascension rate of G-force applied its dragging, clamping pressure upon my body, my skin and organs. It felt like they were being pushed and pulled downwards against my bones until I felt like a vibrating rocket myself, about to take off! The quantum physical shift finally plateaued as the rocket achieved stabilisation at a great distance from earth.

After some time I received word from the Control Tower that I could 'stabilise instruments and take a break ...' That meant I could unstrap myself.

As I did I instantly floated buoyantly in non-gravity, playing with the sense of movement without force. I simultaneously realised that all movement was actually directed by thought. I only had to think and in that instant I was where I had directed the body to go with my mind!

Then I noticed the window above me and decided to float up to it to look out into space. As I began to look over its rim I suddenly realised that everything was happening in the same instant. Time had totally disappeared![1]

There, stretched out before me, was the infinite vastness of inky void – space, splattered with stars. I was looking out ... down and into endless space. I floated higher to look through the very centre of the portal.

A glowing sapphire gem of a ball was hanging in space way below me. As I realised it was the planet Earth, I felt an overwhelming rush of love – I held such immense love for earth and all upon her – I let out a deep sigh as thoughts unfolded ...

'Oh ... Earth! ... Oh ... I'm up here and Earth's way down there ...'

As I looked at the vastness of space I suddenly saw the all-connected continuum and the realisation was then ...

Aah! I am all this! Earth, space, the rocket craft, the body,

[1] In order to explain this, the words convey a sense of linear events yet all occurred in the singular, all encompassing instant! I experienced the true nature of life as both a sequential and instantaneous happening.

all One mind creation – no separation.

In that instant the thought followed ...

As I am all this, I don't need to be in this rocket any more!

So I floated over to the hatch and swung the great latch open. As the hatch opened I was immediately sucked into the non-atmosphere.

I felt and realised the body was simultaneously exploding and imploding!

Skin, blood, bones, sinews, flesh, organs, brains – everything was disintegrating! And in that instant was a whispering remnant of thought ...

'Oh ... I'm disintegrating ... I'm being destroyed!'

Yet in the same instant, the higher awareness shone ... 'Ah! I am all this, not this, all that is ... one beyond body/mind ... I am ... eternal life ...'

Everything, that had appeared to be, exploded and dissolved.

•

I awoke as if from a dream into an awakened eternity of love, being and bliss that was completely beyond time, place, mind, space – and beyond the beyond. I was completely at One, with all-pervading being, infinite beyond any imagining. There, beyond, was the unshakable, unchangeable, limitless power of God, Love, joy, freedom and absolute wholeness.

The love in such absolute beingness was joy beyond belief, love beyond measure – like knowing the absolute entirety of love's eternity and yet knowing there's still limitlessly more!

I stayed dissolved, unshakably in that state, for nine hours. When there was finally a sense of return, the bliss was so immeasurable, I cried tears of joy, love and gratitude for two hours.

From that moment nothing was as it had appeared before.

I still had a memory of what had appeared to have been, yet the state of my awareness was now held in unswerving awakefulness as I knew I was not of the world, the mind, the dream; yet remained as the play and the player, playing the dream.

I saw clearly that what appeared as the body remaining was now only a vehicle for a bridge of spirit – a message of Truth beyond the illusion.

The 17th Attainment

What had been my world was destroyed. This was huge. There was nothing to hold onto any more. There was only the soaring flight of my spirit's eternal journey.

We will all experience the collapse of our worldly identity. Sometimes it's big, sometimes it's small. But no matter what, the falling apart always comes. Our pain is not because of this natural element of life's process. It is because of our resistance to it that we suffer.

The phoenix rises only after being consumed by the fire. When we are left surrounded by nothing but rubble, when we can no longer claim the things of our world as our security, then we discover that our greater power is in the natural process of life as it disintegrates and reintegrates, that we are this rhythm. If we were to stay forever with one place or one event, we would be dead. It is because of the destruction of all events and places that there is renewal and the miracle of eternal life. A lily blooms in the morning and is dead in the evening. That is its beauty. Its momentary fragrance is its gift.

KEY 17.

The Star

KEY 17.

The Star

Having shed all that is conditioned, the light of the soul is unveiled.

Purpose shines from the star of our true being. The Star was calling me forward.

45. *Beyond Choice*

Nothing can return to its previous lesser state.
No mirror can become iron again, no bread again wheat.
There is no return to being a little green apple
after you have gotten the blush of the Beloved upon you!

Jean Houston

Over the following days and months, I entered a process of reflection as I endeavoured to integrate the whole experience of awakening into the context of what remained as the happening of my appearing body-mind reality, which still involved a series of choices.

It came to a crunch point. It was either stay with Jake and my children, and deny the truth of my life – the calling – or make a radical choice and follow it. I chose the latter.

Somehow I just knew it was something even beyond choice – that it was already written. And, it was not just what was written for my own destiny. I knew that by choosing Truth I was equally honouring a destiny that was yet to be recognised by Jake and the children. It was beyond ego, beyond the world's conforming mind. Yet I knew that I would face the great anger, fears and judgments of others in doing so. I knew that on the level of the world such a choice would be considered insane and selfish and something other than love; and that I would be subjected to the lashing rage of such judgments.

It seemed inevitable that in following God's Will I would be judged and ostracised by many. Such things were common to a passage of the soul that followed a calling. All I yearned for was to awaken great love and joy, yet chaos would often erupt in the face of God's Truth. A certain part of me knew that it was simply the work of spirit, awakening, confronting and revealing the work of the ego which would fight against the possibility of freedom beyond all that we had been taught. It was like a monster screaming for its life while its head was being severed by Truth.

Yet I also knew that in the oneness of Spirit that all was possible – 'this too shall pass' – and that Truth would prevail and bring with it peace. I simply knew it was what I had to do. I had to face the disappointment of another to be true to myself. I had to bear the accusation of betrayal in order to not betray my own soul.

So I prayed. I prayed for understanding, forgiveness and peace to come – to Jake, family and friends.

On the second night of my prayer, I was taken to a beautiful place of great height. It was a place from which my soul could see the greater perspective of my journey with Jake.

There I was shown our previous lifetime together in which he had chosen to leave me, preferring to uphold tribal honour. I had chosen to experience the journey of raising the child we had birthed, alone. We had chosen to relive and re-create that experience in this lifetime. Our souls had already chosen the agenda, like a karmic exchange to share some time together and then for Jake's soul to encounter a period of sole commitment for the children we had birthed together. Our children had specifically chosen us as individuals to fulfil their agendas. And all of the life circumstances that came with their parents living two separate lives would provide them with the experience they were seeking for fulfilment. I could see that we were at the intersection now in our life where we had already chosen to follow our separate paths. We had completed what we had come together for. Our separation would lead us all to the greatest fulfilment and completion of our souls' purposes. We each had our own star to follow.

I rested again into my body, breathed in the beauty and perfection of what I had been shown, and sighed out in great relief. Then I took in another breath as I acknowledged it was time to speak: it was time for me to leave.

•

When I finally chose the moment to tell Jake there was a temporary calm, a deep stillness. In that stillness was his fleeting knowing and seeing of the truth and, with it, an acceptance. But it didn't last long. The reality of what was happening began to hit him. Anger was his way of processing his pain. My heart ached. The pain of wanting to see him understand, to come to peace, to know from his soul, tore through me.

For days I cried as I felt his pain. In many moments it was difficult to keep the perspective that it was all a passing process; that it was still nothing more than a play of the illusion.

With each confrontation I put my hands together in prayer and asked for God's truth to be present. Over and over again I saw the reflections of the unconscious self, acting out as guilt, anger, fear and pain – all the symbols of the ego that had taken on the belief of the world as a love-hate reality.

With each appearing 'blow' I remembered the truth that 'I, we' are not the body-mind or fear. There is only God. I saw a state of true forgiveness dissolving what could have been extreme suffering.

I saw that each person's judgment, their aggressions and rejection of me was a projection of the unconscious guilt and fear – the belief in the unreal as real – and that theirs and my state of mind was all truly one of innocence. They truly did not understand, nor did they know what they were doing. In my heart the words reverberated again and again ...

I forgive them, Father, for they know not what they do ...[1]

Now I truly understood the strange paradox of relationship. Over a number of years I had noticed a recurring point of misunderstanding. As differences occurred in my relationships, I would see

[1] Adaptation of Luke 23:34

them as natural points to address. For me, it was a matter of willing observation and commitment to find a solution. For others, what was simply observation by me of these differences could mistakenly be interpreted as judgment and creating division. Actually, by being more conscious and aware I was able to be more embracing and accepting.

Yet I also knew that acceptance does not mean remaining with what is happening, if what is happening does not serve the truth of one's, or the other's, being. In acceptance one observes what is happening without judgment and from the observing simply knows what response to make. Acceptance is not a state of resignation. It is a state of non-judgment in which a clear action may be followed. Acceptance is seeing everything (in all its aspects) for what it truly is, without the projection of the mind, and responding with Truth to the inner and outer knowing, which is all-knowing. I could see that this power of higher discernment was often misunderstood as an ego-driven response.

This had provided many moments of challenging and interesting interaction in my relationship with Jake. It seemed that it was expected that an unconditional love meant one should 'accept' and stay with the circumstance, or behave in a certain way. These expectations caused more conflict. When the expectations were not met it resulted in pain and disappointment and became ammunition to blame and misinterpret the actions of the other as unloving.

Yet I saw, for myself and others, that this often means one's own true purpose and direction in life is compromised. I recognised that this is a very subtle pattern that appears quite complex, yet is necessary to address in order to maintain balance and integrity.

I also noticed the tendency for people to believe that relationships will get better, once they are becoming more conscious. That may or may not be so, depending on the soul's journey and the contracts they are fulfilling in the co-created process of growth. We may be the giver or the receiver in the process of this learning. Even what appears as the conflict may be integral to growth. And there are times where the difference in the degrees of consciousness between two people results in a natural falling away: a completion.

The 18th Attainment

In the realm of space, the power
of creation births each Star.
    Leaving behind all that had been,
I was now ready to fulfil my purpose.

KEY 18.

The Moon

KEY 18.

The Moon

Like the night, the new passage is unclear, not all is seen. Yet within, the light is shining, the power of intuition that leads the way.

The moon is the last initiation of the dark; a symbolic death to be followed by divine resurrection.

Having let go of memory of all as it was, the soul can now truly REMEMBER.

It is time to be as the source of light.

46. *The Move*

Great Spirits have always encountered
violent opposition from mediocre minds.

Albert Einstein

Despite the relentless efforts of others to convince me I was crazy and that I was making the wrong choice, I moved out. I still wanted to be as close to the children as I could, and it wasn't long before I found the perfect little haven for my change. A small caravan park was nestled behind the sand dunes on the beachfront at Port Winya, close to the family house. I was happy to hire one of the small on-site vans. It was small, humble, simple and all that I needed.

Jake and I finally managed to discuss with good understanding all the matters and arrangements around the children. I knew that my life would bring a lot more travel which would be too disruptive for the children, and what I wished most for them was their own stability in their formative years. Jake knew he wanted to be the main carer of the children in the home. He wanted that with all his heart. So I knew it was best to hand over the house and goods to Jake and the children. We both understood the truth of this arrangement. It seemed to be aligned with a higher purpose that Jake was now taking on the role of the main parent and that, beyond reasoning, it was in perfect support of my life's destined purpose.

Naturally we were faced with the challenges of such a life-changing passage. And I knew that in time our understanding and respect for each other would deepen. With a faith in a higher order I was able to accept my destiny peacefully. I watched it all unfolding like a movie, seeing how the play of creation and our journey within it was something more than a linear path. I felt at peace, witnessing a sense of karmic balance at play. I remembered the past-life encounter where I had been left alone with our two children and felt a profound sense of Divine order, as if a contract in loving service was now being fulfilled.

Although I could not yet see all of the steps ahead, I knew that everything would be fine. I knew the children would be fine, Jake would be fine, I would be fine and our lives would be blessed in immeasurable ways.

My time in the caravan was deeply nurturing. The sound of the ocean washed over my mind, the fresh air filled me with invigorated spirit and the clear waters bathed my soul. I spent many hours on the cliff tops, gazing out across the horizon in the wonderment of knowing that everything is always changing and passing. And, despite the enormous change that I had faced, I felt peace in my soul.

My intuition had become my guide in all that I was witnessing and in the movements in my life. It soon became evident that it was time to move again and that I was being called to live closer to the city. For work reasons, Jake wanted to sell the house and move closer to the city, and I wanted to remain close and accessible for the children to continue our shared living arrangements.

I focused on finding a new home for myself. As I considered the type of house that would be most suitable in terms of environment, practicalities and location, I imagined something that would be surrounded by trees, spacious, with enough room for classes and meditation groups, have rooms for the children, be close to the city and Jake, and be affordable. A week later, I signed a lease for exactly the house I had envisaged!

A new passage unfolded in my life as I stepped forward on my path to serve the Love and Truth of the Divine. Many people came, drawn to the lightness of love and the sharing of a Truth that rested deeply in their souls, waiting to be remembered.

I felt deeply at peace and fulfilled.

However Jake still continued to resent me. It came as a shock to me one day, when I reflected on Jake's behaviour, that there was something in me that must still be judging. I could suddenly see that my constant efforts for peace between us were actually directed by the part of me that still had not unconditionally accepted Jake as he was in anger – a state of 'not love'. I wanted him/us to have peace and this 'want' was my own enactment of not-love! It was like a thin gossamer thread that had remained hidden in a deep sub-conscious pocket.

It was such a tremendous 'Oh!' moment, that I stopped dead still.

Jake had dropped the children off earlier that morning and I was feeling greatly concerned for their well-being. I didn't want them to be subjected to such emotional displays. It caused me to reflect really deeply – to look right into the whole situation. I had already learned that the power of awareness and insight increased when I 'looked' at the problem, the unconscious thought, rather than avoiding it. In fact, avoiding the problem actually protected it and kept it well rooted!

So there, in the power of self-reflection, the truth was revealed once again – that it was another reflection of my own non-acceptance! Instantly I chose to love and forgive this unconscious behaviour. I chose to love Jake completely – to welcome and love and respect his state of anger, his fear, his pain, his mind, his whole being. And in doing so I could see the anger and fear as a temporary forgetting of the one Self as God. This meant that fear was a call for love.

In that moment I vowed: 'I no longer choose to *not* love *any*thing.'

The moment I realised this truly and chose to welcome and accept Jake completely as he was, however he was, I felt an immense shift.

When Jake came to pick the children up three days later he was in a very calm state and spoke to me in quite a friendly manner ... his anger had dissolved! That seemed to mark a turning point of a long path to a new relationship – one of understanding, friendship and respect.

Not long after this I learned that Jake was in a new relationship. I discovered that the woman he had started dating was the lady I had foreseen in his coffee cup and that they had been working together for the previous year. I suddenly saw clearly how Jake had been entwined in a developing relationship before we parted. Thankfully, I was able to see the whole thing as innocent from an objective viewpoint. In fact it was now even clearer that our time together had been destined to end. Albeit bizarre, I was able to see the 'is-ness' of our life change – that it simply was destined to be. I didn't see wrong or right. I just saw two people who had come together for a purpose and that it had completed that purpose, which inevitably revealed the next steps. I was totally at peace that those next steps had already been emerging for Jake.

What I hadn't yet resolved was the process of letting go of my children – not actually letting go of my true relationship with them, but instead letting go of society's projections and expectations of how a mother should be with her children. I had been experiencing a deep recurring awareness that I was being called to live in another state and travel more with my 'work' of spiritual service.

Society's model of a 'loving, dedicated mother' would not move to another state even to serve Divine Love. And such a move meant seeing the children periodically in between other travel and events. As far as most people were concerned, that was selfish and unloving. Yet as deeply as I prayed, and as high as I asked, the answer continued coming that, actually, it would be an act of the ego – selfishness – if I denied my purpose to serve Love for all beings. And I knew that this purpose would also include my children.

I felt pulled between the biologically programmed maternal instinct in me and the destiny of unstoppable truth. As a mother I aspired to be physically present with my children for as long as possible.

The shared arrangement of caring was working well on one level yet on another I could also see an element of disruption – that the children weren't able to feel a deep stability of roots in one home. My greatest concern was for my children's wellbeing, and that included their need for stability. I could sense my life was rapidly approaching a passage that could not guarantee that. I saw travel and movement. The visions and inner voice had become more vivid and persistent.

Then one afternoon when the children were in their rooms having a nap, I squatted on the floor in the lounge room. I rocked to and fro on the soles of my feet as, in a deep state of love and devotion, I chanted prayers for the awakening of humanity. I felt so totally consumed in the love that tears flowed freely down my cheeks. All I could think of was to be at one in God, in service.

I opened my eyes. I had a profound sense that I was already fully incarnating this prayer and that I was the living embodiment of such devotion. Then I realised that my form had changed. My hands were small, dark and distinctly masculine. I then noticed that my vision was framed by black, wavy hair that spread out in a wide orb from my head. My body was garbed in an orange dress and my feet were bare.

I suddenly realised I was experiencing the form of a great saint. I burst into laughter as I felt the play of oneness in the greatness of the Divine. More tears followed. I laughed and cried for almost an hour. Then, when I opened my eyes, I was returned to my 'normal' body.

The next morning when I opened the front door there was a small tin on the doorstep. On its lid was a picture of the saint! I opened it slowly. It was full of beautifully scented vibhuti.[1] I stood there staring at it in amazement. Although I was not a follower of this saint I did know of his Divine service.

A part of me realised it was totally normal (in the cosmic sense) that I had been 'visited' and shown my oneness with this being. Yet another part of me found it rather curious, as I had not sought any relationship with him on the physical level. What was most powerful in my awareness was my recognition of the actual living, manifesting

---

[1] Sacred ash used in rituals.

play of the one Self in an endless sea of bodies.

'I', the persona that was the body named Isira, was not claiming to be the *personality* of any God or Saint. It was clearly the Self that is *beyond* individual identity or body that was recognising itself as that which is in all. That essential Self was, is and always will be the same one presence in all beings. It is the Self we all truly are, and the very one same Self that breathed in Jesus, Buddha, Gandhi and Hitler. Saint and sinner: we are all of the one Self!

I puzzled over the world's extent of disbelief in the One within us all. It was evident that most people considered the individual personalities to be inherently separate realities. Yet as I sat there I knew that the transcendent all-unified Self was imminent in all and was more real than humanity's grasping onto any individual separate identity.

The 19th Attainment

Released from the heaviness of ego
I now accepted the Divine Self.
The moonlight of realisation is
integrated with the world. I had
come to the eternal lightness
of being.

KEY 19.

The Sun

KEY 19.

The Sun

'The light of the body is the eye:
if therefore thine eye be single, thy
whole body shall be full of light.'[1]

All things are illuminated through spiritual realisation. All things are growing and beautiful in its light.

Having left the dark night behind, I now bathed in the glory of the soul's eternal dawn.

---

1 Matthew 6:22.

47. *Destiny*

> Our ordinary mind always tries to persuade us that we are nothing but acorns and that our greatest happiness will be to become bigger, fatter, shinier acorns; but that is of interest only to pigs. Our faith gives us knowledge of something much better: that we can become oak trees.
>
> *EF Schumacher*

Outside the air swayed in a gentle warm breeze. To the left of me two tall conifers stood as giant sentinels watching over me, and the gentle morning light laid patches of brightness around the garden. I felt a strange peace, like the depths of an unfathomable lake yet with a gentle stirring upon the surface. I moved from one to the other and back again. Deep within, all was calm. Therein was a solid, tangible knowing in the faith of Divine Will. Yet on the surface was a wind of change that blew ever more persistently, rattling upon the windows of my inner view.

My gaze swept around the yard, taking in the garden I had grown to love. I acknowledged how easy it was for me to make myself a home yet how quickly change would come again. I knew it was only a matter of time before I would have to face my destiny. I could feel it calling me.

Like a wild horse I could smell it on the breeze. It stirred my blood beyond my mind's 'tarry', with full readiness – rearing to run. And yet I was also the rider and my love for my children (with such little time remaining) was like the gloves gripping the reins. The two forces, each so deeply moving, held me in a quivering stalemate.

Then I looked down at the ground. Dry, golden leaves lay upon the path, trembling with the impulse to be moved by an approaching breeze ... then, tumbling, without resistance, they surrendered to the eddying gust.

I smiled.

Back inside I could hear Lilha and Elijah playing in the bedrooms.

I walked into the lounge and stood next to my altar. I looked at the smiling faces of the wise ones I so loved. Lama Zopa, Meher Baba and images of Buddha and Ascended Masters stared serenely.

I prayed quietly, asking that I would be guided by the highest Truth; that I would live and serve as the Divine Will asked of me.

Then Lilha walked into the lounge room. She stared up at me. Her big brown eyes of pure, innocent knowingness moved into me.

'Mummy,' she said. 'you're going away soon ... and that's okay, 'cos you're in my heart and I'm in yours and, well, we've got a special love ... it lasts forever. And, well, you're not just my mummy, you're Isira, you're here to love everyone in the world.'

I stared silently into her deep, loving eyes of wisdom. Lilha stood before me, radiating, like a glowing sun. She smiled and then walked back out of the room.

I could hardly believe it! I sat down on the carpet in complete amazement. My own three-year-old daughter had just confirmed the destiny that was forthcoming! And, she had released me of my concerns for her wellbeing. I felt her knowing and blessing fill me with a deep peace.

Her light of awareness filled the same place of light within me. I felt bathed in the dawn of realisation. All was well. The path ahead was clear.

48. *Ancestral Lineage*

Speak to the earth and it shall teach thee.

The Book of Job 12:8

My life's destiny continued to reveal itself powerfully. Like pieces in a puzzle, events in my life were all beginning to fit together.

The following week I met Mark while I was in the city. We had an interesting connection having met each other at the Mind Body Spirit Festivals several times. His work with sound healing was fascinating and unique in Adelaide at that time. In fact, he was a bit ahead of his time. I had already experienced his healing with crystal bowls and found them profoundly effective in shifting vibrational imbalances.

I approached the Alfresco café, watching him from a distance. His long legs were crossed in the usual relaxed manner as he leaned back into the chair. He must have sensed me coming close as he turned his head to look straight in my direction. I watched his ponytail of silver hair fall over his shoulder and a smile light up his face.

As we were talking about the latest happenings, a young man approached. He was also tall, taller than Mark, thinner and with broad shoulders. His face looked young and fresh, enthusiastic about life.

'Hey! Eddie.' Mark greeted him with great warmth. 'This is Isira,' he said, pointing at me.

'Hi Isira,' he smiled. His face was elf-like yet, took on another dimension due to the height of his long-limbed, lean body.

'What's up?' asked Mark.

'Well, actually, I've got some business coming up with the fellas up north – the Aboriginal community up in the Flinders.'

My ears pricked up and a flash passed through my inner vision: a scene of elders with the ancestors, surrounding me.

'What work's that?' I asked.

'Oh, the Nepabunna mob need some help setting up a centre. John Guv is helping them out a bit too.'

I felt a strong warping sensation of deja vu as I noticed another level of interconnectedness. I had met John previously and knew of his work. And I had received visions and messages related to 'journey work' in the Flinders Ranges. When my granddad had died, I had watched his spirit shining brightly above the great rocky ridges, as if to light them up in my awareness.

I looked at the tall, young man. He seemed open enough, I thought, as I calculated the audacity I felt in asking,

'Hey – um – do you think I could join you? I mean, I'd love to help. And it's kind of coincidental that I got messages about the Flinders Ranges.' He looked surprised yet delighted.

'Yeah, sure! ' he said. 'Actually, I could really do with a driving partner.'

'Great!' I said. 'When do you plan to go? I just have to work out the time around my kids and their father.'

'I'll give you a call, 'cos I've got a few more things to work out,' he said.

'Okay, great,' I replied.

We swapped numbers and then he was off.

Mark smiled. His big blue eyes twinkled.

'Ah, I love the way spirit works!' he said with a chuckle.

I drove home on a wave of excitement. Memories rose up in me with stark clarity: my granddad whispering to me from spirit ... revealing to me his past ... the stolen generation ... his ancestors ...

his light guiding me ... encouraging me not to give up, to follow the signs. He had told me I would meet our relations ... my ancestor's home lands. He had told me it was my destiny, for I was to carry a great fire-stick for the world. I shuddered as I felt the work of spirit moving me to my destiny.

Later that night as I meditated, I received clear instructions that I was to take specific gifts of offerings with me and that I was to take a trip back to Port Winya to collect the offerings.

The next morning I set off without hesitation. As I drove along the coast I breathed deeply as I took in the beauty I so loved. The rolling hills and cliff faces merged with the great wide ocean – golden earth meeting sapphire waters.

Before long I pulled up in the caravan park. The van I had loved to live in was now vacant and sat silently like a little lonely ghost home. I walked past it to the track that led down over the little sand dune. To the right of me were the ochre cliffs that I had marvelled at so many times before. I sat at the base to silence myself and waited for guidance. Soon I heard the clear voice of an ancestor spirit speaking:

'You are to take white and yellow ochre for your father elder, as well as the eagle feather from your altar. White is for the lightning of spirit's message to him from the ancestors, yellow is for the sun and the feather is for the spirit of the eagle that is in him. Also you must collect red and orange ochre for your Auntie elder. Red is for the blood, the power of woman, and orange is for the rebirth of women's lore and creation. You must honour your relations with these gifts. It is the lore of this passage as you return to the heartland of your ancestors.'

I gave thanks for such clear guidance, then stood up and walked over to the base of the cliff. There, on the rock ledge, were fresh fallen clumps of ochres, all within close proximity of each other and in perfect order: white, yellow, red and orange! I picked them up and put them carefully into the paper I had brought with me, wrapped them up and placed them in my bag.

I turned and began walking back along the beach. The cliffs to the south glowed like golden sheaves in the sun, and a lone gull's cry echoed along the vast stretch of white sand.

Later that night I had visions of spirits running across great stretches of red and orange rocky landscapes. I saw them gathering around the Aboriginal people with faces smiling and children laughing. Then the face of a young girl came so vividly that I took out my pastels and began to draw her. Around the edge I drew a window frame of a rock – orange and covered with pale, milky-green lichen – and in the blue starlit sky, a black hawk.

When I finished I stared at it wondering if it were an image of creative imagination alone, or if somewhere, out amongst those rocks, she really existed.

I looked at my watch: 4 am. It was the third week now that I had had abundant energy with very little need for sleep. Most nights I experienced as a time of lucid meditation and creative outpourings of art that rolled into the beauty of dawn being welcomed in by the sweet song of a willie-wagtail. I went and sat on my bed. Deep stillness engulfed me and carried me into silence. Then her song came ... the sweet lilting melody of her morning bird-call, beckoning me to welcome a new day.

At about eleven o'clock the phone rang.

I answered it to hear Eddie's cheery greeting.

With great enthusiasm he asked if I would be able to travel to the Flinders Ranges the following week. It was perfect synchronicity since it fitted in with Jake's plans to have extra time with the children.

•

The sun had not yet risen when Eddie arrived full of energy and ready for our trip. Bags, boxes, tents and eskies were shuffled in order to pack the van. We set off at sunrise with the plan to reach the station by late afternoon. Gradually the suburban landscape disappeared into long stretches of country roads, winding through farming country. Wide fields stretched out on either side. As the hours passed the fields became even wider, and the grasses and gum trees gave way to a more barren landscape. The land's energy changed as we entered more rocky terrain.

Red rocks and hazy blue ranges were rising out of the dusty earth. The sun was shining high in the sky. I looked across the rugged beauty of the landscape with fascination. A sense of synchronicity and significance stirred my soul, as a large red kangaroo appeared, bounding alongside the van as we headed north. Images of my childhood dreams rolled through my awareness. Eventually the roo disappeared into the rocky horizon.

Great round hillocks of orange rocks rose up from the plain like a mother's breasts reaching up to the blue father sky. Tufted grasses, like silvery moonstones, lay speckled across the orange sands. Trees stood to attention upon the hills like a procession of warriors.

As I continued to gaze out of the window I suddenly noticed two massive white light-beings. Their forms, like two huge beams, anchored the sky to the earth and shifted me instantly into a trance.

The word 'valnupa'[1] came echoing like a song. Then a huge mob of tall, black-bodied men and women were running like the wind. Their intent was of such power that the trees and grasses swayed in their wake and clouds of red dust rose from the ground.

The two light-beings seemed like a central vortex as the mob sped excitedly across the land. As they neared a rocky mountain, the light-beings rose above the warriors, their light moving like a willie-willie.[2] The runners ascended to a high plateau and from their vantage point they scrutinised the land before them, looking for special sites for their people to find power. It was very clear their exploration was not just for food and water. They were looking for the places of empowerment, high and low.

Slowly my senses returned to the rattling motion of the van.

I realised I had been in a time-shift. What I had just observed was a past event, thousands of years old, held in the open heart of the all-present now.

---

[1] Creation beings.

[2] A tall spiral of spinning wind and dust like a mini cyclone.

It was also conveyed to me that this was a re-dreaming that ignites consciousness to experience the equivalent interactive encounter, through our physical reality of appearing time in the present. What I was moving towards was an encounter with my ancestral lineage manifesting in the flesh and blood bodies of today. I was about to meet them and our interaction would surely awaken greater levels of the inter-dimensional dreaming.

My mind wandered as I reflected on the guidance and messages that had led me to this place. From my dreams as a child to the presence of the ancestors in my visions, I saw a deep web of wisdom embracing me. I knew the lore[1] was held in my soul and that I was seeking its voice again in my world now. I could feel the pain of disconnection which lived in our indigenous people as the very same displacement in my own life. I felt the ancestors' calling was a cry for bridges to be made, a cry to reunite that which had been divided. There was so much I just seemed to 'know' already, and yet I also knew there were pieces to the puzzle that were still to be revealed.

The ancestors from my home at Port Winya had told me to bring the ochres as gifts; although I didn't yet know who they were intended for, I had no doubt that I would soon be shown.

The van finally pulled off the dirt road, through a gate and into a wide open property. Small native trees hugged the edges between the open, dusty flat and the hilly, rocky landscape that surrounded it. We soon settled in, with introductions unfolding in a typically casual Australian manner. The camp of Iga Warta was a vast expanse of land, sacred to the Adnyamathna people. Its field included a great ridge of ancient trees, including the Iga, the native orange, and a development of housing and buildings for camping and educational holidays.

I was soon 'told' that the white and yellow ochres were for Cliff and the red and orange ones for Christine.

As everyone busied themselves around the camp I made my way over to introduce myself properly to Christine. She was very excited

---

[1] The indigenous system of knowledge and wisdom that sustains sacred respect, awareness and balance of the relationship of all things in creation.

when she heard about the visions and messages that had led me there. Her eyes lit up as if touched by something she had been waiting for.

Then, as I looked into her shining spirit I knew – it was the right moment.

I handed her the parcels.

Her beautiful golden brown eyes opened wide. As I told her what they were, she looked in wonder.

'What does this mean?' she asked.

'My spirit ancestors told me to bring these and that the red and orange ones were for you,' I replied. 'Red is the blood of woman. It is the colour of our earth – I hear the spirits saying 'yurrawey'. Orange is the colour of the rocks – for our people 'Adnyamathna'. It is the light of the womb and colour of creative energy. These are for you and special for the women. Your women ancestors have spoken with me and are giving me messages for you.'

Christine continued staring at me.

'This is what they say,' I continued: 'This land is women's land by the ancient lore. Your spirits have lost some of this power connection. Now it is time – it is important to reconnect. Women need to work together again and find the power through sacred circle.

'There is a cave on a ledge behind Iga Warta – to the south-west. You need to go there. WE, your ancestors, can help you. There is a woman you must speak to for more knowledge. She has curly hair and a round face. Her name is Rosie. She can help you. It is very important now for the women to come together.'

I could feel Christine's heart racing.

'Wow, hey, I have to ask the women to help me, ay? That woman, Rosie, I know her. Yeh, she looks like that! I'll go an' ask her,' she said, with an air of amazed determination.

As we parted company, I realised how deeply we are all woven together by the power of spirit. It is that spirit, the life force which flows in the blood of our veins and whispers a deep knowing of our oneness. It is that spirit, and the people's connectedness to it, which was so painfully judged and severed by the white settlers and missionaries.

The denial of spirit was so evident in the hollowness of our people's eyes and emptiness of soul. I saw it in the longing for acknowledgment and ownership of the indigenous culture, and yet something still seemed so lost.

For the rest of the night Christine stood and watched. Everyone stood, watched and listened. I waited, knowing I would meet Cliff in the morning.

By the next morning some of the story I had shared with Christine had got around. There was a buzz in the background. It wasn't just at Iga Warta, it was at Nepabunna too – the nearest township.

I knew it was really important that I connect with Cliff – the guardian of Iga Warta. I couldn't feel in the right place until my presence was passed by his blessing.

No sooner had I thought this than I could see a sturdy man striding confidently towards us. His black jeans, black shirt and Akubra hat all looked well-worn from working on the land. As I stood close to the campsite I watched Cliff walk directly up to us. The rest of the group were still looking woolly-haired and red-eyed, an effect left over from their drinking the night before.

I turned and faced Cliff straight on. Cliff turned and, from under his old Akubra, his sharp eyes looked straight into mine and he flashed a smile, one front tooth missing. That was my cue.

With parcels in hand, I stepped closer to him.

'Cliff,' I said approaching him with a feeling of great honour welling up in me. 'I have a gift for you.'

'What is it?' he asked, happily curious.

'The spirit ancestors told me to bring these for you. They are ochres.'

I handed them to him with the eagle feather placed on top and he took them with a look of sincerity.

I continued: 'The white is for you – it is your spirit, the lightning bolt that comes from the stars. The yellow is the eagle – he brings your spirit from the sky to the land – yurrawey – earth. This is a wing tip that you may be blessed with the strong flight of spirit. With him you see far.'

Cliff's face was deeply reflective. He looked straight into my eyes.

'You know,' he said, 'this is very important to me. Thank you.'

I felt the fullness of Love's spirit fill me. 'Yes, for me too. Thank you so much. I feel greatly honoured. Thank you.'

Then as I looked into his eyes I saw they were like deep pools and in the corner a tear was welling up. Then Cliff spoke in a deep whisper.

'I have been waiting for this. We knew you were coming ...'

It was in the space of the remaining silence that I received a much larger message, one that was to be confirmed later.

Cliff then invited me over to the 'family' camp. It wasn't long before an older man pulled up in his car. Everyone waved as he approached. His skin was much darker than Cliff's and his hair was snow-white under his black cowboy hat.

'Here's Ron,' said Cliff to me nodding at the approaching man. I was surprised to recognise his face from a previous vision. We smiled and shook hands.

'This Katja's[1] got important news for us,' said Cliff.

'Oh?' croaked Ron. He eyed me with a strange mix of certain authority and familial love.

'Yep! She's had the vision. She's lost family come home.' Cliff nodded.

Ron looked at me, curious and with a hint of suspicion.

Cliff looked at me expectantly. His eyes beckoned me to speak. So I did.

I spoke of the messages and visions I had received. I spoke of the first visitation I had had from my grandfather – how after he had died he came and told me of our ancient blood-line that had been kept secret behind closed doors, and that I would rediscover our family's roots. I told of the ancestors singing me with the language of the land

---

[1] Even though I had taken on the name Isira I was still known to some people affectionately as Katja. Due to its indigenous roots, the name had significance in my relating with the Aboriginal people.

and giving me messages and gifts to deliver. And I spoke of the time-warp I had experienced on the way up through the ranges.

It turned out that everything I had seen and heard was the exact detailed account of the ancestral lineage and that I had indeed come to my ancient roots. I recognised a deep part of me that felt enormous relief. It was the part of me that had felt out of place and had finally come to rest, finally feeling home. It was the connection to family ...

Ron nodded and stared into my eyes with approval, then said: 'Well, you're gonna be initiated.'

I looked at Cliff. His eyes seemed to confirm Ron's sentiment.

The sacredness of our communion soon broke as a young man approached and the meeting shape-shifted into an informality of family chatter.

As the young man got closer I looked at him with curious wonder. He, too, wore an Akubra hat. And as he came closer I felt the lightness of his sprit. Something seemed incredibly familiar in his round, warm face. He broke out in a large grin as he introduced himself.

'Hi, I'm Kristian,' he said.

'Hi ... Katja,' I replied.

'Oh,' he said. 'What are you? Sun Woman?' I wondered if he actually realised the significance in those words and felt a little uneasy as I thought of the possibility that Spirit was watching us closely.

I looked down at the ground, feeling a little unsure.

'Ah ... Katjati mimini?' he chimed. His eyes flashed with a cheeky grin. He enjoyed playing with my name, which I later found out meant *cute girl*.

His round cheeks glowed as the wide grin stretched across his face. Then he offered to show me around the property some more. Along the way I met more of the family. Everyone else seemed to know who I was. It seemed the story had already passed around.

Then a group of children approached, some riding, some running, all of them giggling. And there in amongst them was the face of the girl I had drawn before leaving Adelaide! I looked in wonderment. Her sweet brown eyes sparkled and her rosy cheeks glowed. And, as I looked, I suddenly realised that all the surrounding rocks were also just as I had drawn them, orange with milky lime lichen growing on them.

I looked at the amazing variety of the children's features. Two of the girls were fair – one with golden spirals and brown eyes and the other with even fairer skin than mine had snow-white hair and blue eyes, yet her Aboriginal frame was still noticeable.

Then I met Terry, Cliff's brother. He seemed to take a strong interest in me and decided we should have a walk later. He pinned me down with his green eyes, making sure I was firm in my commitment to meet him.

Later in the day I met Terry as agreed. He walked with me to the top of the hill behind the campsite. The scene was spectacular. An aerial view of Iga trees, swaying gums and great heaped-up hills of red and orange rocks sprawled out before us.

Terry was curious about my visions. Then, without any lead-in, he said I must be initiated if I was going to have my place as an Adnyamathna woman. I really had no idea exactly what that would entail, yet without hesitation I said I was ready. I simply knew it was what I must do.

'Meet me tomorrow before breakfast,' he said. 'Sun-up.' Then he turned and eyed me again with his piercing green eyes, before heading back down the hill.

There was silence until we were nearly at the bottom, then he said, 'Watch Ron, 'ee's got 'is eye on you.'

'Mmm, yeah, I know' I replied. I had already spoken in great depth with Ron and experienced a very powerful telepathic connection with him. However, I didn't yet realise that his interests were more than spiritual. It just didn't seem to apply in my mind. After all, it's not every day a sixty-five-year-old man figures he might be able to get himself a wife less than half his age!

We began work around the camping grounds, helping to clear debris to make pathways.

In the simplicity of being on the earth, working around the rocks and trees I felt an immense peace. There, in the presence of the moment, was a true beauty. I had no need for anything grand: for neither possessions nor rewards. There, in the swaying, being, sweeping, collecting wood, picking up rocks, digging ... there was everything. In that ordinariness was the sacred and profound mystery that filled my heart with a knowing of how extraordinary, yet simple, existence really is. I felt the innocence and beauty of how life must have been for our ancestors and couldn't help but feel a longing well up in my soul for those long-lost days. Yet I knew that same beauty was with me, purely in the now. So deeply absorbed in the moment, I was freed of any clinging to the past or looking for the future. And in such presence was freedom, nothing but sweet joy and fullness.

Then as I walked on the earth, I could feel the pulsing of life beating, rocking, beneath me, in me and all around me. I felt it nourishing me with infinite abundance. Suddenly the sun's golden light engulfed my vision. Everything dissolved into golden light as the inner and outer melted into one great showering of stardust through all.

I stood transfixed. Then I could feel it – the endless ground of creation. In me and all around me was an eternal presence of life – arising from, and commanded by Love! Every point of light that emerged came from the source of love, was moved by love and communicated love! It was truly Love that created and mastered all.

I saw once again how limited the mind is – that it is but a vehicle to serve and give reference to that which already is mastery! I felt an immense relief as I realised there was no longer a necessity to rely on the mind's deductions and stories of structure. Everything is already the perfect orchestration of limitless power, and in realising it, by living in it, there can be no such thing as fear, separation or lack.

I fell to my knees and knelt on the earth. The warmth of her life filled me with joy. In gratitude I laid my head down. Love filled my whole being so immensely that tears began to flow. I felt my Self. I felt all life. And in that moment I knew beyond doubt: 'Love is all I am, Life is all I am, this is all the being I am. Oh, God ... Great Spirit ... Arawatana! Thank you. I am so Blessed. Thank you for this

Blessed Eternal Being.'

A strange dichotomy enveloped me as I realised there is only One – a vast limitless oneness – and I, what I truly am, am it ... being always! Yet within such all-oneness is still an arising perceptive point appearing as this individual, surrounded by all points of the One. I was talking to, thanking myself! Not only that, but that's what Life eternal is always being!

Then the earth felt more solid beneath me again and I realised I was truly never alone ... I was all-one! As I had that thought I suddenly became aware of an elder spirit approaching me with a wise woman lighting his way. Then came their voices, clear and strong.

'Are you ready to be reborn?' they asked.

Through tears of bliss I cried ... 'I am.'

'So you are,' they replied.

As I sat on the red sand I was no longer just 'me'.

I was the ancient Grandmother of the red-roo dreaming ... I was birthing myself into this life. The Grandmother in me fully woke up, her power pulsing in oneness with the land, with all life. I felt the ancient lore emerging from within the depths of me, from the core of mother earth herself and along with it an insurmountable love, a love of protection and sacredness for earth and all her creatures, like my very own children.

In that instant I realised that in the knowing of love there could only be a return to eternal Life – a rebirth – and that all I had believed myself to be before, no longer was. From the rocks and trees the ancestors came to surround me, holding me in their arms. The sun glowed. All was embraced in its warm golden light. In joy we swayed together – one body of love. We were one family. I felt again the purity, innocence and wholeness of life. And in my witnessing was the remembering of how it was ... what it was like for all of our ancestors from all ancient times ... what it was like in lifetimes gone by ... how deeply we were united with all creation ... how we were one family ... one relation.

That night I dreamed.

Beneath my old bare body, the red sand was warm. It felt nourishing. It was the warm embrace of my mother ... earth. I looked at the contrast of colours, my black skin resting in the embrace of my surroundings: red rock, silvery bushes, blue sky. Everything was deeply familiar. It was all a part of me ... alive in oneness ... a pulse of an eternal dreaming, ancient life and the constant vibrancy of the Now. It filled me with a sense of certainty and peace.

Standing up I collected my digging stick and made my way to the cave. Deep in the heart of Uluru was the place where I would sit quietly to receive the words that creation wished me to speak. As I sat in the womb of the great red rock, I could draw – from the very heart of earth herself – her dreaming and her lore. It was a place, a portal of the timeless and the multi-dimensional. It connected the consciousness with all times, with the ancient past, the present and the future; it connected the galaxies and earth, the invisible and visible. It was the lore, the dreaming of these things that I was ordained to receive and give. As a custodian and a lore woman it was my duty to assure that the dreaming was kept alive through the spoken word, art, song and dance. Now that I was so old it was mostly the spoken word that I shared. But, as I loved story-telling, I couldn't help but be animating. The children's eyes would grow big as my hands painted images in the firelight and the young adults would gather close as I drew in the sand.

I stood staring at the great body of rock before me. In the late afternoon she had turned a rich purple colour, streaked with dark stains from the aeons of water that had run down her sides. Before entering the side of the giant rock I lay down my digging-stick and asked the guardians if I might enter. I felt their blessing in the gentle breeze that caressed my back, ushering me to move inwards.

Inside the womb was dark and glowing; the sand, white and cool. I whispered to the ancestors, asking for the blessing of rite of passage before I sat down. I was immediately surrounded by their beautiful light and their lilting song, caressing me with gentleness and strength. And I knew they were showing me that this would be tonight's story. It was the song of Kanyini – the lore of perfect love and sacredness that is the connection and the oneness of all things. This is a thing of such beauty ... a presence of pure awareness that embraces all things.

I contemplated the threads of our lore. Kuranpa – the life force and the love, the spirit of creation – is the eternal power and oneness of all things. It is this that we lived for. The very fact that we are alive is the evidence of our connection to all other things. Tjukurpa, the lore of creation, nurtures us. It is a belief system based on the sacred intelligence of creation: the natural law. The power of Kuranpa, the invisible spirit, gives us the gift, the dreaming into the visible. This spirit forms our Ngura, our world, our homeland that provides all things for our life. And it gives us the living joy of our Waltja, our family, our relations, our people, the creatures, the trees, birds and rocks. All of life is one. We are all one family. And all the parts are perfectly equal, perfectly essential to and connected with the whole. This means our lore upholds the sacred balance and honour of all things. As long as we uphold this we will have a healthy and abundant life. But if this is lost, there is sickness in the world. To us this world, our creation, is such a precious gift and we know we do not ever own it permanently. We are just visitors, passengers for a little while and we have to ensure that it is always left in its wholeness for our children and their children, for all the future passengers.

But then suddenly my heart swelled up with great sorrow.

I began to heave with tears drawn from the depths of my womb place. Once again I saw the same images that had been filling my dreams ... of white men coming to the land with a book, taking the people, severing our sacred lore and way of life, bringing great damage to our mother earth; bringing sorrow, death and destruction to our spirit.

As I cried tears they became a river of light energy. It poured into the sand and disappeared deep in her womb. Then my tears stopped. I saw a great passage of time where the lore was buried. But it was not lost forever. It was waiting for the time to be birthed again; to be dug up and born into the world for a new time; a time when the many coloured skins of the world would have to learn harmony and work together, a time when the only thing that could save us would be the sacred lore.

But tonight, by the dancing light of the fire, I would only sing about Kanyini.

The next morning I met Terry at sunrise. The sky glowed pink as it began to remove the chill of the night air. Terry ushered me to his ute. We got in. Before long we were past the gates and taking an almost unnoticeable track off the main road. The wheels rumbled over rocks and small pebbles until we reached some rocky outcrops.

As Terry got out he motioned me to follow. He took to a rocky plateau that wound around behind rocky hillocks until it met a small flowing stream. The water glistened, crystal clear. We followed it for a way until it turned towards another cluster of rock faces. Then he asked me to stop.

He reached down and scooped up some water and splashed it on me. Then he took a smear of orange silt from the surface of a rock and wiped it on my hands and face. Then he did the same for himself. I looked at his light brown skin. The orange ochre seemed to make his green eyes stand out even more.

Behind the rocks the ledge opened into a low, wide cave that faced due east. The sun was shining straight into it. Inside were ancient Aboriginal paintings of hands, wallabies and kangaroos.

As we sat down he began talking, his voice weaving in and out of English and native tongue. I seemed to know and understand everything he said. And with each tone noted as a question, I replied. He nodded with satisfaction. Then he looked at me and spoke.

'You are one of us ... Adnyamathna ... mmm. You are Sun Woman ... and ...' he paused and looked at the sun. Suddenly a gust of wind blew in from the north. We watched it pick up the red sand on the other side of the stream. 'Mmm,' he continued 'and your spirit rides on the North Wind ... Ororra. Your lore clan is the red kangaroo.'

I looked at him almost in disbelief. The dream I had had as a child came flooding back ... running to the sun ... north-wind blowing, people following ... a giant red kangaroo. As I stared the words fell out of my mouth. When I finished speaking, Terry looked at me. His eyes were glowing with a light that seemed to have come from eternity to shine on me in that very moment. In his look was a presence of the all-knowing. Then he closed his eyes and took my hands.

'May the ancestors always shine on you. May you fulfil your way.'

As I opened my eyes I watched him slowly lift his bowed head. Tears had filled his eyes.

Then we sat. Silence. All that could be heard was the breath of life moving all, as one beat of love.

We returned to camp. All I could think of was the initiation I had just been given. Yet despite the many questions from the others, I kept silent. I knew these things were best kept quiet until the right moment.

I continued working across the yard. I had cleared a good path all the way from the visitor's camp to Cliff's yard. Now I started gathering rocks to line it. Again I felt consumed by the peace of simple being.

The next day Cliff decided he was going to take a few of us around the Mount Serl area. He wanted to take us to an ancient Iga tree

– said to be perhaps the oldest in the area. When we arrived at the base of the mountain we took a steep rubbly track. At the height of the stony peak a lone tree shaded a wide, flat ledge. Cliff sighed as he finished telling us a little more of the history of the Gammon Ranges.

Then I sat down at the base of the tree. As I sat there under the great old Iga I began to dissolve into a symbiotic vibration. I could feel the tree breathing with me. Then as we breathed, together, I was carried into the earth. As I was connected to the roots I was shown the aliveness of mother earth and how we all grow from her as a part of earth itself. I then felt an ascension up the gnarled trunk. A surge of energy rushed through me with a force of great strength, like simultaneous compression and expansion.

It was like a flood of kundalini as I felt my being, at one with the tree, surging ever upwards into the branches and into the leaves, where from a million eyes I saw as the tree could see – a conscious creation journey. From the ground to sapling height and to its greater height, under a sky of infinite winds, blue then cloudy, wet with rain and shining with sun, visited by soaring eagles and people of the land who came to gather in the seasons of fruiting and for storytelling ... all held in the silence of eternal Truth.

•

And so the days passed with work around the homestead and trips to sacred sites: gorges, rivers and ancient rocks carved with old, old pictures of the stars and universes and creatures on earth. In between work, adventure, quests and cultural discussions, I preferred to spend my time alone. I had observed a certain amount of disturbing energy between the others who were a part of our group. In fact, I found it discordant to be amongst people who espoused great knowledge of spiritual matters yet were clearly holding contention with each other. It didn't help that alcohol and marijuana were being used in some strange mixed idea of spiritual practice.

It seemed, more evidently, a blanket of denial to ignore blatant issues of self-hatred and fear. Yet who was I to judge? I saw it as an opportunity to understand and to learn, for I sensed my insights were not something that would be welcome. Instead I chose to be a silent observer, holding compassion from a quiet distance.

Then one morning I found myself sensing the presence of the spirit elders. I had been receiving profound communications on a daily basis. Unlike some guides, the beings of this land expressed themselves deeply through simplicity. Few words were needed.

It was still early when I was 'called' into the bushes to receive some beautiful messages that our fellow light-beings wanted to have communicated to the group. At the time of receiving these messages a few members of the group were bickering between themselves and trying to recover from the unkind things they had been doing to their bodies the night before.

One man in particular considered himself to be the wiser, more learned leader and authority of the group, so there already seemed to be an interesting dynamic of a competitive attitude towards anyone else's wisdom.

I returned to the group in a deep state of peace and love, still feeling the presence of the beautiful spirits. They expressed their desire for me to share the messages with the group, so I began to speak.

'The spirits of the land wish to share some messages with us,' I said.

The 'more learned' man mocked me, 'Oh yeah, what have they got to say this time?'

I could feel his whole energy body pulsing with an angry jealousy towards me. But I knew I had to proceed and remained deeply calm. I continued. 'They have shared with me the depth of love of Life and the Great Spirit Arawatana – of which we are all a part. Their message to us is to BE love; that at this time it is most important to share this for all life.'

The response that followed was certainly contrasting to the loving energy that these great beings were wishing to share. I was able to see the greatness of their wisdom as true teachers. I knew it as deeply as the eternal Truth that lay in my heart and the heart of every other being.

'Well,' he said, 'all this love stuff you talk about is pretty airy-fairy, isn't it?'

In that moment I felt the immensity of the Great Spirit well up in my being and felt simultaneously the wrath and pure compassion of Truth. Without any thought at all words began to pour forth from my mouth. I knew this was a direct response from the eternal truth of Great Spirit – it was the commanding power of Love! It was the lore of sacred respect.

'There is nothing airy-fairy about Love at all. It is the greatest thing of all life. It is the Creator of life! And until you, as individuals, remember this and live it, you will hear this message again and again wherever you go. Become the Truth of this message and you will be walking the light of the greatest wisdom for all people, animals, plants and rocks alike.'

A silence followed, full of humility and knowing.

The group sat down quietly and looked at me as if they knew there was yet more to the message.

This is the power of love, I thought to myself. Then the words continued, pouring forth from the depths of my own ancient knowing.

'All the knowledge of the world could not fulfil you, nor bring you the peace you so ache for. That which your mind clings to, all the structures and formulas of logic, are not even a speck within creation, for they are but an illusion. They pale next to the source itself: Love. It is this which is the greatest power of all, for it IS Creator of all. All the knowledge of the world cannot dispel the illusions of the ego nor heal a single wound when love is absent. For Love is the commander of all life.

'Therefore, go forth with love. Cultivate compassion, grow in loving-kindness. Give more and more of your love to each other that you may cast aside your fears of lack and separation. Only then will you live in harmony. Only then will the blessings you seek be too vast to imagine. Then you will know that God's endless river of love, which flows through you and through all, is the greatest power of all.'

I stood up, put my hands in prayer at my heart, bowed and walked away.

The sun was shining brightly above me. Its warmth filled me. All I could feel was the power of love, within me and all around me. It was so clear to me. All the trivial thoughts and grievances are not real. They are but a fleeting thought that has forgotten to whom it truly belongs. It is merely a temporary forgetting of the True Self – the One and only eternal Self – Love.

From that moment the group was a changed body. From aggressive ego assertions, each one had stepped back into their own centre, and a mood of thoughtfulness hung in the air around them.

•

It soon came time to make our way back to Adelaide. Gratitude was exchanged, and the affirmation of future journeys to be shared was declared. I felt deeply fulfilled.

Upon our return I was eager to develop my photos before Eddie was to drop me home. When I collected them, I flipped through the images with excitement. But there was one in particular that stopped me in my tracks. It was a picture of me with Kristian, Cliff's son, who was now my 'brother' through initiation. I stared at it in amazement. Suddenly I realised what had been so familiar about him.

Our faces were unmistakably alike! In fact there were only a few differences. Obviously, we were of the opposite sex and he had dark brown hair, darker skin and brown eyes and was somewhat chubbier than me. Nonetheless, we could have easily been direct brother and sister. I smiled as I felt a deep core of Truth rippling through me. I had found my relations, the blood of my ancestors!

49. *Chakra Healer*

For us, for our future, our children come
to teach and heal us.

Isira

Once home I went straight to the altar and lit a candle. I smiled to myself as I looked at the eclectic display of sacred items and images. I had everything! Bowls, bells, statues, paintings, crystals, staffs, ceremonial items, candles, feathers, bones and stones, from every source: Tibetan, Hindu, Egyptian, African, Native American, earth spirit, Aboriginal and inter-galactic.

I chuckled as I remembered the curious looks from those who came to visit. Looking at it from that perspective, it was easy to see why they were so intrigued, baffled and inspired.

The days passed into a dreamy haze of worldly normality again as the children came and I resumed schedules of appointments in healing, guidance and meditation groups. Lilha and Elijah both displayed a profound presence of love and awareness nicely wrapped up in the appearance of two very normal, happy, healthy children.

During the day they both still enjoyed a midday nap after lunch – usually for about an hour and a half. So I normally managed to schedule in clients for healings and readings at that time.

One particular afternoon I had a lady laid out on a cloth with crystals placed along her chakras and around her. I had cleared her surrounding auric field and was focusing on the channels of specific blocks and low energy when I could hear a shuffling from the passage. I knew the sound well – Eli's chubby little legs rubbing against his nappy.

I stayed focused on the woman. Elijah made his way up behind me and without a word came and stood next to me. He looked intently at the energy field – eyeing the woman's body from head to toe. Then he focused on the point where I was directing energy, and squatted down next to me (even adopting the same pose).

Then he put his hands in prayer at his heart, closed his eyes and drew a deep breath. With a sigh he opened his eyes and placed his hands right on the point of the body that was most congested. It was exactly the centre that the energy was working on! I then placed my hands on two other points and we both squatted there for half an hour.

The vibration of energy was so clear and high that the woman's body started to pulse and she made sounds that expressed deep relief.

The energy subsided. Elijah put his hands in prayer again at his heart then stood up and walked away. I could hardly believe it! He was only eighteen months old and he had just performed a conscious healing with me! When the woman sat up she shook her head in dazed amazement.

'I feel healed!' she exclaimed. 'That was so powerful! I've never felt anything like it before.'

When I told her about Elijah helping, she just burst into tears of joy and delight.

'Well,' she said. 'My life will never be the same again. Thank you.'

I began to laugh at the absurdity of my mind's surprise. Despite an idea of shock at the constancy of profound encounters that unfolded not only in my own life, but that of my children as well, I really knew it was all quite normal. What a bizarre paradox I thought – that I could still experience surprise for what I already knew!

50. *One Light*

I am the living light within you.

Isira ... *from the voice of God within.*

The front door of my house swung open and shut, open and shut. Shoes gathered on the veranda. Voices uttered in heartfelt whispers. Incense wafted through the air. Candles flickered in the soft glowing light. My doorway became a passage to another place. Strangers were no longer strangers as they crossed that threshold. Eyes lit up. Hearts filled up. Faith arose and spirit took flight. As the months passed, a larger number of people seemed to find their way to my home – all seeking the eternal Truth – asking for guidance and coming for meditation.

During that period I also experienced a deepening of phenomena that had started arising when I was in the Himalayas. Entering a state of deep stillness, I would become aware of a glowing, scintillating pearl of iridescent blue light. It was like the blue of the innermost light of a flame, except it was intensely more vivid.

It had been coming and going for months, hovering, seemingly inextinguishable yet coming and going. This time as I focused on it I determined to discover its source. Within an instant I became aware that it was deep in the sacred chamber of my heart and that its appearance of coming and going was simply that it was rising into my awareness, my inner seeing, which made it appear as if it was floating in front of my third eye.

As I realised this I was suddenly in deep oneness with it and I felt a giant rush ascend my central channel and come out of my crown chakra.

As I would observe this pearl of light it would become even brighter and begin to expand. Its growth emanated at first from within my heart centre, filling the sacred chamber with an exquisite essence that was simultaneously both cool and warm – like the cool water of a vast lake being warmed by the radiant midday sun.

Gradually the orb would expand to encompass a radius of light that far surpassed my physical form. In fact the aliveness and actuality of this light was so potent that it became as if my body were nothing more than a mirage and I was the radiance of this vast, shimmering, blue pearl of light!

During this passage I also experienced another recurring phenomenon of such beauty it seemed as if the heavens were pouring into me. A sweet liquid-like ambrosia elixir would trickle down from the back of my throat. Its exquisite aroma saturated my whole being whilst the light became ever more brilliant.

I moved in and out of this light over a period of many weeks until a moment came when *everything* had been consumed into the luminous field of blue light. Within this radiant field of all-connected light was the vibrant, aware seeing of the one same Divine Self shining in all, and that *I was it,* in which all creation was occurring ... in every thing, in every place, in every dimension of time simultaneously. At first this experience only lasted as long as I sat in a deep meditative state.

But then, after a moment in which I felt such all-consuming saturation in the exquisite blue light, I discovered that it was unending, even as I opened my eyes. What occurred then was unimaginably beautiful beyond all measure ... beyond all comprehension. This light seemed to be so lucid and vivid that it was more real than the light I had seen from the sun every day before that moment.

As I watched I melted into tears of bliss at the exquisite trail of beauty that was Life's supernal, resplendent light all around me.

Everything was engulfed in the brilliant luminous blue light. It scintillated and radiated all around me. Everything was in a flowing stream, all connected in a continuum. I saw that the soul essence, the very life force of all creation was constantly radiating in this light. There was not a thing that was untouched or unlit by this light.

It moved in, around and through everything as one endless radiant constant stream. What had appeared as boundaries melted away until there was nothing but light in every direction.

As I floated in a state of lightness I felt an all-encompassing state of love. It was as if all things were in me, in Love, and I, as Love, was in all things. It was a love beyond anything that could ever be conveyed through words alone.

It soon became impossible for me to do anything but sit down in lotus posture in the lounge room, for days on end.

As I dissolved more and more into the light I felt an explosive rush of bliss. It moved in every direction: a state of infinite expansion that was an all-encompassing, cohesive force of absolute inwardly folding, attractive power that simultaneously reached out infinitely. It was the play of infinity held together by the cohesive force of all centred power.

I was it and it was me – a vastness of One presence, manifest in the infinite array of all united diversity. The love was so intense that I felt its power ... the power of the original Self in utter stillness commanding all life motion, eternally. It was so immense that I felt myself disintegrating into a field beyond comprehension.

Then, from within that spellbinding state, I felt a sense of rippling arising. I became aware again of the field of my body. Golden light was swirling and sparkling in a display of exquisite patterns, so divine that it transcended anything of this world.

After this it took me about an hour to gather the senses back to my body-presence again. When I finally did feel present again, I opened my eyes. All I could see was love-light in every direction. Then a voice spoke in an absolutely clear, physically audible tone. In fact it was so clear I looked for a physical person ...

'Hello, Krishna!' the voice called delightfully.

Puzzled that I couldn't see anyone, I stood up.

I looked all around the house but there was not a sign of any person's presence. Then, just as I shrugged my shoulders, I heard a chuckle from behind me, I turned. But again there was no one there! I couldn't even see a spirit.

Then I went to my bedroom and there was the picture of Krishna on my pillow. It had moved from the side wall to my bed! I laughed as I contemplated the playfulness of creation and, in a state of bliss, all I could do was sing, 'Leela leela, rama rama, leela leela, rama rama,' (divine play, divine play, oh pure joy, pure joy ...).

I contemplated deeply the aspect that was Krishna. He had spoken:

I am the kernel in all things.[1]

I couldn't help but realise that the experience I had just encountered was of the very same essence. The 'I' that was spoken of, was not at all a personality, but the pure all-abiding consciousness that is the source within, and of, all life.

Over the following days I wandered around, on the streets, in parks and on the beach. I was in such a daze of bliss and love that people would look and smile, cross the road to say hello and ask me how I came to be in such joy. All I could feel was a constant stream of all-pervasive love – and everywhere I went people's heads would turn, unstoppably drawn, captivated and yearning for this luminous love.

---

[1] Reference to ancient Indian scriptures.

51. *To Serve Truly*

Angels fly because they take themselves lightly.

Allan Watts

Gradually I managed to find a balance of physical integration through which I could continue to function with a few activities, all of which were a response to an intuitive knowing of where I needed to be.

So, my trips often took me into town where I would occasionally stop for my lunch at the Hare Krishna Restaurant. Dressed in white from head to toe I glided blissfully along the city pathways, past the mundane array of shops, past the general populace dressed in gloomy and black attire. No wonder people stared. I stood out like a glowing beacon.

People continually gravitated to my table wanting to know how to find the peace and joy and bliss that I unmistakeably lived in. Some who were curious were also often keen to challenge me.

'Why do you have to make yourself different? Why don't you wear normal clothes like everyone else? Why do you have to put yourself above everyone?'

The fact that I felt no substance in such things meant there was nothing to say. Mostly I just smiled quietly and shrugged it off. I had become so accustomed to such things. It seemed that there was always something about me that others weren't okay about. I had been told I was mad. I had changed my clothes, my job, my name, my world so many times like a new hat every day. People considered me strange and unstable.

'Why don't you settle down. Don't you know what you want yet? Shouldn't you know better by now? You can't keep going through life so unpredictably. Get a plan. You have to be reliable. Be normal like everyone else.'

But to me I was just free. I was like a river, on a journey, coloured by and not resisting the changing landscape along the way. I was simply being, moving and expressing from moment to moment. I could be the girl next door, on a bike or riding a skate board, dressed in torn jeans, skimpy shirts and jogger's shoes, naive, innocent and simple. I could be the artist, the musician, the writer, tucked away in the field of my mind that knew no boundaries, scattering colours, notes and beauty upon the pages of my life, poetically, romantically fulfilled. I could be the athlete, lithe, focused, fast, determined and absorbed in the performing power of my body. I could be the scholar of life, the student of nature, the explorer of science, impassioned by words, by theory and quantum leaps of thought. I could be the sensualist, dancing like a drunken lover, smelling the roses, garnering the colours of life, swirling in rainbows of skirts and sparkling Goddess dresses, captivating, exuding the air of feminine beauty. I could be a mystic, sitting in a cave, shaved of my hair, dressed in robes, possessions abandoned, desire renounced, married to the infinite endless inner space, free of name, gender and race. I could be a girlfriend, cheeky and playful, silly and ballsy, funny and rude, sexy and fiery, soulful and nurturing, delighting my playmates and synchronising with their mood. I could be a guide, a messenger in the night, a light of insight with cards on a table, with crystals and spirits and psychic cues, and sharing of the soul's message. I could be a wild creature, climbing cliffs and trees, diving in glistening seas, roaming, rambling in walkabout dreaming, lost yet found on earth's great body, filled by an ageless glory. I could be an angel shining, floating in white, silently, smilingly, lovingly washing the streets with rivers of peace. I could be.

I didn't play any one of these stances because I 'needed' to or 'should' do or was 'proving' to ... I just could. I played in the dance of the kaleidoscopic spectrum just because I could, because it emerged from somewhere inside me and danced in the world that embraced me.

Rumours abounded. She's this, no, she's that. She must be a fraud. She must be on drugs. No one can keep smiling and laughing like that for no reason!

It was evident that most people struggled to accept the chameleon nature of my being. They expected consistency. Having been recognised for my 'spiritual' guise I must have been a shock on the occasions that I slipped into something else.

I once walked into an Indian restaurant where the owners had mockingly nicknamed me 'Swamiji'.[1] It had been my courteous habit to greet the staff with a warm 'Namaste', and, wearing robe-like clothes, I had fitted their image of a spiritual teacher. But this time my greeting was met with a derisive and glib smirk. I was on my way to a dance with some friends. Wearing a long pair of my favourite navy-blue dance pants, high heels and a long-sleeved pink top, I skipped in with a little, 'Hello!'

The owner's sister tucked her chin down and looked at me from under her raised brow. 'Oh, Swamiji,' she exclaimed, deliberately eyeing my clothes, 'What happened to Namaste?'

'Oh, Mirni,' I sighed, 'Namaste is in my heart, not my clothes.'

Gradually my presence attracted groups of people with many questions. These happenings turned into spontaneous Satsangs.[2] Before long, more and more people gathered. What struck me about the energy of the people was a certain seriousness. And one thing I had discovered was that liberation was not serious; sincere maybe, but not serious. When we are serious, we are closed and tight. When we are liberated and free, we are open and soft. We don't hold on anymore. So two weeks later, I started opening Satsang with jokes.

'Did you hear about the dyslexic Satan worshipper? ... He sold

---

[1] A respectful form of address for an Indian monk.

[2] Events dedicated to the experience of Truth through conscious dialogue and meditation.

his soul to Santa!'

Some people laughed, others were not impressed. For some, it allowed enough release through laughter to be truly open, to be present. Others were unable to get the deeper message that our religious beliefs may be based on a type of dyslexia – an inverted and false perception of how reality really is – which results in us giving our power away to a fantasy. We bind ourself to an illusion.

The following week those who had not laughed were absent and in their place were new faces. I opened again with another joke.

'What is the last thing to go through a fly's mind when it hits the windscreen of your car? ... Its asshole!'

Some people laughed uproariously. Others looked down in embarrassed disgust. Once again some were able to be released enough to simply experience being. Others were unable to let go of the righteous identity of being spiritual. It was only in a state of openness that anyone could truly embrace the deeper message of this joke. The point is that the fly doesn't think: it just experiences what is. It is a statement of 'no-mind'. If we can get this, we are free of all attitudes; especially of having to be a certain way to validate true spiritual authority. Actually, to be authentic in spiritual awareness we have to be completely free of any such identity.

A month later I came across a wonderful verse from the Tao.

When a superior man hears of the Tao
He immediately embodies it.
When an average man hears of the Tao
He half believes it, half doubts it.
When a foolish man hears of the Tao
He laughs out loud.
If he didn't laugh
It wouldn't be the Tao.[1]

---

1 Lao-tzu.

Despite the controversy of gossiping debates, a steady stream of people continually asked to come for meditation at my home in Campbelltown. I had also discovered another beautiful peace within me. No matter what anyone said about me, it could never change the truth of me. No words or ideas of who or what I was would ever actually change who or what I was!

I renounced the tie between myself and another person's perceptions of me. It was this tie that usually kept people hooked in an entangled web of accusations and defence. This release allowed me the freedom to respect and honour the complexity of other people's perceptions, whilst remaining unaffected by them. It meant I no longer took anything personally. As a consequence there was nothing more to defend. There was no more tug of division and no more cord tying me to them. Whether a person said they loved me or hated me I was free to simply remain me; unmoved by any perception. This gave me an incredible freedom and stillness. It meant that in every interaction with another I was able to simply be present to the uncoloured nature of what was happening. And along with that came even greater understanding, greater compassion and awareness.

•

Before long the Satsangs became very popular. I was asked to provide regular meditation, spiritual enquiry and sacred circles. The numbers grew from a steady dozen to a consistent turn up of around twenty, sometimes even thirty.

It filled me with even greater joy to be able to share the insights that had been such an intricate part of my awakening into the knowing of eternal life beyond the mind/body reality than it had been to experience them. I had truly come to the joy of knowing that giving was far more wondrous than receiving.

Yet my concern remained that the ego's ploys could easily hold deeper agendas for its own fulfilment.

One evening, whilst in a deep meditation I remembered a past life in which I had fulfilled the role of a guru. As I reviewed that memory, I saw a profoundly subtle behaviour that I had overlooked in my dedication to those who were seeking truth. On my deathbed I suddenly saw how elements of the teachings had actually perpetuated a degree of dependency in my students/disciples. I observed how a subtle degree of my concern for how the students' egos would interpret the insights had led me to hold back key points that were essential to their own direct realisation!

The problem wasn't that I didn't offer guidance, but that a gap arose from the degree to which I held some essential insights as secrets. This encouraged the notion that a state of freedom and oneness in God was select and mystical. Also there was a traditional view that to express certain enlightened qualities was a thing of the ego and therefore they should never be mentioned. It kept alive the students' perception that I was special, when actually the truth was far from that. I knew it was the true state of all. And yet in holding back certain details of my own realisations of the true Self, I did not give the most fulfilling tools for each one who came seeking to know it for themselves!

I felt sick as I observed some of the teachings I had perpetuated – teachings that were supposed to give the students a path to liberation.

Of course, I also realised that it was all innocent, an unintentional limitation. Yet in the seeing of this as I lay upon my deathbed, I vowed, that if I were to come again, I would renounce all form and structures that withheld the full knowledge for each one to know and remember themselves as the One Divine eternal life. I could no longer offer support to seekers of Truth through a lineage or tradition that upheld divisions, hierarchy and attachment to conditions, for to do so created its own boundaries. I did, however, understand the part that such traditions played, in the steps towards a higher faith in which the formulas and structures could be surrendered.

What I did see as important was reference to Life's continually present context: the Eternal Now. And also that the teaching and insights needed to be relevant to the individual in their own experience.

I wanted to serve each one to the fullest capacity of the mastery within them, not the mastery in another (whether that was in the form of a hoped-for saviour or a deity to worship). This, however, posed a dilemma, for I knew the role as a guide was still relevant and the work of God's will. For how else could a mind that was blind be led to see? Surely not by its own blindness! I could see the role of one who was seeing was therefore both relevant and essential.

As I contemplated these past-life insights, I wondered how then I could best fulfil this role that I knew as God's will. How could I not be what God had made me to be: a guide for others? And yet how could I be it, free of any subtle ego obstructions? How could I best serve others in the highest capacity possible? I didn't care for acknowledgment or anything in return. It was enough that I felt so immensely humbled to be experiencing such a path of true fulfilment. All I desired was to serve truly for each seeker's own enlightenment.

I cried with the depth of my commitment and prayed that I might be the vehicle of only God's will. 'If I am to serve, then may it be only God's will which works in and through me. Or let me be alone.' Yet even as I thought this, I knew that I could never be alone, for I was no longer here on this earth for myself but for the love of all beings.

I thought about all the people who had asked for teachings from me. I searched inside for the confirmation that it was God's will – that I was ready to serve.

When I raised my head up, I looked straight into Lama's smiling eyes. His photo on the altar allowed me to ask 'another' in moments like these. Was I humble enough? Was I truly at one in God enough that I was ready to serve the teachings that others were seeking? I began to cry and pray from my heart to be shown. And only if my heart was pure enough would I dare to respond to the requests that were coming constantly. Then I surrendered and waited to be shown.

That night I dreamed.

I came to a mountain that was steep. A great trail of steps led all the way up the side of the mountain to the top. There, at the summit, was a raised platform like an open temple. Hundreds of people were making their way up the stairs, some struggling, some slipping, some determined – all gradually making their way to the top.

I suddenly realised that I was on the very top step watching the people who were calling out from the lower levels. They cried with hunger and thirst. They cried with aching souls.

Sitting on the platform, between two pillars, was a wise old monkey, dressed like a king. As I looked into his eyes, he asked me a question.

'All these people are bearing gifts of the world ... What have you brought for me?'

'All I have is my self,' I replied.

The monkey nodded.

'But all these people are hungry and thirsty,' he said. 'What would you give them?' he asked.

'They hunger for the soul and thirst for eternal Life. It is the food of eternal spirit and the fount of limitless love that I would serve them, from the banquet of all-present Truth,' I replied.

In that instant the monkey smiled and was suddenly transformed into my dear Lama Zopa.

He gazed at me steadily.

'As it is that you have arrived at truth and are the food of the soul and the well of love, why then, as Truth, would you not serve those who hunger and thirst?'

I bowed my head as I recognised the intent of his rhetoric.

'Yes ... I can do nought now but serve. For I am full of eternal Life and this love overflows for the giving to all,' I replied.

My heart overflowed from the greatness of Love and Truth and yet no platform was held in my mind. I knew truly the oneness of the simple, humble beauty of being, and that which is great belonged not to any mind or ego but to the divinity within all.

•

As I woke I realised Lama had come once again to test my convictions and answer my prayers.

Once again I saw the inevitable destiny of my life. I could see as clearly as in my dream that every longing, every hunger, every sense of a missing element is the soul's pining for the return to a state of oneness in Spirit – the source of eternal Life and Love. And my heart was full, overflowing with food for hungry souls.

A few days later I was reflecting on the wonder of all that life was revealing to me. And I thought again of the one thing that had perplexed me most: the possibility of the ego leading the whole show. Now I was simply curious.

As I simply sat in that curious observation something profound revealed itself. It was as if I had been struck by a bolt of God's lightning. I could clearly see how all of the 'worry' that the insights and messages of my purpose might be the work of the ego was actually the ploy of the ego! I had suddenly caught up behind it, and witnessed it sneaking in the back door! All of that noise, the holding back 'in case it was ego' was the ego's very own trickery, wielding its authority in some clever attempt to hold me back from simply embracing and living the truth: that which I AM. It was so vivid, so clear and so liberating. I sat on the floor in belly-shaking laughter for the next twenty minutes.

52. *God's Piano*

> He who binds to himself a joy
> Doth the winged life destroy;
> But he who kisses the joy as it flies
> Lives in Eternity's sunrise.
>
> *William Blake*

The city streets looked to me like virtual reality. People shuffled to and fro, looking apparently alive yet oddly dead. The hustle and bustle seemed so rehearsed: strangely automatic and unreal. As I walked through town, I watched the people roaming, wandering as if programmed to act by their minds' little snapshots of hope. Where had the light of their souls gone? Their eyes looked so dull and hollow and each move seemed to be driven by the emptiness inside them. It was as if their happiness was forever behind an impenetrable veil, unreachable, somewhere deep in their unconscious.

That was an illusory veil between them and God, between their mind and their true Self.

Every action was driven by that unconscious yearning – by the mind's veils of separateness from God. I could see the elusive hope of joy stretching out before them: the hope that the new dress would make them beautiful; the hope that a kiss would bring them true love; the hope that the years of boredom would fill their coffers with success; the hope that their new hair would frame them in the hall of glory forever; and the hope that the diamond ring would give them an everlasting possession. Having forgotten the eternal Life, the true Self as Oneness in God, they clung to the body and mind. They clung to the ego and the world of form. And the more they clung, the deeper they fell into the gap of misery.

Yet I could see that any attempt to frame life's passing beauties results in misery. For in this world of form and structure, the attempt to capture some stability, some fulfilment, some lasting joy, is futile. Through losing sight of life's impermanence, there comes the struggle, the fear, the grasping. And yet every move is as futile as trying to pin a stake in a cluster of stardust flying through space – even in the very movement it is being blown apart by Brahma's breath.[1]

I saw how they searched, hungry, in the kitchen of the world, and yet even with a thousand thousand more meals their hunger could never be fulfilled. For, that which ends all hunger is not of this world ...

And upon quicksand did they try to build their homes, from that which is of no substance.[2]

If only they could return their foundations to the rock of Eternity. The true Self, the Oneness in God, is forever unchanged, irreducible and indestructible. The wholeness of eternal life and love is forever our one true and perfect being – the only real thing, the only thing REAL- I-able! My soul overflowed with compassion.

I sighed at the beauty ... the endless beauty that is forever free. That joy to me is like a hand throwing the dove from its cage, kissing each moment goodbye.

---

[1] Brahma is one of the names for the source of all life. It is the life force (the breath) of Brahma that propels the constant change in the manifesting forms.

[2] Reference to Matthew 7:26. This world is a constant flux of the mirage of form that consists of less than one percent of all existence. It is impossible to gain the desired emotional security in the world of ever-changing form by trying to own it: an impossible hope for fulfilment in that which never lasts.

One morning I entered into a slipstream of unceasing conscious awareness, the state known to yogis as 'turiya'.[1] There was no longer a division between any states of awareness. There was nothing but a constant conscious presence. The dream, the dreamer, and the dreaming were all one state of lucid 'awakeful' awareness. I had entered 'Eternity's sunrise'.

Even when I went to bed that night there was an undivided constancy of awareness. I went to sleep. But it was a strange sleep. My body slept, but 'I' was fully awake.

Then, as I flowed in that beautiful light lane of consciousness, I suddenly found myself sitting at 'God's piano'. It was the most beautiful piano imaginable. As I played I instantly dissolved into a timeless state of all-containing creation in which I realised that it was my Self that I was playing and that I was the music arising.

With pure wonderment at Divinity, I realised that I am – as is everyone – the musician, the instrument and the music – all ONE undivided presence ... the play of God. I exploded into a state of utter ceaseless ecstatic bliss. The love and joy was of such an unfathomable degree that tears poured from my being. I had entered into the very fount of Eternal Creation's infinite ecstasy.

The tears of bliss flowed as I dissolved into the infinite field of creation. For a passage of about eight hours my awareness of the body-presence remained merged in that state. And even as the experience of 'God's piano' dissolved into my awareness of the body-presence in the house again, I found myself moved by an unceasing awareness of Life's divine symphony.

Every night for the following week, I kept entering into the same state at God's piano. God was using an instrument that I loved so dearly to reveal to me my true Self. With every moment I seemed to enter more deeply into the undivided consciousness of One presence.

---

[1] A state of consciousness that is beyond waking, dream and deep sleep in which there is a constant stream of pure awareness.

Then one night, when in ecstasy, as I found myself no longer able to lie down, I went and sat at the piano in the sitting room. Suddenly I was in the same experience within the physical 'awake' happening. There was nothing but awake awareness – the dream and being awake were no longer divided. And as I sat at the piano, I experienced the same play of divine oneness in entirety. I was the musician, the instrument and the music – all the play of oneness in God. The music that flowed was so exquisite; it was nothing but a stream of Love's calling, in symphony.

Suddenly, after about an hour of sitting, an impulse intervened to impel me to get out the tape recorder and switch it on. The state remained undisturbed.

I played non-stop for three hours.

Later in the day I turned the tape on to listen to the recording. It was music of such perfection I knew it could never be constructed by mind. Yet in the perfection of unlimited Love as the creator, the gift of mind could serve and behold such wonderment. And so, too, I was the one listening and all that appeared in creation was the eternal communion of God with Self – the one play.

My life had become a flight of never-ending joy.

53. *Poem of Praise*

To see a world in a grain of sand,
And a heaven in a wild flower,
Hold infinity in the palm of your hand,
And eternity in an hour.

William Blake

I sang and chanted with my heart full of glee as my Kombi purred its way along the country road. My heart had been drawn again to my little childhood sanctuary. Like a child I burst with joy as the car passed the sign marked 'Hidden Valley.' The richness of the golden hills and the peace of the rolling waves filled my senses. The sun slowly made its descent. I skipped some rocks across the calm water in the last glimmers of light then made my way back to the van. I lay back for a few moments, taking in the sounds of night.

Unable to sleep I stepped outside again. I wandered across the rocky beaches and hilltops in the great stillness of the night. With each breath my mind dissolved into deeper and deeper oneness with life. Then, as I sat upon the hill, gazing out over the moonlight's silvery trail across the serene ocean, it happened ... I became the vastness of breath itself.

Within that vastness, there was no longer the act of breathing ... there was complete and absolute one breath in every direction, within me and all around me. I was nothing but breath ... the breath in all things. In the same instant, I became aware that what appears as a linear process of breathing is actually all occurring in the singular eternal life of Now.

There, in that vastness, was everything from the infinite, eternal cosmic breath to the most irreducible point of micro-cosmic breath, all breathing simultaneously within the one constant pulse of breath! I was the breath of the adamantine particles, scintillating God particles of moving love-light; the breath of spinning atoms and dancing fire, rocks, stars and cosmic galaxies, of creatures great and small; and the play of every breath on earth even to earth's very own ... the in-breath equalling that of one great Yuga.[1]

I watched as such an in-breath drew in a cycle of great flourishing life and civilisations; how with the out-breath came the falling away of life, the disintegration into darkness; and in the pause between the in-and the out-breath was a moment of sleep, the deepest point of the Kali Yuga,[2] the period of great unconsciousness and darkness on earth. And yet from within the vastness of eternal life's breath, it was still but a sigh in the play of eternal creation.

As I realised my state of oneness in the creation of all things, I simultaneously realised that, at will, I could attune to the awareness within any point of creation. And so, in that instant, I became the Sun ... a great breathing, heaving ball of gaseous fire, breathing in space, breathing out as ecstatic life, emblazoned light in great leaping solar flares. And, upon the light, I travelled into the life of endless diversity.

And so, I dissolved, returned in the limitless power and presence of Self as one breath, eternally breathing in all.

In the hours of the next day, consumed in the ecstatic bliss of the experience I had been immersed in, I wrote a poem of praise.

---

[1] In Hindu cosmology, a cycle of evolution in earth years usually calculated to be about 127,500 solar years.

[2] One of the defined periods of time in the evolution of humanity. A time of darkness and egoic ignorance in which great suffering occurs.

A journey of ever-expanding Self

1.

Far beyond consciousness,
galaxies or time,
Self swayed
In inky void silence.

In stillness sleeping,
a vast and giant rest,
journey of space
from pre-create
eternity's Source
contemplating emptiness.

In farthest reaches
this depth of being lay
pinpointed upon
an infinite map of space.

And entering deep,
this swirling soup,
drew forth upon the breath
of life,
a call within the void ...

I am, I am,
I am ...
Being ...
limitless potential of all,
in a singular point
zero.

Ecstatic, divine,
unstoppable power...
almighty creation
thine
mine
twine
Tri tattvas shrine.

And so,
in an instant
this Self exploded
Bliss
Nanda
Ananda
Sananda
Love of Self.

Knowing ...
no knowledge bound
sees infinite potential
of form to be,
awaiting all to see.

For in this now I am to be,
a brilliant Self decree!
Seen
Seer
Seeing.

Let there be light of me
    and thee,
Where two eyes
are One
for Self to meet Self,
Eternally.

For I am life,
creating all,
giving birth to every call.
I am, I am,
Oh...
Yes!
I AM...
glory be!

Unending delights to see!
I am immensely bright
one infinite light
to illumine the night,
with all reaching sparks
of radiant sight.

Oh the joy,
the ecstasy,
I call,
I sing,
I love!

I seek to know,
to love mine Self,
to create again
and again.

Waves of Bliss
in orgasmic height
spread vibrating ripples
    of sound.

Deep within
the infinite expanse
I am...
lost
and found
to meet myself,
to greet myself,
making love,
in a singular point of now.

In such divinity
I am entranced
Like an unruly child
in abandoned delight,
I divide upon myself
folding and spiralling
so far inwards,
I instantly expand
ever outwards
in a wondrous,
limitless display.

Galaxies upon galaxies
and infinite seas,
I rise and fall,
to know One and all.

So,
Ham
as I AM,
I shall experience all,
now and forever this way.

In every form,
eternally born,
in a sparkling naked array …
a never-ending,
fulfilling play.

And so in all I stay.
Nothing to run from
Nothing to run to
… Being everywhere
… Going nowhere.

Perfect and whole,
I come and I go,
as the moment I flow,
in the ever …
present …
now.

2.

In a great wailing sigh,
she breathed out from her dark
    and fecund womb of void.

Her great vacuous portal hurling
    particles of stardust
through limitless space,
held in the grace of her
    ever-loving embrace,
she welcomed the speed
    of thought.

Gaping open,
she drew him in,
the all-pervading mind,
an ecstatic union to find …

A spiralling staircase of
    galactic gas and heated
    breath,
Brahma
igniting solar fire.

Exploding and leaping,
so far-reaching,
the infinitesimal spark
    expanded upon itself,
to become a galactic sun,
travelling in the void of space.

She draws him in
The swan's sweet song
as he breathes in her,

Aum
Ah
Svah
Ham
entwined in universal embrace,
one singular being ...
an apparition of polarities face.

And so I look within my Self
and see the illumined night,
revealing an endless sight.

In the great silent space
an all-pervading song
reaches out
to infinite shores
and worlds of life beyond.

The greatest depths
of resonant sound,
holds me deep
in love
spell bound.

An infinite call of every scale,
the cosmic AUM
of all life being,
to all expansive heights.

Above,
below,
I do not know,
a point untouched or held within,
this all-pervading sound.

From space to stars,
and planets to Mars
this song gives birth to all.

In the warble of a quail
to a meteor's trail
I am the song of life.

From the thunderous raw
of exploding worlds
to the whispering giggles of
girls,
I am the song of creation's
sound
for the joy of life to be found.

Captivated,
I am
held within
the alluring bliss
of each frequency,
Self looks
within Self.

And in the rhythm
and rhyme of song
a design of form is found.

Riding the waves
of frequencies I feel
my form
take shape
Of nothing create
I look upon the face of Self,
an infinite beauty scape.

Each thought gives birth
to a frequency wave
of exquisite
mathematical
grace.

The quivering waves
of energy dance
and particles bounce in space.

Equations divine,
a tapestry fine,
and a shimmering form takes
shape …
gathering 'round
each cosmic sound.

I condense to make
crystalline
tapestry
weaving
All held within the instant point,
Thought
No thought
form
No form.

Shifting and shaping,
molecules dancing,
space ghosts of void
the perceiver held
yet never meld in swirling trance
forever is one glance.

For I am wonder
of glories asunder …
above and below,
mind shall not know
life's deer shaper
dear.

The dream and the dreamer
of spirit's maker
Heart full
Empty full
Dreamed
No sleep awake.

There I lay,
languishing in space,
in wonder and awe
of such eternal grace.

What could be
my next birthing place?
Death living
destruction
creation?

How, in my image,
could I reveal and seal,
this spirit of joy,
in life's unknowing face?

Again and again,
spinning within,
a galactic spiralling dance.

Billions and trillions of atoms
meet,
swirling around in a cosmic
romance.

Colliding and uniting in ecstatic
bliss,
a symphony of life
in infinite shape.

Each point
a cry
of divine delight,
imploding,
exploding,
far reaching light.

A song is born
of collective design,
of star-dust suspended
in a far off place.

Gathering round,
unto Self be found,
a place to rest
as sacred ground.

To feel,
to touch,
the breath of life,
all to be,
as husband and wife.

The all-attractive
dance gave forth,
the kernel heart of life
Rama na da
Krishna Hari
maha rishi
an infinite cry
of delight
as this Self did behold
the magnificent birth,
of every form to be told.

And within the great cosmic
whole,
the entire infinite
ocean's scroll,
the story of each
drop unique,
did utter forth of life to speak.

Oceans of infinite silence
Gone
Gone
Gone Beyond
Far Gone Beyond
Being none
All
As ONE
So it is
So.

Gate
Gate
Para Gate

Parasam Gate
Bhodhi Swahah!
Ha Ha Ha
HA!

Wondrous creations
of life's great fare,
of multi-dimensions
common and rare,
of races great and children meek,
to express God's Kingdom
and Heaven to play,
a game of hide-and-seek.

Within without,
in all of none,
so in the human,
it shall be done.

A magical journey
of illusion's dance,
a mastery game of
one Self's trance.

So turning within
the cosmic expanse
is a glistening gem
of sapphire bright,
held in boundless
galactic flight.

Breathing in
she expands again,
and pauses in
no breath.
Full breath
All breath
unfolding upon herself.

She is Mother,
a cosmic lover,
of Fathers' great conceptual
force.

And so in a heaving,
swirling dance,
together I filled the great
expanse.

With infinitely small
and magnificent tall,
the micro
the macro,
as One and all.

Soft and hard,
flowing and still,
every expression
could now fulfil.

So in the one,
unity,
I became the expression
me,
you
we.

Weyoume
Shak shi nhi
Empty and full,
light and dark,
I am One,
One
None
Rupa
Eva
Shunyam
Eva, Rupa, Shunyam
eternal art.

As rainbow's song,
omniscient mind
a luminous screen,
fills every space,
a dancing,
playful scene.

So as I stir
the cosmic soup,
I breathe and swirl,
a streaming life
of elements.
Fire of gold
Violet flame
Purity the soul
Silver Water
endless clear.

Flowing rivers of bliss
Space of air
Brahma's breath
Heaving breathing Now.

Earth of love
Chariot of Grace
Serving life the way
Liberation
Is life's little play.

I AM
a story sent,
a glory beyond
all
measures bent.

To create the grandest
    version of all
Self,
Endless
Expression
this illusion indeed
was truly meant,
to be
to enable One
as unity,
to feel the bliss
of loving
me.

Love
Loved
Lover
Beloved
In every form,
magnificence born,
perfect and whole
eternally,
a child of Love's Infinity.

And as the children
so
entranced did be,
in free will mistook
the mystery,
for a woeful
trap
of misery.

And yet
in the darkest hours
did I send,
a shining light
in the shape of a friend.

A hand to hold,
a face to see,
the truth that is always
you and me.

From time beyond,
a love so pure,
that no illusion
of form could procure,
portraying
playing
a portrayal of life's greatest
dream,
the grandest display
of human love to be seen.

For as many
eyes are closed,
yet so it be
a child shall see,
the love in all,
the all in Self,
a design of perfection,
a plan so Divine,
for the Garden of Heaven
shall be the shrine,
of hearts beyond
man's judgment time.

And in the field of Love
shall grow,
each one unique
and of beauty speak,
sweet and gentle,
loving and true,
the bliss of knowing
that I am you
that you are me.

God
Goddess
Being
Nobody All
Free to be
self playing Self
Eternally.

The 20th Attainment

The two eyes that once beheld good
and evil have become single.
The body, mind and soul are Christed,
at one with the all-omnipresent light.

KEY 20.

Resurrection

KEY 20.

Resurrection

The source of light descends to the soul even as the soul ascends to meet it.

Concept becomes direct knowing.

The soul is on the path of return, awake in the universal consciousness of all as ONE, resurrected in the light of the immortal Self.

54. *Liberation*

Faith is an oasis in the heart
Which will never be reached
by the caravan of thinking.

Kahlil Gibran

When I returned home I finally slept. And as my body slept I was awake in a dream.

I approached a great mandala that reached up as a tall mountain. I stood in awe as I recognised that I stood at the edge of a Buddha field. Great wrathful-looking deities guarded each of the directions – east, north, west and south – and golden walls rose up surrounding each of the levels. Intricate symbols and words were inscribed upon every wall and gate, markers and signs only for those who were ready to enter. As I stood at the gate of entry I realised that I was not alone.

Beside me stood a woman. Dressed in colourful ceremonial clothes she was an ordained gatekeeper and protector of the Sacred Lore. That Lore determined the codes of conduct and the authority of Divine Will. I knew it was time for me, and that I must enter. So I approached the first eastern gate ready to make my way into the maze. At each level and gateway, I was required to pass a code of conduct as was determined by the protectors of the mandala, until I realised that I had to hold to the truth of my own codes and that my test was to go beyond the expected. So I passed through the final gate ... alone.

There, on the very top platform, sat the small, wizened body of the Dalai Lama's teacher. He sat there gazing at me, chuckling as he welcomed me and congratulated me for coming.

Then he stared into me with a seriously penetrating look. 'What is it you want in your life?' he asked.

I answered from my heart. 'Nothing,' I said. 'I don't want anything ... I have everything ... I don't need anything.' In fact, it humbled me deeply that I was so completely at one with life, I could truly not ask for anything.

'Yes it is true,' he replied, 'but what is it that you want *to do* with your life now?'

I suddenly realised where the question came from.

He handed me a piece of paper and asked that I write it down. Then, with a glint in his eye, he added. 'Be sure of what you write, for as sure as you ask, it will be done.'

So, without even a moment of hesitation or doubt I wrote, 'I want to fulfil the role of an ambassador for peace, to serve humanity in equality for the knowing of the true Self, as the eternal life of love, oneness and true joy. As this instrument of God's Will, may I touch as many people as possible with the light of Divine Love and Truth.'

I handed the paper to him.

As he cast his eyes upon it, he smiled – a deep knowing smile. Looking upon me, he spoke with an assurance that knew nothing but the power of Truth.

'It is done.'

I sat silently for a moment absorbing the power of certainty that emanated in his message to me. Yet I could not ignore the rumbling whisper that still echoed deep inside my mind.

'So why then is it that I have been continually plagued by doubts? I have been visited by angels and great Ones, I have been given so many messages and signs of certainty, I have even felt that presence beyond question within my own being, and yet still I ask how it can be possible that I can bear such a light for the world.'

He smiled all knowingly. 'My dear child, although you have doubted your task you have not forsaken or forgotten it. All who are sent in the name of Truth have moments of doubt. If it were not for your doubt you would have been yet another impostor, motivated by pride and arrogance. You doubt because you are self-less.'

'But if I am to accept that I am self-less, is that not ego?'

'That which IS, simply *is*. Now go. All that matters is the knowing that you must do what you have been sent for. Go in peace, in Truth.'

The scene faded into golden light and I was engulfed in deep peace.

•

I woke in a state of gratitude and joy flowing within a deep awareness of certainty.

As I reflected on the Lama's message I found a new level of clarity. I could now see that the doubts I had been having were indeed part of the integration of my higher awareness.

Doubts can be either healthy or destructive. When destructive, the mind collapses into depression and the individual ceases to respond effectively to life. Yet healthy doubt stimulates more discernment which cultivates a state of growth, expansion and integrity to Truth beyond the ego, washing away any false assumptions. It widens the horizon to a higher reflection, supporting constructive growth.

By acknowledging my doubts I was able to refine my response to life and align it to the Divine Will. This cultivated a deeper integration between the states of awareness and the embodiment of my actions. Over time I realised that it actually strengthened my faith, which led to another level of accepting my whole self.

I observed how it was the power of acceptance throughout so many moments of my life that had been so significant and pivotal. And I came to understand that it was probably the most important shift for the mind.

Whilst many people continue healing therapies and courses to 'empty out the rubbish' I found it amusing as I had realised that it was best not to collect it to start with!

However, from the perspective of limited thoughts it does not seem so easy. It does require application and commitment. It means there must be a firm decision to leave the past behind and to focus on the present. Ironically this usually causes a greater focus on the belief or event that the individual desires to surrender. It also highlights the feeling and perception of loss, rather than gain. So rather than letting go of the rubbish it is more direct to simply 'let in' to the present. This brings us to a space in which we have already let go! In fact we become aware that there is actually nothing to let go of. The appearing object is only the result of the mind's repetitive focus on something already past. I have realised therefore that there is one supreme response to the question of: How? The how is always NOW.

I felt a deep melting as I rested in this awareness.

I sat in the lounge room. The pink carpet beneath me was like an ocean of rose nectar. Suddenly, I saw indivisibly that it was me. Within the realisation, it was as if I was seeing beyond all that I had even seen before. With wide eyes I took in the entire surrounding. There was no division between anything. It was all me – the one conscious presence of Self in every direction. The floor, the walls, the objects, the window, the view, the trees, the sky, the space ... it was all me!

I saw in utter awake-fullness that there was nothing but the one Self, appearing as all and that I was it ... the all I AM. In this observing, everything was dissolved into the light of love – of God. Nothing was separate. Nothing was lacking. Everything was the play of one whole Self of Being. As a bird sang in the tree I heard my Self, the God-Self singing; as the tree swayed it was my Self, the God-Self swaying; and in the distance the throng of Harley Davidsons was my Self, the God-Self thronging – all the pulse of one infinitely diverse symphony arising from an ever constant all-containing source – its pure point an eternal OM held in infinite silence. Empty-full.

I burst into laughter. It was a laugh from the belly of the universe. I realised the profound joke of the illusion ... that which had ever thought itself to be separate from God or to be asleep, had never even existed. How could I find something that already is when it has never been lost? The quest for enlightenment is based on illusion. Actually, I was never, ever, really the illusion. I realised that all I (and all) have ever been, was, or would be, is the eternal Divine presence – that which is the eternal master, creator, creation, created. To try to find something that already is existing is the most absurd thing. I saw the whole absurdity of trying to be enlightened. It is such a cosmic joke because we are already eternally enlightened. If we already have it we cannot attain it. Enlightenment, liberation, is our very nature! I laughed in profound, uproarious delight.

All I could do was laugh.
I laughed unstoppably.
The minutes passed.

The hours passed.
The days passed ...

into weeks.

And all I could do was laugh ... rolling, shaking, crying, delighting, ecstatically laughing.

Every moment is the one, whole, containing eternal point of Now. And every appearing thing is an undivided field of Self-communion. As I eat, I eat my Self, as I walk on the earth, I walk on my Self, as I turn on a tap, I turn on my Self as the water, flowing in the sink as my Self ... on and on ... infinitely ONE ever-present Self. Everything is the one I AM Self! I laughed non-stop for nearly three weeks.

As I emerged again from those bliss realms I found life performing its usual play of connections. News began to spread about the state I was in, and that my home was open as a space of sharing for meditation and spiritual insight. More and more people had begun to gather around me. Fortunately they had some understanding from previous experiences and stories of 'enlightened' beings. They were at least able to comprehend that my state was not one of madness but the transcendence of madness! To me it was simply that I had realised there was nothing to achieve, nowhere to go, nothing to run from, nothing to be solved, only life to be lived. There is nothing to perfect. Existence is already perfect. Even in what is seen as imperfect ... its imperfection is perfect!

Others recognised something in me that they wanted. They recognised the peace, the love and the certainty of oneness with God. I was not talking concept. I was living the experiencing. And that was like a light for moths.

It soon became evident (with the number of people who wanted to come regularly) that some organised assistance would be of benefit. And of course life had it all magically orchestrated. On one of my regular visits to the Hare Krishna restaurant, I found myself being served by a young woman who was new in the city.

She was obviously a Krishna devotee by her apparel – a sari and the usual tulsi[1] beads. The moment our eyes met it was evident that our connection was profound and ordained as part of a soul's journey on the path of awakening. Tears welled up in her eyes as she looked silently and soulfully at me. Something in her knew I was there for

---

[1] Tulsi is from a sacred basil plant considered by Hindus to be the favourite plant of Lord Vishnu.

her. The tears spilled down her cheeks.

'Oh my God,' she sighed. 'You are the one I've been looking for. Oh my God, I knew you would come. Please let me be with you.' The words fell from her in tender yearning. I nodded, silently acknowledging her and waited for her to finish serving my food before I suggested she come and sit with me when she was finished.

After another hour of service behind the counter she excused herself and came to sit at my table. Tears welled up again.

'Please tell me ... what can I do ... how can I be with you and help you ... I want to learn from you ... all I want is to be truly awake ... to be love.' Her words fell in a cascade of sweet, innocent truth.

'Oh, Maha Aksha,' I said, referring to her large eyes of beauty and love, 'it will be my great honour to serve you and to share with you this service that is for all. And,' I said with a smile curling at my lips, 'it also happens to be that I have a spare room and could really do with some organisational help.'

'Oh my God!' she exclaimed again. 'Really? Wow, could I really come and live with you?' Her eyes opened even wider. 'I am really good at organising, I'm a good secretary and I love to cook,' she said excitedly. We giggled as we both realised the perfection within it all and how effortlessly life had put us together.

It wasn't long before she asked me to give her a spiritual name. I had already heard her soul asking, and in that presence had heard her name echoing back like the song of a sweet child, Aditya. And how appropriate, I thought, for that name means 'child of the infinite'. I could see how pure and child-like she truly was and how deeply she yearned to remember the eternal freedom of that child within her.

Within a matter of days, Aditya moved into my humble little home. It wasn't long before it was evident that my home was a small spiritual centre, a little beacon of light that drew others who were seeking to allow their own light to shine.

It was a great gift that more of the beautiful people who had been coming to my home decided also to live there. I even found one young man, Simon, often sleeping on the couch. He loved being in the space so much that he simply didn't want to go home to his own little place. During the following weeks, I dissolved into deeper and deeper samadhi.

I could no longer perceive solid boundaries. Everything was one luminous field of pure love. That love flowed so deeply, so endlessly, that it poured from me in tears of bliss.

As I sat in the dining room one morning, I felt the power of that love flowing out in every direction for every being. The others had become used to seeing me in such blissful states and loved to sit quietly beside me, silently meditating in the loving energy. Yet this particular morning, there was a sudden exclamation of surprise from Simon.

'Look!' he exclaimed. 'Look! Her tears ... she's crying milk!' Simon stood up and came to my side. He trembled with wide eyes as he slowly stretched out a finger and tenderly took a drop. As he put his finger on his tongue, he let out a sigh.

'Oh my God,' he said ... 'It's sweet, sweet milk,' he said again in wonderment.

Aditya reached out too and, in taking a taste, echoed in amazement. 'Oh my God,' she said, 'It's like milky nectar.' She began to cry. 'Oh Isira,' she said, 'It's your love ... your love for all the children is spilling out of you.'

It became increasingly evident that I had transcended the worldly reality ... unshakably. I no longer saw the world as others did.

On a few occasions, the beloveds who were living at the centre attempted to take me on shopping trips. They seemed concerned for my lack of worldly contact and thought it best that I be kept active. Yet it was all I could do to even walk. The body felt like it was little more than a nebulous field of fluid light. Everything around me had dissolved similarly into a great, all-connected field of streaming light. I could no longer make out distinct solid objects and boundaries.

There was so much beauty in everything, all around me, that its wonder swelled in me in almost unbearable bliss.

It became impossible to do anything but sit in lotus posture or lie down on my bed.

The beauty of bliss and love became so full and constant that it was as if I had been completely consumed by it.

Some say the journey of such arrival is the moment the drop returns to the ocean. Yet for me it was as if all the mind-made membranes of the individual drop had simply dissolved and so the ocean had returned to me. I was it filling me. It filled me, consumed me, drowned me – until there was no longer 'me'. All that remained was the eternal ocean of love.

Within that vastness of pure awareness arose an extraordinary witnessing. I suddenly saw how the world, and all things in it as perceived by the mind as reality, is entirely the play of the one mind in a great web, cast forth from the illusion of separation. It all unravelled as if backwards into its one point of source ... the one momentary thought, an idea of separation from God, the source.

And in the instant of the thought arose the view of such a field of creation ... hurled from the mind as fear and expanding in every direction as if cast out. And so, the Big Bang occurred. In one instant, life became the dream of creation as duality ... inside/outside, this and that, good and bad ... the child perceiving itself to be cast out from heaven whilst in truth, it was still resting – eternally in the deep oneness of God as eternal, infinite life. In one great instant I saw the entire play of the mind's linear dream projection dissolved, returned to the awakened point of awareness from which it had departed.

Oh what ecstatic joy! What liberation! I was truly free! The truth was, I had never, ever left God ... it had all simply been a dream, and I the dreamer was really in truth that which remains eternally awake. I could see that all the seeking was just a validation of the mind's illusion, that there was nothing to seek, only the truth to be seen.

For how can we seek for that which we already are? How can that which is already free need freedom? And yet the dream is a play of the mind that could have a thought, simply to experience separation.

For in the truth of life in which there is no separation there could only ever be the dream of such. And only in believing the idea of separation to be real could we ever perceive ourself to be in bondage. All that ever existed is an endless dance of passing phenomena, none of it ever tied to a single moment.

In the bliss of Eternal God-presence there was only luminous awareness of all life as whole, pure, divine being. Time ceased. This and that were gone. And within that which is, flowed the play of pure presence.

And so the body remained under the loving care of those living at the centre.

Another ten days had passed whilst the Self abided in Nirvikalpa Samadhi.[1]

Then, within eternity, the sense of presence began to emerge in a field of radiant light.

As a radiant light-being I was sitting upon an open lotus on a golden seat. The most intoxicating scent permeated my being as the blazing light of life's adamantine particles shone in harmonic glory.

Then, within the light I saw a form approaching me – it was the great saint again, the one in whose form I had experienced myself. He glided towards me with his hands upon his heart. As he neared me, he knelt down and opened his hands. Therein was the most glorious rose imaginable. It shone in full open splendour. Then, tenderly, reverently, he offered the rose to my heart. In the same instant it became the open blossom of my heart and its fragrance filled the air.

The love that flowed through my being was like nothing ever known on earth. It was so immense that I knew I had

[1] A state of consciousness (deep meditative being) free of thoughts or identity. The 'I', the observer dissolves, and all that remains is the presence of pure conscious radiance.

truly returned to heaven, as heaven was all within me.

A pure awareness enfolded me. I was surrounded once again by a host of Ascended Beings and angels. With clear direction, I was shown that the state to which I had ascended was a point at which it was no longer necessary for me to stay in a body. Essentially, the body was no longer needed for the state of oneness in eternal life. Yet there, in the field of God, I was also seeing the plane of earth and what I would leave behind, if I so chose; the lands upon which so many remained in confusion. I felt earth and every being, every person in me, in the vastness of eternal love.

In the all-containing presence I felt every being's pain, hopes, suffering, longing, dreams and despairs. And I heard every prayer, the reverberating prayer for peace, for love, for fulfilment, for freedom ... In such oneness, I encountered something almost unimaginable. I felt the love of a million, million mothers – and the pain of every being. It was as if I was expanding infinitely, then splitting into billions of points; yet compressed into one presence simultaneously. And yet it was a love and ecstasy beyond measure ... liberated ... totally free of 'self'-suffering.

It simply occurred beyond choice, beyond thought, that I could do nothing but return to earth, to the body. I saw the junction. The choice I had – to leave the body behind – was nothing but a remnant of the mind that had ever thought of a choice for the separate reality of a single me. Now it simply had no relevance. I was totally gripped by a pure awareness that liberation is not for the 'individual' self ... it is *from* the self.

•

In such Love, there could be nothing but the response to stay, to return for those who prayed. For such love could only be to give ... to give to all, as the one Self. I simply could not choose to leave the world, to stay in the eternal field of Love, when so many prayed to know it. I was now beyond choice. I had returned to that which simply is ... the all-embracing, presence that is Love ... purely being. And so I returned to the body.

The 21st Attainment

I and the Father are ONE.[1]

That which I truly am is the omnipresence of perfect, unified existence.

[1] John 10:30.

KEY 21.

Completion

KEY 21.

Completion

There is no self outside of the One Self that is all.

In the source of one's own love, the circle is closed. Through complete awareness, experience and feeling of the true Self, completion is attained. The illusion of separation ends.

The spirit and the body are as one. Life is whole and in balance.

As above, so below.

55. *Home*

> We shall not cease from exploration
> And the end of all our exploring
> Will be to arrive where we started
> And know the place for the first time.
>
> *TS Eliot*

The love did not disappear. In fact, it flooded my whole body with such intensity that it vibrated and shook like a tremendous storm of light and joyous ecstasy. It pulsed non-stop for five days.

And then it ceased.

Stillness remained.

And in the stillness, flowed an eternal spring of love.
Love was all I was.
Peace; Freedom; Oneness.

The child and the cosmos unified.

Love is all I AM.

The 22nd Attainment

The Fool remembers.

She never left home.

The end is but another beginning of that which never began nor ever ended.

Epilogue

> Our journey does not end in a transcended plateau.
> It continues to ripen in the field of unending love where
> the seeds of truth, forgiveness, devotion and love bear
> golden fruits of compassionate service.
>
> *Isira*

The day I 'returned' from the field of pure Love was the single most humbling moment of my life. Whatever had been a 'me' of any significance was dissolved by the power and the magnitude of the Love that consumed me. That Love is an infinite intelligence which reveals the ceaseless, chattering constructs of the mind to be less than specks of dust in the vastness of life.

And, simultaneously, the awareness which remained had merged so completely with the eternal omniscient Source that nothing less than absolute power and 'knowing' graced my whole being. The Self I had discovered myself to be was no longer the mind's illusion of a separate dot existing apart from Life, but the utter omnipotent embrace of God ... one Being.

To this day I remain steadfast in at-one-ment with the glorious Self that is all. All around me I see the scintillating resplendence of an indivisible creation and within me is the life and love of all creatures, great and small. I am consumed by speechless wonder at such immense bliss and peace.

During my journey, over many years, I was so overwhelmed by the bliss and love which filled me that I often also felt a sense of disbelief and bewilderment that I was blessed in this way. I often felt it to be a grand injustice that I could be so blessed when so many were still caught in great fear, suffering and confusion. Now I experience a funny little dichotomy. There is great compassion for those who are still experiencing the apparition of suffering and yet, deep inside, I chuckle because I know that in truth there is nothing 'wrong' – nobody is actually imprisoned in this experience, and that is the cosmic joke of it all.

Now I can say that I feel completely at peace, knowing that it is all the One Self, as one divine play of the evolution of consciousness. And so I watch the radiant light of the one Eternal Life, donning and shedding the costumes of form and personality in a great theatre of illusion.

•

Soren Kierkegaard famously said that life can only be understood in reverse but must be lived forward. And so, looking in the reversing mirror of this life, what can I now see?

I realise that the human challenges, difficult though they were at the time, provided me with the ground of true understanding. Without those moments of challenge I would never have been able to relate fully on a human level, nor could I have been able to share the real possibility of the liberation that lies within us all. I understand that in order to speak as Truth about the journey of awakening, it had to be drawn from direct experience. Anything else would have been more philosophy and concepts.

I have come to see that the 'human' experience of the ego with its arising fears and delusions of separation and limitation is not at all a fault, a sin or a failure. I see now that it is simply a passage in the vast journey of Life – the play of manifestation in evolution – and we are all the innocent children of God growing.

And although I experienced many profound states of God awareness throughout my life, I see now that there was a pattern occurring. Each liberating experience took me both deeper and wider, carrying me through spirals of integration.

During my childhood and teen years I encountered mostly unwilled states of higher awareness, but was also cultivating an intentional ability. Over my early adult years I encountered profound interconnected states that were spontaneous and self-generated. The depth, duration and saturation of these continued to increase through moments of brief satori (such as sudden flashes of the I AM awareness) to awakened kundalini, healing powers and psychic clarity; then deepening unification of many aspects of incarnation. With ongoing cultivation I then entered into turiya states at the age of twenty-eight, followed by permanent samadhi at the age of twenty-nine and Nirvikalpa Samadhi[1] at the age of thirty.

Now, although I experience myself as complete, united with God, I continue to see the marvel of a never-ending journey of creation – unfolding through the endless windows of experience. I, as does all of life, continue growing forever.

And so I am grateful for every step of my own journey, knowing that each and every event has been an essential and integral part of the whole journey.

•

And so it continues with my family.

Jake and I have a wonderful friendship that is growing and maturing.

I have a beautiful and blessed relationship with my children, seeing them regularly, enjoying all of the wonders of their own journey as they grow. They continue to delight me with their own wisdom and joy, sharing a common love, understanding and interest in my larger purpose. We all enjoy and celebrate the beauty of our large blended family.

My parents have continued to unfold in their own growth and deepening love over these years. Our relationship is one that I hold in deep gratitude and honour.

My siblings have each found their own place in life and fulfil their own destinies.

•

I have been teaching meditation and guiding others to be in connection with the inner Self and the powerful presence of Now, for over twenty years. For the last nine of those years I have been giving Satsang and discourses on the true nature of life, Self and creation. It simply followed, after I emerged from samadhi, that others were drawn.

It delights me to see how it is the truth and beauty of the one Self that others see in me and seek to know for themselves: it is their very own Self that they see! And it is my unswerving conviction that the only way to find true freedom, love and joy is for each of us to know that Self as our own true being. Therefore it remains my inexhaustible passion to assist others in reclaiming the power that lies within us all, the power of what IS.

The goal of our human journey is to transform the mind's perception of separation, from our earth and from each other, to the awareness of unity; to lead us from judgment to love, from pain to joy, from war to peace. Although a seed already contains within it the life force of a thousand fruit, it still trembles in its transformation – to die as the seed, to be born as the fruiting tree. Likewise, as humans, we all share the same journey as our ego shakes in its death throes as we grow in love in order to bear the fruits of true wisdom. And everyone who becomes conscious of this transformation always asks: How?

The answer to this ancient question is always the same: by following the path that is lit by love. Not the reduced definition of love as the romantic stuff of fairytales but Love: the acceptance and embrace of all of Life, exactly as it is being and becoming, perfect in its own stage of growth. The choice for tolerance, compassion, empathy, forgiveness, kindness ... this is the choice for love.

What human being does not seek to be fulfilled in love? The journey is inevitable. It is not a matter of if, it is simply a matter of when. And it begins when a simple decision is made deep in the Soul: the decision to wake up and remember the Truth of who we are.

Words flutter like passing phantoms. They can never convey the immensity of my gratitude for this love – because, in truth, this love is immeasurable.

I can never truly express how graced I am, how infinitely blessed, to be forever awake in this witnessing, loving presence of being. Nor how deeply honoured I am to be such an intimate part of the journey of so many people as they each reclaim the Truth for themself: that we are all eternal life, the ONE ... infinite love ... innocence, peace, joy and wisdom.

And I can only say what a great gift it is to serve in this way. For now I see that the only thing I wanted with this life has become a living reality. I travel the world as an ambassador of peace, inspiring others to remember the love we all are and to feel connected again to the wisdom and power that abides in our true essence.

As I travel, I see that so many are touched by, and reaching out to touch, the presence of Love. Gradually, we are joining hands all around the world, embracing the One Self that is in all.

I thank the One that is in all for this gift, for this blessing.

May I continue to serve for the gift that is in all.

May you embrace the power of your own potential. As you move forward to fulfil your vision, know that it is on the path of Love that your true journey begins. And all you ever need to do is take one step at a time.

Love
In the ONE,

Isira.

Glossary

Akashic records	The spiritual record of all events in history and in the lives of every soul. Sometimes called The Book of Life.
amenorrhoea	Absence of menstruation.
ankh	An Egyptian ritual item, a cross with a loop at the top, representing the feminine power – often used in healing and initiation. The ankh is said to be drawn from Isis representing her blood and womb: the power of creation.
asana	Yogic posture to strengthen the body and relieve stress.
ascension	The word ascension is a reference to the raising up of the body-mind into the light-body through communion with the Divine. Although most often associated with Jesus, it is something that has been documented to have occurred to a number of evolved beings throughout humanity's soul journey. Ascension is also referred to as a Christing. Again although this has an association with Jesus Christ, the word Christ/Christing is a reference to the illumining of consciousness, the light that occurs in the atonement with God.
Aum	See Om/Aum
Aum Ah Hum	A mantra which is a self affirmation: creation is the Self I AM in all.
aurora	Unusual phenomena of light and colour in the sky.
Baba Muktananda	A great yogi, saint and spiritual master, who introduced Siddha Yoga to the West in the twentieth century.
bemo	Three-wheeled motor transport with a small carriage for two people.
bhastrika pranayam	The practice of rhythmical breathing that stimulates internal fire, bellow breathing.
Bilbo Baggins	A leading character in *The Hobbit* by JRR Tolkien.
Bodhi Tree	The tree under which Buddha entered into enlightenment.
Bodhisattva	One who is enlightened or committed to the path of enlightenment and has taken a vow to assist in the awakening of all beings. The emphasis is on compassion and service for others.

bogan	A tag name for a roughneck male who is renowned for fighting, driving dangerously and 'living life on the edge'.
Brahma	A Hindu deity: the essence of all creation that consumes the boundaries of the false perception of separateness.
Brahma's breath	Brahma is one of the names for the source of all life. It is the life force (the breath) of Brahma that propels the constant change in the manifesting forms.
Buddha	This word literally means 'awake' … one who is realised.
buddha field	A dimensional state that is sustained by beings of Buddha consciousness.
candida	A bacteria, *candida albicans,* which occurs naturally in the gut but often overpopulates the digestive tract due to a poor diet, particularly of excess sugar and yeast.
chai wallah	Traditional hawker who sells spiced milk tea.
chakra	Energy centre in the subtle body aligned in a path corresponding to the spine. The chakras govern the energy flowing in and out of the body. The energy varies according to the emotional mental and spiritual development of the individual.
channel	Pathway within the body for the movement of spiritual energy.
chapatti	Indian traditional flat bread made of flour, sometimes stuffed with vegetables and spices.
Chitsabhā	The hall of consciousness, the very presence of Shiva, that which is known to be the infinite one Self, the source of all creation in which form/formlessness are the one eternal dance.
chord	Every individual soul aspect resonates with a particular sound, a harmony like a series of musical chords. When we experience an alignment with a message of truth that is in harmony with our soul these chords resonate powerfully sending a harmonic vibration through the body/mind/soul. It is like the vibration of a tuning fork when it is played with a perfectly matching note on an instrument.
Christ	The consciousness of light … the aspect/one who realises the Divine within Self and all.
Christ Self	This reference of Christ Self is not about the incarnation of the individual known as Jesus, but as the pure consciousness of the Divine Self that is the essence of every soul.

Daka	In Buddhist Tantra: a male being, a spiritual messenger or sky dancer, who awakens exaltation.
Dakini	In Buddhist Tantra: a female being, a sky dancer, or spiritual muse who inspires spiritual practice.
Devi/Dewi	Goddess or Divine feminine.
didge	An abbreviation of didgeridoo – a long hollow ceremonial instrument made from native trees of Australia.
dolphin dreaming trail	This trail follows the coast of South Australia where dolphins have been travelling for thousands of years. These trails are sacred to Aboriginals and are a part of the dreaming and connection with the dolphins.
donuted	An energy shift where Isira experienced the creation field dissolve into its own centre – zero point – infinite space – and simultaneously emerge, rolling out from its central void like a giant donut ring only to fold right back around on itself in a continuum. Within this field was the awareness that this pattern was repeating itself in the macrocosm and the microcosm.
dorje	Tibetan word, meaning diamond, referring to a ritual bell in Buddhist practice which represents eternal, immutable knowledge or the heart of knowledge.
dreaming	The conscious connection to the ancestors and creation realms weaving all life together through past, present and future.
dreams, awakeful	The 'dream' state in which Isira's body is at rest yet she is in an awake, conscious state of awareness. These are not normal dreams in which events seem to occur on the unconscious plane. Within this awareness Isira is directly experiencing past, present or future events, in what humanity has, does, or will refer to as 'reality'! In a state of vision Isira experiences a temporary shift of consciousness to events that are outside the environment of her body. Sometimes this is a state of awareness of events occurring in another part of the world. Even though her body is resting elsewhere – she will experience the situation as fully as others in the real event.
Dreamtime	The dimension of place and time that is the origin of creation.
Ganesh	A Hindu aspect of divine incarnation, with the head of an elephant, known as the remover of obstacles and holder of wisdom.
Ganga	The holy river Ganges.

geshe	A lama (like an abbot) who has attained a high degree of knowledge of Tibetan Buddhist teaching, comparable to a western doctorate.
ghat	Landing on riverbank where the deceased is placed on a cremation platform and set afloat.
God	A reference to all that is. That which is the sum totality/ presence and power of creation. May be referred to as the masculine principle of creation. I do not use the word God as a reference to a separate individual or personality but rather as the omnipotent consciousness of the source of all life.
God-bumps	A rush of energy that courses through the whole body and raises bumps on the skin like goose bumps, yet is a communication of the soul. It is a deep response to a stimulus, indicating spiritual significance or recognition of Truth.
Goddess	A reference to the feminine principle of creation: the essence of love and creativity.
gompa	A temple for Buddhist teaching and ceremony.
Heruka	In Tantric philosophy, a male personification of bliss and emptiness.
Hierophant	One of the archetypal figures of The Tarot, a deck of cards used for divination. The Hierophant is a teacher, a wisdom figure, or a message man.
inner eye	This relates to psychic and clairvoyant powers.
Isis	The Mother Goddess of Egyptian religion and mythology; worshipped as great magic; mother of Horus (Hawk-head God); protector of children; associated with the sun gods; represented with the sun seated in cows' horns.
Jewel in the Lotus	Translation of the Tibetan chant: Aum Mani Padme Hum.
Kali	A Goddess principle deity who destroys the ego and time. She represents death as the gateway of eternal life.
Kali Yuga	One of the defined periods of time in the evolution of humanity. A time of darkness and egoic ignorance in which great suffering occurs.
karma	The law of 'cause and effect' which manifests in life experience and often reflects the influence of other lifetimes. Every action has a consequence.

Kaurna	Aboriginal people indigenous to the Adelaide plains of South Australia.
kundalini	Energy that lies dormant in a chakra or energy centre at the base of the spine until spiritual awakening, when it begins to move upwards eventually stabilising in the crown chakra.
Laksmi	A Goddess principle deity who represents abundance, wealth and fertility.
lama	A Tibetan Buddhist who is recognised as having a certain degree of spiritual attainment and authority to teach.
leela	Divine play.
lino	Linoleum – a vinyl floor covering.
loka	Heavenly realm.
lore	The indigenous system of knowledge and wisdom that sustains sacred respect, awareness and balance of the relationship of all things in creation.
mala	A string of prayer beads used for mantra/prayer.
mandala	A geometrical depiction of creation or the hierarchy of a buddha field, often circular, used to focus the mind and raise awareness.
mantra	Sacred Sanskrit words or phrases repeated for prayer or to raise awareness.
merde	A French word meaning crap or shit.
moksha	Liberation – a final release from the cycle of death and birth as Shiva whispers into the ears of the dying.
mudras	Sacred hand gestures that represent and create a flow of subtle energy.
Namaste	An Indian spiritual greeting which means the God within me sees the God within you.
Nirvikalpa Samadhi	A state of consciousness (deep meditative being) free of thoughts or identity. The 'I', the observer, disappears and all that remains is the presence of pure conscious radiance.
Nyung Nye	A Buddhist retreat of fasting, ceremony and meditation.
Om Mani Padme Hum	A mantra that celebrates the eternal conscious sound and presence that remains central to existence – the jewel in the lotus. Om: the eternal, pure sound of creation. Mani: jewel. Padme: Lotus. Hum: within.

Om Namah Shivaya	A celebration and invocation to Shiva, a male aspect of God.
Om swasti astu	Balinese greeting honouring the Divine within.
Om/Aum	The primordial originating and all pervasive sound of creation. Repeated as a mantra in spiritual practice.
pranayama	A practice of directing the breath with specific depth and rhythm to release and raise energy through the channels of the subtle body.
pujas	Prayer events.
Ra	The Sun God; chief God of Egyptian religion and mythology.
rod and staff	The rod and the staff here refer to the covenant of God within us. The rod is the bridge between God and each person: it is the energy that is flowing with limitless power when we are directly connected to God. It is the link between our self (as the microcosm) and our higher Self – God (as the macrocosm). The staff is the central internal channel (the sushumna) through which this God energy (the rod) may flow when the staff is open.
rudraksha beads	The seeds from a sacred tree that was linked to Shiva. Hence the seeds are specifically used for malas for Shiva worship.
runes	Divination tools using stones inscribed with characters from an ancient alphabet representing archetypes.
sadhu	Spiritual wanderer and practitioner.
samadhi	A state of undisturbed bliss in which the perception of a separate self as 'I' dissolves into pure awareness of infinite life-love source which at a deeper level becomes Nirvikalpa Samadhi or moksha (liberation).
samsara	The wheel of suffering.
samskara	Seed of illusion: false perceptions that cause suffering.
sarong	A traditional cloth of Asian people worn around the waist.
satsang	An event dedicated to the experience of Truth through conscious dialogue and meditation.
scape	A word Isira uses to convey a vastness of expanse that is without defined form yet can include form.
seed and the drink	The drink and the seed was an ancient formula that sustained energy for long periods of time which meant the body did not need to take food.

shakti	In Bali the word shakti is often used to refer to spiritual power. In Hinduism, shakti is the female principle and power of creation.
shaktipat	A pure current of Divine energy capable of blessing, healing and awakening consciousness.
Shiva	The central and highest Hindu deity representing God – the male principle of creation.
'singing'	This is an Aboriginal term referring to a particular communication through song in language. The experience both conveys a message to the person being 'sung' and has a powerful spiritual effect. It may be an invocation to deeper aspects of being.
songlines of dolphins and whales	The songlines are the routes that the dolphins and whales have been travelling along for thousands of years.
Sri Yantra	Considered to be the supreme yantra. It represents the process and field of creation – like a diagram of genesis.
stupa	A large structure of worship most often where the burial remains of lamas and masters have been stored.
sutra	Teaching on consciousness and creation, usually Buddhist or Hindu.
swamiji	A respectful form of address for an Indian monk.
sweat lodge	A ceremonial womb-like lodge made of thick canvas, blackened on the inside to block out all light. Glowing red rocks that have been prepared on a fire are brought in and placed in a central pit one by one and sprinkled with water, creating an intense heat. Prayers and chanting are used to guide the participants into a meditative state for vision quest and releasing for healing. It is a Native American practice most often used for purification.
tangkha	Work of art on cloth depicting geometrical designs (mandalas), deities and historic figures to convey Buddhist teachings.
tantric	Referring to Tantra – subtle, secret and mystical teachings about higher consciousness, subtle energy and the raising of sexuality to spiritual dimensions.
Tara	A Buddhist female deity personifying compassion
tathagata wisdom	The wisdom of an Enlightened One.

tattvas	Levels of creation or consciousness. These levels manifest different dimensions of creation from the formless, to the subtle and gross.
theosophy	The study of truth, God, religion and spirituality based on the idea of the unity of all things.
tsog	A gathering for Buddhist ritual practice.
tulsi	An extract from a sacred basil plant considered by Hindus to be the favourite plant of Lord Vishnu.
turiya	A state of consciousness that is beyond waking, dream and deep sleep in which there is a constant stream of pure awareness.
vajra	A ritual item that represents a lightning bolt and/or penetrating wisdom.
valnupa	A creation being.
vibhuti	Sacred ash used in rituals.
Vishnu	One of the principle Gods of Hindu religion
vision quest	A meditation or spiritual gathering for the purpose of understanding with the soul awareness.
Wanjina being	Guardian spirit and keeper of creation dreaming in the Kimberleys (a region in the north-west of Australia).
willie-willie	A tall spiral of spinning wind and dust like a mini cyclone.
wurly	Aboriginal shelter.
yantra	A diagrammatic symbol for a field of energy.
yidaki	An original indigenous word for didgeridoo.
yoni	The female genitalia seen as sacred: the gateway of creation.
yuga	In Hindu cosmology, a cycle of evolution in earth years usually calculated to be about 127,500 years.

References

Key 0
Isira, *Words of One,* The Oracle Press (2004), p. 119

Chapter 1
Wordsworth, William, 'Ode on intimations of immortality', stanza 4 (1807)

Chapter 3
Ehrmann, Max, 'Desiderata' (1948)

Chapter 4
Goodman, Paul, in *The Promise of a New Day,* Hazelden Meditation Series, Collins Dove, Australia (1989)

Chapter 5
Issa, in Jason Elias and Katherine Ketcham, *In the House of the Moon, Reclaiming the Feminine Spirit,* Hodder and Stoughton (1995)

Chapter 6
Rosetti, Dante Gabriel, 'Sudden Light' (1870)

Chapter 8
Roads, Michael J, *Talking With Nature, Journey into Nature,* Reprinted with permission of HJ Kramer/New World Library: Novato, CA (2003)

Chapter 9
Gibran, Kahil, *The Prophet,* Heinemann: London (1980)

Chapter 13
Lewis, CS, in *The Promise of a New Day,* op. cit.

Chapter 14
Tagore, Rabindranath, in *The Promise of a New Day,* op. cit.

Chapter 15
Shakespeare, William (1599) *As You Like It,* act 2, scene 7, line 139

Chapter 16
Lao-tzu, Tao-Te-Ching, translated by Stephen Mitchell, Harper Perennial: New York (1991), ch. 22.

Chapter 17
Gibran, Kahil, *The Prophet,* op. cit.

Chapter 18
Rumi, in C. Feldman and J. Kornfield (eds), *Stories of the Spirit, Stories of the Heart: Parables of the spiritual path from around the world,* New York: Harper Collins Publishers (1991) p. 337

Chapter 19
Merton, Thomas, translated in *Wisdom of the Desert: Sayings of the Desert Fathers of the Fourth Century)* Shambala: Boston & London (1994), p. 16

Chapter 20
Jung, Carl, in Jess M. Brallier (ed), *Medical Wit and Wisdom,* Running Press: Philadelphia (1993), p. 19

Chapter 21
Rumi, in Suzanne Maher (ed), *Philosophy – Inspirational quotations and thoughts,* Affirmations Australia (2005)

Chapter 22
Thoreau, Henry David, in *The Promise of a New Day,* op. cit.

Chapter 23
Castaneda, Carlos, *The Teachings of Don Juan: A Yaqui Way of Knowledge,* University of California Press (1968)

Lennon, John, 'Watching the Wheels' (1981)

Chapter 24
Le Guin, Ursula, from 'The Left Hand of Darkness', in Susan Hayward, *A Guide for the Advanced Soul,* In-tune Books Australia (1999)

Chapter 25
Porter, Katherine Anne, in *The Promise of a New Day,* op. cit.

Lao-tzu, *Tao-Te-Ching,* op. cit, ch. 41

Chapter 26
Wordsworth, William, 'Tintern Abbey', lines 94-102

Chapter 29
Tagore, Rabindranath, in *The Promise of a New Day,* op. cit.

Chapter 31
Lao-tzu, *Tao-Te-Ching,* Richard William edition, Arkana (1985)

Chapter 33
Shaw, George Bernard, in Philosophy – *Inspirational quotations and thoughts,* op. cit.

Chapter 34
Yogananda, Paramahansa, 'Sayings of Paramahansa Yogananda' in *A Guide for the Advanced Soul,* op. cit.

Chapter 35
James, William, in *A Guide for the Advanced Soul,* op. cit.

Chapter 37
Saint-Exupéry, Antoine de, *Wind, Sand and Stars,* Harcourt, Brace & Co: New York (1940).

Chapter 39
Gibran, Kahil, *The Prophet,* op. cit.

Chapter 40
Murray, William Hutchinson, *The Scottish Himalayan Expedition,* J.M. Dent & Sons Ltd: London (1951)

Chapter 41
Einstein, Albert, in P. Crean and P. Kome (eds), *Peace, A Dream Unfolding,* Toronto (1986)

Chapter 45
Houston, Jean, *The Search for the Beloved,* JP Tarcher (1987)

Chapter 46
Einstein, Albert, in *A Guide for the Advanced Soul,* op. cit.

Chapter 47
Schumacher, EF, *A Guide for the Perplexed,* Abacus: London (1978)

Chapter 51
Watts, Allan, *Psychotherapy East and West,* Random House: New York (1971)

Lao-tzu, *Tao-Te-Ching,* Richard William edition, Arkana (1985)

Chapter 52
Blake, William, 'Eternity' (1793)

Chapter 53
Blake, William, 'Augeries of Innocence', stanza 1 (1805)

Chapter 54
Gibran, Kahlil, *Sand and Foam,* Heinemann: London (1926)

Chapter 55
Elliot, TS, *Selected Poems,* Faber and Faber: London (1954)

Every effort has been made to trace and acknowledge copyright. However, should any infringement have occurred the publishers offer their apologies and ask copyright owners to contact them.

Isira's Service

Isira is inter-faith and inter-spirit speaking with a voice of universal awareness and oneness. She offers a range of services for people to connect more deeply with the path of love and awakening. Her goal is to help uplift all of humanity to restore greater wellbeing, peace and harmony for all life.

Through a variety of programs Isira has been a source of great transformation for many people around the world. Below is a general outline for how you may experience the benefits of this service of awakening consciousness.

Short Programs

Satsang/Meditation: Conscious exploration and insights on the heart and essence of existence, including time for your questions and answers and an opportunity to sit together in conscious presence and meditation. Many of these events have been recorded and produced.

Weekend and Longer Retreat Programs

Isira offers a range of events that allow seekers of awakening and Truth to explore and experience their true essence and harmony with life, through simple yet powerful tools of meditation and conscious energy alignment. These teachings and applications are all drawn from Isira's direct experience of the profound states that lie at the very core of us all. With grace, humour and immense love, Isira has the capacity to lead us into a space that allows the most natural depth of consciousness and transformation to be encountered.

Consultations

Spiritual counselling: Isira shares enlightened insight, wisdom, and loving compassion in one on one consultations providing the opportunity to accelerate spiritual and personal evolution.

Transformative Processes: These individualized processes are able to unblock deep conditioning that has held you back from your potential. Isira uses a combination of advanced hypnotherapy, conscious dialogue and enlightened awareness to help access the root of any blockage. Through bypassing the 'critical mind' and tapping into the innate knowing of your higher self - you will be able to find a deep, sustainable resolution so you can better sustain a more balanced life of wellbeing, happiness and purpose.

Books and Recordings

Isira has shared a vast body of wisdom through her published work, satsangs/meditations and longer programs. Many of these are available in written, audio and video formats.

www.isira.com

Lightning Source UK Ltd.
Milton Keynes UK
UKHW011038050821
388368UK00001B/301